More Than a Roof

*The Development
of Minnesota Poor Farms
and Homes for the Aged*

By Ethel McClure

MINNESOTA HISTORICAL SOCIETY, *St. Paul 1968*

COPYRIGHT 1968 © BY THE MINNESOTA HISTORICAL SOCIETY
Library of Congress Catalog Card Number: 68-65534

*This book was published from a revolving fund granted
to the Minnesota Historical Society by the
Louis W. and Maud Hill Family Foundation.*

For
Jessie E. McClure
Marjorie F. McClure
Martha Fullerton McClure

Foreword

FROM THE VERY FIRST PAGE, I found this book engrossing reading. Its author tackled a big job. Her industry in bringing together many hitherto scattered materials on homes for the aged and weaving them into a pattern is to be commended.

More than a century ago, a small group of women founded Minnesota's first "home for the friendless." Today groups interested in such work are not small; hundreds of citizens have made it their public-spirited concern to work constantly toward the goal that no one shall be friendless. A generation ago, such terms as "pesthouse," "poor farm," and "almshouse" were common in the daily vocabulary. Today, thanks to Minnesota's dynamic program for its aging citizens, those words are relics of a bygone era.

Our progress in the field of social welfare has been constant. And it continues. This book is a rich history of that progress.

Morris Hursh, **Commissioner**
MINNESOTA DEPARTMENT OF PUBLIC WELFARE

ST. PAUL, MINNESOTA
June 15, 1968

Foreword

PROBABLY FEW MINNESOTANS recognize the rich heritage the state has enjoyed in the long line of able and devoted men and women who have contributed so much to its development. First as a territory and later as a state, Minnesota has achieved national recognition in many activities, particularly in the broad areas of health, education, and welfare.

The foresight of the first territorial legislature in setting aside public lands in 1849 for the use and support of schools resulted in the growth of a great state university and an outstanding system of public education. In the field of health, examples of citizens' leadership are the establishment of the Minnesota Department of Health in 1872 — the third state health department organized in the United States — and later, in 1913, the provision of state support for the hospital care of tuberculous patients, many of whom had flocked to the area because of the early belief that the cold climate and life in the pine forests would cure this dreaded disease. Today Minnesota boasts essentially low incidence rates in all communicable diseases.

The author of this book has chosen to trace a development that concerns the fields of both health and welfare — the changes that occurred over more than a century in types of care and attitudes toward the aged. Based on the English laws of the 1600s, Minnesota's poor relief system was transplanted to the Atlantic colonies, then incorporated into the laws of the Northwest Territory, and following that into the laws of the territory and state of Minnesota. This system placed the responsibility for the sick, afflicted, poor, and aged upon the local, county, and township governments, which resulted in the opening of county poor farms. Subsequently county and community hospitals and special state institutions for the alcoholic, the insane, the mentally retarded, and the crippled were provided. At the same time, voluntary philanthropic and church organizations were keeping pace by providing facilities for the care of the aged, children, and other needy persons.

Undoubtedly the extensive efforts of private benevolent groups in the fields of health, education, and welfare in Minnesota grew out of the intense interest and the leadership of the area's citizens. This same leadership also resulted in the creation of strong and efficient state agencies. Such citizen concern made it possible for services in these three important areas to survive times of depression and war. Likewise, much of the guidance leading to the adoption of the federal Social Security Act came from the few states, including Minnesota, that had developed facilities and services in health and welfare. Minnesota today is considered a leader in the provision of care for the aged and in the health and welfare activities related to that care.

This book, written by one who has spent a lifetime in the health and welfare fields, should be of value to the present young leaders in the state. Many of them were not yet born during the depression of the 1930s or even during World War II. This history will tell them of the vision, knowledge, and fortitude of their forefathers and give them a knowledge of the rich heritage the state now enjoys.

Robert N. Barr, Secretary and Executive Officer
MINNESOTA DEPARTMENT OF HEALTH

MINNEAPOLIS, MINNESOTA
July 18, 1968

Preface

IN WRITING this account of Minnesota's homes for the elderly — from the first poor farm to the modern retirement or nursing home — I attempted to trace their development in relation to population changes, depressions, wars, changing philosophies, and other forces in state and national history that influenced them. This seemed to call for a chronological treatment, and I decided to carry the story forward by decades, alternating between public and privately owned institutions. For the purpose of this study, the term "public" refers mainly to county poor farms, since only a few cities and villages opened homes before 1960. "Private" means nonprofit ownership: that is, sponsorship by religious, fraternal, or benevolent organizations. Although proprietary (profit-making) homes have an important place in the total scheme of facilities for the aged, little is known about individual institutions established before 1940 and few, even of that decade, are still in existence. They therefore are discussed only as a group.

Obtaining the histories of several hundred institutions would not have been possible without the help of board members, administrators, county auditors, and welfare executives, who answered questionnaires and furnished photographs, brochures, and other material. Officials of a number of homes permitted me to read the minutes of early board meetings; others offered to make them available "if you can read Swedish" — or Norwegian or German. Some translated portions for me, thereby clarifying points which otherwise would have remained obscure.

In drawing a composite picture, it was not possible to give the full history of any one home. Stories of individual institutions are cited only as examples to illustrate trends in the care of the aged.

Even though much of the information provided by the institutions could not be included in this volume, the material will be preserved in the Minnesota Historical Society's collections.

The manuscript of this book was read by several persons long familiar with homes for the aged in Minnesota and elsewhere. For taking time from busy days and for their suggestions I express my appreciation to Morton V. Bjorkquist, executive secretary of the board of social ministry, Minnesota Synod, Lutheran Church in America; Mrs. Campbell Keith, administrator, Walker Methodist Residence and Nursing Home, Minneapolis; the Reverend John M. Mason, director of services to the aging, American Lutheran Church; and Sister M. Laurice, superintendent, St. Francis Home, Breckenridge. Special thanks go to Dr. Robert N. Barr and Morris Hursh for contributing the forewords.

It is impossible to thank individually all the members of the historical society's staff who assisted in this project. My debt to those in the publications department, however, is so great that it must be acknowledged. In suggesting that I write an article for *Minnesota History*, Mrs. Rhoda R. Gilman launched me on this study. Guiding the entire undertaking was Mrs. June D. Holmquist, managing editor. Without her sustained interest and participation this book would not have been completed. Additional help on the manuscript in its various stages was supplied by Mrs. Anne A. Hage, Mrs. Dorothy D. Perry, and Mrs. Mary D. Nagle. Their revisions and verification of sources made this a more accurate and readable account. Typing of the several versions was done by Mrs. Phyllis N. Sandstrom; Mrs. Helen T. Katz compiled the index; and Mrs. Sue E. Holbert prepared tables, assembled pictures, designed the book, and guided it through the press. The society's annual McKnight Foundation Research Grant for 1965 helped defray travel and research expenses.

More than five years of work went into the publication of this volume. They were pleasant years, thanks to Russell W. Fridley, director of the society, and his staff, who made me feel one of their number. Fortunate is the author who has the Minnesota Historical Society as publisher!

Ethel McClure

MINNEAPOLIS, MINNESOTA
August 15, 1968

Contents

1. Minnesota's First Poorhouses 1849–1864 1
2. County Poor Farms 1864–1880 20
3. The Home for the Friendless 1867–1883 39
4. Women of the Churches 1880–1900 51
5. The State Expands Its Role 1880–1900 73
6. Improving County Poor Farms 1900–1920 92
7. Ethnic Groups Provide for Their Aged 1900–1920 108
8. The Poorhouse under Scrutiny 1920–1930 125
9. The Questing Twenties 1920–1930 140
10. From Great Depression to Social Security 1930–1940 156
11. Red Ink and Midnight Oil 1930–1940 172
12. Standards and Shortages during World War II 1940–1950 185
13. Regulations and Ration Books 1940–1950 201
14. Progress in the Fifties 1950–1960 213
15. Changes and Challenges 1850–1960s 231

Illustrations 144–145
Appendix 244
Reference Notes 248
Index 281

More Than a Roof

1

Minnesota's First Poorhouses

1849—1864

"A TIME COMES IN THE HISTORY of all enlightened communities," wrote a Minnesota historian in the 1890s, "when some provision must be made for the aged and infirm poor, who have no means of support."[1] That time came early in Minnesota's history. Although there were few aged among its pioneers, as age is reckoned today, there were many sick, infirm, handicapped, and mentally incompetent persons. Some were penniless, finding it impossible to make a living in the new country — victims, perhaps, of circumstances beyond their control. Not a few had lost their savings to "demon rum"; others were, as the saying goes, "born shiftless." Every community had its deserted wives and widowed mothers. Most communities had at least one or two "fallen women," as an earlier generation termed unmarried mothers; for their infants the poorhouse was the birthplace as well as the first and, all too often, only home.

The relief system established in Minnesota Territory in 1849 had a long heritage. In essence it placed responsibility for the sick and afflicted poor and aged upon the county and township governments. The principles of public and local responsibility upon which it was based can be traced to the English Poor Law of 1601, which was transplanted from England to colonial America by the early settlers of the Atlantic seaboard colonies. From there the principles were carried to Minnesota via the laws of the Northwest

Territory. Those laws had been outlined by the ordinance which organized the territory in 1787.[2]

The English Poor Law of 1601 was the final stage in the codification of a long series of laws that had developed in England over several centuries. Under this act, the parish was the unit responsible for the relief of distress, with the justices of the peace and an overseer of the poor in immediate charge. It was the latter's duty to set able-bodied paupers to work and to provide relief for those unable to earn a living. If necessary, he might furnish a house where one or more families could live — the forerunner of the almshouse or poorhouse. For poor relief purposes the overseer was empowered to levy and collect taxes. The family was not, however, relieved of all responsibility. If of "sufficient ability," the parents, grandparents, and children of "every poor, old blind, lame, and impotent person, or other person not able to work" were required to support their relatives. As for the children of indigent parents, they might be apprenticed by the overseers and churchwardens (with the approval of the justices of the peace) to families who wished to take them.[3]

Because of the problems which arose from the practice of passing on the poor from one parish to another, Parliament in 1662 approved an "Act of Settlement" which permitted the authorities to remove a nonresident pauper to the parish of last legal settlement. This act together with the poor law of 1601 embodied the principles of local responsibility, family responsibility, and legal settlement which were the basis for the poor relief systems of the New World.[4]

The English poor relief system was brought to northeastern America by the passengers on the "Mayflower" who founded the Plymouth settlement in 1620. The colonists were determined that "wilful poverty should find no lodgment in the new England." The poor would be helped, but it must be proved that they could no longer help themselves and had no relatives who owed them support. Moreover, relief — if needed — should come from the governmental unit closest to the individual. The principle that responsibility for the needy lay upon the local community was expressed in an early Plymouth colony statute: "eury township shall make competent puision [provision] for the mayntenance of their poore according as they shall fynd most convenyent & suitable for themselues by an order and genall agreement in a publike towne meeting."[5]

In the early years the duty of aiding the poor devolved upon the board of selectmen, but later this task was given to overseers of the poor.[6] In Massachusetts, as in other colonies, there were four general methods of providing relief: furnishing assistance to the poor in their homes — so-called outdoor relief; farming out individual paupers to families, sometimes by auction; contracting with one person to care for all the town's paupers; and providing a municipal almshouse.[7]

Outdoor relief was seldom given in cash. In the very earliest days it was the sort of charity that kindly neighbors give, suited to the need of the individual. A cow might be assigned to a family for a certain period, or the town might contribute toward the building of a house for the family. Sometimes a section of land was reserved where poor inhabitants were allowed to cut wood, or ground might be set aside for their gardens. It was not uncommon for well-to-do residents to bequeath or give land or a cow for the use of the poor.[8]

As the number of poor persons increased and the giving of relief grew to be more and more of a burden, it became the aim to dispose of these people as cheaply as possible. Thus developed the public auction, where the pauper was awarded to the family who would care for him for the smallest amount or, if he were able to work, to the person who would bid the highest sum for his services. An auction, wrote Robert W. Kelso, "was usually staged at the village tavern on a Saturday night just following the annual town meeting." Here the town fathers and other citizens "could speculate upon the bodily vigor and the probable capacity for hard labor of a half-witted boy, a forlorn-looking widow, or a halt and tottering old man."[9]

Because of its inherent inhumanity, the system of auctioning or venduing, as it was sometimes called, declined in the 1820s and was replaced by care within a single home. Under this system the town made a contract with one individual, who agreed to take care of all the poor for a year. "The result was a privately owned and privately operated almshouse where the profit to the keeper was the object sought, and where the labor of the inmates formed a definite and well-understood part of the legal consideration." This step too fell out of favor. If the poor fared badly, the town decided to go back to the auction at large. If the vendor made a satisfactory profit, it was believed that the town could do likewise. Thus the municipally owned and operated almshouse came into being.[10]

In large communities with numerous poor, the institution known variously as almshouse, poorhouse, poor farm, asylum, infirmary, or workhouse soon became the chosen method. The first almshouse in Boston opened in 1660. Gathered under its roof were all manner of persons: "the widow who was beyond self-support; the little child left orphan or sired by the incompetent; the idiot who was the grinning butt of public ridicule; the maniac; the lame; the halt; and the blind. They were gathered together in the same enclosure, sometimes, but not always, with separate sleeping quarters. It was common to provide a separate room for the furiously mad, as their ravings made life intolerable for the rest. . . . Into the midst of these little children, these widows, and these helpless cripples were thrown the vagabond, the prostitute brought to her lying-in, the drunkard, and the loathsome syphilitic."[11]

In 1820 Josiah Quincy, then a member of the Massachusetts senate, submitted a report on the rapid increase in state reimbursements to the towns for the relief of the so-called "Province poor" — wanderers, vagrants, and others who had no legal settlement. Quincy recommended a system of town or district almshouses in order to place "the whole subject of the poor of the Commonwealth under the regular and annual superintendance [sic] of the Legislature." Other legislative studies followed, and in 1841 Dorothea Lynde Dix commenced her famed investigation of the conditions of the insane in jails, almshouses, and houses of correction. By the mid-nineteenth century Massachusetts had opened not only district poorhouses, but also state hospitals for the insane, thereby siphoning off many persons who did not properly belong in the small almshouses.[12]

While Massachusetts was developing its poor relief methods, other eastern states were also devising ways of coping with the problem. All were based on the English model. In 1823 John Van Ness Yates, New York secretary of state, made a study of the condition of the poor in each county and town in New York. Yates came to the conclusion that almshouses provided children with a better education "for future usefulness" than did outdoor relief, and he recommended the establishment of county "houses of employment" where paupers could be maintained with their children. In 1824 the state legislature acted on Yates's recommendations and inaugurated a county almshouse system, a version of which was later to become common in the Midwest.[13]

The New York experiment, however, proved disappointing. It became apparent that the almshouse was not the answer for children, nor, indeed, for many other kinds of dependents. In 1856 a senate investigating committee found appalling conditions in the institutions of New York. "The poor houses throughout the State may be generally described as badly constructed, ill-arranged, ill-warmed, and ill-ventilated," the committee reported. "The rooms are crowded with inmates; and the air, particularly in the sleeping apartments, is very noxious." Provisions for educating children, despite Yates's findings of some thirty years before, were defective, and the treatment of insane paupers consisted largely of punishments designed to break their will. The committee's report also touched on another group: "persons of great worth and respectable character, reduced to extreme poverty, not by any vice or fault of their own, but by some inevitable loss . . . Poor houses, if properly conducted, might be what they were originally designed to be, comfortable asylums for worthy indigence."[14]

An investigator for another state legislature was also concerned with the plight of older persons in poorhouses. He was Thomas R. Hazard, who in 1851 investigated the poor relief system of Rhode Island. Hazard too found many children and insane persons in almshouses and contract homes. However, it was the older persons — more than one-fourth of the total population in the homes — who made a special appeal to his sympathies. Arriving late in the day, Hazard found that old men who had been engaged in labor seemed worried and fatigued. In his opinion, the overseers were often too young and too preoccupied with management problems to understand the needs of the elderly. For them Hazard preferred small individual boarding homes in the old person's immediate community to a large, more central facility. "To separate an old person from a home that they have long been accustomed to, *be it ever* so homely," he said, "is very much like tearing an old tree from the ground, *be it ever so poor*, in which it has grown . . . they will both, in all probability, soon wither and die."[15]

As the eastern states made studies of their poorhouses and other methods of care, the new states of the Midwest were developing similar systems of poor relief. "The principle of local responsibility," wrote Josephine C. Brown, "was carried westward by the pioneers and formally recorded in the statutes of the Northwest Territory in 1790." The statute of 1790 provided for the appointment of overseers of the poor, who were charged with the duty of reporting to the justices of the peace both worthy persons who needed help and vagrants who might become a charge upon the township. In 1795 the territory enacted a comprehensive poor law adopted from the legislation of the original states, principally that of Pennsylvania. The provisions of the 1795 law, as summarized by a recent historian, included "setting the able-bodied poor to work, giving relief to the disabled poor, binding children out as apprentices, making the relatives financially responsible for the poor, providing elaborate qualifications for legal settlement, and establishing procedure for removal." The act also authorized the levying of taxes for "providing proper houses and places, and a convenient stock of hemp, flax, thread and other ware and stuff, for setting to work such poor persons, as apply for relief." In 1799 the administration of the poor law was transferred from the justices to county commissioners.[16]

On these statutes were based the poor laws of the six Midwestern states formed out of the Northwest Territory — Ohio, Indiana, Illinois, Michigan, Wisconsin, and Minnesota (in part). During their territorial and early statehood periods, they passed innumerable laws on poor relief, borrowing from the eastern commonwealths concepts and terminology which dated back to the English Poor Law of 1601. At first these old methods were used with little or no attempt to adapt them to the changed circumstances of a new country, and it is not surprising that the laws were amended many times. In Michigan, for example, more than a dozen poor relief laws were enacted in the 1820s and 1830s. One writer has commented that the "continual enactments, repeals, and modifications in the poor relief legislation of this period indicate the efforts of the legislators to deal with unfamiliar problems."[17]

Although the states created from the Northwest Territory eventually passed laws to establish poorhouses, many counties continued to place the poor with individual families. Many also turned over the operation of the county-owned poor farm to a single contractor, usually the lowest bidder. Most early poorhouses were very small and overcrowded, but early settlers were used to small and crowded abodes. What made them such miserable places was the fact that, when a county established a poorhouse, the commissioners were disposed to use the new facility for everyone who needed aid. The poorhouse consequently was filled with the sick, the aged, the handicapped, and the orphaned, as well as able-bodied paupers and their children. It also became the home for the mentally ill and deficient who had previously been confined in the jail — although, as one writer has observed, "It may well be doubted whether or not the condition of the insane was improved by a transfer from the jail to the poorhouse." It was not the overcrowding, therefore, but the wretchedness of the inmates and the herding together of all ages and classes of unfortunates which made the poorhouse of the Middle West, as of the East, an unsatisfactory institution for the care of the destitute, the insane, and the feeble-minded, and such a poor home for the very young and the very old.[18]

The poor laws developed so laboriously in the older states created from the Northwest Territory eventually migrated to Minnesota. This came about because the eastern and more settled portion of present-day Minnesota was formerly a part of Wisconsin Territory. When Wisconsin became a state in 1848, a movement got under way to create a new territory on its western boundary. Under the Organic Act establishing Minnesota Territory, which was passed by Congress on March 3, 1849, the laws that had been in force in Wisconsin continued to be valid in the new territory until its government could be organized and a legislature elected. Thus from Massachusetts, New York, and Pennsylvania, by way of the Northwest Territory and Wisconsin, came the foundations of the poor relief system established in Minnesota. Local governmental responsibility, family responsibility, and legal settlement — the three principles expressed in the English Poor Law — were transplanted some 250 years later to a new Midwestern American territory.[19]

The Wisconsin law which became operative in Minnesota vested county boards of commissioners with the "entire and exclusive superintendence of the poor, in their respective counties." The boards were authorized to provide relief and if necessary to appoint agents who would "oversee and provide" such relief. Members of the immediate family, "father, grand-father, mother, grandmother, children, grand-children, brothers or sisters," were required — if of "sufficient ability" — to support a poor relative who was "unable to earn a livelihood, in consequence of bodily infirmity, idiocy, lunacy, or other unavoidable cause." Destitute children or those likely to become a charge upon the county were made the wards of the commissioners, whose duty it was to bind the minor as an apprentice to "some respectable householder of the county." An applicant for relief was required to furnish proof that he had been a resident of the county during the preceding twelve months. If not a resident, the applicant might be returned to his own county or served with a notice to depart. A nonresident who was not a pauper, but who became ill in the county and was unable to pay for board, nursing, or medical aid, was to be assisted by the "overseer of the poor of the proper township." Expenses would be paid from the county treasury. A fine was to be levied on any person who knowingly brought or left a pauper in a county where the pauper was "not lawfully settled."[20]

Although poorhouses were not specifically mentioned, workhouses were. The term apparently was intended to cover both a workhouse for the able-bodied poor and an almshouse for county charges who were unable to earn a livelihood. The Wisconsin law provided that the "Board of County Commissioners . . . may, if they think proper, cause to be built or provided, in their respective counties, work-houses for the accommodation and employment of such paupers as may, from time to time, become a county charge; and said work-house and paupers shall be under such rules and regulations as said Boards of Commissioners may deem proper and just."[21]

In 1849, when the law became operative, Minnesota was little more than a wilderness, and St. Paul, the territorial capital, was "just emerging from a collection of Indian whisky shops and birch roofed cabins of half-breed voyageurs," with here and there a frame building, some warehouses, and the foundations of a hotel.[22] Nevertheless St. Paul was an exciting place in 1849. "The whole town is on the stir," reported the *Minnesota Pioneer* of April 28, "stores, hotels, houses, are projected and built in a few days." All that year the newspaper was filled with notices of land transactions, long lists of building materials and merchandise for sale, and reports of elections and other activities connected with the organization of the new government.

Minnesota's first legislature convened in St. Paul on September 3, 1849, and shortly thereafter created nine counties: Ramsey, Washington, Benton, Dakotah, Itasca, Mahkahto, Pembina, Wabashaw, and Wahnahta. (The first three comprised the area on the east side of the Mississippi River which had been ceded by the Indians and was thus open to settlement.) The law specified that there be organized a "board of county commissioners in each county in this Territory," the first members to be appointed by the governor, with succeeding members of the three-member board to be elected at large.[23]

Ramsey County, which then comprised all or portions of present-day Ramsey, Aitkin, Anoka, Hennepin, Isanti, Kanabec, Mille Lacs, Pine, and Washington counties, was the earliest to be or-

MINNESOTA TERRITORY *showing the original counties 1849–1851.*

ganized. In November, 1849, the voters elected as the first county commissioners Louis Robert, Roswell P. Russell, and Benjamin Gervais. These men brought to the board a variety of backgrounds and experiences.[24]

Russell, the chairman, was a New Englander who had gone to Minnesota in 1839 at the age of nineteen. In 1850 he was operating a mercantile business in St. Anthony. He was characterized by a contemporary as a "quiet, honest, honorable gentleman, very popular and very greatly esteemed by those who know him." Of the three commissioners, Russell was the only one able to write his name.[25]

This does not mean that the other men lacked qualifications for their positions. Louis Robert, thirty-nine years old, was already one of St. Paul's outstanding citizens. "Though without the advantages of education in early life," said a biographer, "he had a large fund of information, gained by travel and contact with men, and was gifted with excellent business capacity and judgment." Born of French parents in Missouri, he became an Indian trader, real estate investor, steamboat captain, and politician. A man of decided convictions and great energy, Robert served five years on the county board. In early life Benjamin Gervais, the third commissioner, farmed in the Red River country, worked for a fur trading company, and then settled near Fort Snelling in 1827. Eleven years later Gervais opened a farm in St. Paul, later moving to Little Canada. In 1850 he was sixty-three years of age.[26]

The new board members found plenty to do when they took office in January, 1850. In four meetings held that month, they divided the county into school, road, and assessment districts and appointed the necessary officials. They also selected jurors, issued ferry and liquor licenses, ordered official stationery, and issued a notice offering ten dollars for the best plan for a new courthouse. Turning to relief matters, the board appointed James M. Goodhue as county overseer of the poor "at a salary of twenty dollars per Annum." Thus Minnesota's first newspaper editor also became the area's first overseer of the poor. And on April 1 the board authorized payment, in county orders, of the first poor relief bill: "Twenty two dollars and eighty three cents to Bartlett Presly for keeping Shipler's child (Pauper)."[27]

Despite the fact that two of the commissioners could sign the courthouse bonds and building contract with their marks only, the board had great respect for written records. In April it resolved that "the treasurer be required to appropriate the first money that comes into his hands for the purpose of purchasing a fire proof safe for the safe keeping of the records of the County." As it happened, Louis Robert advanced the money with which the purchase was made.[28]

Immigration to Minnesota increased after 1851, when two treaties with the Sioux Indians opened the territory west of the Mississippi River for settlement. As more and more boats discharged their passengers on St. Paul's levees, the town continued to grow and prosper. "The year 1854," a chronicler later recalled, "began to open up a new impulse. . . . The little cluster of houses grew wonderfully fast; new streets were opened; new hotels erected; new enterprises inaugurated; new blood infused in the community." A real estate boom was under way.[29]

It was in 1854 that the Ramsey County board bought what was to be Minnesota's first poor farm. How much need there was for a poor farm at that time is not known. From the nature of the transactions and the amount of land acquired, it appears that the board members may have been smitten by the same land fever which infected nearly everyone else in this period. On December 23, 1854, the board, now comprised of Louis Robert, James P. Wilson, and Joseph Le Bonne, met "to receive bids to buy a farm or piece of land to make a pauper farm." Two bids were received. One was later rejected because the land was adjacent to a church; the other was submitted by William P. Murray, Robert's close friend and attorney. Murray's offer of 202 acres in Mounds View Township south of Snail Lake, in what is now Shoreview, included 80 acres owned by Robert. On December 30, when the board met to examine the bids, Robert was excused from voting. At this meeting an offer of another 80 acres near Murray's land was received from Abraham Bennett, who had just been elected commissioner and soon replaced Le Bonne. The board, accepting both offers, purchased 282 acres in Mounds View Township.[80]

Several years later the purchase came in for criticism because of the unsuitability of the land for farming and the rather large amount of acreage acquired — mistakes which other counties would also make in buying poor farms. At the time, however, these faults seem not to have been evident, and the board prepared to start farming operations. At the January 16, 1855, meeting, "Rolly & wife was employed as superintendent to work on poor farm for one year from 1st April and do all work necessary . . . at the rate of $450.00 a year for him and his wife." Although bills were allowed that spring for such items as "hauling to Poor House" and "one wagon for county farm," the records do not show whether this first facility was used to house the poor. It is certain, though, that other forms of relief were provided. The county board continued to pay for wood and provisions for families in their own homes, to reimburse an occasional woman for "attending" a poor person, and to send sick indigents to St. Joseph's Hospital, which the Sisters of St. Joseph had opened in 1854 in a new building.[81]

The care of sick indigents was apparently becoming more and more of a problem in St. Paul, for in 1855 the board considered establishing a county hospital on the poor farm grounds. A correspondent whose letter appeared in the *Minnesota Pioneer* on March 23, 1855, protested such a move. "I have learned with much surprise," he wrote, "that our County Commissioners have notified the Sisters of St. Joseph, who are in charge of the Hospital built by the benevolence of the Right Reverend Bishop [Joseph] Cretin, that they are about preparing a building expressly for the use of the sick of the County, which as soon as ready, they will have such removed to." The writer recalled the devotion of the sisters in attending victims of an earlier cholera epidemic and expressed the opinion that the public would not support the board's proposal. To this statement the editor added his comment: "This step on the part of the Commissioners, appears to us a very strange one, and one which we think will receive the condemnation of every liberal minded citizen of the County."

The board temporarily gave up its idea of opening a county hospital and continued to send patients to St. Joseph's. It then learned (if it did not already know) that there is no pleasing everyone. A letter in a St. Paul newspaper complained that too much money was going into St. Joseph's. Replying to the attack, Sister Seraphine Coughlin, the mother superior, stated that during 1855 "sixty-eight patients were admitted into our Hospital at the charge of the county; some stayed one week, and others six months, according to their diseases, and order of their physician." For their care the hospital had received only $1,623.60, and she believed the "charges moderate for attending day and night on those patients, considering our pay was in county orders." Sister Seraphine concluded: "It will be a gratification for us to receive gratuitously, or at a low price, many patients when the Hospital shall have received charitable donations."[32]

It was not only physically ill patients who created a problem for the county board. Provision for care of the mentally ill was also the commissioners' responsibility. Minnesota did not as yet have a hospital for the insane, and it was necessary to transfer patients requiring hospitalization to the Iowa State Hospital at Mount Pleasant. Violent patients were sometimes confined in the St. Paul jail. In 1856 the city considered establishing a special "Maniac Hospital." Although the county commissioners passed a resolution endorsing the city council's proposal, such an institution did not materialize.[33]

When the county board was confronted with the necessity of providing for the mentally ill, the commissioners considered the problem carefully. It is worthy of note that the Ramsey County board did not immediately consign such patients to the poorhouse. In February, 1858, for example, the board's attention was called to "the danger of permitting to go at large one Abner Ramsey an insane person." The board, now comprised of Bennett, Nathaniel McLean, and Edmund Rice, asked the overseer of the poor not only to obtain a "mental report" from the county physician as to whether the person was insane, and if so to have him "safely taken care of in a comfortable manner," but also to seek the district attorney's advice about the possible future disposition of the case. When the county physician reported that "said Ramsey was foolish yet harmless," the board left him in the community. At the same time it took the precaution of ordering "that if at any time he should become dangerous to run at large that he be safely kept or locked up."[34]

In March, 1857, the county board purchased another farm — a sixty-acre tract in McLean Township in the area near the Mississippi River known as Pig's Eye. (The land at one time had been settled by Pierre "Pig's Eye" Parrant, a notorious whisky dealer with one blind eye.) Nathaniel McLean, chairman of the county board, later explained that in negotiating for this farm he thought he had made a good bargain. "At least two individuals were anxious to get the Pig's Eye tract at the price paid by the county." The board continued to hold the first poor farm, but it moved the poorhouse operation (if, indeed, one had existed) from the Mounds View farm to the new location.[35]

Only one other Minnesota county experimented with the establishment of a poor farm during the decade of the 1850s. Few details of its story can be found, but those which are known reveal that except in magnitude its problems were similar to those faced by Ramsey County. In 1858 the Washington County board of commissioners purchased 207 acres of land about five miles north of Stillwater. There is no further record of action until June, 1859, when the board thriftily agreed that "bringing under cultivation more land on the Poor Farm, is an Object to be constantly pursued, with a view of making it self-sustaining."[36]

At the same meeting the board appointed John S. Proctor as superintendent of the poor farm and also gave him general supervision over all matters relating to county relief. It was further decided "that all aid and assistance that may be required, shall be rendered at the Poor Farm as far as in his [*Proctor's*] Judgment shall be deemed practicable." The board's generous delegation of powers to the new superintendent is not surprising. Proctor was a highly respected citizen of Stillwater, and when he became warden of the state prison in 1860 even his political opponents called him the "very best man whom Gov. Ramsey could have selected from the Republican ranks of this city."

Before long the officials of Washington County, like those of

Ramsey, were confronted with the question of caring for the insane. On September 13, 1859, apparently prompted by an emergency, the board authorized the committee on the poor "to enlarge the Barn and build a Suitable Lock up for the Safe Keeping of a Crazy man on the Poor Farm." The resolution raises several unanswered questions. Was this lockup to be part of the enlarged barn, a separate structure, or an addition to an existing house already on the site? What provision had been made for an attendant? Although New York investigators only three years earlier had found mental patients confined in shacks at the almshouses, it does not seem likely that the worthy citizens of Washington County would have relegated even a violent patient to an isolated building or to a section of a barn. The records do not reveal whether there was a house on the farm in 1859, but apparently one existed in 1860. In that year Joseph N. Masterson, overseer of the poor, was instructed to provide the "necessary supplies and provisions for the house upon the poor farm." Was this the log cabin with barred windows which stood, within living memory, near the "old poorhouse"? Used in early years for refractory and disturbed inmates and known as the "'jail," the structure had three rooms, one of which conceivably might have housed an attendant. But whether this cabin was the lockup built in 1859 and whether it was also the "house on the farm" in 1860 are matters of conjecture.[87]

As late as the early 1860s the number of inmates never exceeded three, and the Washington County board continued to provide relief to some paupers in their homes and to board others with private families. Little is known of the farm's first residents. Presumably they are buried in the poorhouse cemetery now covered by a thick tangle of underbrush. Only a few broken slabs remain, and the inscriptions, which might at least have revealed the names and ages of those buried there, are almost entirely obliterated. No grave marker is needed, however, to perpetuate the memory of one inmate. Known only as "Hannah's Louise" (said to have been the addlepated child of an unfortunate girl), she wandered away and was drowned in the lake north of the home. The unhappy event, so legend tells us, gave Lake Louise its name.[88]

Poor relief in Minnesota took on a new dimension when on August 24, 1857, the Ohio Life Insurance and Trust Company of New York failed, triggering a nationwide panic. Because of intense speculation in land and high interest rates, Minnesota was severely hit. "With many, even those who had but shortly before imagined themselves wealthy, there was a terrible struggle between pride and want," wrote a St. Paul historian of the period; "few had saved anything, so generally had the reckless spirit of the times infested all classes."[39]

Despite hard times Minnesota proceeded with preparations for statehood, and on May 11, 1858, was admitted to the Union. In an attempt to make government more democratic, the first state legislature established a new system of county organization, based on that of New York. Under Minnesota's Township Act of 1858 each county was to be divided into as many "towns" as there were townships, and each town regardless of size was to have an elaborate organization with numerous officers. The old county board of commissioners was replaced by a county board of supervisors comprised of the chairmen of the town boards. Most counties were sparsely settled, many having only a few hundred inhabitants, but the areas they encompassed were often very large. As a result, even counties of small population could have twenty or more townships, which meant that their county boards were also very large.[40]

The law was characterized by John P. Owens, an early St. Paul journalist, as "perhaps the most inordinate piece of recklessness indulged in by this Legislature." Owens severely criticized "the magnitude of the machinery and expenditures which it [*the law*] contemplated in this then comparatively unsettled State and impoverished people, who were importing their bread and meat, and scarcely knew when one scanty meal was consumed, where the next was to come from."[41]

From the standpoint of organization, Ramsey County was perhaps fortunate in having only six townships — Rose, Reserve, White Bear, McLean, Mounds View, and Little Canada (renamed New Canada). The towns organized promptly, and by June, 1858, the new ten-member Ramsey County board of supervisors was ready to function. In addition to the six town chairmen, each of St. Paul's four wards was represented.[42]

Besides its administrative unwieldiness, the act offered a further difficulty in its definition of the roles of county boards and town overseers of the poor in the matter of paying for relief. The new law stated: "It shall be the duty of the Board of Supervisors to take charge of the poor, and the management of the Poor House, in their respective counties . . . and the Overseers of the Poor of the several towns shall be accountable to, and their compensation shall be audited by the Board of Supervisors, and paid by the county." The exact division of responsibility between county and town was not clear to many boards, and a number of them asked their attorneys for an interpretation. The law was generally construed to mean that primary responsibility for care of the poor rested with the county, but at least one board took the precaution of having a local auditor examine, and the town chairman approve, all bills before authorizing payment.[43]

In Ramsey County the question of jurisdiction was complicated by the presence of large numbers of nonresidents, many of whom became ill in St. Paul. The city paid a physician to care for its paupers, but there was "always a question as to who were properly city or county patients." The county board finally hit on a partial solution by "investing one person with both offices."[44]

One of the first acts of the new Ramsey County board of supervisors was to appoint a committee to examine the books and to report on the affairs of the county. At the July meeting the committee advised that in its opinion "the poor farm (so called) is far too small. While we would recommend a reasonable economy, we would urge the humanity of providing all such comforts as shall seem desirable and proper." The county physician called the buildings "entirely unfit to protect the sick from the inclemency of the weather during the severe winter."[45]

In its strategic position as the head of navigation on the Mississippi and the port of entry for most immigrants seeking homes in Minnesota, St. Paul received more than its share of the indigent poor and sick. Those left by the boats and unable to get farther remained in St. Paul, making the city's relief problem unique within the state. As the financial situation following the panic grew worse, the county was soon "supporting poor all over the city," and the board tried to lessen the drain on the county treasury. In August, 1858, it gave notice to the "Captains of boats landing at the Port of St. Paul that they will be held responsible for all cost sustained by the County of Ramsey from their landing paupers at said port." The board also asked that the county physician consult with the township overseer of the poor before arranging to hospitalize patients.[46]

The idea of a county-operated hospital was as attractive to this board as to its predecessor, and on August 14 the members decided to sell all the poor farm lands and use the proceeds to build "a good and complete County Hospital . . . Where each Township shall send their sick and be taxed for accordingly. And be it further resolved that each Township shall support its own Poor." The board's committee on the poor, to whom the resolution was referred, recommended that a hospital be erected within the St. Paul city limits.[47]

Apparently it was not easy, however, to dispose of the old poor farms. In October, 1858, the overseer of the poor, after calling attention to the serious increase of pauperism and the heavy expense of caring for the indigent sick at St. Joseph's Hospital, recommended that a county hospital be erected near the existing poorhouse. At the same meeting the board received a letter from C. B. Gallagher, offering to sell a tract of land adjoining the Pig's Eye poor farm. Because some members did not consider it prudent to buy a new farm until the Mounds View land could be sold, the board took no immediate action.[48]

When it became known that the county board was considering the purchase of another farm at a cost of $3,000, the *Daily Pioneer and Democrat* was aroused. Although the reporter had passed up the January meeting because "we have not stomach enough for the effluvia generated by their [the board's] presence and that of the public interested in their proceedings in the small room used for the meeting," he did attend the February meeting and was further disenchanted with what he found. Not only was the meeting noisy and lacking in any semblance of order, but it appeared that "the supervisors had authorized an indebtedness of over $30,000, since they had come into office: and judging from the disposition to create an indebtedness for a poor farm and additional poor buildings, the end is not yet."[49]

Despite the newspaper's criticism, the county board on February 8 purchased the sixty-acre Pig's Eye tract and began planning for a new building. Ramsey County now owned a farm in Mounds View Township and two farms at Pig's Eye, which the *Daily Pioneer and Democrat* dubbed Poor Farms 1, 2, and 3. On February 11 the newspaper reviewed the details of the purchases and commented on the poor bargain the county had made. The journal reported that the land on Farm 1 was poor and that only ten acres of Farm 2 could be cultivated at all. As for the third acquisition, "This farm, Mr. [Martin D.] Clark, one of the Supervisors, thinks is well calculated for the purpose, and that hereafter the poor farms will support the poor." On March 4, 1859, the board of supervisors let a contract for a ten-bed "Poor House and Hospital." The specifications called for a "frame building 36 by 40 feet, two stories and attic high, to be built in a plain manner." For the amount awarded — $290 in county orders — it could hardly have been elaborate. With the completion of the building the supervisors ordered the transfer of five paupers from St. Joseph's Hospital.[50]

The question of whether the poor farm should be used primarily for "permanent invalids and infirm," with outdoor relief provided for those who could remain at home, was argued in the press. At least one result of caring for invalids at the poor farm was to precipitate the removal of St. Joseph's Hospital to smaller quarters. On August 20, 1859, its board of trustees announced: "The average number of patients at the Hospital during its existence has not exceed[ed] three or four, and other provisions having been made by the County and City for the care of the rich and poor, the necessity no longer exists for a Hospital at least to such an extent as to justify the Sisters in maintaining so large an establishment."[51]

During the remainder of 1859, the *Daily Pioneer and Democrat* continued its criticism of the county supervisors. On September 8 the newspaper pointed out that although St. Paul had two-thirds of the population and taxable property in the county, the city was represented by only two-fifths of the board's membership. The journal also accused the board of assessing property unfairly and of extravagance and reckless spending which had brought the county to bankruptcy. "This ponderous institution met yesterday in the auditor's room in the county jail," said the editor on September 14, "but if justice ruled the hour, other and smaller and stronger rooms in the jail would be fitting places for the actors."

By this time it was evident to many observers that county boards of supervisors were too large for efficiency, and that their members often were more concerned with the interests of the towns they represented than with the welfare of the county as a whole. In his outgoing message to the 1860 legislature, Governor Henry H. Sibley noted that "experience has shown that the system is better adapted to populous and wealthy States, than to a sparsely settled region like Minnesota. . . . The machinery of county government is not only expensive, but useless." Responding to Sibley's suggestion, the legislature repealed the Township Act and reinstated county commissioner boards representing districts rather than towns. A county which had cast 800 or more votes at the last general election was allowed five members; in other counties the board was to consist of only three commissioners.[52]

In 1860 prospects for recovery from the 1857 depression appeared bright. Immigrants were again arriving in the state, new buildings were going up, business had begun to revive, and a good harvest was anticipated. In the ten years from 1850 to 1860 Minnesota's population had increased from 6,077 to 172,023. St. Paul was now a city of 10,401 persons.[53]

Despite the good times, care of the sick and dependent occupied, as in the earliest days, a considerable portion of the time of public officials. Although poor relief was again administered as it had been under the old Wisconsin law, the question of county versus city or town responsibility continued to plague the county boards. In 1861 Ramsey County obtained a special law to exempt any township which supported its own poor from paying county taxes for poor relief.[54]

For most Minnesota counties the period from 1849 through 1863 was one of organization and adjustment. Only two counties acquired poor farms, and in Ramsey County the emphasis was on providing a facility for the sick. Public responsibility for the aged (as distinct from other groups of dependent persons) was not a problem of any magnitude. In the matter of poor relief, the state — through its adoption of the Wisconsin law — was committed to the system brought from old and New England by way of the Northwest Territory. Primary responsibility rested upon county governments. Although the law placed some responsibility on families, it did not contain guidelines for determining when relatives were of "sufficient ability," and enforcement depended on the commissioners' general knowledge of the situation and their powers of persuasion. The law also stressed the responsibility of the "county of residence," but a migratory population and the constantly changing county boundaries made this provision almost meaningless. In the succeeding hundred years the principles of the English Poor Law would be further eroded as state and federal governments took over a larger share of responsibility for the poor and the aged.

2

County Poor Farms

1864—1880

IN 1864 THE MINNESOTA LEGISLATURE took an action which, in effect, established the county poor farm as a vital part of the state's poor relief system. A comprehensive new law passed that year made the county the only unit for poor relief and provided for the appointment of an overseer of the poor who would have immediate charge (under the supervision of the commissioners) of both county dependents and the poor farm. The old law had specified only that the commissioners, if they thought proper, might establish a workhouse for county charges. The 1864 law now made it mandatory for every county to provide a poor farm or a suitable substitute, unless the board members found that the number of poor persons was too small to warrant such an expenditure. The board might then provide for their support in any other "judicious and suitable" way. The importance attached by the legislature to indoor relief, however, is indicated by the large amount of detail relating to the acquisition and management of poor farms, and by several references in the law to the support of dependents "at the place provided."[1]

That the legislators still thought of the poorhouse as a sort of community woodpile where vagrants could work out their board and keep is suggested by the statute's frequent use of such terms as "work house," "employment," and "manual labor." On the other hand, the legislature completely dropped the hated term "pauper" in favor of the words "poor person," although county boards for many years to come would continue to refer to all their dependents as "paupers."

The law became effective on March 4, 1864, near the close of the third year of the Civil War. The time hardly seemed propitious for the buying of poor farms. In February and again in April the war department issued heavy calls for men. In May the draft was extended to fill the quotas of some Minnesota districts which were delinquent. "That these frequent and heavy drafts for men produced a feeling of doubt and despondency can not be denied," wrote one historian. The feeling of uncertainty and foreboding was intensified by the continuance of a widespread drought which had begun the year before. Currency was inflated, prices were high, and agricultural labor was scarce.[2]

County treasuries were being depleted by the demands put upon them. The draft could be satisfied by paying a substitute to replace a man who was needed at home, and county boards frequently appropriated commutation money as well as bounties to volunteers. Even very sparsely settled areas joined in this effort. St. Louis County, with a population of only a few hundred, had already furnished its draft quota of sixteen men, but in April, 1864, the commissioners nevertheless appropriated $600 "for the purpose of paying Bounties for volunteers or for paying the Commutation money of any citizen . . . who may be drafted." In September the county appropriated another $1,500.[3]

In spite of these drains, county boards proceeded to buy poor farms. In the two decades covered by this chapter, twenty-one more counties — including nearly all of the larger ones — joined Ramsey and Washington in purchasing land for this purpose. With the exception of St. Louis and Chisago counties, the twenty-one were largely located in the southeastern portion of Minnesota. Most of them had been created by the legislature between 1853 and 1855. Their people had shared many of the same experiences: the pouring in of settlers during the early 1850s, the depression of 1857, the terrors of the Indian outbreak of 1862, the special problems of the Civil War, and all the challenges, hopes, and disappointments involved in opening up a new territory.[4]

In this process of development the county boards played an important part. On them rested the responsibility for transforming a raw area dotted with tiny, isolated settlements into a cohesive, functioning political community. It was their job to lay out roads and bridges, divide the county into school, election, and assessment districts, provide county buildings, assess property, and set tax rates. Now, under the new law of 1864, they were also solely responsible for poor relief and, if the need dictated, for providing a poor farm. Sooner or later, after the courthouse and jail had been erected, almost every county considered the propriety of buying a poor farm.

There were several reasons for thinking of a poorhouse in terms of a poor *farm*. A farm, it was argued, would provide food and other products essential for the maintenance of the inmates, who might labor to some extent and thus contribute to their own support. The idea of a farm as an investment also appealed to many boards, for it was felt that with the growing population land would increase in value.[5]

In January, 1864, even before the new law became effective, the Goodhue County board appointed a committee to select a location for a poor farm. This county on the Mississippi River had come a long way since that day in June, 1854, when its newly appointed commissioners held their first meeting on a lumber pile in the heart of what would become the main business district of Red Wing. Or, for that matter, since 1858, when the board of supervisors, split between Democrats and Republicans, came up with a tie vote for chairman and two men presided at opposite ends of the table. Much water had run under the bridge since then, and there was certainly no disunity in 1864 as the county board took measures to help the war effort and to aid persons on the lengthening relief rolls. But the county felt the financial pinch; perhaps, the commissioners reflected, a poor farm would solve the problem.[6]

In reporting this decision to purchase land, the *Goodhue Volunteer* of Red Wing gave the commissioners' reasons and added some of its own. "They want a good farm to support poor people. . . . The poor of the county must be provided for, their poverty is frequently their misfortune, without being their fault. Now the cost of supporting the poor is considerable and as the population of the County increases it will grow larger and larger. Money invested in land in this County cannot be a bad investment; and if a farm of 621 acres is bought, and judiciously managed, it will be but a short time before our poor will be able to pay their own way, a thing they will greatly prefer, to being indebted to the county. The sooner the land is bought the cheaper it can be got."[7]

The *Goodhue County Republican* of Red Wing saw the farm as

a financial asset. "Such an institution can in a few years be made to pay its own way and put money into the county treasury," prophesied the paper on April 1, 1864. "As a measure of economy and humanity, we hope Goodhue County will not long be without an asylum and farm for the poor." Alas for the editor's expectations. Although on April 23 the county purchased a fine farm of 200 acres in Burnside Township about three miles north of Red Wing, the early inmates were "mostly old persons or children, and immigrants" — not a very promising labor force. The farm did not pay for itself, and bills for its operation mounted.[8]

Hennepin County was the next to buy a poor farm. Its first board of commissioners had met in 1852 at the home of John H. Stevens — in the first frame house built on the west side of the Mississippi River in Minneapolis. The county grew rapidly, and by 1864 the board was already assisting a number of individuals in their own or in boarding homes. In those days little thought was given to making relief palatable, or even respectable, and the names of recipients were listed in the board's proceedings, which were published in a local newspaper. Everyone knew, for example, that the board had voted "To pay Mrs. Murnan, a pauper, $1.50 per week for the next four weeks." It was also common knowledge that the board had made "a temporary arrangement, closed at their option, with Christopher Hankes, living beyond Lake Calhoun, on the Minnetonka Road, to keep all adults at $2.00 per week," except for "Mrs. Dee, an insane woman," for whom three dollars would be allowed. Hankes also agreed to keep "children at graduated rates according to age."[9]

Few items were so explicit, however, as one in the *State Atlas* of Minneapolis for May 4, 1864. "It was determined . . . to allow Mr. Streeter, of Minnetonka, $3.00 per week to board and take care of Mr. McGann of that town, who, made drunk by Minneapolis whisky, last winter, froze both feet off on his way home, and is made a County expense for life." Whether the commissioners were more irked by the "expense for life" or the "Minneapolis whisky" is not a matter of record.

In March, 1864, the board discussed the "propriety of purchasing a farm for the purpose of erecting suitable buildings thereon for the use of the poor." It advertised for a parcel of land between 160 and 400 acres in size "situated not less than four nor more than eight miles from Minneapolis." The *State Atlas* hailed the move as being the "most feasible, as well as the most economical way to maintain the unfortunate poor." The editor was especially pleased with the proposed location: "One thing is certain, the farm will not be in the immediate vicinity of Minneapolis. Thus the temporary rush of idle vagabonds during the winter months will in a measure be obviated. All inmates capable of working will be kept busily employed."[10]

The commissioners were not able immediately to find a suitable farm, and it was January 4, 1865, before the poorhouse opened. The 400-acre tract was in Hopkins, about nine miles from the center of Minneapolis. A report in 1869 commented at length on the crops and stock, but referred only briefly to "the subjects of charity at that house, numbering about twenty" who seemed "reasonably neat, clean and well cared for."[11]

The year 1865 saw the end of the Civil War and the beginning of an era marked by economic expansion and an impressive growth of population. An intermediate census taken by the state, though probably incomplete, indicated that the population had increased by at least 45 per cent since 1860. By 1866 the stream of settlers moving into the state had become a torrent. "They are pouring into all sections of the State with great rapidity," reported the *St. Paul Pioneer* on June 28, 1866. "They come by boat and by wagon; sometimes in squads, sometimes in companies, and at other times singly. Twenty-seven thousand five hundred and twenty-three acres of land were entered under the homestead act at St. Peter. . . . Between two and three hundred Norwegians were landed at our levee yesterday and every arrival brings more or less, besides the hundreds who stop at points below."[12]

In spite of the general prosperity, there were, as in earlier years, many persons who became county charges because of age, illness, mental incompetence, intemperance, or just plain bad luck. Under the pressure of mounting relief loads and the compulsion of the 1864 law, several counties hastened to acquire poor farms. One of the first to buy in the post-Civil War period was Dakota County. Whether the action was precipitated by an incident that took place early in 1866 is not known, but since the newspapers made the occurrence something of a *cause célèbre*, it may well have influenced the commissioners' decision. On February 13 the *Stillwater Messenger* reported that an insane woman had been admitted to the Washington County poor farm on the representation of friends that she lived in the county. A little sleuthing on the part of officials revealed that "the unfortunate woman" was really a resident of Dakota County, and the sheriff escorted her back across the county line. "Our Dacota friends didn't play the dodge very fine," commented the *Messenger*. A week later, on February 20, the newspaper reported that "Dacota County officers fought the return of their patient with much resistance, but finally yielded to law and justice — thus saving an expense of at least two thousand dollars a year to our county." The estimated saving seems a little high for the times, but the patient's hasty removal from Washington County pointed up the problem of caring for mentally ill patients.

A few months later the Dakota County board took steps to acquire a place for its dependents. Curiously enough, this county did not acquire a farm but rather it bought a poorhouse in town, and in a dying town at that. In July, 1866, the board voted to accept "the proposal of G. B. Reed to sell to the county lots 11, 12, and 13, in Nininger, with the buildings thereon for [a] poor house . . . $525 to be paid on delivery of the deed and $150 in one year, with interest at ten per cent."[13] At that time Nininger — once a booming townsite on the Mississippi River north of Hastings — consisted of little more than the handsome dwelling of Ignatius Donnelly, politician and author, who was then serving as a United States congressman from Minnesota.

In buying such a poorhouse the commissioners may have been wiser than they knew. To judge from the bills for medical care, most of the residents were invalids who would have been of little assistance on a farm. Within a few years the number of nursing cases increased so sharply that the board's chairman was "authorized to employ assistance for the Poor Master in taking care of sick paupers at an expense not to exceed $3 a week."[14]

Like Dakota, Nicollet County may have been moved to action by the necessity of caring for a mental patient. According to a local historian, "the first public need of any measures . . . for the care of paupers" arose in 1859, when the board of supervisors entered into an agreement with Josiah Horner to provide "Napoleon Brisbo, a lunatic and pauper, with wholesome food, clothing and lodging for the space of one year for the sum of $300, to be paid monthly at the rate of $25 per month." Horner also agreed to keep other Nicollet County paupers and "furnish them all necessary food, clothing and lodging for the sum of $12.50 per month."[15]

Poor Napoleon Brisbo was a sore trial to the county board and a terror to the countryside. More than sixty years later Jennie Pettyjohn Tyler described a childhood incident which had made a lasting impression on her mind. "One forenoon," she recalled, "when our men and boys were harvesting in the southeast corner of our field, mother called us little girls in, took the ax and after closing up the lower part of the house, we all went upstairs, where she hung a white sheet from the window. . . . Away down the road a man was coming on the run. Where the weeds were low, he would crouch down and run, sometimes crawling; then, where they were high, near the outside of the fence, how he would run!" The description reminds one of the old poem:

> Rob, the Pauper, is loose again.
> Through the fields and woods he races. . . .
> He hath broke him loose from his poor-house cell;
> He hath dragged him clear from rope and fetter.

Old Rob, hunted with dogs and guns, was brought down by a bullet, but Napoleon was, perhaps, more fortunate. As he raced toward the house, four or five men, driving their team from the field at top speed, were upon him. "It took three of them, strong men all," wrote Mrs. Tyler, "to overpower him and tie him to the rack, my father and two of the men taking him back to his keeper . . . whom father threatened with dire results should his charge, a murderous maniac called Napoleon, again escape him."[16]

In March, 1867, Nicollet County made a substantial purchase of land — 260 acres in Granby Township — for use as a poor farm. In an editorial commending the board for its action, the *Saint Peter Tribune* reported that "the building provided for the accommodation of the poor is a plain log structure, but well adapted for the comfort of the inmates. The room is provided with clean, comfortable beds, and those now supported by the county are living as well, if not better than very many of our border settlers." In the summer of 1870 the county built a new poorhouse on the farm.[17]

Most counties acquired poor farms in the hope of substantially reducing expenditures for poor relief. For example, at a meeting on May 20, 1867, the Dodge County board decided "that it would be [an] economy for the county to purchase a small farm for the use of the county poor," and solicited proposals of not less than 80 or more than 160 acres. In reporting the decision, the *Mantorville Express* of May 31, 1867, gave the board a pat on the back. "We think the Board, who seem to have the best good of the county at heart, would do a wise and beneficent act to thus provide for those who are unable to provide for themselves. Last year the county disbursed to its poor, over thirteen hundred dollars. With the proper management of a poor farm, the county officers could do more for the needy, at less expense." Whether the county board was too particular in its requirements or whether people were not ready to part with their land (this was an inflationary period) is not known, but in spite of continued solicitations for offers, the board apparently did not find what it wanted until two years later. In June, 1869, it voted to buy the farm of A. Everts, in Wasioja, renting it that fall to Daniel Weaver for one year with the understanding that he would board paupers at $3.50 a week and give the county one-third of the crops.[18]

The Le Sueur County board also received praise from the press when it decided in January, 1868, to open a poorhouse on the farm it had acquired some time before in Kilkenny Township. The *Le Sueur Courier*, after approving the board's action, recommended that the county farm "be managed so that in a few years it will be able to support such poor as the county has on its hands in a comfortable condition and add very slightly to the general expense." Actually the term which appeared in the board's published proceedings was not "comfortable," but "inhabitable," and the preparations for furnishing the home did not seem to assure many comforts: "Commissioner [Julius] Hielscher was authorized to procure, for the use of the poor on the county farm, one table, two chairs, two towels, one pail, one small looking glass, one broom, one dipper."[19]

A self-supporting county farm required land that was suitable for farming, but it was not always easy to determine the fertility of the soil in advance. As a result, there was considerable selling and trading of farms during the early years. In 1868 the Olmsted County commissioners, finding it necessary to "provide a home for the indigent on their hands," bought the Silas N. Howard farm, a 240-acre tract in Marion Township, and made arrangements to open a poorhouse. This proved to be literally a poor farm, and in 1874 and 1896 the county traded for others. Although the third was a "fine piece of land," it was larger than needed and proved an encumbrance that kept the county "land poor."[20]

Blue Earth County was more fortunate. On November 27, 1867, its board authorized the "committee on poor farm" to purchase land when, "in their opinion, the interests of the county shall justify." The interests of the county apparently demanded prompt action, for three days later the committee purchased from Columbus

Ballard 160 acres in Rapidan Township. On January 9, 1868, the board authorized arrangements to "build a suitable house and procure such animals, farming utensils, and furniture as may be needed." Two days later it appointed Hiram Yates as overseer of the poor farm; his services were "to include himself and wife and two cows." At that time the farm was situated in the center of a large wooded area, and during one week nine or ten deer were shot in the vicinity. But after the woods were cleared, a local chronicler reported, "no better farming land could be found anywhere."[21]

Fillmore County was not getting a pig in a poke when, in the spring of 1868, the board purchased 400 acres of land in Canton and Amherst townships. This was a first-class farm, and after a three-story frame house and other buildings were completed that fall it was quite a show place. In October the board appropriated $3,000 to buy stock, furniture, and other supplies. With improvements the farm was valued at $15,000. This seemed a good deal of money to put into a poor farm, but the county's expenditures for poor relief had nearly doubled within a year (from $2,188.81 in the fiscal year of 1866–67 to $4,347.44 in 1867–68). If the county was to own a farm, it wanted a good one.[22]

Although the location was generally less important than the quality of the land, a few counties, like Carver, made an attempt to place the poor farm near the center of the area. Carver had been settled by thrifty people, many of whom emigrated from Germany. Long before the board decided to buy, the commissioners made a careful study of poor expenses, and they used the same cautious approach in locating the farm. On February 3, 1870, the *Valley Herald* of Chaska reported: "The County has affected the purchase of 200 acres of land of Bernhard Rudiger of Dahlgreen for a poor farm. The County paid $1,000 down, balance in one, two and three years — whole amount $3,950. We are informed that it is a most desirable farm, about equally divided between clearing, timber and meadow and some say, would make an excellent place for the location of the county seat." The newspaper added the suggestion, which no doubt fell on deaf ears, that the "county officers could cut and haul their own wood, a saving of several hundred dollars per year to the county."[23]

If it was not always easy to determine the quality of land in advance, neither was it easy to predict where the center of population would fall in future years. In 1867 Wabasha County located its first poor farm in Hyde Park Township, which it considered "central and well adapted for purposes intended." Five years later the board members concluded that the farm was not as well located as they had hoped. On September 3, 1872, they noted that "the County poor farm . . . is too far from a public thoroughfare, [and] That it is too expensive to convey paupers to the farm." A committee was appointed to sell or exchange the land and relocate the farm close to Wabasha, Lake City, or Plainview. A thirty-two-acre farm was found on the edge of Wabasha, and the poorhouse operation was moved to that location.[24]

At least two counties obtained poor farms not so much because they needed them, as because land was readily available. Freeborn County, for example, became the owner of the ghost town of Bancroft, which it obtained for unpaid taxes. Like many other promising villages of the 1850s, Bancroft faded away after it lost out to Albert Lea in a hotly contested election for the county seat. In 1870 the land was auctioned for unpaid taxes, and the property passed into the possession of the county, which built a poorhouse on the site of a former store.[25]

Faribault County obtained its poor farm at a sale of school lands. Under the Organic Act establishing Minnesota Territory, sections sixteen and thirty-six in each township were reserved for the support of schools. In 1868 the state offered a section of land in Prescott Township, and Faribault County purchased the north half. When the county's plan to open a poorhouse failed to materialize, the property reverted to the state, probably because the county failed to make the payments.[26]

Although a number of elderly persons applied for relief in Brown County during the 1860s and the board bought a farm in 1870, it did not operate a poorhouse until some years later. The Brown County board believed strongly that children should support their elderly parents when able to do so. For example, the county records of March 11, 1868, show that "Mr. Laudenschlaeger presented a bill for boarding a poor old man, father of Oliver Mathew. . . . He stated that the old man was left in his house sick and unable to help himself; that Oliver Mathew, son of the old man, had driven him off and did not want to support him. After thorough investigation of the matter the auditor was instructed to notify Oliver Mathew to take care of his old father immediately and said notice to be sent to said O. Mathew by the sheriff. Mr. Laudenschlaeger's bill was disallowed." A year later the board faced a similar case in the "Application made by Phil. Gross that he be relieved of taking care of Carl Neun, and [sic] old helpless man, father-in-law of German Friton. . . . Board ordered that sheriff be instructed to inform German Friton that he immediately take care of Carl Neun, his father-in-law, otherwise the county commissioners would be compelled to take care of him at the expense of said German Friton." A day after issuing this order, the board made a final disposition of the case: "Sheriff instructed to take Carl Neun to German Friton."[27]

Brown County, Minnesota, was not the only area where grown children occasionally neglected their elderly and destitute parents. The most powerful voice raised in America on behalf of needy old people was that of a country editor in Hinsdale, Michigan, who often visited the county poorhouse and saw there old people who had put their property into the hands of their children and now were "on the town." Although Will Carleton was not quite twenty-six years old when "Over the Hill to the Poor-house" appeared in the June 17, 1871, issue of *Harper's Weekly,* his tale of the old mother who had worked "summer and winter" to raise her six children and then found that "no house is big enough for two families" is a penetrating study of family relationships. The ballad immediately caught the public's fancy, and the phrase "over the hill" became a synonym for "poorhouse."[28]

> Over the hill to the poor-house I'm trudgin' my weary way —
> I, a woman of 70, and only a trifle gray —
> I, who am smart an' chipper, for all the years I've told,
> As many another woman that's only half as old.

Although life was hard, things went pretty well for the old mother until Charley, the last son left in the nest, brought home a proud wife with an "edication." One word led to another:

> So 'twas only a few days before the thing was done —
> They was a family of themselves, and I another one;
> And a very little cottage one family will do,
> But I never have seen a house that was big enough for two.
>
> . . .
>
> I went to live with Susan, but Susan's house was small,
> And she was always a-hintin' how snug it was for us all;
> And what with her husband's sisters, and what with
>   child'rn three,
> 'Twas easy to discover that there wasn't room for me.

An' then I went to Thomas, the oldest son I've got,
For Thomas's buildings 'd cover the half of an acre lot;
But all the child'rn was on me — I couldn't stand their sauce —
And Thomas said I needn't think I was comin' there to boss.

An' then I wrote to Rebecca, my girl who lives out West,
And to Isaac, not far from her — some twenty miles at best;
And one of 'em said 'twas too warm there for any one so old,
And t'other had an opinion the climate was too cold.

So they have shirked and slighted me, an' shifted me about —
So they have well-nigh soured me, an' wore my old heart out;
But still I've borne up pretty well, an' wasn't much put down,
Till Charley went to the poor-master, an' put me on the town.

After the poem appeared, Will Carleton is said to have received many letters from poorhouse superintendents who reported that children were withdrawing their parents, shamed into filial duty by the ballad. It is impossible to measure the poem's effect, for there are no figures on the number who left institutions, nor any information on how many of the aged had sons and daughters able to support them.[29]

In St. Louis County, Minnesota, neglected old people were not the principal problem. Rather it was the sick and disabled for whom no care was available and the families who needed the bare necessities in order to exist. This northern county was growing at a tremendous rate — between 1860 and 1870 the population jumped from 406 to 4,561 — and people were still pouring into the area. In 1869 the county board opened a very primitive "two-mattress" hospital (there is no record of bedsteads being provided), and a year or so later began to allow more and more payments for provisions, house rent, and merchandise for the poor. St. Louis County, which stretches from the tip of Lake Superior north to the Canadian border, is extremely cold in the winter, and "wood for poor" was prominent among the items provided.[30]

Some time before 1873 the county procured a timbered tract northeast of Duluth on what later became Rice Lake Road. It is possible that this was the first, and perhaps the only, poor farm in Minnesota which originally served as the county wood lot. In January, 1873, the board advertised for "proposals for chopping the wood on 15 acres, more or less . . . and delivering and Piling the same in the Court House Square." Several bids having been received by February 1, the board "adjourned to the Poor Farm to locate land to be cleared." As the commissioners tramped through the woods, selecting the trees to be cut, they must have pondered the rising cost of caring for the county's poor. In the past several months there had been a substantial increase in the number of bills submitted for provisions and merchandise, and there had been expenses for boarding out paupers. Lately several bills for "coffins for paupers" and "hauling pauper to grave" had made their appearance.[31]

If the commissioners had not already thought of using this county land for a poorhouse, the sight of it may have given them the idea. Perhaps, they reasoned, here was a place where the poor could cut their own wood, and where the overseer, if necessary, could "haul pauper to grave" without extra charge to the county. At any rate, less than two weeks later, the board was advertising for plans and specifications for building a poorhouse; seven months later on August 16, 1873, the building was completed and ready for occupancy.[32]

As the St. Louis County commissioners accepted their new poorhouse from the contractor, they resolved: "that on and after Saturday the 23d day of August, A.D. 1873, no provisions be allowed nor any help granted any parties in this County other than those residing at the Poor House . . . and that all those at present receiving help from the County, be requested to appear at the Auditor's office . . . and show cause why they should receive help from the County." Six women and one man apparently were able to "show cause" and were granted from $4 to $8 each per month.[33]

The move to concentrate dependents in a newly acquired poor farm was not an unusual reaction. Olmsted County had taken the same step in 1868, soon after making its decision to buy the Howard farm. The board announced that "all arrangements heretofore made with any person for weekly or monthly aid or stipend for support of indigent persons" would expire on May 1. Thereafter "indigent persons, except by special arrangements with district commissioner, will if entitled to public support be received at the County poor farm." And in Wabasha County, after the new poorhouse was in operation, the board resolved that because of the mounting expense for poor relief and the fact that the county now had a comfortable place for paupers, each commissioner would be limited that year to spending not more than $15 for any one family outside the poor farm.[34]

If there seems to have been a certain smugness on the part of some counties in allowing the poor, as one historian expressed it, to "share the bounty, a beneficent hand is pleased to bestow," how did the poor themselves feel? There is no doubt that for many "over the hill to the poorhouse" was the last ignominious stretch of an unhappy road. When, for example, Ramsey County was debating the question of a city-county hospital in 1872, the local board of health was informed by the health officer that people felt "a perfect horror . . . at the thought of going to the poor house — in fact, starvation and death were considered preferable to removal to that establishment."[35]

Many, of course, were resigned to it — they had little alternative — but occasionally there was rebellion in the ranks. Perhaps the most dramatic display of spirit occurred in Faribault County, which, it will be recalled, had a farm but not a poorhouse. The needy were lodged with friends and relatives throughout the county. In 1874 the board decided to concentrate its charges at one place, and on March 4 "the keeping of the County Poor was let to Ebenezer Raymond for the sum of $2.00 per week each person, this being the lowest bid received." The board then notified the sixteen persons being supported by the county "to repair to Mr. Raymond's, where comfortable quarters had been prepared for them."[36]

A local historian painted a graphic picture of what followed when he wrote: "But lo! only three obeyed the order! The others refused, on the ground that they were not going to the poor house! not they, they could do better than that — they had not become so poor as that yet! Not quite! So long as many of them could live comfortably among friends and relatives, and the county pay their expenses, it was all right, but this thing of going to the poor house, they could not stand." The historian concluded: "We are compelled to honor the spirit they manifested . . . still they seemed to make a great distinction where there was not much difference. The county, at all events, was by this action relieved of their support."

The problems of county administration during the 1870s were compounded by the severe financial panic which followed the collapse of the Philadelphia banking concern of Jay Cooke and Company in September, 1873, and by a series of natural disasters, especially in the southwestern section of the state. Although Brown County seems to have been particularly unfortunate, its experience in the 1870s was shared by other areas and can be cited as an example of the difficulties which several boards of commissioners faced. In July, 1871, a severe hailstorm destroyed the crops of many farmers, and during the fall prairie fires caused further damage. Brown County's commissioners were kept busy in their respective districts investigating "the losses sustained by each farmer." In January, 1872, when the county received $200 from a state relief fund created by Governor Horace B. Austin (from donations contributed by individuals in more fortunate counties), the board distributed this money to the most needy. Then it set up a general meeting to receive the continuing applications and claims from sufferers by hail and fire. On January 7-9, 1873, a blizzard of such intensity and violence that it was called the "Arctic Cyclone" swept over the state, causing great suffering and considerable damage. But what really took the heart out of the farmers was the visitation of grasshoppers in the summer of 1873 and thereafter until 1877.[37]

The grasshoppers precipitated a major disaster, for they devoured not only crops but all vegetation, as well as items of clothing and other articles left exposed. By March, 1874, the Brown County board had received about 200 applications for relief, including 125 from persons "who were entirely destitute and without any means to procure the necessary seed grain" for the spring planting. During the next few years Brown County received several appropriations from the state legislature, and the board distributed seed grain, pork, and flour through local committees. The county did not, however, rely wholly on outside help. In September, 1874, the board allocated a thousand dollars for purchasing flour, and during the summer of 1875 it was paying bounties for dead grasshoppers. At last in 1877 the grasshoppers left the state as suddenly as they had appeared.[38]

Throughout the five years of grasshopper plagues, the board of commissioners was busy acting as the liaison between Brown County and the state government on measures aimed at destroying the insects and dispensing relief. Thus it is not surprising that the members did not see fit to take on the establishment of a poorhouse on the farm that had been acquired in 1870. The board's records for January 3, 1871, show that it "ordered that Mr. Mason, renter of the poor farm, be paid $3.50 a week for taking care of and furnishing board and washing for Pardon Spooner, a poor feeble old man," but there is no indication that the farm was used for other county charges. Most of the persons applying for relief during the grasshopper plagues were not poorhouse candidates. What they needed was seed grain and food to tide them over until they could get back on their feet.

The hardships of the 1870s effectively checked poor farm buying for the next five years and gave impetus to a movement toward township responsibility for care of the poor. As we have seen, the idea of township responsibility was not new. In the short-lived Township Act of 1858, the Minnesota legislature had attempted to take the government closer to the people, not only in matters of poor relief, but in many other areas as well. A different kind of argument was now advanced for shifting tax burdens to the towns. Many persons believed that local control would inhibit a tendency toward general extravagance. Because the town officers had a better knowledge of the applicants, they would be able to match the relief to the need, giving only what was absolutely necessary. It was also argued that the applicants themselves, especially "unworthy" persons, would be more reluctant to ask for help from local officials whom they knew.[39]

After 1875 a number of counties shifted to the township system of poor relief in an attempt to reduce the costs of caring for the indigent. Ramsey County, it will be remembered, had taken this step in 1861, and Freeborn became the first of some eighteen counties to follow the example during the 1870s and 1880s. In decentralizing poor relief, however, local officials faced again the vexing problems posed by residence requirements. Many of the laws enacted to permit counties to shift from one system to the other made no provision for the relief of a pauper who was a resident of the county, but not of any organized municipality or township; additional legislation was often necessary to fix more accurately the areas of county and town responsibility. In their squabbles over jurisdiction, the authorities seemed occasionally to overlook the fact that it was not merely a tax burden, but a human burden, they were shuttling — sometimes quite literally — between county courthouse and town hall.[40]

The county did not lose its powers to operate a poor farm under the township system, but adoption of the latter seems to have had a deterring effect.[41] Three counties — Freeborn, Carver, and Le Sueur — promptly closed their poorhouses after obtaining special town plan laws. Some counties apparently postponed the purchase of farms in the expectation that the towns would eventually take care of their own poor. One which dragged its feet was Stearns County. As early as 1868 the board appointed a committee to negotiate for a farm, but, according to a county historian, the "records do not show that any report was ever made." Following public protests that the county poor were being unfairly treated, the board in March, 1870, asked for "propositions regarding the purchase of a poor farm or other methods for the care of the poor." Again the matter seems to have been dropped. Four years later a committee was once more appointed to select a poor farm. The members went so far as to visit some farms offered for sale, but their report was laid on the table. In 1876 the board adopted a resolution asking the Stearns County legislative delegation to secure "the passage of an act requiring the different towns in the county to support their own poor." The town system law was passed the following year and the board gave up the idea of operating a poor farm.[42]

By 1878 the economic situation in the state had improved, and that year the Houston County board bought an old wayside tavern three miles from Hokah in Union Township and opened it as a poorhouse. In 1879 Murray County bought a farm but did not open a poorhouse until nearly twenty years later. From 1854, when Ramsey County acquired its first poor farm, to 1880, twenty-three Minnesota counties purchased farms or buildings for the care of their homeless dependents.[43]

Most of this activity occurred in the 1860s. The disasters and depression of the 1870s brought retrenchment and a re-examination of the respective roles of county and town governments as well as a new emphasis on poorhouse care as the cheapest form of relief. By 1880, however, the county poorhouse was firmly entrenched as the major institutional resource for needy persons. It held this position in spite of the creation of specialized state institutions. While the early establishment in Minnesota of a state prison, a state reformatory, and a county jail system undoubtedly eliminated certain types of criminals who at one time flooded the almshouses of the East, the shiftless and the intemperate often found refuge at the poor farm. By 1880 the state also had two hospitals for the insane, schools for the deaf, dumb, and blind, an institution for the feeble-minded, and — for a brief period from 1872 to 1878 — a home for soldiers' orphans. But these institutions were overcrowded or not available to all who needed specialized care and treatment. Consequently, the county poorhouses were often filled with mentally ill, mentally deficient, and handicapped persons.[44]

In rural areas the poorhouse was also the sole resource for many homeless women, delinquent girls, and dependent children. All but one of the private benevolent institutions open to these groups of unfortunates in 1880 were located in Minneapolis and St. Paul.

COUNTY POOR FARMS 37

The few hospitals in the state for the acutely ill were also situated in the metropolitan areas; needy persons who became sick in rural counties were sent to the poorhouse for such care as the matron could give.[45]

A word picture drawn by an Iowa observer conveys the heterogeneity of the poorhouse population of the period. In a paper given at the National Conference of Charities in Chicago in 1879, C. S. Watkins, a delegate from Iowa, described a typical rural poorhouse. "The average number of inmates . . . seldom exceeds twenty-five or thirty," Watkins reported, "exclusive of the pauper insane who are sent there whenever the State hospitals are too much crowded for their reception, as almost constantly is the case. Of this average we generally find the sexes in nearly equal numbers. The individual details usually include two or three foundlings or orphaned children; two or three half-grown boys and girls of feeble intellect, and accompanying low grade of moral perceptions; two or three adults with constitutional antipathy to manual labor."[46]

After observing that persons in this last group were prone to constant complaints about ailments which restricted their movements except, conveniently, at mealtimes, Watkins commented: "It is, however, noteworthy that these cases are almost invariably of the 'male persuasion.' In our pauper inspections we seldom find a chronic case of female laziness. In fact, the women in a poorhouse are the only pauper workers."

Having thus described the major types of poorhouse inhabitants, Watkins continued: "To all these add a few adult imbeciles and cases of destitute old age, these last being chiefly of foreign birth, and coming to this country only when nearly worn out by field-labor at home; and add also, with more or less frequency, cases of homeless boys and girls waiting till the county officials can 'bind them out' to respectable farmers; also cases of friendless men and women, forced by temporary or chronic illness to seek this refuge, for the county poorhouse is also the county hospital; and add the almost constant sheltering of several of those social outcasts of either sex, who, without committing any decidedly criminal act, yet constantly pollute the very atmosphere of every place they occupy."

If Watkins passed lightly over the "few" cases of "destitute old age," this is not surprising. Old people, unless physically or mentally ill, were not usually a source of trouble in poorhouses, and care of the aged had not yet become an obvious problem for the community. Nevertheless, although people were generally unaware of it, the phenomenon known as the "aging of the population" had already begun. From 1870 to 1880 the ratio of persons sixty-five years of age and over to the total population increased from 3.0 per cent to 3.4 per cent in the United States as a whole, and from 1.9 per cent to 2.5 per cent in Minnesota. Poorhouse populations would eventually be affected by this aging trend, as well as by the exodus — only then beginning — of mentally ill, defective, and handicapped persons to state institutions. But the outcome of these tendencies was not clearly apparent in 1880, and the county poor farm remained the catchall for every age and condition of society's unfit.[47]

3

The Home for the Friendless

1867—1883

IN 1857 HARRIET E. BISHOP, St. Paul's first schoolteacher, predicted that in the "drama of events which are to precede the millenial glory," Minnesota's women would play a large part. "Man may bid the tall forest tree to bow; he may make the waste places smile with plenty . . . or he may hold the scepter of power: but to WOMAN a higher, a nobler work is entrusted." Although Miss Bishop had in mind primarily woman's role in "training the twig," she did not exclude any activity which would make a better environment for all, including the aged.[1]

Miss Bishop herself took part in what was probably the first organized activity carried out by Minnesota women in behalf of a worthy cause. When the winter of 1847–48 closed in on the little settlement of St. Paul, the women of the few white families then living there wondered what "rational, social pleasure" they could devise to elevate the moral tone of society. The answer was suggested by a man: form a ladies' sewing society and raise funds for the erection of a schoolhouse, a building which could also be used for lectures and other public gatherings. "Accordingly," said Miss Bishop, "the 'St. Paul Circle of Industry' was formed, with eight members, and several gentlemen as visitors." By plying their needles, the ladies earned money to provide the first payment on the lumber; then they solicited subscriptions to complete the building.[2]

This was only the beginning of women's activities in Minnesota. As new arrivals poured into the territory in the 1850s, charities were practical though not always organized. The women helped their needy neighbors or members of their churches, and it was not long before they formed ladies' aid or missionary groups. During the Civil War the women organized volunteer aid societies — so-called because their object was to help army volunteers — and raised money to provide hospital care for wounded soldiers and assistance for their families. In addition they sewed uniforms, scraped linen, rolled bandages, and sent to the men at the front comfort bags filled with "combs, pins, needles, court-plaster and black sewing cotton."[3]

After the war, in that period when county commissioners were buying poor farms, the women again found plenty of scope for their energies. While the poor farms might care for many of the destitute and defective, they could not accommodate all who needed help. The women began to look for ways of assisting the growing number of widows, deserted families, orphaned children, homeless immigrants, and girls who had gone astray.

One of the first of the postwar organizations was the Christian Aid Society of Minneapolis, of special interest to this study because it later opened a home for the aged. On January 27, 1866, after five preliminary meetings, "some twenty ladies and children" gathered to consider what might be done to serve the community. They decided on the following objectives, which were incorporated into a constitution: "to provide homes for the destitute as far as possible among those who are concerned, to read the Holy Scriptures with meditation and prayer — also to provide food, clothing, religious and literary instruction for the needy irrespective of class or church." Going two by two in apostolic fashion, the women of Minneapolis called on the poor, visited the state prison, collected clothing for freedmen in Tennessee, and supported the temperance cause. (Visitors among the poor were exhorted to "make use of the 'Total Abstinence Pledge' as a means of doing good.")[4]

Harriet Bishop had a hand in a similar undertaking in St. Paul which was to result in the founding of the first private home for the aged in Minnesota. On May 4, 1867, after several preliminary meetings, twelve women gathered in the vestry of the First Presbyterian Church and laid the foundations for what is now the oldest private home for the aged in the state — the Home for the Friendless (later renamed the Protestant Home of St. Paul). Miss Bishop took the first minutes. "Twelve women from the Evangelical Churches of St. Paul (as by appointment at a preliminary meeting)," she wrote, "met . . . to consider the need of, and measures requisite for a 'home for the homeless'; for which work God had seemingly opened up the way. The command 'Go Forward'! could not be mistaken or misunderstood. Facts developed the need, and His children 'have a mind to work.' "[5]

The need was plain, for the "homeless" were to be found everywhere — in the boardinghouses along Fourth Street, at the doors of the churches, and on the levees by the river. In 1867 the homeless were not mainly the aged, but immigrants. St. Paul already boasted a population of about 16,000, and newcomers were reaching the city on every stagecoach and river steamer. To some observers those arriving from foreign shores appeared to be "a stout and hearty lot of settlers." But the trained eye of at least one physician saw that the immigrants, in many cases, brought with them "constitutions broken by the hardships and privations of peasant life abroad." Many bore the "marks of malnutrition, the flush of fevers, the deep pits of small pox." There were American-born settlers, too, seeking relief from pulmonary disease in Minnesota's much vaunted salubrious climate.[6]

The first boat in the spring of 1867 docked at St. Paul on April 21, and many of its passengers were stranded.[7] Five days later the city council, at the request of the Chamber of Commerce and the Board of Trade, opened a "Home for Emigrants" in a warehouse on the upper levee. "All of them need cheap accommodations for a few days," observed the *St. Paul Daily Pioneer* of May 18, 1867, "a thing they could not get at a crowded hotel or boarding house, where rates are generally exorbitant. These poor ignorant immigrants are generally badly imposed on, and swindled by parties who prey on the ignorant." The newspaper did not mention the ninety-two saloons listed in the city directory, but no doubt they too received a share of the immigrants' meager hoard.

At the new emigrant shelter a family could rent, for fifteen cents a person per day, an apartment furnished with bunks and straw, and have the use of stoves and fuel for cooking. But this was temporary housing, a place to stay until work and a permanent abode could be found. With the arrival of each boatload of newcomers that year, the number of jobless immigrants increased, and it was clear that by the end of the summer the situation would be almost intolerable.[8]

The urgency of the problem is reflected in the speed with which the women of St. Paul organized and set to work. Most of the city's Protestant congregations were represented at the May 4 meeting. The delegates named a committee to prepare a constitution, and its members immediately began collecting information on similar projects in other states.[9]

By 1867 benevolent organizations in the East and in many of the southern and central states were conducting institutions of various kinds: hospitals; orphanages; homes for invalids, working girls, and unmarried mothers; temporary abodes for the "homeless"; and permanent homes for the aged. More than forty institutions throughout the country received aged or homeless persons. More than a third of them were church-sponsored, and others may have been church-affiliated. The first religious groups to enter the field were the Episcopal Church and several orders of Roman Catholic nuns, notably the Sisters of Charity.[10]

Homes for women predominated. Of the 43 known to be receiving aged or homeless persons, 24 were for women only; 12 for women and children; five for men and women; and one for men, women, and children. Only one limited its intake to men — the Sailors Snug Harbor at New Brighton, New York, founded in 1833 for "aged, decrepit, and worn-out sailors." A few homes were selective as to church affiliation; one specified "respectable" aged women; another admitted "wayfarers."

The purpose of a home was often spelled out in its name. Typical were the Pennsylvania Asylum for Indigent Women and Single Women, the Lutheran Orphans Home and Asylum for the Aged and Infirm, and the Home for Aged Indigent Females. Few names seem to have been designed to make the prospect of entering the home attractive. How much of an inducement the "Widows and Old Men's Home" offered probably depended on the individual applicant.

The years after the Civil War showed a marked increase in the establishment of private benevolent homes, especially institutions for "friendless" persons. From 1865 through 1867, the number opened was double that of the preceding five years. In view of this national trend, which may have been due to the mobility of the population and the disruptive effects of the war, it is not surprising that when the women of St. Paul's Protestant churches held their first meeting in 1867 their original goal was to establish a "home for the homeless." Within a few weeks, however, the project had assumed a larger and different aspect. The organization, now named the Ladies Christian Union, decided that it would undertake to "relieve, aid, and provide *Homes* for the homeless, the destitute and unfriended especially women and children[;] also to visit the fatherless and widow in their affliction; to instruct and assist those in prison; to afford protection to young persons exposed to contagion from the moral evils that are rife in society, and to surround all who may become objects of attention with kindly and saving influences."[11]

It was a big order, and the Reverend Frederick T. Brown of Central Presbyterian Church ventured to suggest that "the house was too large for the occupants." But the founders of the group were not to be discouraged, for behind them stood the women of their churches. They immediately adopted a constitution, solicited funds, organized auxiliary societies, and set up in each member church a committee to visit the poor, the sick, and the destitute. Other committees were formed to attend to home-finding and employment, finances, and devotional exercises.[12]

After electing officers, the ladies devised strict rules for the conduct of their meetings. All meetings were to begin precisely at the time fixed and no one was to be seated during opening exercises. In order to ensure a more businesslike atmosphere, the rules also admonished: "As many valuable suggestions are lost by whispering and talking in groups, and as such practices tend to discord and confusion, it is expected that every lady will address the Chair."[13]

On July 5 the women decided to keep open the lecture room of the First Presbyterian Church on each Thursday, when one or more members of the home-finding committee would be present to interview strangers. Almost anyone who needed help of any kind received it. The group found a boarding place for Mrs. W_____, helped Mrs. C_____ of Tenth Street obtain employment, and assisted widows and children. In addition to furnishing "necessaries and comforts" for the sick and destitute at the emigrant shelter, the women left word with the superintendent that "application might be made for future supplies . . . during the period before the close of navigation."[14]

By the end of the first summer the group had employed as "Bible Reader and City Missionary" a Miss McNair, who had done similar work in St. Louis. Introduced at the October meeting, she reported that "she had visited several families, chiefly Romans." Miss McNair requested tracts, and there is some evidence that Bible reading was of greater interest to her than finding homes for the homeless. She remained only until the following July when, despite the offer of an additional five dollars a month for the use of a carriage in her work, she returned to St. Louis.[15]

In spite of, or perhaps because of, its ambitious program, the Ladies Christian Union soon suffered a slackening of interest on the part of its members. For some time in 1868 the ladies found it impossible to obtain a quorum. Diagnosing the causes of the difficulty as organizational unwieldiness and departures from the original purpose — the establishment of a home for destitute women and children — the women took steps to remedy the situation in the fall of 1868. By December they had rented a house at 47 Walnut Street and opened it as a temporary home until a permanent site could be acquired.[16]

This determined course of action helped to revive interest, and the annual meeting held in January, 1869, was well-attended although not entirely harmonious. A reporter from the *Daily Pioneer* observed: "For the quick transaction of business, the ladies have a very decided advantage over men. They have no long, tedious speeches to inflict upon a patient, long-suffering public. When they do talk, though, they are wont to talk together. The confusion caused by this proceeding, however, is amply compensated for by the fact that the talking is all done at once, and thus the sooner got through with."[17]

The group agreed upon a new name — the Ladies Relief Association — and adopted a new constitution. Some of the purposes set forth in the earlier constitution were deleted. Although the women would continue to surround "with kindly and saving influences" all who became objects of their attention, they would no longer attempt to visit everyone who was afflicted, in prison, or exposed to the moral evils "rife in society." Henceforth, their aim would be simply to "provide a 'Home for the Homeless' destitute and friendless women and children and engage in such works of Christian Charity as may be appropriate and incident to the aforesaid general purpose and plan."[18]

The rented house on Walnut Street was not satisfactory as a permanent home, and the reorganized group renewed its efforts to find a suitable property. On May 4, 1869, the organization bought for $3,300 a house and approximately an acre of land on Collins Street, near De Soto and Lafayette (then Herkimer) streets. The new Home for the Friendless, as it was almost immediately known, now became the reason for the association's existence and the focus of all its endeavors.[19]

There is little information about this building, which was to serve the organization for nearly fifteen years. Although thoroughly renovated by order of the city physician, it was described a few years later as "very old, very small, and almost insufferably cold." These defects must not have been evident at the time of purchase, for after the building was repaired and cleaned the women "were gratified at the appearance of comfort."[20]

Certainly they lost no time in filling the home. Not until later did they develop intake policies, make investigations, and, as new agencies came into being, consider alternative solutions to an applicant's problems. During these early years, the simple need for care and shelter was the deciding factor, and action was prompt. For instance, one day in February, 1870, "Mrs. [John B.] Sanborn brought up the case of a newly arrived destitute Virginian family and it was voted to receive the Mother and daughters for a time. . . . Mrs. Sanborn at once sent her sleigh for them and they arrived before the close of the meeting."[21]

Many of the first persons admitted to the Home for the Friendless were ill as well as penniless. In 1869 St. Paul had only one hospital — St. Joseph's — and it could not accommodate all who needed care. Some of the illnesses were contagious, although their potential danger was not always recognized at the time. When a destitute woman with typhoid fever was recommended for admission, "Mrs. Fairchild was appointed to consult with Dr. Smith as to the propriety of taking the woman to the Home, as her case is not a very serious one and it is supposed will yield to cleanliness and good care." In 1870 the association voted as a matter of policy to accept some invalids and to charge $6 a week for ordinary cases. There was pressure to do more. St. Paul physicians wanted the group to open a women's hospital, and it was even suggested that they build an addition and take in sick mariners. But the women kept their eyes on the main purpose — to operate a home, not a hospital. Although they continued to take in a few sick persons, the latter were usually homeless and destitute as well. In October, 1871, the board considered "an urgent request that the Home should receive . . . an aged Methodist minister and wife, poor, homeless and sick." They were perhaps the first residents accepted for permanent care.[22]

To support the home, it was necessary for the organization to tap new financial resources. There was little in the way of fund raising that these women did not try; their projects ranged from amateur musicals and lectures to theatricals and charity balls. Gradually the home became famous for two regular events: a strawberry festival each summer and a donation party each fall. Items received at the latter included everything from carpet rags to pieplant and a cord of wood. The only failure occurred on October 10, 1871, and was described in a terse comment: "Small attendance at Donation Party. Cause Chicago Fire." The strawberry festivals held at the home must have added greatly to the gaiety and sparkle of life in old St. Paul. For these occasions the spacious grounds were illuminated with Chinese lanterns, and an "arbor, flower tables, candy stand, & lemonade fountain beautified the front yard." Freezers of ice cream, cakes, and strawberries were donated in abundance.[23]

As St. Paul's population doubled in the 1870s, there was a corresponding increase in the number of persons requiring care. For the first few years, the Ladies Relief Association felt equal to almost any demand made upon it. "Affairs in most prosperous condition," noted the minutes of January 29, 1873, "[the home] free of debt." But in the financial stringency which accompanied the panic of 1873 the women discovered that some works of charity must of necessity be left to others. Fortunately, St. Paul already had a number of city missions, ladies' aid societies, and mutual benefit or fraternal societies which stood ready to assist members in sickness or distress and to provide relief for their widows and orphaned children. When the hard times arrived, additional agencies came into being, and it was no longer necessary for the Ladies Relief Association to attempt to care for all of the sick, needy, and erring of St. Paul. Its first project — helping immigrants — was now shared with the Scandinavian Ladies Emigrant Society and other organizations assisting newcomers to the city.[24]

St. Paul also had one home for "fallen women," the House of the Good Shepherd, which the Sisters of St. Joseph had opened in 1869 in a building originally planned as a Presbyterian college. In November, 1873, a second rescue home for women and girls was opened in the city. Its history went back to December, 1872, when a sixteen-year-old girl asked assistance from Mrs. Daniel S. B. Johnston, president of another organization of St. Paul's Protestant churchwomen called the Women's Christian Association. The girl was homeless, Mrs. Johnston's biographer wrote, "no kin on earth that she knew — betrayed — an outcast; lying, foul mouthed, and thievish." After Mrs. Johnston had helped this girl and several others, "five girls[,] all inmates of houses of ill fame, came in a body seeking help to turn from lives of shame." At Mrs. Johnston's suggestion her association rented a house on Bradley and Woodward streets and opened the Women's Christian Home. After that the Home for the Friendless referred erring women to the new institution.[25]

In 1876 a group of prominent St. Paul men, including Alexander Ramsey, Henry M. Rice, Henry H. Sibley, William R. Marshall, Daniel R. Noyes, and other political and civic leaders, organized the St. Paul Society for Improving the Condition of the Poor, later named the Society for the Relief of the Poor, to assist with food, clothing, employment, and loans. Persons requiring relief were then directed to, or sought voluntarily, this new organization.[26]

As other agencies took over some of the activities formerly handled by the Ladies Relief Association, the organization restated its purposes. "The design of the Home," declared the annual report for 1876–77, "is to provide temporary shelter for destitute women and children." In accordance with this policy, the association tried to find employment for women who were capable of supporting themselves. The ladies went about this in several ways: they might, for example, find a position as a maid for a young woman or provide "clothing suitable to enable her to go to a place of service."[27]

In 1873 St. Paul's second hospital — St. Luke's — was incorporated and opened. The city also acquired a site for a city and county hospital. The Ladies Relief Association had earlier resisted pressures to establish a women's hospital, and the opening of the new institutions made it easier to refuse patients who were properly hospital cases. The association did, however, continue to receive some "persons who are not entirely destitute, but are in too feeble health to maintain themselves with their limited means. Of such we receive the nominal sum of three dollars per week for board."[28]

The Home for the Friendless made no change in its policy of accepting children. Even though St. Paul had both Protestant and Catholic orphan asylums, and the state opened a home at Winona for soldiers' orphans in this decade, there still were not nearly enough facilities for the proper care of dependent and neglected children. In fact, in 1875 the Ladies Relief Association discussed the question of adding a separate building for children, but decided that its financial resources were insufficient.[29]

While the group wished to "prevent long tarrying" by persons who could find homes elsewhere and on occasion insisted that women accept employment offered to them, the annual report of 1876–77 also noted a distinct trend toward long-term dependency: "To some, however, the Home becomes a permanent shelter. Aged, infirm, without friends or relatives able to assist, there is nowhere else for them to go, and their declining years are passed in all the comforts that a good home can give."[30]

In 1877 the group's name was changed. The annual report noted: "On account of the confusion arising from the fact that the name by which we are known is not the real name of our society, an amendment was offered early in this year (1877)" to change the name from the Ladies Relief Association to the "Home for the Friendless Association of the city of St. Paul. On consulting a lawyer, Mr. C[ushman] K. Davis, it was found that the simplest way to effect the change was to have it done by a special act of the Legislature. By the kindness of Mr. Davis an act was drawn up and passed during the present session."[31]

From the time the society purchased the Collins Street property with its inadequate building, the women had hoped for a new location. "We are working for the future," wrote Kate Nicols in her secretary's report for January, 1871. "When St. Paul shall have rounded out the circle of its growth, a stately edifice will stand where we to-day in weariness and perplexity lay humble but firm foundations."[32]

Although St. Paul had not "rounded out the circle of its growth" by 1878, the association voted that year to establish a building fund and appoint a building committee. Architectural plans were adopted in 1881, and in November, 1883, the Home for the Friendless moved into its new building, a structure that attracted considerable attention. With the Hennepin County poorhouse, it was one of the earliest buildings in Minnesota to be designed expressly for the purpose of caring for aged and destitute persons. According to the home's annual report for 1883, the women successfully raised $8,240 to erect the building.[33]

As recently as 1966, it was not necessary to draw entirely on the imagination to picture that structure. It still stood at 469 Collins Street, occupied by the Crispus Attucks Home for the Aged. There had been some changes, including the addition of a stucco exterior. Gone long ago were the original floors, the gas fixtures, and the stoves which in the 1880s old ladies might have in their rooms for the price of a cord of wood. In many respects, however, the building remained much as it had been on that November day more than eighty years earlier. The twelve-foot ceilings were still intact, as well as the stairway which led from the front hall to the second floor where there were about fourteen bedrooms. After the attic was finished in 1886, it was used to accommodate working women. A reporter, visiting the home several years after it opened, commented: "The home looks like a home. It has nice high ceilings, many windows, light, pretty wall paper. . . . The wood work's all light, everything's desperately clean, and it doesn't smell of cabbage."[34]

Where the women of the association found space for all the persons admitted and how they managed to keep the building presentable challenges the imagination. In some years they cared for more than 200 women and children, and the average number of occupants was frequently reported at from 40 to 50. Not surprisingly the informal admission policies of early years were replaced by formal rules adopted after the new building was opened. Because they served as a model for later homes, the regulations are of some interest. The first rule provided "That a committee on admissions be appointed by the board, whose duty it shall be to inquire into the circumstances and character of those who make application and report to the board all the facts relating to each case. They shall also keep a record of names of applicants, ages, place of birth, residences, date of application, persons by whom recommended, time and terms of admission and any other facts deemed important. The case of no applicant for admission will be considered which is not recommended by the committee on admissions."[35]

Rule two stated that "Applicants [for the women's department] must be persons of good character, in reduced circumstances, not less than sixty years of age and must have been resident of the state not less than two years." A third regulation required approved applicants "to pay an admission fee of $300," and stated that "no person will be received even as a temporary inmate, without an entrance permit signed by the admission committee." The final rule stipulated: "All inmates shall be received on a probation of six months, after which time the board shall act definitely on the case of each one so received, and if not made a permanent inmate the admission fee (deducting board at the rate of $3 per week) shall be returned. But no probationary inmate shall be received until she shall have signed an agreement . . ."

The agreement was a model of brevity. It addressed the applicant as follows: "Do you understand, consent and agree, that your admission to the home is not by any reason of any right, or in consideration of any payment on your part, but because the proper authorities, so far as they now know you, think you are worthy of its care; that you are at all times to be subject to and to obey each rule for the regulation and management of the home and the conduct of its inmates; that you cheerfully and without question will render such assistance in the necessary work of the home as the matron shall require of you; that your remaining in it is to be wholly within the control of the board, and that, if at any time, a majority of the board present at any regular meeting, for good reasons, shall think it expedient, they shall have a right to expel you from it and cause you to be removed therefrom; provided, however, that if it shall be within one year after your admission, the sum paid on your admission shall be returned to you, less three dollars for each week you shall have been an inmate of the home."

When the Collins Street home adopted these policies in 1883, the county poor farm was still the chief resource for Minnesota's needy and homeless of all ages. Like the poorhouse, the Home for the Friendless had at first attempted to care for all manner of people: destitute women, homeless immigrants, children, the sick, the erring, and the aged. It was the only private benevolent facility in the state that had been established to cope with the broad range of problems faced by the publicly supported poorhouse or poor farm. As new, specialized, private philanthropies emerged after the Civil War, the home's sponsors limited the scope of their activities to the care of destitute women and dependent children. Despite the fact that a need to care for elderly persons had been demonstrated (and the Home for the Friendless would later become such an institution), no facilities — either public or private — specifically for the aged existed in Minnesota as the 1880s dawned.[36]

4

Women of the Churches

1880–1900

THE 1880s WERE YEARS of notable growth and great activity. In Minneapolis an early settler named Charlotte Ouisconsin Van Cleve watched the rapid development of the city with awe and amazement. When she first knew it in the early 1860s, Minneapolis was a small town. "But the immense water power [*of the Falls of St. Anthony*] kept up its music," she wrote, "the mills ground flour and sawed logs and made paper, and, all unconsciously, we were growing great and preparing to become the wonder of the world."[1]

St. Paul was equally enterprising. Mark Twain, who visited the city in May, 1882, reported: "St. Paul's strength lies in her commerce — I mean his commerce. He is a manufacturing city, of course — all the cities of that region are — but he is particularly strong in the matter of commerce."

During the decade of the eighties there was a great expansion of private charitable agencies in both cities and, to a lesser extent, in other parts of the state. "The people are large-hearted," said Mrs. Van Cleve, "and ready to take hold of anything which has for its object the good of the community or the amelioration of suffering in any form." Additional hospitals, more orphanages and rescue homes, and a wide variety of relief and missionary societies appeared. There were new kinds of projects: kindergartens, recreation centers for newsboys and bootblacks, women's work exchanges which sold on commission homemade articles and foods, and industrial schools where volunteers taught women and girls some of the simpler household arts.[2]

The depression of 1893 slowed for a time the programs of the established organizations and changed somewhat the direction in which new agencies developed. Special emphasis was placed on the prevention or alleviation of poverty and the protection of children. The humane society movement, for example, spread in Minnesota during this period. The pioneer organization, the American Society for the Prevention of Cruelty to Animals, which Henry Bergh had started in New York in 1866, had found it necessary to form a separate branch in 1875 for the protection of children. In Minnesota, already "supplied with many admirable and efficient children's societies," one organization covered both children and animals. Although St. Paul's society had been started in 1870, most of Minnesota's humane societies were organized in the early 1890s. By 1894 Minneapolis, Duluth, and many smaller communities — Anoka, Mankato, Owatonna, Red Wing, Rochester, and others — also had chapters.[3]

Along with an interest in protecting children, charitably inclined groups were becoming increasingly aware of the needs of the elderly. The pressure of a burgeoning population, which at the same time was growing older (by 1900 the aged represented 3.8 per cent of the total population) resulted in the establishment of several homes exclusively for the elderly as well as others for both old and young.

By 1900 Minnesota had ten privately sponsored homes for the aged, which will be discussed in this chapter. Seven were in the Twin Cities of Minneapolis and St. Paul; three were in rural communities. While they had many similarities, no two of these first ten homes were exactly alike. However, in types of sponsorship, methods of raising funds, and ways in which they developed, the homes established certain patterns which were followed or paralleled by many of the institutions which came after them.

The sponsors can be described in two words: "women" and "churches." Or, it might be more accurate to say, "women of the churches." There was usually a pastor in the background, perhaps even as the instigating force, and men served on advisory boards and made generous donations when called upon. But it was the women who created the organizations and carried on the work. They came from all walks of life. Among them were the wives and daughters of the most prominent men of the day. There were also women whose only social outlet was the cause for which they worked. There were nuns dressed in the garb of the Breton peasant, and there was the Lutheran deaconess from Omaha, Nebraska, with her crisp white apron over a long plain black dress, and her tiny bonnet with a huge bow tied demurely under her chin. In two respects all these women were alike: they were deeply religious and they had the faith that can move mountains.

That faith was sorely needed. Most private benevolent homes started in a very limited way, in a small rented dwelling or a building which had outlived its original purpose. Only one (the Jones-Harrison Home in Minneapolis) began its service with an endowment. Early records are filled with references to problems which, at the time, seemed insurmountable. Frequently, Providence came to the rescue in the form of a needed donation of money, groceries, or wood. More often the women put their wits to work and devised a new way of raising funds to meet the crisis. Of women's fund-raising activities in this period, a social critic has unkindly suggested "that the small affairs where women contribute the things sold, and then induce their husbands, relatives, and friends to buy, indicate an unsatisfactory condition of financial servitude on the part of the women."[4] In Minnesota, however, it is doubtful that the women begrudged their time and effort. Fundraising activities were often tied in with social events, and people of the 1880s and 1890s had the prodding finger of a favorite charity to thank for many of the musicals, theatricals, lectures, strawberry festivals, and charity balls which enlivened their days.

Just why a benevolent home was started in a given place at a particular time is not always clear. The decision to open such an institution was seldom preceded by much planning or study. "All early charities were more or less indiscriminate," said a social worker some years later. "Giving was impulsive, rather than thoughtful. While often necessary and always kindly, it was usually without system or reference to its effect, further than immediate relief." The precipitating factor might be the need of a single individual for a place to stay, or a gift of land or money made with the proviso that it be used for an old folks' home. Often the work grew out of another field of service. Six homes for the aged founded before 1900 also cared for children. In general, the benevolent homes catered to women; the county poorhouses took care of the men.[5]

Because these early homes set important models, it may be useful to trace the development of a few typical institutions. The following accounts carry the stories to the end of the century and give, insofar as information is available, the who, when, where, why, and how of each home.

Although the ways in which the groups went about achieving their aims varied with their sponsorship, three broad patterns are recognizable. One was that of the women's society, with its emphasis on organization. The second was set by orders of Catholic nuns who started their homes to fill a community need and drew on the community for support. The third pattern was the sponsorship by a Protestant church body, which usually became involved after the home had been initiated under the impetus of a pastor or a member of the congregation.

The women's organization usually started by calling a meeting to discuss the problem; next the women proceeded to choose temporary officers, appoint key committees, adopt a constitution, elect permanent officers, and create additional committees as occasions arose. In due time these came to include a men's advisory board on financial and legal matters, which were deemed to be beyond the ken of women. With careful regard for the propriety of their actions, the ladies put every proposal to a vote and meticulously recorded it in the minutes. Many matters were considered at the business meetings, which were faithfully attended, but perhaps the major portion of the women's time was taken up by the search for a site or a building and by their numerous fund-raising activities.

As we have seen, this was the way in which the Home for the Friendless developed in St. Paul. Two Minneapolis homes were also sponsored by women's organizations, although, in each case, the group was involved in another form of service when it launched its old people's home. One of these — the institution now known as Stevens Square — had as its first purpose the care of homeless children. It was started as the Children's Home in October, 1881, at a small rented house at 520 Second Street in northeast Minneapolis, and there are at least two versions of how it came into being. One explanation records that two ladies "happened . . . upon a little girl, turned adrift by a heartless mother." When inquiry revealed that there were many such waifs, the ladies told the story to a few acquaintances "with whom to hear was ever to help. The little house in East Minneapolis was opened, money was provided for its modest wants. . . . The Children's Home was born."[6]

A second version tells of a man walking the streets of Minneapolis, carrying a baby in his arms and leading a small boy by the hand. This father was trying to find a home for his children, whose "mother had been a victim to the typhoid epidemic that was sweeping through the town. . . . Hour after hour he traveled . . . until he met a lady on the East Side, whose life has been spent in helping the unfortunate. She found two other women, and they, with sublime faith in the generosity of the citizens of Minneapolis, at once rented a small house . . . taking the motherless ones with four others to their arms."[7]

Both stories could be true. The records of the Children's Home for October, 1881, show the admission of a twelve-year-old girl whose mother "refused to care for her," as well as of a five-year-old boy and a baby girl whose mother may have died of typhoid fever. About the identities of the large-hearted ladies, there is no question. At the first annual meeting of the Children's Home Society, as the organization came to be named, the president stated that it was begun through "the united efforts" of three women — Mrs. Charlotte Van Cleve, Mrs. Jane M. Glidden, and a Mrs. Drake — who were "moved to compassion by the sight of so many neglected children."[8]

The three women prevailed upon Mrs. John S. Pillsbury to call a meeting. The *Minneapolis Tribune* of October 28, 1881, carried a notice in which she invited "All ladies interested in organizing an Orphans Home" to meet at the temporary residence on Second Street Northeast. Twenty-five ladies gathered to hear Mrs. Van Cleve present the problem and describe what had already been accomplished. The group elected temporary officers and appointed a committee to frame a constitution.[9]

A second meeting five days later brought out 150 women representing various religious denominations and geographic areas of the city. Mrs. Pillsbury was elected president, a position she accepted with reluctance. As the governor's wife, a director recalled years later, "her duties in State, Church, City, and home affairs were many and pressing. . . . In the end she yielded to the unanimous wish of those who were willing to enlist under her leadership."[10]

In August, 1882, the rented building on Second Street was sold by its owner, and on September 23, 1882, the Children's Home Society voted to purchase the Isaac Atwater property at 2200 South Sixth Street. This building soon proved inadequate for the increasing numbers of children needing care; within three years the organization had purchased land on Stevens Avenue between Thirty-second and Thirty-third streets and was making plans for a new structure.[11]

In the meantime the society was carefully considering its future program. Cadwallader C. Washburn of flour-milling fame died in May, 1882, leaving a bequest of $375,000 to establish the Washburn Memorial Orphan Asylum in memory of his mother. Almost immediately some members of the society questioned the propriety of asking the public for building funds in the face of Washburn's gift for the support of a similar charity. It was the consensus of the group, however, that the organization should not go out of existence. If it developed that the children's work was no longer needed, they reasoned, there were other areas of service.[12]

One field not yet covered in Minneapolis was the care of aged persons in a nonpublic facility. The society's secretary, in her report at the annual meeting of October 7, 1884, summed up the situation: "we are frequently met with the reminder that the Children's Home, through the beneficence of another institution, amply endowed, will become a superfluity, and our work will be taken out of our hands. But... there still remains... a grand work for friendless children, and the other extreme of the cycle of life, friendless age — and even now the need of an Old People's Home is very evident, and the 'Home of the Friendless,' will be one of the most necessary institutions of our city."[13]

When the women gathered at a special meeting on June 23, 1885, to approve the purchase of the new Stevens Avenue property, the Children's Home Society became the Home for Children and Aged Women, and the articles of incorporation were amended to state its new purpose: "to provide and maintain a home or asylum for . . . infirm women and children." Plans for the new building were speedily completed, and on September 9, 1885, the cornerstone was laid.[14]

The following month the women began another activity which brought renown to their organization. It was a charity ball, one of a series usually held annually until World War I. For the 1885 ball, as for many subsequent ones, John T. West offered the use of his elegant, new West Hotel, and the ball soon became the culmination of the Twin Cities social season. Each year local newspapers devoted entire columns to listing the guests and describing their attire (140 gowns with accessories were described in detail that first year). Throughout the years each ball was considered bigger and better. "The combined blandishments of 'sweet charity' and social enjoyment," commented a reporter in 1887, "proved irresistible to the society element," adding that the current ball was "the most successful, in both a social and pecuniary sense."[15]

On May 1, 1886, the staff and thirty-one children moved into the half-finished new building. At first there was a dearth of applicants for the aged women's department. Several reasons may be suggested. This was the first home of its kind in the city, and the popular image of an old people's home as an "asylum" undoubtedly deterred many elderly women. Perhaps too the board had overestimated the number of homeless women in Minneapolis, although across the river in St. Paul the Home for the Friendless was even then filling its rooms with more and more residents. Other deterring factors may have been the entrance requirements and the fee. An article in the *Minneapolis Tribune* of September 16, 1886, noted that the "old ladies quarters are at present unoccupied. The general understanding that this part of the house is open to homeless aged women without means is an error. $300 must be deposited." The writer conceded that the women would have a comfortable home, but added that during her stay a resident was "expected to do her own work and if time permits sewing and knitting or light work for the Home."[16]

Two days later the same newspaper printed a spirited reply from a member of the home's board of directors. "The idea of old ladies entering the home being obliged to work for their living has never occurred to any director," she said. "In the matter of the fee for the admission of any old lady . . . the rules . . . have had the united wisdom of all the best similar institutions in the country to cull from." The director pointed out that the home could accept needy persons, and if "the institution ever becomes sufficiently munificent [the] fee can be done away with." The directors believed that "$300 would be consumed more quickly by any old lady who attempted to live on this amount outside the home than in the home." As for those who might conceivably have to leave after their money was used up, it was the board's "hope not to turn any out of the home quite penniless."[17]

The first woman resident entered on November 10, 1886. After that relatively few applications were received from women wanting a permanent home on a lump-fee basis, but there were some requests for temporary care at a monthly rate. On May 3, 1887, the board voted to "take such boarders as we had room for."[18]

The financial stress of 1893 and the years immediately following pointed up the need for an endowment fund. The annual report for 1895 noted that the directors were "often obliged to refuse worthy women admittance," and suggested that an "endowed institution could do a great work among the aged who apply to us. . . . we could fill the present Home entirely with careworn and neglected persons, who have worn themselves out ministering to others, and now find no comfortable place or cheerful welcome." In 1899 the dream became a reality when John S. Pillsbury, former governor of the state, presented to the institution a gift of $100,000.[19]

That year the old ladies' department housed thirteen permanent residents and three boarders. Every room was filled and the board was obliged to turn down seven applicants for admission. Great as was the demand for beds for elderly women, however, the need for additional facilities for children was apparently even more pressing. The number of children increased from 53 in 1886 to 66 in 1899 and continued to grow in the following decade. In 1899 the board purchased two additional lots with a view to adding new buildings and more playground space. In 1902 a hospital annex was constructed to replace the inadequate infirmary in the children's department.[20]

The Twin Cities now had two homes started by women's organizations — the Home for the Friendless opened in 1868 in St. Paul, and the Home for Children and Aged Women in Minneapolis begun in 1881. A third such institution was the Jones-Harrison Home of Minneapolis, established in 1888 after the sponsoring group coincidentally received a large cash bequest and a gift of real estate. The story of the Jones-Harrison endeavor really began some twenty years earlier with the founding of the parent organization, the Christian Aid Society of Minneapolis, later known as the Woman's Christian Association. This group, which had long cherished the idea of opening a home for the friendless in Minneapolis, saw its hope approach reality in 1886 when it received a bequest of $30,000 from Mrs. William M. Harrison and 80 acres of land from Edwin S. Jones, a banker and judge.[21]

Judge Jones's gift, a tract of wooded land on Cedar Lake, included a large house and two double cottages. The house had been built in the 1860s by Ebenezer D. Scott, an English-born Methodist minister and merchant, who at that time was in his early forties. In his way Scott may have been as much of a philanthropist as the eminent judge, for he is said to have built the house with the aim of eventually using it for an orphan asylum or some other charity. In 1870, however, he and his wife were operating it as a combined resort and hotel for invalids. Oak Grove House, as it was called, was a large four-story octagonal building with a cupola on top. Advertisements described it as a "palatial structure, containing forty rooms, heated by furnace." In the 1860s and 1870s Minnesota had a national reputation as a health resort, especially for tuberculous patients, and Oak Grove House was patronized by visitors from Pennsylvania, New York, Chicago, New Orleans, and other distant points.[22]

The subsequent history of the building is not clear. According to one historian, after Scott spent more than $40,000 on improvements the mortgage was foreclosed. Although Scott was allowed to retain possession for several years, the property eventually passed into the hands of Jones. The opportunity to use the building for a worthy purpose came on the heels of Mrs. Harrison's $30,000 bequest to the Woman's Christian Association, and on June 11, 1886, Mrs. Jones, who was a member of the board, read a communication from her husband offering the buildings and as much land as would be needed for the establishment of a home for aged women and ministers and their wives.[23]

Accepting both gifts, the association engaged a man and his wife to put the house in order and to clear five or six acres of land. The parent organization also adopted a separate constitution for the Jones-Harrison Home, providing for its own board of directors. On May 29, 1888, the home opened with one old lady in residence. Three more women entered in 1889. Mrs. Isabel C. Ramsey, secretary of the Jones-Harrison board, pictured "this happy family" in her report for 1891. "Mrs. Odell is busy with her patch work," she wrote. "Mrs. Ashley is happy over some Harper's publications and Home Journals, Mrs. George is sewing a little and Miss Bues spends most of her time in writing letters. . . . It is a beautiful charity, this care for the aged."[24]

In August, 1890, the association decided to admit disabled ministers and their wives. These couples were to be housed in a cottage that was being made ready for them, and they were to board in the big house, now known as the Old Ladies Home. Before this plan could be put into effect, however, it became necessary to vacate the large residence. "The octagon house, so pleasant and commodious was found to have been poorly constructed, and being pronounced unsafe had to be abandoned, and the cottage, a few rods distant, built for the accommodation of disabled ministers and their wives . . . was put in good order and the family entered it November 20th." During the summer of 1892 the octagon house was demolished.[25]

Applications were now increasing, but the limited quarters prevented the acceptance of many who applied and the plan to admit disabled ministers was given up. "A large house is an imperative necessity," stated the annual report for 1897, but for some years there was no money. Eventually, a bequest of $10,000 from W. S. Benton, together with large gifts from Mrs. Benton and Mrs. Charles S. Pillsbury, enabled the directors to build a two-story brick structure which accommodated about forty persons.[26]

"The hopes and aspirations of years have been fulfilled," the secretary proclaimed in the annual report for 1901: "our new Home . . . which has been the dream of the Directors for ten years, now stands completed and on the site of our long lamented building rises a vastly superior one. Its erection has meant much work, constant care, great anxiety and often deep perplexity; but now this is all forgotten, and we see only the perfect result of all our labor."

A second pattern in the establishment of homes for the aged was set by orders of nuns who responded to requests to meet a community need. They solicited funds and received gifts and bequests from persons who had been made aware of their work. It was the nuns, however, who made the pertinent decisions, within the framework of the rules of their religious communities with the approval of the bishop or archbishop, as the case might be.

The first Catholic home in Minnesota — and the first to be opened exclusively for the care of the needy aged — was started by the Little Sisters of the Poor, who arrived without fanfare in St. Paul on September 26, 1883.[27]

At that time the Little Sisters of the Poor were conducting homes for the aged in France, Belgium, England, Spain, and some twenty-three cities of the United States. Their first home had come into being in 1839 at Saint-Servan, France, a small town on the Breton coast, when Jeanne Jugan, a former servant, came across a blind and half-paralyzed old woman alone in a hovel. Taking the woman into the tiny apartment she shared with a friend, Jeanne gave up her own bed to the invalid. Soon she was asked to receive other guests. As the requests mounted, more young women joined Jeanne. They took a larger apartment; then they remodeled an old convent building. In time the little group took on the appearance of a religious community. Its members wore dark blue dresses and the round white bonnet of the Breton peasant — a garb they retained until 1967. Eventually they came to be known as the Little Sisters of the Poor, an order dedicated to the care of the needy aged. As news of its work spread, the order was asked to operate homes in one city after another.[28]

The St. Paul home was opened in response to a plea from members of the Catholic diocese, who believed that their community needed an institution of this kind. Four months before the arrival of the first French sisters, the people began to raise a subscription to purchase a home. Eventually about $6,000 was collected. A local newspaper, the *North-western Chronicle,* kept a running record of the pledges received throughout the summer of 1883. The journal pointed out that the home would be open to the aged poor from all parts of the state and to "both sexes without distinction of race or creed." The only requirements, the paper said, were that the applicant "need help" and be over sixty years of age.[29]

The Little Sisters were to find a warm welcome in St. Paul. Their first home at 19 Wilkin Street was a large three-story stone house originally designed for use as a Presbyterian college. Built in 1855, it had been occupied since 1869 by the House of the Good Shepherd, a home for "fallen women." The sisters purchased it for $10,000. The location was attractive; the twenty-eight-year-old structure stood on high land overlooking the Mississippi River and the adjacent countryside. In addition to the stone house, which was used for women, the property included a two-story frame building which became the men's department.[30]

The Little Sisters did not have long to wait for their old people. On October 3, 1883, just a week after taking possession of the property, they received their first guest. The *North-western Chronicle* described the circumstances. "Passing along the streets the Sisters were stopped by a poor old man who asked if they were the Little Sisters of whom he had heard. On being told they were he begged them for God's sake to take him in and care for him." By the end of the year the Little Sisters had admitted eight men and six women.[31]

To care for these old people, the sisters began their *quêtes,* or collections. This method of raising funds went back to 1841 and the days of Jeanne Jugan. After she had exhausted her small savings, she picked up a basket and went out on the first *quête*, the begging excursion for which the Little Sisters have since become famous all over the world. With a horse and wagon driven by one of their old men, the Little Sisters of St. Paul made their way to the market that fall of 1883. "We went to the butchers, the vegetable vendors, and others. The merchants were charitable." Although the sisters soon became a familiar sight on the city streets, they did not establish their home without hardships. During the winter of 1884–85 they lacked a supply of water, which, as they wrote, "was quite a shortcoming. This winter the cistern is dried up and it is difficult to get [water]. We have now and then to melt the snow to wash the clothes."[32]

By December, 1885, when the home had been operating a little over two years, ninety-three persons had found refuge within its walls. Men outnumbered women five to four. The median age was sixty-nine years. Nearly three-fourths were Irish, born for the most part in Galway, Tipperary, or County Cork. They came with few tangible possessions: a number of feather beds, an occasional rocking chair, a few pieces of china or glassware. These belongings and their memories were their links with the past. While the women darned and mended and visited, the men gathered in their smoking room in the house next door and told stories.[33]

In that winter of 1885 the population included twenty-seven Irishmen. It is to be assumed that their collective adventures would fill a book. But it took an eighty-year-old Frenchman, one Benois Villincourt, born in Quebec, to dredge out of his past adventures so colorful that his story eventually reached France and in time was included in a book on the homes of the Little Sisters.[34]

Villincourt, so the tale went, guided Sir George Simpson, the famous governor of the Hudson's Bay Company, on a trip of exploration to the Far West in the 1820s. On his return the young Frenchman encountered a tribe of Indians near the Mississippi River and traded some coins and a few jugs of brandy for a vast tract of land which included the future sites of St. Paul and Minneapolis. Later, according to the story, he was robbed of his property and "when drunk tied on a raft and left to the mercy of the great river. . . . After many adventures, he reached Algeria with the French soldiers at the time of the conquest. We find him in 1848 at Paris, fighting at the barricades." In his old age, Villincourt appeared in St. Paul and asked for admission to the Little

Sisters' home overlooking the Mississippi Valley. "There, seated in his arm-chair, he could view his past possessions and without regret for what he had lost, he used to say: 'After all, God has been good to me for he has brought me, out of many adventures, to end my days in peace in the place where I had made up my mind to spend my life.'" If the tale itself seems a little tall, this much, at least, is a matter of record. On October 26, 1885, Benois Villincourt, son of Louis and Mary Michaud Villincourt, was admitted to the Little Sisters of the Poor Home, where he remained until his death on April 13, 1891. And in this home someone listened to his story — else how could it have traveled so far?

Having someone with whom to share memories was undoubtedly the lodestone which drew many old settlers to the home and accounted perhaps for the increasing number of aged persons who sought admission. Even before the end of the second year it became apparent that a larger building would shortly be required, and by 1888 the need was critical. At that time the rules of the order did not permit the Little Sisters to solicit funds beyond the money and supplies required for their daily operations. However, in 1889 they decided to build, "trusting in Providence to provide the means."[85]

The general design for the home was prepared by the mother house in France. ("When you have seen one of our homes, you have seen all," a member of the order told the author in 1962.) The plan, however, was approved by the local bishop, and the contractor was J. C. McCarthy of St. Paul. "During the month of March [1889]," reported the order's historian, "we commenced clearing out the land for the construction." The new building, which was still standing in 1967, was located close to the street in front of the old stone house. By the end of the year it was practically completed, and on February 9, 1890, it was blessed by Archbishop John Ireland.[86]

The Little Sisters had borrowed $25,000 to cover construction costs, and hanging over their heads was the necessity of repaying the loan. On one occasion, when an installment was due, they were the recipients of a "stroke of good luck from St. Joseph. We needed $2,500 for a payment. We prayed to our Good Protector: after which the Little Begging Sisters, obedient to the spirit of faith, went to find Mr. J. Hill, protestant, very rich, who even had a feeling against us because we were not building in the area which he would have wished. To our great astonishment he received the

Little Sisters very kindly and without being surprised by their request . . . he remitted to them the same day the $2,500 which they had asked." On many later occasions this same "Mr. J. Hill" — James J. Hill, the "Empire Builder" of railroads in the Northwest — was to help the Little Sisters.[87]

Others also came to their rescue. Such was the case on a memorable Friday in 1890. "Every week on Friday," the sisters' historian recorded, "we received a large quantity of fish, enough for the old folks' dinner. One week the fish did not come." As the dinner hour approached, the Little Sister who was cooking told the one who was responsible for supplying the food to go to the market. "The Little Sister remarked that the merchants would not have any more at this time, but nevertheless went. On arriving at the market they saw three wagons. The first man threw a few fish into their wagon, as did the second. At the third wagon the merchant was in an argument with two gentlemen who were contesting for a big fish lying in the wagon. Good St. Joseph! If we had that fish, it would be enough for the whole house. After a time, the merchant got impatient with the men and said: 'No, you won't get that fish. I would rather give it to the Little Sisters of the Poor.'" So they got their big fish, a haddock, and the hungry old people had their dinner.[38]

The 1890s were years of financial stringency. For some time a chapel had been planned, but it was not until the spring of 1897 that the mother house authorized the St. Paul group to proceed with its construction. With some help from the old people, the stone house was demolished and on its site arose the chapel, which was completed on January 23, 1899. The Little Sisters then set their sights on further improvements: a stable for the horse, a brick wall to afford privacy and keep their aged charges from wandering away, and a convent for themselves and their novices. By the end of the century all these additions were well under way.[39]

In the meantime, the order had started in Minneapolis a similar venture, now known as St. Joseph's Home. Apparently it was in prospect as early as 1884, when the St. Paul Little Sisters wrote: "Until there is a foundation in Minneapolis, we have permission to go begging in Minneapolis." "Those indefatigable angels of charity," as the *Chronicle* called the Minneapolis sisters, opened their home in a building at 313 Third Street Northeast on February 7, 1889. "The house is fitted up in the usual manner," the newspaper reported, "and the Little Sisters are prepared, from this time forward, to receive aged and infirm old people, tenderest care for whom it is their mission to exhibit." On opening day the home admitted its first resident, a shivering, miserable old man who came to the door and was warmly received. In May the home sheltered twelve aged persons, and by the end of 1890 the sisters were caring for an average of thirty-five. Early in 1891 an assistant-general on a visit from the mother house observed that the Little Sisters were badly housed, but not until June, 1895, were they able to buy land and begin construction of the building that later became the central portion of their home at 215 Broadway Northeast. On April 1, 1896, just after the heaviest snowstorm of the year, the sisters and their charges moved into the new structure with the assistance of some of the old people from the St. Paul home.[40]

The Minneapolis Little Sisters also found it necessary to rely on Providence to meet many of their needs. There was the time, for instance, when it appeared there would be no wood for winter. "The Good Mother encouraged them, told them that Divine Providence did not fail. Right after discussing it they came out into the yard and what did they see but nineteen wagons full of wood." In this case, it was later learned, Providence had appeared in the guise of the employees of a nearby wood company. With more and more aged persons seeking admission, the Little Sisters did not let difficulties in obtaining food and fuel stand in the way of needed expansion, and at the turn of the century they were considering the purchase of additional land for a larger building.

Another Catholic order entered the field when the Franciscan Sisters of the Immaculate Conception founded St. Otto's Home for the Aged in Little Falls. The work was started in 1891 at the suggestion of Bishop Otto Zardetti of the St. Cloud diocese, in whose honor the home was eventually named. In addition to the elderly, the sisters also cared for orphaned children and sick people of all ages. This association with a hospital was to be typical of Catholic homes started in Minnesota during the next forty years.[41]

The Franciscan Sisters had arrived at Little Falls in 1890, but they lacked official status until March 1, 1891, when their constitution was approved by the bishop and they were formally received into his diocese. About the same time Ashby C. Morrill offered the sisters five acres of land for the purpose of starting a hospital.[42]

Little Falls was then a thriving central Minnesota town. The 1890 census showed a population of 2,350 — more than four times greater than that of 1880. The air fairly crackled with talk of prosperity and progress. Railroad lines extended in four directions; a newly completed dam in the Mississippi River furnished power for paper and flour mills and other industries to come. The town already boasted a waterworks, and a new courthouse was under construction. With this growth, a hospital was needed.[43]

The sisters lost little time in starting the building which was to serve as combined convent, hospital, orphanage, and home for the aged. The citizens of Little Falls watched its progress with interest. "The partition walls of the convent portion of the Franciscan Sisters building are up one story," reported the *Little Falls Transcript* on July 10, 1891, "and a large force of workmen are employed. It will require more brick to fully complete the building than were used in the court house." The cornerstone of the hospital section was laid on August 23, 1891, amid much pomp and ceremony.[44]

The sisters had started the building largely on faith, and they needed additional funds to pay for it. An eloquent plea for their cause appeared in the *Morrison County Democrat* of Little Falls on January 2, 1892. "Everybody is pleased to see this new convent, which is an ornament to the city," the writer said; " . . . it is destined for a great work of charity; the care of the sick and the education of the orphan. The sisters had no means to erect such a structure. What did they do? They begged everywhere and we have the result before us. . . . These sisters are poor in dress, but poorer at their table. They have nothing. . . . They will call on the people once in a while, to solicit charity to help them in their great work."

On December 15, 1891, the sisters admitted their first aged person, an eighty-year-old man from a nearby town. Six months later an elderly woman was received and in another six months an aged couple. These and other older persons who entered later were cared for in a separate section of the convent building.

Meanwhile, by January, 1892, the sisters were ready to receive sick persons in the section of the building referred to as St. Gabriel Hospital. The work with the children was growing; following the 1893 panic, the number of orphans greatly increased, and by the summer of 1895 the order recognized that a suitable building was needed to house them. Plans were prepared for a three-story structure, 50 by 100 feet, similar in appearance to the convent-hospital building. Construction proceeded rapidly.[45]

With the removal of the children to the new St. Otto's Orphanage following its completion in 1895, there was more space in the hospital for the elderly. Thirteen persons were admitted during 1895, and at the end of the year eighteen were in residence. Although the institution now had a well-defined old people's department, the home for the aged was for a long time overshadowed by the hospital and the orphanage.[46]

A third pattern can be discerned as large Protestant church organizations became involved in caring for the aged. This occurred in the late 1890s, when homes were more or less wished on denominational bodies by zealous pastors, members, or women's groups. It was not until after the turn of the century that the establishment of church homes for aged members came to be considered a duty of the synod, conference, or district. A forerunner of this Protestant movement was the Church Home of Minnesota, started in St. Paul in 1894 by Sister Annette Relf, the first consecrated Episcopal deaconess in Minnesota.

Sister Annette was a remarkable person. Born in Kentucky in 1840 and trained in Pennsylvania as a deaconess, she went to Minnesota in 1871. There she found a fertile field for her activities. Following an initial period as a parish teacher in Faribault, Sister Annette moved to Minneapolis, where she served from 1877 to 1882 as matron and nurse in charge of the Cottage Hospital (now St. Barnabas). In her spare time she started a Sunday school at St. Jude's Mission. Resigning from her hospital position in 1882, she began the work that led to the establishment of the Sheltering Arms home for children. "With your approbation and blessing last August," she wrote Bishop Henry B. Whipple on May 12, 1883, "I rented a house and made a beginning of a Church Orphanage. Though expecting aid and sympathy of the Church throughout the Diocese, I assumed responsibility of all the debts. . . . There is a pledge of $500 towards a new building. . . . It is God's work and he will provide the means."[47]

Sister Annette then surrendered the institution, at that time located at Twelfth Street and Twenty-seventh Avenue South, to a board of trustees, and in May, 1885, turned her energies to a new venture — the Church Home for Babies at 2110 Fifth Avenue South. "The object of the home," said a contemporary report, "is to prevent mothers from giving away their babies, by providing a home 'within their income, allowing them to see their children often, thereby keeping up the parental love.'" The mothers paid $1.25 a week toward the support of the home. When informed of her new undertaking, Bishop Whipple is said to have remarked: "God will provide for Sister Annette." During her years at the Sheltering Arms and the Church Home for Babies, wrote a biographer, "she received no salary, but on the contrary, used her own money in her work, while her clothing, be it spoken with reverence, could hardly have been more expensive than that of the Blessed Lord himself."[48]

In 1894 Sister Annette approached the Reverend John Jacob Faude, minister of Gethsemane Church in Minneapolis, with the idea of establishing a home for aged and infirm persons of the diocese. The project was not successful in Minneapolis (if, indeed, it was ever started there), and on the advice of Bishop Mahlon N. Gilbert of the diocese of Minnesota, Sister Annette moved to St. Paul. She took a house at 719 Martin Street, where she opened a home for children and aged women. In a year or two she moved to 527 John Street. In 1897 the diocese took over the home and incorporated it as an institution of the Protestant Episcopal Church, caring primarily for aged women. Sister Annette remained at the home as matron, nurse, and finally resident until her death in 1915.[49]

During its first years the Church Home of Minnesota had a difficult struggle. Without generous donations from Andrew Schoch and other St. Paul merchants and the efforts of board members who drove their carriages to the South St. Paul stockyards to return with loads of ham, bacon, and lard, it is doubtful that the home could have survived. At one time only a check for $100 from James J. Hill kept the doors open. During this period the home made many moves: in 1898 it was located at 549 Olive Street; in 1899 at 509 Lafayette; and in 1905 on church property at 587 Fuller Street, where it remained for some fifteen years.[50]

A second Protestant venture, the Augustana Home of Minneapolis, grew out of the missionary efforts of the women of the First Augustana Evangelical Lutheran Church and was the realization of the dream of its pastor, Carl J. Petri. For some time Reverend Petri had felt the need for missionary activity among the people of his own church, and on August 2, 1894, he presented the problem to the Ladies' Aid Society. Although the group made an appropriation of $50 for the support of a deaconess, it was more than a year before Sister Cecelia Nelson arrived from Omaha, Nebraska, to begin her work. Her monthly reports told of "days spent in caring for sick in the homes, distributing food and clothing where needed, helping in parochial and Sabbath school, visiting hospitals and institutions for correction."[51]

In October, 1896, the Ladies' Aid Society decided to open a "mission cottage" as a center for benevolent activities. For $10 a month the society rented a small frame house at 1307 Eighth Street South. The first persons received for care were an aged woman, a blind girl, and a small child. Some years later Reverend Petri recalled: "In this Cottage on 8th Street, many important meetings were held. One cold and gloomy December morning in 1897, five interested persons gathered here and decided to rent premises to open a Swedish Hospital in our city. As a result, in January, 1898, the Swedish Hospital began its work." This was the inception of a close tie between the hospital and the Augustana Home which has continued to the present.

The last of Minnesota's church-related homes of this period — the Lutheran Home for the Aged — was established at Belle Plaine by the Evangelical Lutheran Synod of Wisconsin, Minnesota, and Michigan, chiefly because Mrs. Sophia Boessling, an elderly resident of the town, offered land and money to found a home for orphans and aged persons. Meeting in the summer of 1897, the synod unanimously accepted Mrs. Boessling's offer, but took the precaution of appointing a committee to "see that the offer was sufficiently secured," according to the *Belle Plaine Herald* of September 1, 1897. The newspaper expressed the hope that the good work would proceed without interruption: "A charitable institution of this kind would not only be a lasting monument to the donor and synod which erected it, but would be of great benefit to our borough."

The committee evidently found the offer sufficiently secured, for on October 20, 1897, the *Herald* reported: "We understand Mrs. Sophia Boessling turned over the block . . . upon which the building is to be located, also her residence and two lots, and $2500 in cash and notes. It will add another fine structure to our town and should be encouraged and assisted." On May 11, 1898, contracts were let for a two-story brick building, 45 by 60 feet. The cornerstone was laid on July 13, and preparations were made for dedicating the home.[52]

"A Big Day in Store for Belle Plaine," announced the *Herald* in November. "The Home for Orphans and Aged People is receiving its finishing touches and will be ready for the dedication services on Sunday next [*November 6*]." It was expected that special excursion trains from the Twin Cities and New Ulm would bring persons who wished to attend. As it happened, the special trains could not be obtained, and it fell to old-fashioned but reliable teams of horses to transport the immense crowd of people who came from neighboring towns to view the "magnificent structure" and share in the potluck dinner which the townspeople provided for twenty-five cents.[53]

One final home, established under the auspices of a group quite different from those discussed thus far, made its appearance at Anoka during the decade of the 1890s. The Ladies of the GAR Home for veterans and their wives was one of the early projects sponsored by the Minnesota Department of the Ladies of the Grand Army of the Republic. This organization, which came into being at a convention in Minneapolis in February, 1893, was composed of wives, mothers, daughters, and sisters of Civil War veterans. For the first few years the members spent most of their time organizing local circles throughout the state, donating flags to schools, assisting in Memorial Day observances, and furnishing relief to needy veterans and wives who came to their attention.[54]

Precisely when the idea of establishing the Anoka home was born is not known. Although destitute veterans received care at the Minnesota Soldiers' Home in Minneapolis, their wives were not at first eligible for admission. As early as 1896 the Ladies of the GAR petitioned the legislature to build houses at the soldiers' home for the wives of men in residence there. A chronicler later reported that the "State had provided a home for needy comrades," but their wives had to be "supported outside, by patriotic organizations. . . . We felt this was an injustice to the women." When the legislature took no action on their request, the ladies evidently decided to go ahead on their own and build cottages where destitute veterans and their wives could live together. The city of Anoka donated about six acres of land for the project.[55]

In August, 1899, the president informed the membership that the "Ladies of the Grand Army of the Republic Home Fund has with the very efficient help of our Anoka friends and the bountiful donation at the last Department Convention by the comrades all over the state, succeeded in building one cottage with prospect of another before winter."

As various circles furnished the money, additional cottages were erected and named Garfield, Lincoln, Howard, and Logan, in honor of Civil War leaders. For the first six years of the institution's existence, the organization maintained it without help from others. But when "the 'Old Folks' building was erected by the state at Minnehaha," reported the home's historian in 1927, "and a large sum appropriated for its maintenance, we asked the legislature to assist us. We received $500.00 for several years and a gradual increase until the amount reached $5,000.00 per year." This appropriation continued until at least 1940. As members of the organization became fewer and fewer, there was less need for the home. It closed early in 1960 when the regional board decided to abandon the building rather than make the extensive repairs necessary to meet fire protection standards.[56]

Sponsors of early homes for the aged were embarking on a field of service which was, to a large degree, experimental. The experience available to them from homes in older parts of the country lay chiefly in the realms of organization and fund raising. The women lacked the kind of information that would have helped them anticipate many of their future problems, particularly in matters of intake and budget — whom to admit, whether and how much to charge, how to fit expenses to income. The prevailing philosophy was to provide for the needy, regardless of ability to pay. The immediate problem was to get the home started; the future, perhaps, would take care of itself. Several homes had prepayment plans under which a lump sum ensured care for life, although, as sponsors later discovered, these fees did not always meet the cost of that care. As described by an early observer of the social service scene, this payment was "really a life annuity for somewhat less than its money value."[57] But even homes that had this requirement for admission usually found a way to finance the care of a worthy applicant who lacked the necessary funds. Others asked no payment or only a very nominal one; most homes had flexible arrangements and suited the plan to the individual situation.

By the end of the century the private benevolent home for the aged was established in Minnesota as a useful social institution, a resource for the growing number of older persons no longer able to maintain homes of their own, and a desirable addition to the local community. Almost invariably newspaper editors welcomed a new benevolent home for the recognition and trade it would bring to the area and, in some instances, because adding a new building or improving an old one would enhance the appearance of the town. It was seemingly taken for granted that the home would be a benefit to those fortunate enough to live in it. Certainly, the ten homes which had been opened by 1899 found no dearth of applicants for admission. As the century closed, all were making plans to expand, and several additional institutions were in the offing.

5
The State Expands Its Role
1880—1900

THE LAST TWO DECADES of the nineteenth century were especially notable for the expanded role of the state in the care of its unfortunates. In this period Minnesota not only increased its facilities for the defective and mentally ill and extended its care to two additional groups — dependent children and needy war veterans — but also began to supervise nonstate institutions, including the county poor farms. Outside the counties in which they were located, information on poorhouses had been almost completely lacking. How well or how badly they were conducted was left to the consciences of the commissioner boards and of a generally indifferent public. With the creation of a State Board of Corrections and Charities in 1883, the legislature in effect recognized the responsibility of the state for knowing what kind of care its needy citizens were receiving.

The step toward state supervision was in line with a national trend. Massachusetts had been the first to adopt a general plan for overseeing its charitable and correctional institutions. Its board was created in 1863, primarily for the purpose of controlling expenditures for the care of paupers who had no legal settlement in any town and for whose support the state, therefore, had assumed responsibility. Gradually, however, the legislature added other functions until, in 1879, the board of charities was superseded by the Massachusetts Board of Health, Lunacy, and Charity, which was responsible for all public charities, public health, and the mentally ill.[1]

In the post-Civil War period the movement spread to other states. The new boards did not all have the same functions, nor apparently did their courses run smoothly. In 1879 Frank B. Sanborn, secretary of the American Social Science Association and a former member of the Massachusetts State Board of Charities, reviewed their development. "The boards created in New York in 1867, in Pennsylvania, Rhode Island, and Illinois in 1869, and in Michigan and Wisconsin in 1871, were all, to some extent, modelled after the Massachusetts board, though with many variations and some improvements," he said. By the end of the 1870s similar boards existed in Ohio, Kansas, and Connecticut.[2]

In New York the board of charities at first was responsible only for institutions receiving financial aid from the state. However, in the course of its duties the board discovered that almshouses had changed very little since 1856, when the senate investigating committee had found such appalling conditions. Several reasons for extending state control to county almshouses were given in 1869 by Theodore W. Dwight, a member of the board and professor of municipal law at Columbia College (later Columbia University). As a rule, Dwight said, there was little popular interest in the care of the poor, due largely to lack of knowledge. The local boards of supervisors, sensitive to political effects, were reluctant to appropriate sufficient funds. Dwight also found that the "management of the almshouses is purely *official*." Boards lacked the humanizing effect, he felt, that would come from the presence of public-spirited citizens to watch and advise.[3]

Ten years later Frank Sanborn offered further reasons for state supervision: "perhaps you will say that public charity, which, like all charity, 'begins at home,' should stay there, and should not spread out so as to become a State affair. But, if you will consider for a moment, you will see that there are some kinds of public dependence (that created by insanity, for example), in which the power and wealth of the locality are insufficient to meet the emergency, and the State must come in to build and regulate the hospital or asylum. . . . The inspection and authority of the State," he continued, "is also useful to produce economy of expenditure in the localities, uniformity of treatment for the sick and infirm, the removal to their proper place of those poor persons about whom the separate localities may be in doubt or dispute, the correction of local grievances and abuses, and for the dissemination of a wider knowledge and more correct principles concerning the whole care of the poor. This last duty of State Boards of Charity," said Sanborn, "is best fulfilled when carried to its furthest extent in such conferences as this, where the representatives of States and of cities meet to compare notes with each other, and to disseminate . . . the results of experience and close observation."[4]

The meeting at which Sanborn made these remarks in 1879 was the sixth Conference of Boards of Public Charities, an organization founded in May, 1874, by delegates to the American Social Science Association from nine states. The membership was soon expanded to include all persons interested in charitable or penal work. In addition to providing a forum for reports and discussions, the conference promoted the collection of uniform statistics by state boards.[5]

At the eighth conference, held in Boston in 1881, Minnesota was represented by Dr. William H. Leonard, a member of Minnesota's first lunacy commission, and by E. W. Chase, secretary of the St. Paul Society for the Relief of the Poor. The next year, when the conference was held in Wisconsin, nineteen distinguished Minnesotans were commissioned by the governor to attend. They included social workers, physicians, clergymen, institution officials, and educators. At this time it apparently was taken for granted that Minnesota should have a state board of corrections and charities; the only question was what kind. Generally state boards were of two types: one having powers of control over state institutions; the other having powers of inspection and report only. The delegates found that convention members as a whole favored an advisory board without mandatory powers.[6]

The attendance of the state delegation and the report which its members brought back stimulated a good deal of interest in Minnesota. As a result, the legislature in 1883 established the State Board of Corrections and Charities. The agency was primarily a fact-finding body; its duties were to "investigate the whole system of public charities and correctional institutions of the state, [and] examine into the condition and management thereof." Comprised of six members appointed by the governor with the consent of the senate, the board was unsalaried and nonpartisan. Governor Lucius F. Hubbard, who served as its first president, selected the following prominent citizens as members: Reverend Malcolm M. Dana of St. Paul; Charles H. Berry, Winona; William M. Campbell, Litchfield; Reuben Reynolds, Crookston; Henry R. Wells, Preston; and David C. Bell, Minneapolis.[7]

The new board was empowered to employ a full-time secretary. For this position it selected Hastings Hornell Hart, a thirty-two-year-old Congregational minister who had served a Worthington church for the preceding three years. From the time it became known that Hart was being considered for the position, the *Worthington Advance* kept its readers informed of developments. "This is an important position," the paper noted on May 31, 1883, "and is no small compliment to Mr. Hart's efficiency and executive ability." There seemed to be some reservations, though, about the selection of a clergyman: "He will do the work well and thoroughly," said the *Advance*, "if any minister in the State will." The *St. Paul Globe,* perhaps fearing that Hart would be too trusting, urged him not to "commit the absurd mistake of giving the persons in charge of these institutions a notice so that they can get up a good dinner and clean up house for the occasion." Commenting on this advice, the *Advance* stated: "We have no doubt of Mr. Hart's integrity, energy and good intentions. . . . But he has a difficult work before him. He will find that wherever he discovers anything that would reflect upon 'the party,' or the church, or some minister, it will cost him his good name to make an honest and impartial report."[8]

Hart "had made no application for the appointment," wrote Minnesota historian William W. Folwell, "and it was not until after long consideration that he accepted it. His acceptance was received by the board on July 10, 1883, and he began work soon afterwards." Making an "honest and impartial report" was not to cost Hart his good name. Rather he was to become Minnesota's "Apostle of Charities." "For his position," Folwell wrote, "Hart was fitted by natural endowment, character, and temperament. His extensive knowledge of the field and his readiness for service in any emergency commanded the confidence of his board and the respect of legislative committees and governors." Certainly he attacked the problems awaiting him with enthusiasm and industry. Combining the attributes of student and preacher, he not only amassed facts, but also communicated his findings and philosophy with the zeal of an evangelist.[9]

Although the county poorhouses were only a part of the board's responsibility, Hart visited them in his first year on the job. By October, 1884, he had made at least one inspection of all but two

THE STATE EXPANDS ITS ROLE 77

of the twenty-four county institutions. At that time two western counties of small population — Pipestone and Yellow Medicine — were using temporary buildings in towns. Two other somewhat larger eastern ones — Anoka and Scott — contracted with families to board county charges. The Rock County poorhouse in the extreme southwestern corner of the state had no inmates at all. The poorhouses were of all kinds, Hart reported, "from the substantial building of Hennepin County, with suitable accommodations for one hundred and fifty paupers, to the so-called poor house of Rock County, which does not afford adequate provision for the overseer's family, not to speak of any paupers."[10]

Hart found that the occupants, too, were a varied lot, representing all ages and conditions of physical and mental health. Sometimes they did not even speak the same language. In the Lyon County poorhouse, said Hart, there were "only three paupers at the time of the visit, one old woman and two old men. The woman was Norwegian and talks no English; one pauper is a Welshman and an imbecile, and talks no English. The other is a Scotchman so that there is little communication between the paupers."

In charge of these ill-assorted groups were overseers employed under a multiplicity of financial arrangements. As the county boards drew up their contracts, they considered not only the amount to be paid for care, but also the disposition of proceeds from the sale of produce from the farm. Would this income go to the county or to the overseer? Who would provide teams, wagons, and machinery for working the farm? Furniture, bedding, and clothing for the inmates? Who was to pay for farm and kitchen helpers if such workers were employed? Should members of the overseer's family receive wages and pay board? Usually the county settled for the person who agreed to board paupers at the cheapest rate or who would take the position at the lowest salary. In one county an overseer agreed to provide everything at his own expense in exchange for use of the farm rent-free. "A bad system," commented Hart, "since it makes the overseer's profits depend upon the meagerness of the fare and thinness of the clothing of the inmates."[11]

A few of the overseers were characterized as capable and vigilant administrators. In Houston County, Hart reported wryly, the man in charge was a "good one, and the county evidently intends to keep him, for at a salary of $150 [a year] he will inevitably become a permanent inmate." Some managers were plainly incompetent and indifferent. In St. Louis County Hart found the overseer and his wife both absent when he visited the home. As he left Hart met the man who "was intoxicated, swaying to and fro in his seat, urging his horse at a rapid rate up the stony hill. In the wagon was a coffin, containing the body of a woman destined to the county burying ground. The old song was literally exemplified: 'Rattle his bones over the stones, He's only a pauper that nobody owns.'" In the main, however, Hart considered the overseers to be well-meaning and hard-working, and he believed the defects of operation were due largely to "inexperience and inattention, rather than to lack of disposition to care suitably and humanely for public wards."

Hart noted that the caretakers were hampered by inadequate facilities and equipment and by the generally poor condition of the buildings. With few exceptions the poorhouses were frame farmhouses, ill-adapted for use by more than one family. Many were in bad repair, hard to heat, and difficult to keep clean. The floors of the second story of the Wabasha County home had large cracks and could not be scrubbed because the boards were "so leaky." The Fillmore County poorhouse, which had been the show place of the countryside when it was built in 1868, was now in such poor repair that Hart ended his description with the simple comment: "General air of decay." Sanitation problems were numerous. In Winona County Hart reported that water was supplied "from a well in the barn yard — a very objectionable source." Most of the buildings had no hallways, Hart found, and slops from the bedrooms were of necessity carried through kitchens or dining rooms. The problem of vermin was ever-present and drastic steps were sometimes necessary. "The beds had been treated with Paris Green to destroy vermin," Hart reported of the Hennepin County home, "which is very effective, but rather suggestive, not to say picturesque." Bathing facilities were far from adequate: "There are only five bathtubs in the poorhouses, and eighty per cent of them are in the Hennepin County Home."[12]

Since the Hennepin County poorhouse, completed in 1884, was one of the first structures in the state designed expressly for the care of aged and destitute persons, Hart's description of the new building is of some interest. He reported that it was situated on the 400-acre farm which the board had purchased in the 1860s near Hopkins, and that 200 acres were under cultivation. The structure, he said, was "of brick, in the form of a capital letter H, the dining room forming the connecting link. Each section 40 x 80 feet. Basement under the whole building; with steam-heating apparatus, vegetable and pork cellars; two cisterns, with joint capacity of fourteen hundred barrels; laundry, which is a nuisance, damp and unwholesome . . . Women's department in front half of south wing, first floor. Hospital 14 x 14 x 14; looks east; linoleum on floor; large bath room adjoining, with bed for lying-in patient. Women's sitting room, 14 x 28 x 14, looks south; comfortable settees and rocking chairs; wash room, 7 x 14, adjoining; scullery, 10 x 14, in rear of wash room. Second floor: Dormitories, each about 14 x 14 x 12, and containing three double beds.

"Women's department separated from men's department on second floor, by securely locked door; on first floor by dining room for both sexes . . . Kitchen in north wing, 14 x 34; good range; sink twelve feet long, with pump . . .

"Males occupy west half of south wing. First floor — hospital, 15 x 34 x 14; looks to the south; sunny and cheerful; linoleum on floor; badly ventilated; dormitories each about 14 x 14 on first and second floors, with two beds each. . . . First floor — Men's sitting room, 38 x 38, an admirable room; windows on three sides; comfortable settees, tables, etc. . . .

"Overseer's apartments: kitchen and pantry, dining room and sitting room on first floor; all commodious and convenient. Five family sleeping rooms.

"A ten-foot hall runs through the south wing and half way through the north wing. Stairways, front and rear, in each wing. . . . Ventilation by transoms, and flues near floor and ceiling in each room. Furniture, good and substantial. Iron bedsteads; all those recently purchased, having woven wire springs. Wadded comforters are used on the beds. They favor filth and vermin, and should be discarded. . . .

"*Bill of fare* — Meat twice a day; (fresh meat in winter three times a week, and in summer twice a week). Coffee twice a day; tea once a day; butter three times a day in summer, and once or more in winter, and apple sauce or sorghum syrup to take its place at other meals. Dinners: stew once a week; soup and meat once a week; meat dinner on Sundays. Good supply of potatoes, onions, etc., raised on the place."

Hart concluded his summary by saying: "This is the only adequate, convenient and suitable poor house in the State," although he felt it had "minor defects." "On the whole," he said, "it is a first class institution, a credit to Hennepin County, and in most respects a model."

Although the Hennepin County poorhouse had room for 150 persons, only 120 were in residence in 1884. Hart found this to be the exception rather than the rule. Most buildings were overcrowded, sitting rooms and even dining rooms being used as bedrooms, especially for the infirm who could not climb stairs. In Fillmore County in "the women's sitting room, 16 x 16 feet, slept a man and his wife, a woman 84 years old not related to them, and an idiot girl 14 years old, mute and helpless." And in Nicollet County in a "room 9 x 20 feet were a stove, two double beds and a single bed. There being no closets or storerooms, a quantity of old clothes and rubbish was under the beds. The single bed was occupied by an old bed-ridden man. One double bed was occupied by the old man's wife and idiot daughter, the other by two women not related to this family."[18]

The housing of men and women in the same room, or even on the same floor, was a matter of grave concern to Hart. After a visit to the Winona County institution, where women were supposedly housed on the first floor and men on the second, he reported: "The great lack in this poor house is proper separation of the sexes. Some of the infirm paupers cannot use the outside staircase in bad weather, and the result is that the women's part is more or less a thoroughfare. Sometimes the first floor is full and a woman has to room on the second floor. Scandals have occurred in the past and are liable to occur again. The overseer stated that in suspicious cases he had to lock both parties in their rooms over night." To Hart's query, "What if the house should take fire?" the overseer replied, "Oh, they have to take their chances on that." The commissioners of Otter Tail County apparently found it impossible to remodel the building to provide for separation of the sexes, but Hart reminded them: "There is among the inmates one simple-minded girl who has had one child; there may be a repetition of this at your poorhouse; you cannot allow such a state of affairs. It costs $150 per year to support a pauper child, and $150 is interest on a pretty large sum of money."

Hart was also concerned about the absence of proper provision for the sick and the mentally disturbed. "The lack of suitable hospital facilities is general," he said. "In several poorhouses the sick are kept in the paupers' sitting rooms. In Blue Earth County, an infirm woman had her bed in the dining room." Several homes had detention rooms in the basement or attic for refractory or mentally disturbed persons. At the Dodge County farm there was an outside building which had been designed for mental patients, "a terrible place for the insane," said Hart, but "happily never used for them." In Goodhue County a "code of rules is prescribed by the . . . commissioners, for violation of which the overseer is authorized to confine inmates in a strong room, on bread and water."[14]

During that first year Hart met with boards of county commissioners, studied contracts between boards and overseers, and set up a system of uniform reporting. He asked for statistics on the composition and movement of poorhouse populations, as well as on operating expenses and the costs of farms and improvements. Tables prepared from the information thus gathered were included in the board's published biennial reports. These statistics made it possible for the first time to compare counties and to relate Minnesota's efforts to those of other states.

Hart's findings showed a wide variation in county expenditures for poor relief in Minnesota. Some were generous to the point of extravagance; others allowed so small an amount per inhabitant as to suggest complete lack of concern. Among the twenty-four counties operating poorhouses in 1884, Hart found that expenses per capita of population varied from a high of 58.3 cents in Goodhue County to a low of 3.0 cents in Hubbard County. Although the immediate responsibility rested with the county commissioners, Hart refused to blame them wholly, pointing out that the "commissioners, coming into office, find established customs of dealing with paupers, which can be changed only with difficulty. Increased expenditure in economical counties is criticized as extravagance. Decrease in extravagant counties is denounced as oppression of the poor. The remedy lies in the increase of knowledge on this subject among the people, and the conscientious discharge of their duty by county commissioners without fear or favor."[15]

An analysis of the statistics he obtained and his own personal observations led Hart to conclude that the cost of operating poorhouses and poor farms was influenced by the quality, or lack of it, of the overseers. Methods of hiring left much to be desired, and in some counties a competent person could not afford to enter the competition for the position. In general the management of the farm and house was left too much to the discretion of the overseer, and little control was exerted over finances. Farm proceeds, Hart said, should be turned into the county treasury; bills should be audited and paid by the treasurer. In small counties it might be more practical to pay the overseer a fixed weekly sum for boarding paupers, but in the larger ones he recommended that the commissioners set a fair salary. In any case the overseer should be selected on the basis of his competence. The practice of hiring an overseer on bids and for only a year's tenure did not assure obtaining the best man for the position.[16]

From a comparative study of poorhouse expenses in relation to the number of inmates, Hart came to the conclusion that counties of small population could not "afford to run poor houses." He found that six counties — Freeborn, Marshall, Martin, Murray, Redwood, and Swift — owned farms in 1884, but were not operating poorhouses. In at least two instances he was successful in dissuading boards from building until such time as the county really needed a place. The Marshall County board was advertising for bids when Hart met with the commissioners at their request to review the plans; after exploring the whole problem the board postponed its decision to build and later sold the farm. Stevens County did not own a farm but was taking steps to purchase one. Again, after a thorough review of the costs of caring for paupers in and out of poorhouses, the board decided against buying a farm.

One solution to the problem for a small county, suggested Hart, was to "make contracts with neighboring counties having poor houses, for the board and care of paupers." A similar idea was put forward by the auditor of Yellow Medicine County, who wrote in 1884: "I think it would work well if four or six small adjoining counties purchased and run [sic] a poor farm or poor house in common." However, when the legislature enacted a district poorhouse enabling law in 1899, the board of corrections and charities was not optimistic: "We believe this is a good law, but must frankly confess that there seems small prospect of its being used, because each of the co-operating counties cannot be the seat of the district building." The board was right. No counties took advantage of the new law.[17]

In buying poor farms, most counties purchased at least 160 acres, and it was not unusual to find 300-acre tracts — far more land than was needed for a poorhouse operation. "I find a growing conviction among officers of the more populous counties that a large poor farm is undesirable," Hart said. "The overseer has enough to do in the supervision of a large poor house, without running a farm.

... There should be ample grounds about the house, a well tended garden of several acres, which will employ all inmates able to do outdoor work, and land enough besides to afford sufficient pasture and hay for a good number of cows." In answer to the argument that farms afforded opportunities for paupers to share in the work, Hart stated: "There are very few able-bodied paupers in the poor houses of Minnesota. The popular idea that pauper labor ought to be utilized would find little useful material to utilize."[18]

Hart also criticized the practice of buying farms in advance of need. He pointed out that the land did not always appreciate in value as anticipated, and that the low purchase price was more than offset by interest charges on the loan and the removal of the property from the tax rolls. Then too a farm purchased in advance of a county's need sometimes proved to be badly located or unfertile. "Mower and Olmsted counties exchanged their farms for others," said Hart, "and several other poor farms ought to be exchanged." Hart also observed that a purchase made in the early years of a county's development placed a relatively higher burden on its taxpayers than an acquisition made in later years after the county's taxable valuation had risen. Finally, the practice was not fair to the earlier settlers who were paying for something they could not use.

Hart's observations were not limited to expenditures. He commented also on the practice of housing children on the poor farms. Nearly 11 per cent of the total number of persons cared for during the year ending September 30, 1884, were children under fourteen years of age. Many were with their mothers, but Hart recommended that "in cases where the mothers are not likely to become self-supporting, homes should be found for the children elsewhere, for children brought up in poor houses seldom turn out well."[19]

Hart was not alone in this view. Observers had long contended that children who grew up in the atmosphere of the almshouse were unfit for work by the time they were old enough to be useful. In the nineteenth century several organizations attempted to solve the problem by sending vagrant and orphaned children to other localities, especially to rural areas, where homes could more easily be found for them. The chief agency of this type in the United States was the New York Children's Aid Society, founded by Charles L. Brace in 1853. Each year this organization transported literally thousands of children to southern and western states, there to be claimed by residents, many of whom were farmers. The adopting family promised to give the child an education and to pay him

$100 when he reached his twenty-first birthday. In exchange for board, room, and education, the child was to perform such work as was required by his foster parents.[20]

This child-placement program was both praised and damned by social workers and others, and the Children's Aid Society became the object of many investigations. Hart conducted an inquiry into its efforts in Minnesota, and his report was widely accepted as the most comprehensive and unbiased available. During the winter of 1883–84, he made a study of 340 children who had been placed by the society in southern Minnesota counties during a three-year period. By means of records, correspondence, and interviews, he attempted to learn whether the organization was sending out "vicious and depraved" children and placing them without proper investigation and supervision; whether the children were ill-used; and whether they were becoming paupers or criminals. (One earlier critic had posited the theory that the "reduction of juvenile crime in New York might be attended by an increase of juvenile crime in the West.")[21]

Although Hart's conclusions were generally favorable, he recommended greater care in the selection of homes and closer supervision for the children so placed. Of the forty-one children found to have done badly, thirty-two were thirteen years of age or older. "The younger children appear to be uniformly doing well," he reported, "but we are of the opinion that the system practiced by this society is not well enough organized to make the introduction of the older children safe for the State or the children." How many of the children found their way into poorhouses is not known (seventy-eight children had moved elsewhere by the time the study was made), but the report did effectively check the importation of children into Minnesota by this agency. When, some dozen years later, it resumed the practice, the legislature passed a law requiring that any agency bringing children into Minnesota must first file a bond of $1,000 to ensure that it would observe good practices and would remove any children who became public charges.[22]

A development which had a far greater effect in reducing the number of children in poorhouses was the movement toward placing them in state-operated public schools. Since 1856, when the New York senate committee had delivered its sweeping criticism of the care of children in county poorhouses, state governments had become more and more convinced that the "collection of children in alms houses had been a serious mistake" and had passed a series of laws designed to bring about their removal. Some states required that all children except defectives and the very young be placed at state expense in private orphan asylums or family homes; others provided alternative methods of care. One of the latter was Michigan, which, after making a study of children in almshouses, established a state public school in 1874.[23]

During Hart's first year as secretary of the board of corrections and charities, he had visited the state school at Coldwater, Michigan. He was impressed by the cottage plan and the concept of providing temporary care only until a good family home could be found for the child. In his message to the 1885 legislature, Governor Hubbard recommended that a similar institution be set up in Minnesota. In December, 1886, the new Minnesota State Public School for Dependent and Neglected Children opened at Owatonna under the supervision of Galen A. Merrill, former assistant superintendent of the Michigan school.[24]

As the buildings neared completion, the board of corrections and charities began a state-wide search for children who were eligible for admission. By September, 1886, between thirty and forty had been located, about twenty-five of them in poorhouses. The board expected that the school would "hereafter relieve the county poor houses of all children of sound mind and body." Although children in poorhouses numbered between 50 and 72 during the depression years of the mid-1890s, the prediction eventually was borne out. During the year ending December 31, 1899, only fifteen children were cared for in the poorhouses of Minnesota.[25]

In 1887 the state entered another field of care — one which would have considerable impact not only on poorhouses but also on private benevolent homes for the aged — when it established the Minnesota Soldiers' Home. A leading role in this endeavor was played by the Grand Army of the Republic, which estimated that the state had some 30,000 war veterans and noted that "no adequate provision had been made for their comfort and care by the general Government." The reasoning behind the concept of government responsibility was succinctly summed up by Josephine Brown: "On the theory that men in the armed services of governments are employees of those governments in work of a peculiarly hazardous and 'seasonal' kind," she wrote, "needy soldiers and sailors have been for many years the beneficiaries of special state legislation."[26]

When it was started, the Minnesota institution was intended primarily for men without families. For veterans with dependents the state provided a monthly allowance, an unusual feature at that time. According to Henry A. Castle, the first president of the board of trustees, "all the [other] state homes, with a few exceptions, separate the veteran from his family, and leave the latter more than ever exposed to life's vicissitudes. It was the aim of the Minnesota law to avoid this error."[27]

For the new home the city of Minneapolis donated a scenic site at the confluence of Minnehaha Creek and the Mississippi River. It was, said Castle, a "broad, level tract of ground . . . surrounded by magnificent forest trees, forming a most attractive park." Funds for building were not immediately available, but "owing to the pressing necessity of providing for many disabled veterans who were then cared for in poorhouses or by charitable societies, a temporary home was opened on November 21, 1887." During the first year some eighty-three old soldiers were admitted. The first two permanent buildings were completed and occupied in 1889. In order to achieve a homelike atmosphere, the institution was developed on the cottage plan. But the design also offered a reminder — if the men wished it — of "tenting tonight." According to Castle, a "number of men usually occupy one room, just as they occupied a single tent during the war."[28]

Operating funds came from several sources. Although Congress appropriated $100 (later reduced to $80) annually for each resident, it contributed nothing toward the support of militiamen who had fought on the frontier during the Sioux Uprising of 1862. But "certainly no one," noted the board of corrections and charities, "will consider them less welcome on that account." The state legislature usually provided $20,000 a year, and inmates who received federal pensions were required to surrender all but $4 per month to the state.[29]

The number of soldiers cared for increased each year (reaching nearly 400 by 1898), and successive legislatures appropriated funds for new buildings as the need arose. Within five years the state constructed a hospital, an additional cottage, a separate kitchen and dining room, and a much-needed administration building. In 1894 the home experienced a "great increase in the number of inmates, caused partly by the growing infirmities, and partly by the hard times." As the board explained, in previous years "almost any man who was able to do chores or light work could find someone who would keep him," but during the depression of the mid-1890s, this type of accommodation was no longer available.[30]

The board of corrections and charities did not see any prospect of an immediate decline in the number of veterans needing care. "Those who are most familiar with the subject," said the board's 1895–96 report, "believe that the number of dependent soldiers will still continue to increase for several years to come, until the advancing death rate overbalances the increasing infirmities of the men." The board observed, however, that there were relatively fewer dependent old soldiers in Minnesota than in many other states. "The old soldiers of Minnesota are for the most part a thrifty and independent class of men, and the proportion who become dependent is much less than in the older states from which the more active and thrifty class emigrated to the Western States."

By 1898 the financial picture had brightened, and work was again available for some veterans who otherwise would have been in the soldiers' home. Under improved economic conditions and the trustees' adherence to a policy of accepting only homeless men, the population declined. A potential new source of applicants appeared that year, however; the Spanish-American War had been fought, and in time its survivors would need care. "It would seem proper," said the state board's report, "to amend the law so as to allow the admission of ex-soldiers of the late war on the same basis as the ex-soldiers of other wars."[81]

In the period immediately following the panic of 1893, the state's poorhouse population, like that of the soldiers' home, increased markedly. During 1892, 706 persons received care in poorhouses; by 1896, the peak year of the decade, the number had increased to 1,052. The board of corrections and charities began to urge the larger counties to make more adequate provisions. "Heretofore the number of paupers requiring almshouse care in this state has been so small as to hardly justify the counties in erecting permanent and suitable structures," said the 1893–94 report, "but the time has now come when this state must take up the work. From the fact that we have practically no permanent buildings, the State of Minnesota has great opportunity to make a record on poorhouse buildings equal to our excellent record on the character of the county jail buildings."[82]

The board had long been concerned about the counties' apparent lack of interest in replacing old farmhouses and other poorly adapted structures. As early as 1884 the board strongly advised against "additions to old farm houses or badly constructed buildings," and each subsequent report repeated its criticism of expensive makeshifts which frequently stood in the way of permanent improvements. The law which created the board in 1883 had also specified that "all plans for new jails and infirmaries shall . . . be submitted to said board for suggestion and criticism," but the agency had little opportunity to participate in the planning of suitable poorhouse structures until 1889, when the Goodhue County home was destroyed by fire. Through the heroism of its overseer, all the inmates were rescued, but the building was a total loss.[33]

At the request of the county commissioners the board offered advice on plans for a new poorhouse. The resulting brick structure, "well built and conveniently planned," opened about January 1, 1891. For some years thereafter it was considered the best in the state. The board's report described it as "finely located in a grove of trees about 200 feet back from the road. . . . The basement contains janitor's room, furnace room, smoking room, sitting rooms, bath room and closet. The first floor contains the overseer's office, sitting room and dining room, women's apartments, bath room, closets, men's sick room, day room, paupers' dining room and kitchen. The second floor contains sleeping rooms for the overseer's family and dormitory for male paupers."

On April 1, 1898, Hart resigned his position to become superintendent of the Illinois Children's Home and Aid Society. His successor was James F. Jackson, formerly executive secretary of the Associated Charities of St. Paul, who carried on the statistical, inspectional, and educational work started by Hart. The use of old structures for poorhouses continued to engage the attention of the board. In order to stimulate interest in properly designed buildings, that body in 1900 commissioned an architect, J. Walter Stevens, to prepare model plans for the guidance of county authorities. Designs were drawn for poorhouses of three sizes, accommodating twenty-three, forty, and fifty inmates. All plans provided separate quarters for the overseer's family, men, and women, "as well as the special requirements for proper and economical care of this especial class of people."[34]

The model floor plans were published in a pamphlet issued by the board in 1900. In addition to offering concrete suggestions on location, construction, and layout, the pamphlet stressed the possibility of future expansion — a point the counties had not considered in their conversion of old farmhouses. Local officials were also told that efficiency in operation was more important than economy in construction. "Good management," said the state board, "is very difficult in a poorly constructed building." In order to provide a homelike atmosphere, the pamphlet suggested that volunteer committees be enlisted to furnish books and pictures.[35]

The board's efforts met with a gratifying response, and the pamphlet was "the subject of flattering comments in other states." However, with the exception of the twenty-three-bed Becker County poorhouse, for which plans were approved on July 10, 1900, the members of the board of corrections and charities did not have the satisfaction of seeing new homes materialize under their jurisdiction. In a move to streamline state government, the legislature of 1901 abolished the board, along with a number of others, and turned its duties over to the new Board of Control of State Institutions.[36]

Even though the poorhouse buildings in use in Minnesota at the end of the century were far from satisfactory, the board of corrections and charities could take pride in many accomplishments during its eighteen years of existence. The inauguration of uniform reporting on the movement of poorhouse populations, the amount of pauperism, and the cost of both indoor and outdoor relief gave a much-needed basis for comparison among the counties. In several instances, by pointing out the small number of potential inmates, the board deterred counties from purchasing land or buildings in advance of need. Although responsibility for the proper administration of poor relief rested upon the local commissioners, the role of the poorhouse superintendents was not overlooked. Suggestions made by Hart must have done much to make overseers more aware of the needs of the people in their care. By gathering and publishing information on the poorhouses of the state and on developments in other states and at the national level, the board in this period made available a vast amount of new information.

Probably few of its actions had more far-reaching effects on the care of Minnesota's needy, by both public and private agencies, than the board's initiation in 1893 of an annual State Conference of Charities and Correction, patterned after the national conference. "It is a forum open to every lover of humanity for the discussion of live questions affecting the care of dependents, defectives and delinquents," said the board in 1900. "It continues to be valuable in educating the public sentiment of our own state, and is highly regarded in other states." Although the meetings were well attended, the board was disappointed in the relatively small number of public relief officials who came. These men, the board pointed out, had little opportunity to acquire the expert knowledge which their work required. The board suggested that the attendance of county commissioners and poorhouse superintendents would result in substantial improvements in their institutions, for it had noted that poorhouses "in the counties whose commissioners are regular attendants upon the conferences are the best managed in the state."[87]

At the end of the nineteenth century Minnesota had thirty-four poorhouses in operation — ten more than in 1883 when the board of corrections and charities had begun its work. Forty-six of the eighty-two counties which had been organized by 1900 had acquired property intended for the care of their needy. Six of these — Faribault, Marshall, Big Stone, Swift, Brown, and Martin — had not opened poorhouses, although Brown and Martin would do so in future years. Six others — Le Sueur, Carver, Todd, Redwood, Morrison, and Renville — had opened poorhouses which were now closed. The state-wide poorhouse population had increased from 625 persons during the year ending September 30, 1884, to 917 persons in the year 1899.[88]

More significant than the increase in the number of homes and inmates was the change in the character of the population. The county poorhouse was no longer thought of as a workhouse for the poor, and it was beginning to lose its status as a catchall for people of every age and condition. Throughout the nation, as the states established institutions for persons requiring specialized treatment, the population of almshouses was partially siphoned off to the new facilities.

By 1900 Minnesota had a well-developed system of state institutions: five hospitals or asylums for the insane; a soldiers' home; separate schools for the blind, the deaf, and the feeble-minded; a school for dependent children; the nucleus of a hospital for crippled children; and three correctional institutions. By 1900 too a host of private benevolent organizations had developed programs for the needy and had opened institutions for the homeless, including ten residences for the aged. In the meantime, however, the state's population had increased from 780,773 in 1880 to 1,751,394 in 1900, with an especially high jump in the number and proportion of persons sixty-five years of age and over. During the last two decades of the century, this group grew from 19,190 to 66,771, constituting 2.5 per cent and 3.8 per cent respectively. Benevolent homes for the aged could not begin to care for all the needy older people, and because most private institutions required that the resident be in good health when admitted, there was a demand for other facilities for the chronically ill and infirm.[39]

The "differentiation of charitable work," wrote Amos Warner in 1893, "has left the old, the infirm, the decrepit, and the chronic invalids and paupers for the almshouse of the present time." Nearly all the 917 persons cared for in Minnesota poorhouses during the year 1899 were there because of insanity, idiocy, sickness, loss of limbs, deformity or accident, blindness, or old age. More than half (52 per cent) were sixty years of age or over. At the end of the century county poorhouses were well on the way to becoming old people's homes — or, perhaps more properly, infirmaries.[40]

6

Improving County Poor Farms
1900—1920

As THE TWENTIETH CENTURY OPENED, one historian observed, the advances in transportation and communication "had done much to break down the cultural isolation of rural America . . . but they had not altered in any important respect the institutional life of the people." Outside the metropolitan areas, most of the basic arrangements of American society remained unchanged. "The family, the church, and the schools, lyceum lectures, and local governments, the county poor farms, the prisons, and the hickory stick, the general merchandise store, the traveling salesman, and the fringe-topped surrey . . . were fundamentally what they had been for generations."[1]

Yet new developments were under way. The early years of the twentieth century were a period of questioning and of searching for fresh approaches to solutions of long-standing problems. In the words of a Minnesota historian, "old ideas jostled with new." This process was particularly evident as county commissioners wrestled with the issues of poor relief.[2]

By 1900 the thirty-four counties operating poorhouses were becoming more interested in how their institutions compared with others and in what might be done to improve them. The medium for answering these questions was the State Conference of Charities and Correction. Before 1900 very few county officials had attended these meetings, but in the fall of that year the conference program

IMPROVING COUNTY POOR FARMS   93

included a session on poorhouse management. So far as is known, this was the first time that Minnesota members of county boards and superintendents of poor farms had an opportunity to air their problems in a general meeting. Other participants joined in the spirited discussion, with the result that several future sessions were planned around the poorhouse and its role in the field of social service.[3]

Although persons over sixty years of age constituted only a little more than half of the poorhouse population in 1900, it was evident in the discussion on management that the participants were thinking primarily of their older inmates. Their comments revealed some interesting differences in outlook concerning old folks in these institutions. In the view of commissioners and superintendents — those persons most closely involved in administration — the elderly often behaved like children who should be guided in every aspect of their living. For their own good, and that of the institution, a highly regimented mode of life was necessary. On the other hand, private agency workers and state officials tended to regard the inmates as people who had managed their own lives for many years and who were entitled to individualized treatment.

The opening paper by Mrs. J. L. Hendry, matron of the Ramsey County home, was largely concerned with the rules she had found necessary for her institution. In the interest of order and cleanliness, she wrote, inmates were not allowed to occupy their rooms during the day or to bring in the "accumulation of clothing and various other things that a pauper always finds." In regard to bedding, Mrs. Hendry had found that straw ticks and blankets were more sanitary than mattresses and quilts. Inmates were required to take a weekly bath, even against their inclinations. The matron had known old people "who would rather leave and try their luck elsewhere than wash."[4]

Ramsey County discouraged idleness: "Inmates' time must be employed as much as possible." The men worked on the farm, sorted vegetables in the root cellar and did light work inside the house. Finding suitable work for the women was not so easy, wrote Mrs. Hendry: "they are for the most part feeble and have poor eyesight, with all sorts of imaginary diseases; so they mend and patch for themselves, as their sewing is not satisfactory to me."

The bill of fare, always a bone of contention, was standardized, beginning with Sunday morning's breakfast (also Monday's, Wednesday's, and Friday's) of bread, butter, potatoes, and coffee, and ending with Saturday night's supper of bread, tea, and boiled rice — one of four meals during the week when potatoes were not on the menu. "Luxury in the way of tobacco is allowed, a sack or plug weekly, with the privilege of raising some for themselves." More labor went into tobacco-raising, Mrs. Hendry observed, than into any "necessary work."

Mrs. Hendry believed firmly in systematic discipline, "each day having its own work and ready for inspection at any time." As for refractory inmates, a short confinement on a diet of bread and water usually sufficed, but this was admittedly a drastic measure. Mrs. Hendry warned that supervisors "must be extremely careful not to ask anything unreasonable or show any partiality in the treatment of these people."

George Jarchow, superintendent of the Washington County poor farm, agreed with most of Mrs. Hendry's rules, but urged that couches be provided in the sitting rooms so that inmates could lie down during the day "if they feel so disposed." He too had discovered that the "average pauper and labor are not the best of friends" and that the "average inmate does not enjoy bathing." Jarchow's bill of fare was also built around potatoes, but it included pancakes, fried mush, and graham muffins for breakfast, and pickles five days a week.[5]

Charles E. Faulkner, superintendent of the Washburn Memorial Orphan Asylum in Minneapolis, opened his remarks by saying that "in the absence of the representative from one of the poorhouses, I would like to account myself a pauper just for a moment." In this role Faulkner had several comments on the subject of baths: "Of course, we are indisposed to taking very many of these; . . . but possibly there might be something . . . as a substitute for the ordinary poorhouse bath tub. . . . some of us are a little squeamish about that — we are accustomed to bathe in creeks and out doors." Besides, he intimated, there might be a reason for the sqeamishness. The bathtub should be eliminated entirely and thrown out "for the pigs to use for a trough." If a substitute could be provided, such as "the shower and the spray in the little stalls made as they make them now in the most delightful sanitariums," Faulkner said, "we would consent to take many more baths."

Asked for his comments, J. C. Boller, overseer of the Winona County poor farm, said that his experience had been much like that of the other superintendents. His institution was conducted under the township relief system, and "when you go to speak to any of these paupers about work, about cleanliness, about this or that . . . well, then they are going to see the supervisor of their town, or . . . speak to the jurymen from their district about how they are abused, and I never saw a pauper yet but what thought he was abused." Boller also questioned whether poorhouse inmates were entitled to more comforts than the taxpayers who supported them.

James F. Jackson, who was still serving as secretary of the board of corrections and charities, agreed that many taxpayers did indeed live under wretched conditions, but he maintained that it was "not consistent nor dignified for a county to keep its guests in squalor." Jackson expressed considerable sympathy for the persons in charge of poorhouses, especially the superintendent's wife, whose life was particularly confining. While her husband could get to town occasionally, she associated with the inmates almost constantly, seldom seeing anyone else or receiving a word of encouragement. "I have more sympathy with the superintendents' wives than with any other class of people in the State of Minnesota," said Jackson. These women had great opportunity, he pointed out, to brighten the lives of inmates, but too often their efforts were not appreciated. "I wish that some of the women's clubs or somebody else could expend some of their sympathy on the superintendent's wife and through the superintendent's wife upon the institution."

The idea of enlisting support from the community immediately caught hold, and several persons suggested groups that might become interested in visiting or other similar activities. A social worker from Wisconsin urged that, when an inmate died, a minister be invited to the poorhouse to conduct a "decent, Christian burial." Under the practices prevailing in some localities, an overseer simply placed the body in a wagon and hauled it to the burying ground without benefit of mourners, flowers, or any kind of religious ceremony. Jackson agreed that the matter should be brought to the attention of clergymen in the various communities, but added, "more important than a respectable burial of the dead is a respectable care of the living, and it is that I would again urge upon your attention."

The 1900 conference was the last in which the board of corrections and charities participated. In 1901, it will be remembered, this agency was replaced by the Board of Control of State Institutions. Influenced in this action by developments in Wisconsin and Iowa, the legislature established a single, full-time, salaried board, appointed by the governor, to take the place of the numerous unpaid boards which had previously managed charitable and penal institutions.[6]

The three new members of the board of control continued the participation in the State Conference of Charities and Correction which the previous board had started, but the county commissioners soon took over the sessions on poor relief. In November, 1902, hoping to stimulate the attendance of more county officials, the commissioners formed an organization in order to become "better acquainted with each other and with their duties in the general work of charities and correction." The Minnesota Association of County Commissioners functioned as a section of the conference, but it also held one or more separate meetings each year. Poorhouse problems, as a subject for discussion, gave way to other issues: county versus township systems of poor relief; the causes and prevention of pauperism; the care of the sick poor, including the tuberculous and the insane; and the relative merits of boarding-out and poorhouse care.[7]

The system of boarding paupers in private homes had many supporters. In 1908 Chris Heen, Todd County commissioner, pointed out two objections to the poorhouse. In the first place, he told his colleagues, the words "almshouse" and "poor farm" were repugnant to most people. In the second place, the grouping together of many kinds of paupers was "not conducive to the comfort or peace of mind of the average deserving county charge." The boarding-out plan, on the other hand, had many advantages. Heen felt that it was more humane, because it surrounded "the unfortunates with the influence of a home." It also permitted each commissioner to supervise closely the boarding homes located in his neighborhood and to remove the paupers in the event of mistreatment. Furthermore, Heen said, the poor farm could not handle all relief cases; most of them were not candidates for the poor farm, but rather persons who needed only temporary help. The county had to rely on the "direct aid system in order to complete its charitable work." Taking everything into account, Heen concluded, the boarding-out system in his county not only produced better results but was cheaper than maintaining a poor farm.[8]

A few commissioners presented similar views, but on the whole the poorhouse seemed to be the preferred type of care. This conviction was brought out in revived discussions of county and township systems of poor relief, which culminated on February 12, 1910, in the adoption of a resolution recommending the county system because it facilitated the "conduct of a small farm, with good buildings, equipped in the most modern way — sewage, water, heat and light." Poor farm care, the resolution added, was "humane, commendable and inexpensive." To "give it strength," the association readopted the resolution at its November, 1910, meeting.[9]

While the commissioners' actions might have strengthened in their course the forty-four counties which already were maintaining poor farms in 1910, it had little perceptible effect on those without them. By this time the buying of poor farms had practically ceased in Minnesota. Of the twelve counties which purchased farms in the 1900–20 period, only two — Lake and Traverse — made the acquisition after 1910. Most of the twelve counties were located in the heretofore sparsely settled northern and western sections of the state. In acquiring farms county commissioners followed the usual pattern: a committee selected a suitable location, and the board voted on its purchase; the board then arranged for any necessary remodeling, or secured plans for a new building, and instructed the county auditor to obtain proposals from prospective managers.[10]

In at least one county — Koochiching — the poorhouse evolved from a pesthouse, that forerunner of the contagious disease hospital. When smallpox or scarlet fever struck a community, the victims were isolated, the place depending on the circumstances. Often town officials quarantined such persons in their own homes, with a placard tacked to the front door and the yard roped off from the neighbors' premises. Sometimes a guard was posted to keep out intruders. (A favorite pastime of neighborhood children was to see how far they could duck under the rope without goading the guard into giving actual chase.) Some communities owned or rented a small pesthouse outside the town. Even when not in use, it had the aura of a haunted house, and children invariably quickened their steps as they hurried by.[11]

During the early years of the nation's development, poorhouses and pesthouses were often closely connected. In Minnesota, contagious disease cases were cared for at times in poorhouses, but only four counties are known to have had separate pesthouses on their farms. Aside from the fact of their existence, little is known about such facilities in Ramsey, St. Louis, and Aitkin counties. The arrangements made by Koochiching County are, however, a matter of record. When that county was established in December, 1906, one of the earliest acts of its board was to open a pesthouse. After renting buildings in International Falls for a time, the board on

October 6, 1908, voted to purchase a nearby farm. The main building was used as the poorhouse, and until as late as the 1920s a small outbuilding held contagious cases. Sometime after 1922 the county enlarged the main building and sealed off a new wing for the isolation of contagious diseases. Years later a window opening from the corridor into that unit was pointed out to visitors as the place where food had once been passed to the sick inmates.[12]

Although most of the poorhouses which opened between 1900 and 1919 utilized existing buildings, many of the pre-1900 homes were replaced by new structures. The state had weathered the depression of the mid-1890s, and conditions were generally favorable for building. Then too county boards were beginning to realize that in the long run it was an economy to replace their remodeled farmhouses with permanent buildings designed for the purpose. In their interest in improving physical plants, the commissioners were undoubtedly influenced by discussions at the State Conference of Charities and Correction and at their own association meetings.

A third important factor in the construction of new buildings was the pressure exerted by the state board of control, particularly after 1908 when it added to its staff a full-time inspector of institutions. In addition to the management of state-operated institutions, the new board — like its predecessor — was responsible for investigating the "whole system of public charities, and all charitable and correctional institutions in the state." For the first few years, however, board members were preoccupied with the problems of state-operated institutions, and the inspection of poorhouses was carried out by agents with other duties.[13]

When the laws were revised in 1905, the board's jurisdiction over prisons, jails, infirmaries, asylums, and public hospitals was made more specific. Then the question was raised as to exactly what facilities came under its purview. The board was of the opinion that its inspections were mandatory, but it was not sure that privately owned hospitals, which were rapidly increasing in number, were "public" hospitals. In 1907 the attorney general ruled that "any hospital open in a charitable way to the general and unrestricted public is subject to an investigation by the State Board of Control, whether its ownership and management be of a public or private nature."[14]

After receiving this opinion, the board resolved to appoint an agent whose sole duty would be to "investigate all the various institutions . . . and to report their condition on such blanks as this board may provide for that purpose." One member objected to the creation of the position, on the contradictory grounds that local officials already inspected jails and that the examination of asylums, hospitals, and poorhouses was "of too much importance to be delegated to an employe." The majority overruled him, however, and the board appointed as the first institutional inspector Louis G. Foley, who was then serving as supervisor at Anoka State Hospital.

Foley assumed the post on January 1, 1908, and in the next six months visited 208 lockups, 41 jails, 25 poorhouses, and 132 hospitals. For the inspector's use the board provided simple report forms which could be readily completed during a visit. Those for county poorhouses included questions on construction, sanitation, fire protection, and other data on physical plant; number of employees, number of inmates, and movement of population in the preceding year; type of record forms in use; and general conditions throughout the building.[15]

A genial, soft-spoken person, Foley was both liked and respected by the persons in charge of the institutions he visited. Despite the lack of regulatory control, he accomplished much by persuasion and practical advice. Although the board lacked the power to condemn buildings, Foley was able to exert pressure by calling attention to the dilapidated condition of some poorhouses. "The buildings in these several counties should be condemned," he pointed out in 1918, "but the Board of Control is without the necessary power." On another occasion he noted: "This matter has been brought to the attention of the county commissioners of these counties repeatedly, but definite action has been postponed owing to alleged lack of funds. . . . There seems to be no reason why the poor should not receive the same attention at the hands of the state, as regards sanitary and health conditions in public buildings, as is given criminals."[16]

One of Foley's duties was to examine the plans submitted for new construction. The board continued to recommend the model designs that architect J. W. Stevens had prepared in 1900 at the request of the board of corrections and charities. With some modifications these plans served as the pattern for county poorhouses constructed in the state during the next thirty years. In the light of modern standards the plans had many defects, but they did provide the "special requirements" deemed necessary: substantial construction; complete separation of the sexes except, perhaps, in the dining room; and a separate apartment for the overseer, including office, sitting room, dining room, and three or four bedrooms. Because the inmates were expected to stay out of their bedrooms during the day, sleeping quarters were not spacious but dayrooms and dining rooms were very large.[17]

As in previous years, most of the new poorhouse buildings were located on farms. Those known to the author were large, solidly built rectangular structures of two or three stories, often set back from the road in a small grove of trees. A typical county home of that period could usually be spotted at a distance; any doubts about its identity were dispelled on closer view by the appearance of a dozen or so old men clad in ill-fitting suits, the coats and trousers of which never matched.

There was a marked sameness about the interiors, as might be expected in buildings evolved from the same model designs. Although the original plans did not show a center hall, one was usually provided, giving access to porches at both ends of the building. Ordinarily separation of the sexes was accomplished by situating the men's and women's quarters at opposite ends of the building, with the overseer's apartment between them. Rice County, however, took unusual precautions when it completed a new poorhouse in 1903. The overseer's apartment occupied the extreme north end of the building; the long south section was divided into east and west units for men and women, separated from each other by a double hall so that men and women did not even traverse the same corridor.[18]

The overseer's apartment frequently occupied a disproportionate amount of space, especially as the number of inmates increased. Moreover, the front entrance belonged to the overseer, and visitors who went to the front door were informed that "these are private quarters" and directed to the "paupers' entrance" at the side or rear of the building. As it happened, there were few callers other than those brought by duty; visiting the inmates of poor farms was usually reserved for the Christmas season when various groups put on annual entertainments. Few people were really aware of the place in the country except when some unusual occurrence brought it to their attention.

Public reaction to the new buildings varied from community to community. In some counties, especially where the new structure replaced an existing building, there was little publicity. When the new home was sufficiently completed for occupancy, the inmates simply packed their belongings and the superintendent hauled them to the new facility without special ceremony. Other counties took considerable pride in the provisions made for their dependents, although the term most frequently applied to the new building — "palace for the poor" — seems a little condescending. When Brown County dedicated its new $20,000 poorhouse on January 25, 1908, some 300 people attended the exercises. The committee in charge "wanted everyone to know what was being done" and visitors listened to speeches in Swedish, German, Czechoslovakian, and English. "The worthy poor, of which there are now nine at the poorhouse," reported the *Brown County Journal*, "were the guests of honor and sat down to a table ladened with a sumptuous repast." In congratulating the citizens on their public spirit in providing this building, Andrew J. Eckstein, chairman of the county board and a frequent participant in the state conferences, warned them against complacency: "When we cease to take pride in these institutions or to replace them from time to time with better ones no other evidence will be needed to show that we are on the decline."[19]

The *Martin County Independent* was not sure that the rural location of the area's new poorhouse, completed in November, 1915, would be entirely pleasing to the paupers, who previously had been housed in the town of Fairmont. It did not, however, question the benefit to the public. "While some of them [*the paupers*] who have been in the habit of spending their time loafing and begging on the streets will probably not like the change in spite of the fine building in which they are located[,] it will be better for them and better for the public[,] who have been more or less annoyed by the presence of some of the county charges on the streets and at public gatherings."[20]

A number of counties constructed buildings in response to prodding by the board of control, and it was sometimes difficult to explain to taxpayers why a new home was needed, especially in areas where economic conditions left something to be desired. At its August, 1920, meeting, the Pine County board let a contract for a new building to be erected on its existing poor farm. In reporting the action the *Hinckley Enterprise* of August 20, 1920, explained: "The present buildings are good farm buildings, but never were suitable for a poor farm." The new structure, the newspaper noted, would be "fireproof with soundproof inside partitions, steam heated and scientifically ventilated and with numerous bathrooms." When the voters defeated a bond issue designed to pay for the building, the commissioners imposed a tax levy for the purpose. Persistent complaints about the "expensive building for the poor" eventually led to a grand jury investigation, which revealed only that "the board of control had ordered [sic] the erection of a new building which had to be built according to their specifications."[21]

In the administration of poor farms, there had been virtually no change since 1884, when Hastings Hart called attention to the varied and unsatisfactory arrangements under which overseers were appointed. Now generally referred to as superintendents, they were still selected on the basis of the least cost to the county. Compensation, as in earlier years, might be in the form of a fixed salary, the payment of a stipulated boarding rate per inmate, or the use of the farm in return for the services set forth in the contract. How detailed such agreements could be is illustrated by the offer which the Houston County board received from one Peter Klein: "For use of the house farm and barn, board for myself and family and $2.25 per week for a hired girl, I will take proper care of all the paupers brought to the poor farm during the year 1902; I will keep all fences in repair free of charge, the county to furnish the necessary material, I will go after coffins for paupers when needed, free of charge and will pay my own expenses when absent from home on business for the county. I will furnish garden vegetables needed during the summer months and one acre of potatoes from the crop raised in 1902 free of charge; I will furnish 3 cows and 100 chickens their products to be used in the house; I will do all mending for paupers free of charge." The only other bidder did not offer nearly so many free-of-charge services, and Klein's proposal was accepted. Whether he or the county got the better bargain, probably neither could have said.[22]

Turning the farm over to an individual who provided care at a stipulated rate per inmate gave the overseer too much latitude, in the opinion of the state board of control. "It is desired to emphasize what has been said in former reports concerning the so-called 'farming out' of the poor to the lowest bidder," Foley wrote in 1916. "This practice cannot be too strongly condemned. The easy escape from responsibility which it affords to county officials, together with the impracticability of efficient inspection and supervision from our office, is most detrimental to the welfare of the poor." Fortunately, Foley added, the system was "meeting with growing disfavor in all parts of the state."[23]

Judging from reports submitted by superintendents from 1900

to 1920, the poorhouse population included a very large number of persons who were admitted because of illness, disability, or the infirmities of old age. The question of what to do with them recurred frequently at the state conference of charities. Suggestions ranged from expanding the general hospital system to establishing separate county hospitals or infirmary departments at the poor farm. The inadequacy of poorhouse facilities is illustrated by the account of a physician who attended patients at the Becker County home. "The county infirmary . . . is a model to a certain extent," he said. "It is a commodious frame building, well finished inside and out, full basement, steam and waterworks. It is not ventilated as well as it should be, is lighted by lamps and there is no elevator, a defect most easily noticed after one has carried a two-hundred-pound woman in his arms from the front yard, through two halls, up a narrow flight of stairs and deposited her upon an operating table." (Such defects, it might be noted, were also common in many small rural hospitals of the day.) [24]

The problem of caring for the incapacitated loomed so large that many commissioners believed it could be solved only with help from the state. In 1911 their association discussed the desirability of a state hospital for the poor, "especially the deformed, cripples, helpless people from age and decrepit," and adopted a resolution favoring such an institution. When the proposal came up again at the 1914 meeting, Charles E. Vasaly, chairman of the state board of control, reminded the group that his board has been advocating this action for a number of years. The board's report for that year again recommended the establishment of a state home for the aged and senile "to care for from five hundred to one thousand persons." [25]

Although this particular proposal was not carried out, the period did bring a solution to another problem which the county boards faced. For many years the poor farms had cared for tuberculosis patients who, for whatever reasons, could not be kept at home. In many poorhouses little attempt was made to segregate them from other inmates; in others some isolation was provided. Robert Hall of Olmsted County reported in 1901 that when he first became a commissioner he had arranged for an isolated room to house consumptives. "Now," he said, "we have more or less of that in the poorhouse all the year round. We have two there now. We thought best to have them isolated so as to prevent infection, and we find it works admirably." [26]

A plan to care for tuberculosis patients at the Ramsey County home in the 1890s backfired when Dr. H. Longstreet Taylor provided "tents to accommodate a few persons . . . during the summer months." Not surprisingly, the action was unpopular in the neighborhood, and "in order to prevent the tents from being pitched the following summer" local residents took steps to have the field "plowed in the spring and planted to potatoes."[27]

After the turn of the century public health authorities pressed hard for measures to prevent, control, and treat tuberculosis. Although counties had not been disposed to unite in building district poorhouses, their boards joined medical and public health organizations and other agencies in a movement to set up district tuberculosis sanatoriums. In 1909 the Minnesota legislature passed a law enabling counties to co-operate in constructing and operating such facilities. When this act did not produce the desired results, the legislature decided to appropriate matching funds for the construction and maintenance of sanatoriums. Under the terms of a 1913 law, each county could receive an amount equal to its own appropriation, up to a maximum of $50,000. This act offered the needed incentive, and five years later the state had fourteen county or district sanatoriums. "Minnesota has provided institutional care for a larger proportion of her tuberculous population than any other state in the Union," a magazine in the hospital field observed in 1917. "She has not merely provided this care; she has brought it to the doors of her citizens."[28]

The new facilities were to have somewhat more far-reaching implications for the aged than simply permitting the removal of patients who did not belong in poorhouses — important as that measure was to the control of tuberculosis. The buildings were well constructed, substantial, and designed for hospital care. These factors became important some thirty-five to forty years later when the sanatoriums were considered for conversion into county nursing homes.[29]

While county boards gave considerable thought in this period to the care of the sick, they were also concerned about other segments of the poorhouse population and about the causes of pauperism in general. "Looking at the different cases of the poor in my county," said Mathew Bullis of Pine County in 1914, "they would seem to me to be divided into six different classes." The first three included the "worthy poor": respectable old people who had become dependent through age or adversity, families deserted by the fathers, and people who were destitute because of illness. A fourth class consisted of "spendthrifts," who had not saved for their old age. For this group county boards had scant sympathy. Describing one applicant who freely admitted his misspent life, Bullis said: "Tears ran down his cheeks and he was deeply moved, if the board was not." The fifth group was made up of the mentally deficient, who required relief on a daily basis. If assistance is given them "too freely," said Bullis, "they waste; and if too sparingly, they want."[80]

Bullis' sixth and last category of county charges included alcoholics, who made up most of the poor farm population in his area. "The left over product of the saloon," he reported, "is usually the class we have in the Poor House. At least, that is so in our county, being about a dozen, most of the time. While we try to make them contented and comfortable, they are unappreciative, create more or less trouble with our housekeepers and managers, and give nothing in return." Bullis' remarks on the "drinking class" struck a responsive chord among county commissioners. Practically all poorhouses, it seemed, housed men with alcoholic problems. Not many, perhaps, found them as troublesome as the institution whose superintendent stated in a report that "he should have had three males, but that they were all away on a drunk that night."[81]

A state law prohibited saloonkeepers from selling liquor to inmates of public institutions, and county commissioners were authorized to black-list a drinker at saloons he was likely to frequent. Many inmates, it seemed, had ways of getting around the hurdle. "Our biggest trouble," said C. B. Waddell of Hennepin County, "is the town a half mile away from the county farm, where there are ten saloons. Our old men get out and go over to the town, and a great many people seeing the old men loafing around, ask them to have a drink — and they take it every time they are asked, you may be sure."[82]

If the cause of poverty was indeed the saloon, the remedy, suggested John Kelly, Wright County commissioner, lay in seeing that the laws were enforced, but the commissioners' fears of being hurt politically sometimes stood in the way. Kelly believed it was necessary to invoke assistance from another source — women — the wives and mothers of drunkards who had observed the evil effects of strong drink. "And I want to tell you," Kelly concluded, "with all the sincerity and eloquence that I am capable of, that if you give the women the vote . . . ten years from now your poor houses will be empty."[83] But Kelly proved a poor prophet. Neither the

Eighteenth Amendment, ushering in national Prohibition in 1919, nor the Nineteenth Amendment, which brought woman suffrage a year later, had any noticeable effect on the continued existence of county poorhouses.

Nevertheless, even in 1919 a few observers predicted that these institutions would disappear from the American scene. In that year Mary Vida Clark, a New York social worker, suggested that the poorhouse was an anachronism. "In a generation of railways, trolleys, telephones and automobiles, with an era of aircraft in sight, the county is too small a unit for the practical operation of curative and custodial public institutions and agencies," she pointed out. "The multiplication in any populous and extensive state of almshouses and jails is extravagant and ineffectual to a degree seldom realized, because these institutions are too uninteresting to be contemplated by the modern health or social worker long enough to be understood. . . . Let the expert in state finance picture these scores of little institutions, with their miscellaneous and unclassified population, purchasing supplies and running farms, each according to its own self-selected plan, in its own political milieu, generally changing such policy as it may have and losing most of the experience it may have gained with every election of county officers."[84]

During the first decade and a half of the century, Minnesota's social workers and public officials had made an attempt to understand the state's poorhouses and poor relief problems. At their annual conferences they raised questions, shared experiences, and suggested courses of action. The most tangible result, perhaps, could be seen in the new structures which replaced the old farmhouses and other makeshift buildings. For a time there were indications that the exchange of ideas would also result in other improvements, but after the first flurry of interest poor farms attracted relatively little attention, especially in the years immediately following World War I. Too many other developments engaged the attention of county commissioners, including the pressing problems of road and bridge construction in the expanded highway system. Among social workers interest in the new child welfare programs crowded out consideration of activities concerning the aged poor. In 1917 the Minnesota legislature enacted a body of laws for the protection of defective, illegitimate, dependent, neglected, and delinquent children. To administer these acts, which became famous as the "Minnesota Children's Code," a children's bureau was created in the state board of control, and volunteer child welfare boards were organized in counties where the commissioners requested them. This new program and others, such as the inauguration of county public health nursing services, left little time for the contemplation of possible poorhouse improvements.[85]

It would not be long, though, before the poorhouse became a focus of attention on both national and state scenes. Eventually not only health and social workers but also legislators and laymen became interested in replacing this institution with some more acceptable form of care for the needy aged.

7

Ethnic Groups Provide for Their Aged

1900–1920

DURING THE FIRST TWO DECADES of the twentieth century, twenty-three new benevolent homes, more than twice the number started in the nineteenth century, opened their doors. At the same time the earlier homes increased their capacities by replacing old buildings, adding new wings, or making space available in sections previously used for other purposes. The period of experimentation was over: there was no longer any question as to the need for places where homeless older persons could live and receive care.

As private groups expanded their activity in this field, new patterns emerged in the types of sponsoring organizations and in their general purposes. The years from 1900 to 1920 saw greater involvement with hospitals and the first conversions of old hospitals into homes for the aged. Another distinct trend, formerly discernible only in veterans' facilities, appeared in the establishment of homes for special segments of society. A fraternal organization opened a home for members of its order; a St. Paul group founded a residence for needy Negroes. Several nationality groups provided places for their aged countrymen and countrywomen. More large church bodies entered the field — a movement which led to the founding of additional homes in later years.

ETHNIC GROUPS PROVIDE FOR THEIR AGED 109

In the wake of the great wave of immigration which hit American shores at the end of the nineteenth century, new churches tended to be set up along ethnic lines. As benevolent homes for the aged were established in the next decades, it was hard to say which was the more influential factor — religious denomination or national origin — for the two tended to be inseparable. By 1900 the three largest national groups in Minnesota's foreign-born population were Germans, Swedes, and Norwegians. All but a handful of the new institutions were started by these three groups.

Generally speaking, homes opened by Germans, both Catholic and Protestant, began as hospitals. In time they came to number among their patients many people whose only affliction was old age. The first of the hospital-homes in Minnesota to achieve a separate identity was St. Joseph's Home for the Aged in St. Cloud, conducted by the Sisters of St. Benedict. This history of the hospitals started by the order in this German community went back to 1885, when the sisters opened St. Benedict's Hospital in a large brick structure on Ninth Avenue. In April, 1886, after a tornado swept through the city, the hospital functioned as the center for rescue work, and the sisters proved their worth. Four years later, needing more room, they acquired a large tract of land east of the Mississippi River and built a new hospital. But they soon found that this location was too remote for hospital purposes; in 1900 the sisters built a third hospital — St. Raphael's — on their old site in St. Cloud.[1]

As work proceeded on the new hospital, the question arose of what to do with the old building on the edge of town. The answer was not long in coming. The hospital was already caring for aged patients, eight of whom wished to remain where they were. The sisters, therefore, decided to convert the structure into a residence for the aged, to be known as St. Joseph's Home. By the end of 1900 there were twenty guests, all of whom had been born abroad in some one of the German states. Although they ranged in age from sixty to eighty-four years, they must have been unusually agile. The rules of the home encouraged the old people to go outdoors and to take walks on the grounds, but forbade them "to cross fields or climb through fences when going to the City or visiting neighbors."

One of the first institutions that planned from the beginning to care for infirm and aged persons was St. John's Hospital in Springfield. The institution opened in 1901, but it did not have separate quarters for older persons until some years later. The campaign for a hospital was spearheaded by J. George Appel, pastor of St. Paul's Evangelical Lutheran Church in Springfield. Although the institution was established by a community association, it was placed under the supervision of Reverend Appel's congregation. Ferdinand Schwartzrock donated a five-acre site, and in March, 1901, the directors let the contract for an "elegant building," three stories high, with a full basement largely above ground. The first patient was received on November 9, 1901. By 1903 it had become necessary to provide larger facilities for the old people.[2]

Fourteen years later responsibility for St. John's Hospital and Old Folks Home was transferred to the Lutheran Synod of Ohio and other states. The synod provided $7,000 to pay the home's debts, reported the *Springfield Advance* of February 1, 1917, and "those who worked so ardently and faithfully for many years to make the hospital a paying proposition, besides heroically attempting to pay off an old indebtedness, may now breathe easier." A year later, on January 24, the *Advance* took note of the continuing growth of the old people's department: "That the Old Folks Home ministers to a long-felt want in this district of the Ohio Synod was evidenced by the many applications. . . . All the rooms of the Old Folks' Home are now occupied and the board is planning additional rooms." Other German or Catholic hospital-homes of this period were St. Alexander Home, connected with Loretto Hospital in New Ulm, which achieved separate identity in 1913; Bethel Home in Mountain Lake, which began as part of the German Mennonite Hospital opened about 1904; and St. Ann's Home in Duluth, sponsored by the Sisters of St. Benedict and opened in the former St. James Orphanage building in 1910.[3]

Scandinavian national groups were particularly active in opening homes for older persons. Their extensive endeavor in this field doubtless resulted from their familiarity with both state and private institutions for the elderly in their native countries.[4]

The most numerous of the Scandinavians in Minnesota were the Swedes, second only to the Germans among the foreign-born in 1900 and outnumbering them in the next decade. Swedish immigration had reached substantial proportions by the 1880s and 1890s, and many who arrived then as middle-aged adults, together with survivors of earlier migrations, were now joining the ranks of the elderly. One agency which took note of the situation was the Minnesota Conference of the Augustana Lutheran Church, comprised in the early 1900s of nearly 400 Swedish Lutheran congregations in Minnesota and neighboring states. The idea of a home for aged members was born at the group's annual convention in 1902, when the Reverend Carl A. Hultkrans, superintendent of the conference-supported Bethesda Hospital in St. Paul, suggested that a committee investigate the feasibility of erecting an old people's home. The committee recommended that a home be built and suggested a location in St. Paul. The participating congregations apparently did not share the committee's belief that a home was needed, for an appeal for funds brought in exactly $16.[5]

The energetic Hultkrans was not discouraged. For several years he had kept his eye on a tract of land at Chisago City, which he considered particularly suitable for an old people's home. When the property unexpectedly came on the market, Hultkrans lost no time in persuading the Augustana board to buy the land and the Chisago district pastors to help in raising funds. It is not surprising that the area's ministers were interested or that the conference was favorable to the location. The Chisago Lakes area was the first permanent settling place of the Swedes who came to Minnesota in the 1850s. The Minnesota Conference, forerunner of the Augustana Synod, was started there in 1858. The site proposed for the home was a beautiful wooded tract of twenty-three acres on Green Lake, near the Zion Lutheran Church at Chisago City.[6]

Plans were immediately developed for an eighteen-room structure. The building committee was composed entirely of men, and when the Bethesda Old People's Home (now the Chisago Lutheran Home for Aged) was completed, it has been said, there was not a clothes closet or shelf in the place. Someone devised a novel way of stocking the new residence with china. Each person who came to the dedication exercises on November 10, 1904, was requested to "bring his own dishes for lunch and donate them to the Home." The first inmates arrived later in the month, and it was not long before the home was filled.[7]

Although most of the church bodies and some of the other groups that sponsored homes in the 1900–20 period were dominated by men, women did not entirely give up this field of work. A half dozen women's organizations opened homes in the tradition of earlier institutions, but with some differences. These women, less impulsive than their nineteenth-century sisters, developed plans more carefully and stated their objectives more clearly. They started homes to serve specific nationality groups or to provide care for the chronically ill. The period also saw several notable examples of intercity co-operation — a far cry from the unfavorable reaction in the mid-1880s when someone in St. Paul urged that a home projected for Minneapolis should instead be turned into a joint institution serving the two cities. "The suggestion," the *Minneapolis Tribune* commented on September 9, 1885, "was for good reasons rejected and no project akin to it has since been received."

The Swedish women who sponsored the Twin City Linnea Home in St. Paul not only developed it as a joint project, but also proposed from the beginning to serve people from their native country. At first, however, they had in mind a younger age group. Several founders of the Linnea Society had worked as domestics; they knew from experience that immigrant servant girls often were "compelled to board at lodging houses, sometimes surrounded by unwholesome conditions and associates." The women planned to open a home where the girls could stay while awaiting employment and where they could spend their vacations.[8]

The Linnea Society began as two separate organizations, of which the Minneapolis group, organized in March, 1904, was the first. The St. Paul society, although started some months later, appears to have been the more active. The initial step in its establishment was taken by Mrs. Charles (Anna) Bennett, who lived in a hotel where she and her husband served as caretakers. On December 6, 1904, she invited six women, including her sister, Mrs. E. M. Rystrom, to meet Ida Nihlon Kindwall, founder of the Minneapolis society. This was not the first time that Mrs. Bennett had attempted to start a movement on behalf of persons who needed help. Several years before, following a midwife's suggestion that she put her talents to work "doing good," Mrs. Bennett had invited several prominent St. Paul women to a coffee party to discuss some worthy but still undefined cause. For the occasion she and her sister had baked a variety of Swedish cakes and cookies, taken down their best dishes, and made a huge pot of coffee. But, alas, not one of the invited guests showed up. Somewhat daunted by this rebuff, Mrs. Bennett gave up her project for the time being. When she renewed her charitable efforts in 1904, the women she invited were plain Swedish housewives like herself.[9]

The St. Paul women decided to call their organization the Linnea Society, "because like the little lovable linnea flower small and insignificant it spreads its influence among the poor and needy along life's way." The society grew rapidly but, with a fifty-cent membership fee and ten-cent monthly dues, building up the treasury was a somewhat slower process. As an aid to obtaining more funds the group incorporated in 1906. "Now that the society has incorporated," reported the *St. Paul Pioneer Press* of October 24, 1906, "several promises of assistance will be fulfilled."[10]

By 1909, when the St. Paul and Minneapolis groups merged and incorporated as the Twin City Linnea Society, they had received several applications from aged women who wanted to enter the projected home when it was opened. The new organization decided to establish a residence midway between Minneapolis and St. Paul which would care both for "old and worthy indigent Scandinavian women" and for needy young women "dependent on their own labor for their living."[11]

Several years elapsed before the group was in a position to build, and it was not until October 21, 1917, that the cornerstone of the present Twin City Linnea Home for the Aged was laid on a site at 2040 West Como Avenue in St. Paul. By February, 1918, the structure was ready for occupancy. The society had previously voted to admit men as well as women, and the first resident was a man. By October of that year all rooms were filled.[12]

Among the foreign-born in Minnesota's population, Norwegians ranked third in 1900 and second in 1920 — outnumbering Germans whose immigration dwindled with World War I. The state's earliest home entirely for aged Norwegians — the Lyngblomsten Home in St. Paul — also owes its beginnings to women of Norwegian descent in both of the Twin Cities. The idea seems to have originated with a Minneapolis group, which met informally each month "to exchange lofty thoughts and ideals." In September, 1902, eight of the women gathered at the home of Mrs. Karl (Anna Qvale) Fergstad to form a literary club. The women soon decided, however, that some kind of benevolent project would be more satisfying.[13]

At the October, 1903, meeting Mrs. Fergstad painted for the membership a vivid picture of the snug little huts along the coast of Norway which the government provided for widows of fishermen who had lost their lives at sea. "Right here in the Twin Cities," she pointed out, in "the heart of the Norwegian settlements," many old men and women sat alone and forgotten. She suggested that even a small group like theirs could provide a home for a few deserving countrymen. On October 19, 1903, eleven members of the literary club formed a new organization. To symbolize the way they envisioned their movement might grow, they adopted the name of the Norwegian national flower, the sturdy *lyngblomst,* which "quietly grows and spreads through the rocky crags of Norway."

In Minneapolis, and later in St. Paul, the membership increased to the point where it became necessary to break up into circles. Branch groups were formed in Madison, Duluth, Mankato, Brainerd, Moorhead, and other cities of Minnesota, and in Wisconsin and North Dakota. The organization accumulated funds and in 1909 acquired a tract on present-day Midway Parkway at Pascal Street in St. Paul. At that time the sponsors of new homes did not always consider future needs in acquiring property. One contributor — James J. Hill — apparently foresaw the possibility of expansion, for he gave $500 with the stipulation that it be used only to buy land. The additional ten acres thus acquired became important some fifty years later when the Lyngblomsten Society combined with the American Lutheran Church in the development of the present Lyngblomsten Retirement Center.

Before long inquiries began to arrive from aged persons who wanted to enter the home. This show of interest spurred the women to even more fund-raising endeavors: raffles, socials, quilting parties, waffle luncheons, and lutefisk suppers. One of their projects was a lunchstand at the Minnesota State Fair, where the St. Paul branches served waffles. After the fair was over, the women found that a week's hard labor had netted them only $9.12. However, they had gained a great deal of know-how, or perhaps more accurately know-how-not, and in subsequent years the state fair venture was more profitable. The Lyngblomsten Home opened on November 5, 1912. In the next twenty years 157 elderly people were received.

The influence of their churches was a strong factor among Norwegian Americans in establishing homes for older persons. In fact, one of the largest church sponsors of homes for the aged in the nation as well as in Minnesota is the body which, as the Norwegian Synod, opened the Glenwood Old People's Home in the west-central part of the state. For some time the synod had been conducting a home for the aged at Stoughton, Wisconsin, and when the question of its expansion came up in 1911, someone proposed that a facility be established farther west.[14]

As it happened, a Norwegian Lutheran academy at Glenwood closed that year, and its building became available. The trustees lost no time in suggesting that the structure be used as a home for elderly Norwegian Lutherans, embodying this proposal in a letter to the church council. It took longer, however, to work out the details of transferring the academy's stock, setting up a local organization to administer the venture, and raising funds to remodel the building. Not until December, 1914, was the home ready to open.[15]

The academy had occupied a large, square, three-story structure of typical schoolhouse design, even to the bell tower and flagstaff on top. About $20,000 was expended to remodel and repair it. This renovation, stated the *Glenwood Herald* of December 10, 1914, "is without question the most important improvement made in Glenwood this year. . . . The building . . . is beautiful architecturally and presents an impressive appearance. The inside wood work is white enameled and the rooms are light, airy and comfortably large. . . . The Home is a distinct business asset to our city and is deserving of the united support of the people of this community."

Concerning its future, the *Herald* was optimistic. "After the building is paid for the institution will be self supporting as it will have a fund paid in by the inmates which will be ample to meet all of the running expenses." Within one week thirteen residents had arrived, including seven from Minnesota and two each from Illinois, Wisconsin, and Iowa, and many others had applied for admission. Life-care fees ranged from $1,000 to $1,500. Since the home had a potential capacity of thirty, it was believed that the admission fees would assure a substantial fund at the outset and that this would be augmented as new guests arrived to replace those who died or left. In 1914 neither the newspaper nor the institution's directors could foresee the devastating effects that increasing longevity and the reduced purchasing power of the dollar would have on homes which depended on lump sums paid in for life care. When the home opened that December day, the future appeared rosy and the guests well satisfied with what their money had purchased. "All of the inmates with whom we have had an opportunity to talk," said the *Herald's* editor, "have expressed themselves as highly pleased with their care."[16]

In 1915, shortly after the Glenwood institution opened, a group of Minneapolis business and professional men took the steps which resulted in the founding of the Ebenezer Home, the largest Norwegian Lutheran residence for the aged in the United States. With a convalescent home in mind, the group invited men belonging to six church bodies — the Norwegian Synod, Hauge's Synod, the United Norwegian Lutheran Church, the Lutheran Free Church, the Eielsen Synod, and the Society of Brethren (Lutheran) — to join them. The results of a preliminary investigation among the hospitals of Minneapolis showed, however, that the need for a convalescent home was not as great as had been supposed. A more necessary project, it appeared, was a facility for the "many aged poor and homeless people among Norwegian Lutherans" who could not afford the admission rates of the existing Norwegian homes.[17]

This idea met with favor, and the men's group rapidly grew into a society of some 400 members. Employing a field agent, the organization inaugurated a program of public information and fund raising, with an immediate goal of $3,000. After this amount had been collected, a house was rented at 3017 Portland Avenue in Minneapolis. "On April 17, 1917 we . . . began to make the frame house ready," a member later recalled. "On May 7 the Home was opened, soon ten old people filled the rooms." It was obvious that a larger building would be needed, and in 1919 the society purchased the present site at 2545 Portland Avenue. By the middle of December two floors were ready for occupancy. "Thirty needy old women are to move into the Ebenezer Home tomorrow," the *Minneapolis Tribune* reported on December 14, 1919. Work on the third floor was rushed to make it possible for an additional twenty occupants to enter by Christmas.[18]

Except for the hospital-connected homes, the institutions discussed thus far were opened primarily to care for the aged. Bethesda Homes near Willmar (with a Danish as well as a Norwegian background) grew out of a child-care service. The children's home had its beginning in Lamberton, Minnesota, where the Reverend Nils S. Haggerness of the Norwegian-Danish Conference (Lutheran) opened his home in 1897 to three children from a broken family. The people in the area took up the cause and formed an organization which purchased land in the town and erected the Lutheran Home Asylum of Lamberton. When it became apparent that individuals alone could not support the institution, the founders applied to the Norwegian-Danish congregations for funds. Before long the building became too crowded, and in 1905 the institution changed its name to Bethesda Homes and moved to a site about five miles north of Willmar. Although two elderly men were given temporary care in 1905, a home for the aged was not definitely established until 1910, when a separate building was provided for them.[19]

Still another ethnic-religious association of women was responsible for the founding of a home in St. Paul in 1908. The Jewish Home for the Aged was established after long years of planning by a devoted group of Jewish women. Originally known as the Charity Loan Society, the organization was started in 1890 to help needy families with small loans. After thirteen years of struggle, the society was all but crowded out by newer organizations and only eleven members remained. In 1903 the group reorganized as the Charity Loan Society and Old Women's Home, built up its membership, and accumulated funds.[20]

In 1905 Mary Burton, a woman of great organizational ability, became president; under her leadership the society began to plan actively for a home for aged and infirm Jews. The women found a desirable location at 75 Wilkin Street in St. Paul. The house, built in 1855 by William L. Banning, was a mansion of imposing appearance. Tall pillars supported a second-floor balcony, and wide steps led to the front porch. (The steps were probably not greatly appreciated by the old people who had to climb them.) The fine grounds, on the banks of the Mississippi River, were "spacious and well wooded and beautifully laid out, affording a splendid airing spot for inmates." The women made a down payment of $2,000, leaving an indebtedness of $6,000. Finding it difficult to assume such a responsibility, the group in 1907 turned over the management of the home to a new organization representing a wider segment of the Jewish community. The only woman on the new board was Mrs. Burton, who was elected vice-president.[21]

The home opened on June 14, 1908. At that time, according to W. Gunther Plaut, historian of Minnesota's Jewish community, the home appealed "exclusively to the East European portion of the population. The German group considered the sending of its aged to an institution socially inadmissible." Like other institutional administrators of this period, the home's managers believed that strict rules (which actually resulted in considerable regimentation) were necessary for smooth operation. For example, the residents were informed: "Inmates desiring to lie down to rest during the day shall be first assigned a place to lie down in a special room by the superintendent." At mealtime, the rules specified, "All food shall be placed in large platters. When all are seated, the platters will be passed." The regulations even covered daily attire: "The women will wear white aprons each day except while at work, and the men will wear black skull caps." Everyone was assigned an hour's work a day unless excused because of illness. The rules apparently did not deter old people from entering the home, and it was not long before the sponsors were considering ways of obtaining a larger building.[22]

Meanwhile, a women's organization in Minneapolis had made considerable progress toward opening a similar residence in that city. The group gave up its project, however, when it became known that the St. Paul sponsors were thinking of replacing the Wilkin Street home. "In a unique inter-city and inter-group meeting of one hundred Twin Cities leaders," wrote Plaut, "a joint new institution was planned and property purchased in the Midway district. . . . Quite beside the beneficent effects a new home had for the aged, it performed a function in community building which had a far-reaching importance of its own." With the opening of the new Jewish Home for the Aged of the Northwest in 1923, the old home in St. Paul closed.[23]

During the first two decades of the century, Minnesota's Negroes, constituting less than 0.5 per cent of the state's population, were mainly concentrated in the Twin Cities, particularly in St. Paul. It was natural, therefore, that the earliest home for aged Negroes in Minnesota should be started in that city. The Attucks Industrial School, Orphanage, and Old Folks Home, which opened about 1908, was, according to its founders, the first institution in the Upper Midwest "designed for the betterment of the Negro race, to provide a home for the orphans, the aged and the indigent of our race variety." The home took its name from Crispus Attucks, a mulatto who was killed by English soldiers during the Boston massacre of 1770 and who is referred to as the first man to die in the American Revolution.[24]

The Attucks enterprise was founded by James W. King, a Methodist minister who with his wife, Fannie, moved to St. Paul from Denmark, Iowa, in the late 1890s. Shortly thereafter the Kings started a mission at 168 Acker Street, moving in 1904 or 1905 to 228 Acker Street. For a short time they operated an industrial school where boys learned to make paintbrushes. The house on Acker Street proved too small for the expanding work, and sometime in 1908 interested friends, including several prominent white citizens, helped the Kings procure a five-acre farm with a small house at 1537 Randolph Street. During the first winter, men and boys were housed in a shack intended as a brush shop.[25]

Although the sale of brushes provided some funds, the chief support came from donations and benefits, including charity balls. In July, 1909, the public was invited to a picnic held on the grounds of the home. There was a good turnout, and the visitors were said to have been impressed by the magnitude of the work. At that time the small building housed twenty-two men, women, and children and was exceedingly crowded.[26]

In 1916 the organization learned that the building owned by the Home for the Friendless on Collins Street was for sale and made efforts to raise the purchase price, a reputed $5,000. In this endeavor it was aided by the city's Negro community. On April 25 the group sponsored a grand charity entertainment with no fewer than 135 patrons and patronesses. Several women's clubs worked regularly for the home, and on Thanksgiving Day all the Negro churches of the city held a union service, with the offering going to the Attucks Home. On December 9, 1916, the *Appeal* reported: "The Crispus Attucks Home moved this week to its new location at 469 Collins Street. This property is a large frame structure containing twenty rooms, and will furnish ample accommodation for the benefit of the inmates of the home." The care of children was discontinued a few years later.[27]

The Minnesota Odd Fellows Home in Northfield was established not for a specific racial, nationality, or church group but for members of a fraternal organization. Some twenty other states had Odd Fellows homes when the Minnesota institution opened in 1900 after a long period of study and planning. The history of the fraternity in Minnesota goes back to 1849, when the first lodge was established at Stillwater. In 1853, with four lodges in Minnesota Territory, a grand lodge was organized. Twenty-eight years later at a meeting in Winona Gideon S. Ives, former lieutenant governor of Minnesota, suggested the founding of a home to care for aged members, as well as for their widows and children. In 1885 a committee began to accumulate the needed funds. Contributions poured in at first, but the financial stringency of 1893 checked further donations, and the board could not proceed with its plans until 1898. After investigating tempting sites offered in Winona, Minneapolis, Montevideo, Owatonna, and other cities, the lodge purchased a farm within the municipal limits of Northfield.[28]

The Odd Fellows building, completed in 1900, consisted of an administration center connecting two large wings, one for men and boys, the other for women and girls. Designed in Dutch colonial style and constructed of red brick, the building stood imposingly on a slight rise in a wooded area. The town was proud of its new institution and turned out enthusiastically for the dedication. "Friday, June 15, 1900, was a red letter day," proclaimed the *Northfield Independent*, "not only for the Odd Fellows, but also for the people of Northfield, when the members of the order gathered here to witness the dedication of the Home. . . . store windows were handsomely draped, both depots thronged with people watching for special trains." A mammoth parade featured five bands. The Rebekah Assembly of Minnesota took on the job of furnishing the home. Seeking "uniformity of design and quality," they solicited cash contributions rather than completely furnished rooms, as was the usual custom.[29]

Most homes for the aged in Minnesota provided care for residents who became ill or infirm after admission, but in comparison with other states facilities for those who required special care from the outset were slow to develop. As early as the 1850s and 1860s there were homes for "incurables" in Massachusetts, New York, and Ohio; by 1900 some twenty states had institutions for the crippled, the tuberculous, and those with other types of chronic illness. Caring for incurables was a favorite charity of a wide variety of benevolent organizations — churches of several denominations, orders of nuns, King's Daughters, the Young Women's Christian Association, and private philanthropic corporations.[30]

The need for facilities to care for long-term patients in Minnesota was called to the attention of benevolent agencies as early as 1890, when Hastings Hart pointed out the "many sad cases of persons who have been completely disabled from disease or accident and who need more tender and kindly care than can be provided in the alms-houses of the state. Such persons are not suitable inmates for hospitals which are intended for the cure of the sick, and it is well worth the consideration of the benevolent whether such institutions should not be established."[31]

Nearly a quarter of a century elapsed before any private benevolent organization accepted Hart's challenge. The Bethesda Invalid Home, or Invalidhem as it was called, of St. Paul was perhaps the first private institution established specifically for the care of chronically ill aged persons. It was opened in 1914 by the Minnesota Conference of the Augustana Lutheran Church which had earlier sponsored the Chisago Lutheran Home.[32]

The leading spirit in this new venture — as in the founding of the old people's home — was Reverend Hultkrans. In his capacity as superintendent of St. Paul's Bethesda Hospital from 1891 to 1915, Hultkrans became familiar with the plight of the chronically ill and disabled. Early in the century he began to preach the need for a facility where the crippled, paralyzed, and very feeble could receive more care than was obtainable in the poorhouses or usual homes for the aged. "There is an urgent need of an Invalid Home," Hultkrans noted in 1906. "At present we have seven invalids in our hospital, and there are several invalids in every township in the state, but there is not a suitable place where these unfortunate brothers and sisters of humanity can be cared for. . . . We have been hoping that this report might fall in the hands of some well-to-do generous person, who would give us 50, or better still $100,000 to start the work with." No generous person came forward with even so much as fifty dollars.[33]

In 1913 the church took advantage of an opportunity to buy a summer resort on the shores of Lake Gervais northeast of St. Paul. Largely as the result of Reverend Hultkrans' efforts, the conference purchased the property and remodeled the old frame hotel building into a thirty-bed home for invalids. Long open porches extending the length of the building were favorite gathering places for the residents. The home opened on July 6, 1914, and was almost immediately filled. Hultkrans himself lived only a little more than a year to see the fruits of his endeavors.[34]

During the same decade two women's organizations opened non-profit nursing homes that later developed into homes for aged and chronically ill persons. One was the Women's Welfare League of Minneapolis, organized in 1912 to "secure better social and moral conditions surrounding girls and women in this city." Among the organization's projects were a vacation camp for girls, a recreation center, a woman's occupational bureau, and the promotion of legislation bearing on women's affairs.[35]

The idea for a Home for Convalescents was broached by Gratia A. Countryman, Minneapolis librarian and first president of the league, during the summer of 1913. The group lost no time in acquiring a building at 2925 Park Avenue and on October 1 opened a home where women could recuperate from illness. In the next few years the board members, like the founders of the Ebenezer Home, discovered that the need for a convalescent home was not as great as they had supposed. They also learned a good deal about the problems of financing an institution where stays were short and the number of inmates fluctuated from month to month. In particular the summer season — with its low incidence of pneumonia and other respiratory diseases requiring long periods of convalescence — brought little demand for this type of service. Nevertheless, the group persevered with the project and in 1916 moved to a large duplex at 1801 Park Avenue.[86]

During the influenza epidemic of 1918–19, the institution was better patronized, and for a time at least it had a waiting list. After the epidemic subsided members of the welfare league sought in various ways to promote the home's usefulness. They met with the county medical society, visited the social service departments of hospitals, and issued descriptive brochures. They even removed their sign from the front of the building, fearing that some persons might be deterred by the implication of charity in the word "welfare." Despite suggestions to convert the operation into a home for the aged, the group was reluctant to turn from the original purpose, and it was not until 1921 that the superintendent was instructed "to take enough patients, chronics or incurables[,] to put the Home on a paying basis." Eventually, in another location, the institution became a home for aged women.[87]

The second women's organization to enter this new field of service was the Woman's Christian Association which, in addition to conducting the Jones-Harrison Home, was engaged in a long-range program of maintaining residences and clubs for working women and girls. In 1919, as a result of the nursing shortage which followed World War I, the association underwrote a new endeavor — the training of practical nurses. In co-operation with the Minneapolis Board of Education, the group opened the Woman's Christian Association Hospital at 1714 Stevens Avenue in a residential building vacated by another of its projects, the Transient Home for Girls. In addition to the two-year practical nurse program, the hospital furnished work experience for nursemaids enrolled in the city's Vocational High School.[88]

Important as these training programs were, the women soon found that the institution also met a real community need in caring for aged and long-term patients who were "not welcome in the larger hospitals." In 1927 the work was taken over by a group of graduates of the practical nursing course who continued it under the name of the Vocational Nursing Home.[89]

By 1920 thirty-three institutions under private benevolent auspices were operating as, or on the way to becoming, homes for the aged. In each case the enormous financial effort necessary to launch a home totally absorbed the attention of the sponsors, and it was not until later that governing boards began to pay serious attention to the question of financing daily operations. No doubt they expected to tap the same philanthropic sources which had furnished funds for the buildings. In addition, they depended on two forms of revenue from the inmates. A certain amount of income came from residents who made monthly payments which varied according to their ability. A second source was the entrance fee, a lump-sum payment which was supposed to assure care for life; this was customarily a fixed amount, regardless of how long the person might stay or how much care he might require. Neither system was closely related to the cost of living. Despite rising prices, most early homes were slow to increase their fees. The Home for Children and Aged Women in Minneapolis, for example, set a fee of $300 in 1886; not until 1923 was that charge increased to $500. The Lutheran Home in Belle Plaine, which started with an entrance fee of $500 in 1898, had made no change as late as 1913. The new homes that opened between 1900 and 1920 generally charged higher rates, but even these were not realistic.[40]

With the entry of the United States into World War I, problems of financing and operation multiplied. How the war affected a typical home was related by the historian of Lyngblomsten. Less than five years earlier, its sponsors had rejoiced because their project was finally completed, but they now knew that the task had only begun. The problems which they faced were made even more difficult by their personal involvement in the war. "The Board meetings were almost transformed into consolation gatherings," the home's historian recalled, "where messages, letters, and news from distant loved ones were read and discussed. . . . But the management of the Home had to be carried on. . . . An extensive conservation program was adhered to by both the old folks and the Board."[41]

Improvements were postponed and essential repairs accomplished as far as possible by donated labor. Wartime price rises, especially in food items, increased the running expenses of the home. Pork rose to .40 a pound, and a sack of flour cost $4.50, related the historian, "even though bought directly from the mill. The ridiculous price of $30.00 was paid for 100 pounds of sugar. And at that the women had to beg most earnestly for it." In order to reduce costs, the home increased its flock of chickens, did all its own baking, raised vegetables, and made preserves. Male residents cut grass along nearby boulevards and put up hay for the home's four cows.

The influenza epidemic that began in the fall of 1918 brought additional trials to homes for the aged, as it did to households throughout the state. Residents became ill, nurses were scarce, and all employees had to put in long hours merely to keep the homes going. Because of a ban on large gatherings, boards were unable to carry out many of their former fund-raising activities.

Fortunately for several homes in the Twin Cities, the birth of the community fund movement offered some hope of financial relief. Federated or united fund raising for social agencies has been called "the most characteristic development of social work in this country." Although some experiments in budgeting expenses, setting goals, and co-operative raising of funds had been carried out in Cleveland, Cincinnati, and other cities, the movement was greatly influenced by the war chests of World War I, which combined local, national, and overseas appeals. More than 300 communities are said to have had these organizations. At the end of the war the joint appeal, which was started in Minneapolis in 1918, became the Minneapolis Community Fund. The St. Paul Community Chest was established two years later.[42]

Not everyone favored a united appeal, nor did all the eligible organizations join the agency. Many homes for the aged had large followings of loyal patrons who, it was feared, might be lost to them in a joint appeal. Homes which served large areas, the entire state, or several states, could not always see the advantage of allying themselves with the fund of a single city. Other institutions lacked the staff necessary to prepare budgets and carry on the accounting procedures required. A number simply preferred greater independence in raising and using their money.[43]

The Lyngblomsten Home in St. Paul, on the other hand, saw in the united venture a real hope, not only for itself but also for many similar agencies which had suffered because of the war as well as from the maldistribution of the city's charitable donations. The board's officers believed that the "new plan would bring about a fairer division of charity gifts as well as relieve the business men of the constant annoyance of solicitors." For institutions which did participate, united fund checks were a most welcome addition to their budgets.[44]

Recovery from the hard times of the war period was rapid both in the nation and in the state. By 1920 Minnesota's thirty-three private homes located in sixteen counties were well established — many in new structures built for the purpose. Nearly all these homes, confident of the future, entered the new decade with plans to expand and improve their existing facilities.

8

The Poorhouse under Scrutiny

1920–1930

THE DECADE OF THE 1920s WITNESSED THE BEGINNING of important social and economic movements. As Clarke A. Chambers pointed out in *Seedtime of Reform*, novel lines of action were being tried out in the "confused twenties," though they were perhaps not clearly discernible at the time. In 1921 Congress passed the Sheppard-Towner Act, a grant-in-aid program to the states, designed to give nonurban areas the kind of maternal and child health services that had helped reduce infant death rates in the cities. A committee of social work agencies, organized in 1922 to study methods of preventing juvenile delinquency, promoted child guidance clinics and visiting teacher services. Settlement houses experimented with new kinds of activities. Undeterred by setbacks and delaying tactics, social reformers continued the long struggle to abolish child labor, trying now for an amendment to the Constitution. Forty states had passed mothers' pension laws by 1921, although much of the legislation was permissive only. The principle might be adopted, but questions about eligibility, the effect on the aided families, and sources of funds were argued endlessly.[1]

Though programs to improve the welfare of children absorbed much of the energy of reformers, it became apparent as the decade progressed that changes were needed on other fronts. The war was over; the country was adjusting to woman suffrage, Prohibition, the automobile explosion, the restriction of immigration, and advances in technology. A brief depression in the early 1920s was followed by nearly eight years of good times, but for many people the general prosperity was more apparent than real. Midwestern farmers saw the value of their crops decline; bank closings and farm mortgage foreclosures were common. Factory workers found it harder to obtain and keep jobs as industry became mechanized. Whether or not there was such a thing as "technological unemployment," a subject of much dispute, it was true "that the number of the unemployed, judged by such imperfect statistics as were available, rose steadily from 1922 to 1929; and that in 1929, relief agencies, both public and private, were struggling with a volume of unemployment that approximated the number of unemployed at the peak of the depression of 1921."[2]

Among the unemployed were the aged, who by now constituted a clearly visible group both in absolute numbers and in proportion to the total population. For the country as a whole the ratio of persons sixty-five years and over rose from 4.7 per cent in 1920 to 5.4 per cent in 1930. In 1926 Louis I. Dublin, a statistician for the Metropolitan Life Insurance Company, attributed the increasing number of aged persons to two factors: "first, the remarkable decline in mortality at the younger ages and, second, the very heavy immigration of adults during the last three or more decades, who now are swelling the ranks of the aged. That explains why 27 per cent of the aged are foreign-born."[3]

For Minnesota, with its steady stream of immigrants, the increase was even more noticeable. In this state "the big jump in the rate of increase of the aging came between 1920 and 1930," wrote Isaac L. Hoffman. During the decade the number of aged increased from 110,766 to 163,480, and their proportion rose from 4.7 per cent to 6.4 per cent.[4]

Even as the number of the nation's older people increased, their opportunities to earn a livelihood became scarcer. "The depressing fact is that while there are more old people there is a smaller percentage employed and the tendency is steadily downward," John A. Lapp, president of the National Conference of Social Work, told the Minnesota conference in 1926. "In some industries there are few men past 50; in others men are not employed after 45. The mechanization of industry has brought a demand for the young and the nimble and has taken away the chance for the older and less supple. It is a bitter irony that life has been lengthened for the aged and the means of living have been lessened."[5]

What was true of the nation was also true in Minnesota. "During the past thirty or forty years," reported a state legislative committee in 1929, "the advent of labor saving devices and machinery, duplicating nearly all formerly purely manual operations, has taken away employment from thousands of aged people, and left practically no jobs for the old man or woman." Some of the reluctance on the part of employers to hire older workers, the committee found, was due to the operation of a compulsory workmen's compensation act, passed in 1913. Older men were more likely to be injured on the job and less likely to recover rapidly, making them greater financial liabilities to insurance companies.[6]

Limited opportunities for employment, coupled with factors that made saving difficult for old and young alike — the substantial increase in the cost of living and a general lack of unemployment insurance and sick benefits — meant that many persons reached old age without adequate financial resources. The legislative committee also noted that the loss of savings through speculation in unsound investments increased materially in Minnesota during the 1920s. It concluded: "The old man or old woman with no means to provide for his or her own support is an actual condition confronting us."[7]

If, in addition to lacking money for daily expenses, these men and women were without homes of their own, where would they live? Many old people moved in with sons or daughters, but for some this was not a good solution. John R. Brown, executive secretary of the United Charities of St. Paul, noted that "in an industrial community where houses are small, where the care of old people is thrust upon a father who is scarcely keeping his head above water, not only unhappy family life but often economic disaster follows."[8]

Some elderly persons could enter benevolent homes for the aged and practically all homes reported long waiting lists. Many other old folks, however, found such accommodations out of reach. "The majority of private homes," said Anne F. Fenlason in 1926, required "entrance fees ranging from $500.00 to $900.00" and had restrictive intake policies limiting applicants to certain religious affiliations or fraternal connections.

For many of the state's elderly people, therefore, the poorhouse offered the only answer to the question of where to live. This institution, unfortunately, received scant attention in Minnesota until the late 1920s, except for routine inspections made by the board of control. The State Conference of Charities and Correction, which in earlier years had devoted so many sessions to public relief and poorhouse problems, had become a widely representative group interested in many fields of endeavor. Its membership was drawn from a variety of health and social agencies, particularly the newly created county child welfare boards. In keeping with its "enlarged social scope and social vision," the conference in 1920 was renamed the Minnesota Conference of Social Work. Its programs were geared to child welfare, and the few papers concerning the poor and the aged dealt primarily with the old age pension movement. In 1924 Blanche L. La Du, a member of the board of control, pleaded in vain for legislation to improve the management of poorhouses.[9]

After 1923 county commissioners attended the social workers parley only as members of an Associated Conference for Officials Charged With Enforcement of Laws Relating to Children. Their own annual meetings, held at other times and places, were devoted to such questions as how to get patients into the University Hospitals; how much of the gasoline tax should go for county roads; whether the landowner or the county should put up snow fences; how to get people to cut their weeds under the new weed control bill; and whether to ask the legislature to increase the bounty on wolves. All of these were new programs; poor relief was an old story. Except for opinions (mostly adverse) on old age pensions, and experiences (many unfortunate) with mothers' aid, they brought to their consideration of poor relief functions little that was new. In discussions that were reminiscent of the early years of the century, the commissioners debated county versus township systems, enumerated how much money their counties were spending on relief, suggested cheaper methods of caring for the sick poor, and outlined the causes of poverty. "We have three kinds of poor," a commissioner observed sourly in 1925, ". . . the worthy poor, the crippled poor, and I won't works. The biggest one of the three is the I.W.W's." One commissioner asked wistfully for information on how to provide poorhouse residents with something interesting to do, but no one had an answer.[10]

Although the emphasis during this period was on financial considerations, no statistics were collected for the state on costs per inmate or on how poorhouse care compared in expense with other forms of relief. Elsewhere, however, observers had begun to gather such information and, further, to question the value of the poorhouse as a place of refuge for the old and infirm. Was it the best,

THE POORHOUSE UNDER SCRUTINY 129

or even the most economical, solution to the problem of the indigent aged?

On the national level two comprehensive studies were made by departments of the United States government and a third was conducted by sixteen national fraternal organizations. The three surveys took different approaches. In 1923 the bureau of the census carried out a special enumeration to learn how many persons were cared for in almshouses, the length of their stay, and personal facts about them. These findings were compared with those of previous censuses, and many tables showing regional and state differences were published in 1925.[11]

In November, 1923, the bureau of labor statistics began a yearlong investigation into the costs of almshouse care, compiling information on property values and maintenance and operating expenses for 2,183 public institutions — approximately 93 per cent of the nation's total. The bureau also collected data and recommendations from state welfare boards and other official agencies. The printed report, prepared by Estelle M. Stewart, appeared in 1925.[12]

The study by fraternal organizations was made in co-operation with the labor department — the latter concentrating on financial aspects, while the private agencies studied the physical and social conditions of the inmates. The idea for the survey originated with James J. Davis, long-time director general of the Loyal Order of Moose and United States secretary of labor from 1921 to 1930, who had become concerned about the problems of aged and dependent workingmen. The brief but informative study, directed by Harry C. Evans, was published in 1926 under the title *The American Poorfarm and Its Inmates*.[13]

In Minnesota a close look at the poorhouse was taken by a committee of the state legislature toward the end of the decade. In 1927, as part of its investigation of a pension plan for the aged poor, an interim committee of five senators under the chairmanship of George H. Nordlin of St. Paul set out to put the cost of poorhouse relief in perspective. The committee's first action was to compile statistics on county poorhouses, including the number of inmates, amount of income, and costs of buildings, maintenance, and operation for each year from 1920 to 1927.[14]

What did the findings of observers on the state and national levels reveal about the poorhouses of the 1920s? In the nation as a whole, the poorhouse population apparently had reached its peak.

From 1880 to 1910 each census enumeration indicated an increase, but in 1923 for the first time the number of inmates showed a decline. On the other hand, in Minnesota, with its younger system of poor relief, the poorhouse population — which constituted slightly less than 1 per cent of the state's aged — was still on the increase. The number of inmates rose from 994 in 1920 to 1,385 by 1927. The neighboring states of Wisconsin and Iowa reported almost twice as many inmates, but North and South Dakota and most of the western states had far smaller numbers.[15]

Although the nation's almshouses were increasingly becoming institutions for the aged, as yet only a little more than half the inmates were sixty-five years of age or over. Poorhouse populations still included — as they had for decades — children, the ill, the feeble-minded and insane, the deaf and blind, as well as able-bodied and mentally capable paupers. Minnesota's poorhouses were farther along toward becoming old people's homes. In 1923 nearly 63 per cent (650 persons) of the poorhouse populatin was sixty-five years of age or older.[16]

The years had brought little change in methods of management. The bureau of labor statistics found that 88 per cent of the institutions were managed by county officials through a salaried superintendent. The remainder operated on the contract system, under which overseers were paid a specified rate per inmate rather than a fixed salary.[17]

How many homes in Minnesota operated under each system is not known. That there were at least some contract homes is indicated by state board of control reports. In 1924 Mrs. La Du told the Minnesota Conference of Social Work: "The practice of letting out contracts for the boarding of these unfortunate individuals to the lowest bidder (in some cases as low as $2.39 per week) prevails in some counties, the superintendent of the county poor farm being hired on that basis." Even where the superintendent received a fixed salary, his compensation was set at a minimum level by competitive bidding. "One of the most difficult situations we have had to meet," said Foley in 1926, "is the employment of superintendents for these homes, as this is done by accepting the offer of the lowest bidder for the keeping of the institution and the inmates."[18]

The expense of poorhouse care was very great, whether measured by investment in physical plant and total operating costs or calculated in relation to the number of persons receiving care. In land, farm equipment, buildings, and furnishings, the nation's 2,183 almshouses represented a property value of more than $150,000,000 or $1,752 per inmate. The value of Minnesota's poorhouses was $2,424,264 or $2,351 per inmate.[19]

The operating cost per inmate, the investigators discovered, was directly inverse to the size of the institution: the smaller the number of persons, the higher the per capita cost. This was true both in Minnesota and in the nation as a whole. In 1923 the state had 13 poor farms caring for 10 or fewer persons; the average annual operating cost was $718 per inmate. Twenty poor farms housed between 11 and 25 persons at an average cost of $415. For all Minnesota institutions the average cost per inmate was $491, considerably more than the national average of $334. Comparing costs with other findings, the bureau of labor statistics concluded that "unnecessarily high cost, inefficient methods, and inadequate care are the result of the multiplicity of small almshouses."[20]

Throughout the nation poorhouse buildings included a motley collection of old frame farmhouses, primitive cottages, and remodeled buildings in towns, with a sprinkling of fairly modern brick structures in various states of repair. Probably most observers would have agreed with the eastern official who said of his state's homes: "In a few cases there has been marked improvement in the county almshouse beyond the conditions outlined in the 1909 report. . . . On the whole, however, the chief difference between . . . [1909 and 1924 is] merely 15 added years of depreciation, neglect, and decay." Of Minnesota, which had acquired many new structures in the 1900–20 period, the Evans report said in summary: "While conditions are extremely bad in places — generally conditions are above the average. Little effort is made anywhere to afford inmates recreation or religious services. Contaminating diseased inmates and feeble-minded are not segregated. No [physical] examinations of inmates are made." In addition to these general comments, the Evans report included brief descriptions of ten Minnesota institutions deliberately selected, as they were in the rest of the nation, to exemplify the worst to be found. Certainly the Minnesota examples revealed deplorable conditions, ranging from poor food and clothing to filthy, crowded, vermin-infested buildings without plumbing or adequate protection against fire.[21]

As for social conditions, the national investigators discovered innumerable instances of neglect, mistreatment, and lack of regard for the individual's self-respect. What must have been the feeling, for example, of a person who had been law-abiding all his life on being sent to a poorhouse which was combined with a prison? Or of the person who had known better days when he found himself in a place with "sagging doors, broken walls, soiled, ragged wallpaper . . . haphazard, broken furniture, trampled, frowsy front yard"?[22] In several poorhouses whipping was still the accepted method of punishing those who refused to work. Illegitimate births to feeble-minded women and girls were common. And despite the trend toward mothers' pensions, whole families of children were still found in poorhouses. Appalled by the picture of human misery and debasement which his report delineated, Harry Evans declared that the poorhouse had become a symbol of "the composite horrors of poverty, disgrace, loneliness, humiliation, abandonment, and degradation."[23]

Concerning its value as a welfare agency, the bureau of labor statistics concluded: "Taking into consideration the amount of money tied up in more than 2,000 institutions which, even when they are fulfilling their mission . . . are doing so against tremendous odds; the amount of money required annually to maintain them even as indifferently as they are maintained; the thousands of acres of idle land; the duplication of effort and the extent of unproductive employment — it is difficult, indeed, not to subscribe unreservedly to the conclusion . . . that — 'measured by any decent standard of social efficiency the county home is a failure.'" Harry Evans concurred. "Poor farms should be abolished," he said emphatically; there is "no justification for their existence; the entire system should be uprooted and abolished."[24]

The Minnesota senate interim committee reached a similar conclusion. Its members were particularly disturbed by the fate of the so-called respectable aged — the decent, law-abiding citizens who in increasing numbers were forced to end their lives among the diseased and the "morally derelict." Further, the committee deplored the effects of institutionalization, which removed the aged person from his familiar environment and social relationships, deprived him of all independence of action, and reduced him to a cog in the institutional machinery.[25]

But it would take more than legislative reports, more than action by elected local officials, more than recommendations from state boards with little power, more, even, than the arousing of an indifferent public to wipe out overnight the country's 2,183 almshouses, which cared for nearly 80,000 people.[26] If the poorhouse was a failure, as charged, how were these people to be cared for?

To many observers the most practical answer seemed to lie in changing rather than closing poorhouses. If the obstacle to efficient administration was the extremely small size of most almshouses, why not have fewer but larger institutions serving wider areas? "There is . . . almost universal agreement," said the bureau of labor statistics, that "the establishment of district almshouses, well planned, well equipped, and well managed, with the main idea in mind, the care of the poor, seems to be the most practical and efficient solution of the problem at this time." Other authorities believed that "political differences and community bickerings [would] make the success of a joint venture very doubtful." They suggested that a single county own the institution to which other counties would send their dependents.[27]

Along with the idea of larger institutions, there also were suggestions for making the almshouse more specialized. Such a proposal had been advanced by Mary Vida Clark some years before. "Suppose we were to select from the almshouse group," she wrote, "the one best located in or near a city or town easily reached by train or trolley from other parts of the district, and set this apart as a district home for the aged and infirm, where the respectable aged poor might receive home and infirmary care, in a place accessible to relatives and friends, from which they might themselves be privileged to emerge to visit their friends or enjoy the life of the streets, the church and the 'movies.'" Physical plants not suitable for conversion into residences for the "respectable aged poor," Miss Clark suggested, might become homes for the "tramp or vagrant class," or perhaps colonies for the subnormal. If the plant were good enough, she thought, it might even be converted into a tuberculosis sanatorium. At a 1926 conference, welfare officials of eastern states recommended that almshouses be converted into infirmaries or hospitals for the chronically ill.[28]

Other reformers believed that the welfare of aged citizens would be improved if the states assumed greater responsibility. By this they meant that the states should take over the direct care of the elderly rather than merely tighten the conrol of state supervisory agencies. "In the social evolution of the past quarter century," noted the bureau of labor statistics, "the care and treatment of tuberculosis and insanity have become State functions," as well as care for the blind, the feeble-minded, the epileptic, and orphaned. The next logical step, said the bureau, was the establishment of institutions for destitute old people.[29]

At one time or another state and county government agencies in Minnesota had considered all these proposals and had taken steps to put some of them into effect. While there had been no great movement to close small poorhouses, neither were counties actively acquiring new farms for this purpose. Only one new poor farm had been added in this decade. It was located in Norman County, and it had been the gift of Laurits H. Borger, who conveyed to the county in 1926 a 181-acre site for a home for the needy poor. Donations of sites and buildings to establish benevolent homes were not unknown, but the presentation of land for a public facility was extremely rare. Norman County's expression of appreciation no doubt set some kind of precedent; in accepting the gift the board assured Borger that if he at any time desired care in such a home, it would "be given him cheerfully and without charge."[80]

As to the suggestion for district poorhouses, Minnesota had since 1899 possessed a law enabling counties to pool funds for the construction of multicounty homes, but none had seen fit to do so. Moreover, while the idea of boarding county charges in the poorhouse of another county was favorably received, it did not result in large poorhouses. In 1923 only eight of the state's poorhouses held more than twenty-five inmates.[81]

The concept of direct state care of the aged also was not unknown in Minnesota.[82] By establishing the soldiers' home in the late 1880s, the state had undertaken responsibility for one group of aged persons. In the early 1900s the board of control had recommended that the state establish a home for aged and senile patients who did not belong in state mental hospitals. While this proposal was not put into effect, it did receive considerable attention. Now, in the 1920s, the state considered a new form of participation, borrowed from the successful experience of counties in obtaining tuberculosis sanatoriums with state aid. Called the "sunset home movement," it was, so far as is known, unique in the country.

The proposal to build sunset homes was introduced in 1920, following the appointment of Minnesota's first commission on aging by Governor Joseph A. A. Burnquist. Similar bodies were already functioning in such other states as California, Massachusetts, Ohio, Pennsylvania, and Wisconsin. Many were legislative committees, and the majority were set up specifically to study old age pensions. The Minnesota commission differed from all the others in directing its efforts largely toward obtaining sunset homes.[83]

The initial idea for such homes originated with E. C. Teachout, a Methodist minister then serving in Winnebago, who for some time had been distressed by the conditions under which many of his aged parishioners were forced to live. Teachout served as chairman of the Minnesota Commission on Aging. The other members were Charles E. Vasaly, superintendent of the state reformatory for men at St. Cloud and a former member of the board of control; Charles E. Faulkner, superintendent of the Washburn Memorial Orphan Asylum in Minneapolis; Frank E. Putnam, a state senator whose home was in Blue Earth; and John B. Sanborn, a member of the state tax commission, who was a resident of St. Paul.[34]

The commission's purpose, as described by Teachout, was to "provide comfortable care under the guarantee of the state for the self-respecting aged . . . in their last years." The beneficiaries would include the "self-respecting" homeless aged who were ineligible for, or unwilling to enter, other refuges for the elderly — the private benevolent home, the poorhouse, and the insane hospital. In urging the 1920 state conference of social work to support his proposal, Teachout declared: "We are taking infinite care of our fish. . . . We are spending large amounts to cultivate our swine, our chickens, horses, cattle. . . . But we have left, so far, to the care of our various church organizations and our pauper home (some of them good and some of them not so good), the care of our aged. . . . I believe that we need a home for the aged . . . where all may retire and have a home, where we can be honored and self-respecting . . . [until we] enter into the great beyond."

The governor's commission prepared a bill for introduction in the 1921 legislature as well as a synopsis of its plans in circular form for general distribution. The main features included several ideas which were revolutionary at the time. The sunset homes were to be established with the consent of the voters by joint action of the state board of control and county boards of commissioners. Counties might unite in building homes, and they were to share maintenance costs with the state on a fifty-fifty basis. Control of each home would be vested in a special commission — working under general rules drawn up by the state board of control — composed of the chairman of the county board, the county attorney, the probate judge, and four others, including two women. At the time of admission residents would make a payment of $750, which would assure care for life. Persons of sufficient means, however, could be required to make additional payments to defray the costs of their support. To be eligible, the applicant had to be over seventy years of age (or over sixty-five if unable to maintain himself) and meet certain requirements in regard to health and character. No "insane, feeble-minded and venereal diseased persons" were to be admitted, and no paupers for whose maintenance a governmental unit was responsible. "We must differentiate," warned Teachout, "between the reputable citizen desiring to have a reputable existence, and the pauper with the pauper mind."[35]

A bill incorporating these features was introduced in the senate on January 19, 1921, but failed to pass. Although Teachout continued to press for its approval during much of the decade, it was never enacted into law. How the sunset home plan would have worked had it been approved is a matter of conjecture. It seems unlikely that counties already operating poorhouses would have appropriated money for a new kind of institution from which their "paupers" were excluded. Thus the state might have witnessed the creation of a dual system of county institutions for the aged: in some a poorhouse for the penniless and in others a superior type of residence for those who had $750 to invest in a plan for life care. Although giving credit to the commission and Teachout for "creating and maintaining an interest in the aged of the state," one knowledgeable observer felt that the proposal did not offer any real solution to the problems involved in their care. Except for the fact that they operated under public auspices, Mrs. Fenlason said, the sunset homes would not have differed from existing benevolent institutions.[36]

It is possible that a modified sunset home plan or some other proposal to provide a large number of homes for the aged might have gained acceptance had it not been for the simultaneous development of the old age pension movement, which its supporters believed would make institutional care unnecessary. The idea of pensions for the aged was not new. In the late 1790s Thomas Paine had proposed the creation of a national fund from which would be paid the "sum of Ten Pounds per annum, during life, to every person now living, of the age of fifty years, and to all others as they shall arrive at that age." Throughout the nineteenth century others advocated and in some instances set up old age pension plans. As more and more people came to depend upon wages for their livelihood, reformers pointed out the necessity for some form of social insurance to protect the wage earner and his family against loss of income due to sickness, accident, involuntary unemployment, old age, and death. When the decade of the 1920s opened, a number of retirement systems were already in effect. The federal government had long provided pensions for members of the military services and civil service employees. In many cities policemen, firemen, and teachers were retired on pensions at a specified age. At least thirteen national churches had some retirement plans for their clergy. As early as 1884 the Baltimore and Ohio Railroad set up a pension plan, as did many other industrial employers in the years after 1900. In the six years from 1910 to 1916, for example, nearly seventy systems were established by various corporations. Several fraternal organizations and trade unions also provided pensions for their members, and a few insurance companies offered them in the form of purchased annuities. Yet, in spite of all the plans, only a fraction of the country's aged population was covered.[87]

By the mid-1920s pensions for the needy aged began to receive accelerated attention. At first the emphasis was on state rather than on federal systems. Proponents were not sure, however, whether the money should come from tax revenues or from a fund to which recipients had made prior contributions. At the 1926 session of the Minnesota Conference of Social Work, Amelia Sears, assistant superintendent of Chicago's United Charities, discussed the merits of both plans and stated that she favored a combined approach. "A contributive pension," she said, "would not meet the immediate need nor satisfy the insistent public demand. A combination of an immediate non-contributive pension paralleling a contributive system based on actuarial computations could be devised. Such a combination pension plan would meet the immediate need and would at the same time utilize the present productive power of our future aged citizens." It would satisfy, said Miss Sears, the objectives of the humanitarian and the strict economist.[88]

Before Minnesota decided on any plan, suggested Mrs. Fenlason at the same conference, the state should gather more information on its aged citizens. "An analysis of the condition of the dependent or partially dependent over the age of 65 would be enlightening," she said. "Is not the time now ripe for the State of Minnesota to ascertain the exact condition of its aged citizens and to plan a program which will insure their protection and their care?" A year later, in 1927, the Minnesota senate set up the interim committee whose findings on poorhouses we have already reviewed.

In the meantime national leaders in the movement organized the American Association for Old Age Security. George Nordlin, chairman of Minnesota's senate committee, attended at his own expense the organization's first national conference in New York in 1928. While there, he consulted with "dozens of the leading public welfare workers and educationalists of the country."[39]

By the fall of 1928 Nordlin had gathered sufficient information to be able to compare the costs of poorhouse care with the probable expenses of a pension system. In an address delivered at the state conference of social work, he anticipated the recommendations his committee would make to the senate. "Under the poorhouse and poor farm systems," he said, "an initial outlay must be made for land and buildings, and equipment, amounting in 1925, in Minnesota, to about two and one-half millions of dollars, the average, per inmate being $2,351.41. The interest on this investment alone, in this state, amounts to considerable. Then the salaries of superintendents, and employees, and the general upkeep of the institutions . . . must be provided for, and the general experience is that the actual keep of the unfortunate aged inmates is a very small part of the total per capita expense." Referring to the labor department's finding of an annual per capita operating cost in Minnesota of $491, Nordlin said, "No American pension plan calls for more than $360.00, so that the drain upon the taxpayers is conceivably less under the pension system, than under our present system of poorhouses and poor farms."[40]

Nordlin's committee reviewed the data gathered, the reports of similar commissions in other states, and a study made by the Fraternal Order of Eagles. It also held a public hearing on October 9, 1928, to obtain the "views of social workers and others, who have given years of study to these questions." It then recommended to the 1929 legislature a limited old age pension law. The bill, introduced on January 21, 1929, was considered intensively during the month of February. Passed by both houses, it became effective on March 1 when it was signed by Governor Theodore Christianson. It provided that a county might establish a pension plan if the county board and the voters approved. The board was empowered to appropriate funds, prescribe rules, and acquaint the public with the law, but the district judge was to hold hearings, investigate, and act upon applications for pensions. To be eligible an applicant had to be at least seventy years old, a United States citizen, a resident of the county for at least fifteen years, and own no property worth more than $3,000. Pensions were not to be granted to any "habitual tramp or beggar," nor to inmates of prisons, insane asylums, and charitable institutions.[41]

THE POORHOUSE UNDER SCRUTINY   139

By October, 1929, ten states and Alaska had noncontributory old age pension laws. "As long as prosperity held," a later historian explained, "most proponents of government assistance to the dependent aged preferred the principle of granting pensions out of the general revenues of the state to the newer concept of contributory insurance." All pension laws provided for county systems, but the laws did not make them mandatory, and except in Wisconsin the cost was borne by the individual county. The bureau of labor statistics made a special study of the operation of the program in six states — Colorado, Kentucky, Maryland, Montana, Nevada, and Wisconsin — which had obtained their legislation prior to 1929. It was one thing, the bureau found, to have a law on the books, and quite another to have an effective program in operation. In the states studied only 53 of the 264 counties which reported had adopted pension plans. The reasons given for their failure to do so ranged from alleged inability of the county to finance the system, especially where the county had money invested in an almshouse, to disapproval of the principle of noncontributory pensions. Some authorities believed that such pensions pauperized and degraded the recipient; others considered them merely an extension of poor relief.[42]

Minnesota's program was too new to be included in this special study. The plan, however, seems to have aroused little interest in the state, and it took several years and two amendments to the law before old age pensions became a reality in even the most limited way. In the meantime, the poorhouses continued to care for hundreds of aged persons without means. In spite of the various studies and proposals for alternative methods of care, the 1920s saw relatively little change in Minnesota poor farms. One county — Norman — opened a poorhouse in this decade; two others — Chippewa and Wilkin — discontinued their operations, although both held on to their farms. Several counties, notably Pine, Hennepin, and Washington, put up new buildings, but in most respects poorhouses remained static in this period.[43]

9

The Questing Twenties
1920—1930

FOR BENEVOLENT HOMES IN MINNESOTA, the 1920s at first glance appear rather uneventful. Although thirteen new homes were opened during these years, the trail blazing had occurred in the preceding decades, and the 1920s generally saw little change in types of sponsorship or methods of development. But to say that the decade held little significance for philanthropic institutions in Minnesota or in the nation is to overlook the fact that the private home, in this period, became an object of interest to social reformers. For the first time, perhaps, an effort was made to find out what it was like to live in a home for the aged. Solutions would not be agreed upon, but the ideas generated in the questing twenties would be debated far into the future.

By the 1920s the private benevolent home was a facility which was taken for granted but about which relatively little was known. What was its role in relation to other community resources? If intake policies limited admission to special segments of the population or to the aged in good health, how vital a need did the home serve? Should it become primarily an infirmary or a chronic disease hospital, as some advocated, or should it be supplanted, as in the children's field, by family boarding homes? In the millennium when all the aged had public pensions or private income, how many would choose to live in an institution for the elderly? What was the older person's attitude as he contemplated the possibility of entering a home? What were his feelings after he had been there for some time?

Much of the inquiry into these questions took place in the latter part of the decade, and in Minnesota at least seemingly had little effect on the opening of new facilities. The 1920s, it will be recalled, were the years when the number of aged increased dramatically from 4.7 to 6.4 per cent of the state's population.[1] Practically all homes had long waiting lists. The pressure for more beds was met both by enlarging existing homes (more than half of them added beds during the decade), and by opening new ones. Interestingly, there was no great acceleration in the rate at which institutions were established; new homes — as in the preceding two decades — averaged about one a year.

The thirteen homes which opened in this period followed previously established patterns. World War I and the falling off of immigration had made the country "America conscious," but the roots of elderly people remained deep in their old traditions. Churches retained their ethnic associations, and homes for the aged were still founded for members of specific nationality groups, although in some places this occurred because the community itself was largely composed of a single ethnic group rather than because of any restriction imposed by the sponsor.[2]

Hospital-connected homes, in particular, generally accepted patients and homeless old people regardless of creed or national origin. At least two hospital-homes opened in the 1920s had German backgrounds, and both were Catholic. The Sisters of St. Benedict, who already operated St. Joseph's Home in St. Cloud, proved that history repeats itself when they built a fourth new hospital and converted the old one into St. Raphael's Home for the Aged in 1928. In the southeastern Minnesota town of Wabasha, the Sisters of the Sorrowful Mother began to take old people into St. Elizabeth's Hospital after they found there were not enough patients to fill the new wing which was completed in 1920.[3]

A third hospital-connected facility was St. James Home in the south-central Minnesota city of St. James. It was opened in 1922 by the Sisters of the Third Order of St. Francis of Our Lady of Lourdes, who moved from Rochester to operate the local hospital and immediately announced the opening of a department for the elderly of all faiths.[4]

St. Paul's Church Home in St. Paul was started by a single German Protestant congregation to meet the need of one individual.

The story began in 1922, when Mrs. C. W. (Lillian) Seng, a member of St. Paul's Evangelical Church, was serving as secretary of a drive to help starving children in postwar Germany. Into her office one summer day came William Rascher, a St. Paul truck farmer. Aged and ailing, he nevertheless wanted to contribute $50. In 1925 Rascher's widow, Katherine, remembering Mrs. Seng's kindness, asked her help in finding a place in an old people's home. When it turned out that no home in the city had a vacancy, Mrs. Rascher donated her own house on Cook Street. St. Paul's Evangelical Church became the sponsoring organization. Through members of the church, Mrs. Seng located a housekeeper, and it was not long before the place was filled. In 1927 the organization procured the old Ashland Hotel building for a permanent home.[5]

The 1920s produced six new Scandinavian homes. Of three Swedish institutions, two were church-related: Bethany Covenant Home, started by the Swedish Evangelical Covenant Church in Minneapolis in 1929 as the second Minnesota home to be sponsored by this religious body, and the Elim Old People's Home in Princeton. The opening of the latter in 1927 brought a new denomination — the Swedish Evangelical Free Church — into the field. The third Swedish institution — Svithiod Home — had fraternal sponsorship. It was started in 1928 near Excelsior by the Independent Order of Svithiod, which had been organized in Chicago in 1880 for "immigrants who felt a need for fellowship outside the religious sphere."[6]

A Norwegian women's group was behind the Aftenro Home in Duluth. In the early years of the century the women were affiliated with the Lyngblomsten Society of the Twin Cities. In 1911 the need for a similar home in Duluth caused them to sever their connection with the parent organization and start their own building fund. It grew slowly until 1916, when a windfall of $40,000 from an anonymous donor gave impetus to the movement. Not until 1921, however, did the women have sufficient money to build the kind of structure they had in view.[7]

Although another Norwegian institution — the Pioneer Memorial Home in Fergus Falls — was established by members of Lutheran congregations, it was from the beginning essentially a community project. In the campaign for funds "solicity squads" covered the city, and by May, 1928, the organization was able to purchase a site at Sheridan and Channing streets. An old house on the grounds was wrecked and a new building constructed. Dozens of women made curtains, hemmed towels and table linens, and performed other tasks to get the building ready for opening day early in December. The idea of honoring old settlers was expressed not only in the name of the home, but also in a memorial room where pictures of local pioneers were displayed.[8]

The sixth Scandinavian institution — the Danebo Home in Minneapolis — was founded in 1925 by a group of Danish men and women. Their belief that a need existed for such a residence for their aged countrymen was confirmed when nine persons entered the home on opening day. Contrary to the experience of many benevolent institutions, Danebo admitted more men than women (seventeen men, twelve women) in its first three years.[9]

Another national group entered the field in 1925 when the Czechoslovak Baptists purchased the F. A. Bean residence in New Prague, and opened it under the name Czechoslovak Baptist Charitable Association of America. Although New Prague was largely Roman Catholic, the town had a small settlement of missionary Baptists, followers of Joseph Vaněk, a preacher who settled there in 1915. "There was much enthusiasm among some members of the Convention when this institution was established," commented the historian of the Czechoslovak Baptists in 1941, ". . . but weighing the results of this work, it is seen that not much was achieved by the Convention in purchasing this building. It was an expensive project which has not yielded a missionary return." The home was taken over in 1938 by the Northwest Baptist Home Society, an act for which the Czechoslovak convention was duly grateful.[10]

A home for aged members of the Moravian Church in America was discussed as early as 1911 by its Western District, which comprised the six states of Illinois, Iowa, Michigan, Minnesota, North Dakota, and Wisconsin. Little was done, however, until 1921, when John Holtmeier of the Laketown, Minnesota, congregation offered half his 130-acre farm on the condition that the church purchase the other half. After long deliberation the district agreed to buy the site — a beautiful area on the shore of Lake Auburn about a mile from the town of Victoria. In line with the trend to start out in new buildings, if at all possible, the church built a two-story, colonial style, fire-resistive structure, which was dedicated on Armistice Day, 1928, as the Lake Auburn Home for the Aged.[11]

Only one new institution of the decade had neither ethnic nor religious sponsorship. It was the Minnesota Masonic Home, opened at Bloomington in 1920 after a long period of study and planning. The person most active in organizing this endeavor was Gideon S.

Ives, who some forty years earlier had initiated the development of the Odd Fellows Home at Northfield. When the Masons' temporary facility opened in the Marion W. Savage farmhouse on the Minnesota River in Bloomington, it was named Ives Lodge. In 1925 a bond issue permitted the construction of a new building, which was dedicated on September 3, 1927, before a "very appreciative assembly" of more than 5,000 people.[12]

The dedication of the Masonic Home was not the only one which attracted large crowds. The desire to view places where other people live is almost universal, and the interest in new homes for the aged — especially the first in any given area — was usually lively. As members of the sponsoring organization and other guests toured the building, they frequently commented on the comforts provided and spoke of the good fortune of the residents. No doubt the visitors were sincere in their praises, but it is doubtful that they themselves looked forward to living in such a home. As a social worker observed some years later, these residences were "the means we think of first for other aged people in trouble, but the last means we choose to use for ourselves if we can avoid it."[13]

National leaders in the field of the aged believed that only an assured continuing income, such as a pension system, would give older Americans real freedom of choice in their living arrangements. The attainment of this goal engaged their energies throughout the 1920s. The agitation for old age security measures, as Clarke Chambers pointed out, began with an investigation of existing conditions and the "elaboration of a rationale for state pension action." Among those who explored the situation were labor leaders, social workers, university professors, and government officials. While the poorhouse received the closest scrutiny, the benevolent home also came under the spotlight of investigation. The light was never so glaring, though, as that directed on the poorhouse, nor was it suggested that the private home for the aged be abolished. On the contrary, observers generally agreed that institutions conducted by religious or philanthropic organizations offered important resources for certain of the elderly who were unable to live alone or who preferred the companionship to be found in homes for the aged. But did the homes really offer this companionship and the other services old people required? How many institutions were there, and how available were they to those who most needed this type of care?[14]

The most far-reaching study of private homes was conducted in

ROSWELL P. RUSSELL *(left) and Louis Robert (center) were named in 1850 to the first Ramsey County board of commissioners. James M. Goodhue (right), Minnesota's first newspaper editor, was Ramsey County's first overseer of the poor. Among the commissioners' many duties was the establishment of a poor relief system. Roswell engraving from Horace B. Hudson, ed.,* A Half Century of Minneapolis *(1908); Goodhue daguerreotype taken about 1850.*

RAMSEY *in 1854 became the first county to invest in land for a poorhouse. These structures, still in use in the 1960s as the Ramsey County Home, were built at 2000 White Bear Avenue in St. Paul in 1915. They replaced facilities erected at this and other locations. Photograph taken in 1925.*

WASHINGTON COUNTY'S *poorhouse, located near Stillwater on a site acquired in 1858, was a typical frame structure. George Jarchow, superintendent from 1895 to 1913, is shown (seated) with his family and employees in this picture taken in 1904. Photograph courtesy Washington County Historical Society. John S. Proctor (inset) was the county's first poor farm superintendent in 1859.*

THIS ILLUSTRATION *appeared with Will M. Carleton's poem, which began "Over the hill to the poor-house I'm trudgin' my weary way," in Harper's Weekly, June 17, 1871. The poem made the term "over the hill" virtually synonymous with "the poorhouse."*

HENNEPIN COUNTY *was one of the earliest Minnesota counties to build a poorhouse for its needy residents. Its first such structure was opened in 1865; a second was built near Hopkins in 1884 and was used until 1926, when the third building pictured here was constructed. It closed in 1953. Photograph taken in the 1930s, courtesy Mrs. Byron W. Johnson, Minneapolis.*

THE *Dakota County board purchased land and buildings for a poorhouse in the dying town of Nininger in 1866. Photograph taken in 1937.*

HASTINGS H. HART *(left) was employed in 1883 as the first full-time secretary of the State Board of Corrections and Charities. He ably filled the position until 1898, when this tintype was taken. James F. Jackson (below) succeeded Hart as secretary and remained in the job until 1901. Photograph taken about 1887.*

THE STATE BOARD *participated in planning the second Goodhue County poorhouse at Red Wing, which opened in 1891. At that time it was considered the best in the state. It closed in 1963. Photograph courtesy* Red Wing Daily Republican Eagle.

MODEL PLANS *for poorhouses were published in a pamphlet issued by the state board in 1900. This plan, which appeared in the booklet, was followed in building the Becker County poorhouse. The structure was used by the county from about 1900 until it was leased for private operation in 1936; it closed in 1940.*

THE STATE BOARD'S *building plans were designed for twenty-three, forty, and fifty inmates. Becker County utilized this twenty-three-bed plan, which was published in the state board's pamphlet.*

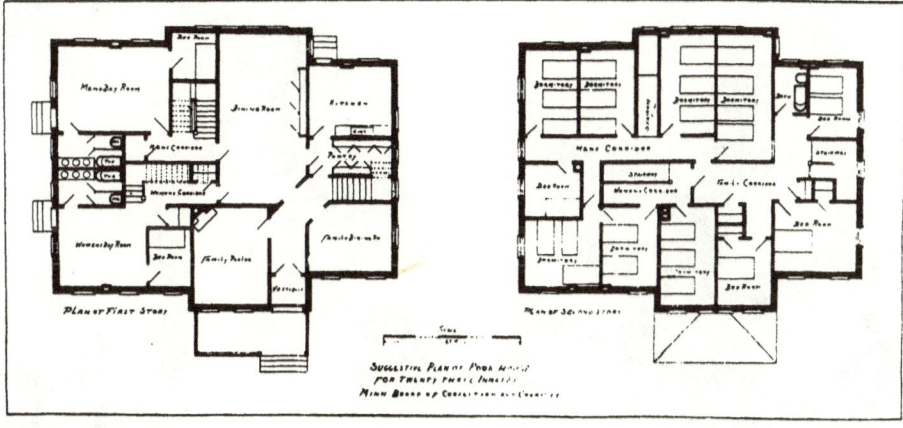

THIS BUILDING in Shakopee was completed in the 1860s as St. Gertrude's Convent and Academy of the Benedictine Sisters. About 1889 it was sold to Scott County and was used as the county poorhouse until 1938, when it became St. Francis Hospital and Home for the Aged operated by the Franciscan Sisters of the Blessed Virgin Mary of the Angels. Photograph taken in 1936.

LEGISLATION in 1951 enabled counties to establish nursing homes. Chisago County reassumed the operation of its leased poor farm near North Branch in 1954. Renamed Green Acres Nursing Home, the building was remodeled and enlarged in 1956 and 1959. Photograph 1968, courtesy of Green Acres Nursing Home.

AFTER *the passage of a federal old age assistance program in 1935, many Minnesota counties closed their poorhouses or leased them for private operation. The present Holznagel Boarding Care Home at Hinckley was Pine County's poorhouse until 1937. Photograph courtesy of home.*

BROWN COUNTY'S *poorhouse at New Ulm was opened with ceremony in 1908. It was leased for private operation in 1938 and closed in 1965. Photograph taken soon after 1908, courtesy Brown County Historical Society.*

ITASCA COUNTY'S *former poor farm at Grand Rapids became the county nursing home in the 1950s. Facilities built since then include a chapel and a recreation pavilion. Photograph taken in 1968, courtesy of the home.*

THE MINNESOTA LEGISLATURE *in 1909 and 1913 enacted laws enabling counties to co-operate in building district tuberculosis sanatoriums. By 1918 the state had fourteen sanatoriums. In the 1950s many of them were converted to county nursing homes. Buena Vista Sanatorium at Wabasha, shown as it looked in the 1930s, was erected in 1917. In 1956 it became Buena Vista Rest Home operated by Wabasha County.*

LATE *in the nineteenth century, the state expanded its role in caring for the needy and dependent. Shown below are temporary buildings of the Minnesota Soldiers Home in Mineapolis used from 1887 until two permanent structures were completed in 1889.*

MINNESOTA'S FIRST PRIVATE HOME *for the aged was the Home for the Friendless (later renamed the Protestant Home). It was founded in St. Paul by a group of Protestant church women including Harriet Bishop (above). Opened in 1868, the home moved in 1883 to this structure on Collins Street. From 1916 to 1966 the building pictured above housed the Crispus Attucks Home. Below is the Protestant Home in 1962; photograph by Eugene D. Becker.*

THE MINNEAPOLIS INSTITUTION *now known as Stevens Square began as the Children's Home in 1881. In 1885 the women's group that founded it changed its name and its purpose to the Home for Children and Aged Women. The building on Stevens Avenue pictured above was occupied in 1886. Photograph taken in 1892.*

MRS. JOHN S. PILLSBURY, *wife of the governor, was elected president of the Children's Home Society in 1881.*

BENEVOLENT GROUPS *raised funds by sponsoring balls and other events. The story at right appeared in the* Minneapolis Tribune *of November 23, 1887, to describe the charity ball of the Home for Children and Aged Women.*

A WOMEN'S GROUP *formed in the 1860s dreamed of opening a home for the friendless in Minneapolis. The idea became a reality in 1888 after the group received a cash bequest and a gift of the building on Cedar Lake known as Oak Grove House. This octagonal structure, which had been operated as a resort for invalids, became the first Jones-Harrison Home. It was later demolished and replaced. Broadside published in 1870s.*

IN THE *1920s comprehensive studies of private homes for the aged focused on the needs and wants of residents. It was found that lack of recreation and meaningful activity often caused the old people to lapse into apathy or senility. Attitudes toward independence and recreation varied from home to home. Shown here are croquet players at the Jones-Harrison Home about 1925.*

A FORERUNNER *of the movement of large church organizations to provide care for their aged was the Church Home of Minnesota. Pictured at left is its founder — Sister Annette Relf — the first consecrated Episcopal deaconess in the state, who opened the home in St. Paul in 1894. Photograph courtesy Church Home of Minnesota.*

THE INSTITUTION *founded by Sister Annette was taken over by the Protestant Episcopal church in 1897. After a series of moves, the organization built a new home on Feronia Avenue in 1933, adding a wing in 1964. Photograph by Becker, 1968.*

THE LITTLE SISTERS *of the Poor, a Roman Catholic sisterhood dedicated to the care of the needy aged, arrived in St. Paul in 1883. They opened their first home in the structure shown at left. Built in 1855, it served the Little Sisters until 1890, when a new home was built at the same location.*

TAKEN ABOUT 1925, *the upper photograph shows the Little Sisters of the Poor in the dark blue dresses and round white bonnets of the Breton peasant that were worn by the order until 1967. Below is the home of the Little Sisters in Minneapolis, photographed by Becker, 1968. The central portion was constructed in 1895.*

THE RESIDENTS of St. Otto's Home for the Aged, another Catholic facility operated by the Franciscan Sisters at Little Falls, engage in many activities. At left is the jazz band formed by men at the home. Photograph courtesy of home.

ST. ANN'S HOME at Duluth was used as a hospital and as an orphanage before the Sisters of St. Benedict opened it as a home for the aged in 1910. The building pictured here was closed in 1956. A new St. Ann's opened in 1963. Photograph courtesy St. Scholastica Priory, Duluth.

IN 1936 the Franciscan Sisters of the Blessed Virgin Mary of the Angels started St. Mary's Home in St. Paul. It was the first Catholic facility in the Twin Cities open to persons who were able to pay for their care. At left is the portion completed in 1936 and enlarged in 1939; the section at right was erected in 1957. Photograph taken in the early 1960s, courtesy St. Mary's Home.

WHEN residents of St. Francis Home at Breckenridge were invited to share in the institution's operation, they organized the Busy Bee Club to sponsor activities. This is the club's popcorn stand. Photograph courtesy St. Francis Home.

A GERMAN PROTESTANT congregation began St. Paul's Church Home in 1925 at the urging of Mrs. C. W. Seng (inset). In 1927 the organization obtained the former Ashland Hotel building; the wing at left was added in 1962. Photograph of Mrs. Seng from a brochure entitled St. Paul's Church Home; photograph of the home taken by Becker in 1968.

AUGUSTANA HOME of Minneapolis, which grew out of the efforts of the women of the First Augustana Evangelical Lutheran Church and of its pastor, Carl J. Petri, served a Swedish-Lutheran group. Shown above is the home's first building as it looked in the 1890s. Reverend Petri is seated in the center. Photograph courtesy Augustana Home.

BETHESDA INVALID HOME at Lake Gervais near St. Paul also had Swedish-Lutheran origins. It opened in 1914. Photograph from Emil Lund, Lutherdom i Amerika [1926?].

THE Reverend Carl A. Hultkrans was the moving spirit who initiated both the Invalid Home and the Chisago Lutheran Home. Photograph from Lund, Lutherdom i Amerika.

SWEDISH WOMEN of *Minneapolis and St. Paul established the Twin City Linnea Home in St. Paul to serve their countrymen from both cities. The building on West Como Avenue, which the home still occupies, was opened in 1918. This photograph was taken in 1925 soon after an addition was completed.*

BETHESDA HOMES *at Willmar was established by Lutherans of Danish and Norwegian descent. The institution began as a childcare facility at Lamberton; after it moved to Willmar in 1905 a few elderly people were received. A separate building for the aged was opened in 1910. Photograph, late 1930s, courtesy Bethesda Homes.*

LYNGBLOMSTEN HOME *in St. Paul was started by a women's group in 1912 to serve aged Norwegians. Pictured above is an early board of directors. Only a few of the women are identified: (1) Mrs. Karl (Anna Qvale) Fergstad, founder; (2) Mrs. L. P. Foster; (3) Mrs. Ernest Reiff; (4) Mrs. O. Brecke; (5) Mrs. Peter Clausen; (6) Mrs. A. Hanson; and (7) Mrs. A. Leland. Below, a community fund poster of the 1920s depicts a Lyngblomsten resident; the home is shown as it looked a few years after its opening.*

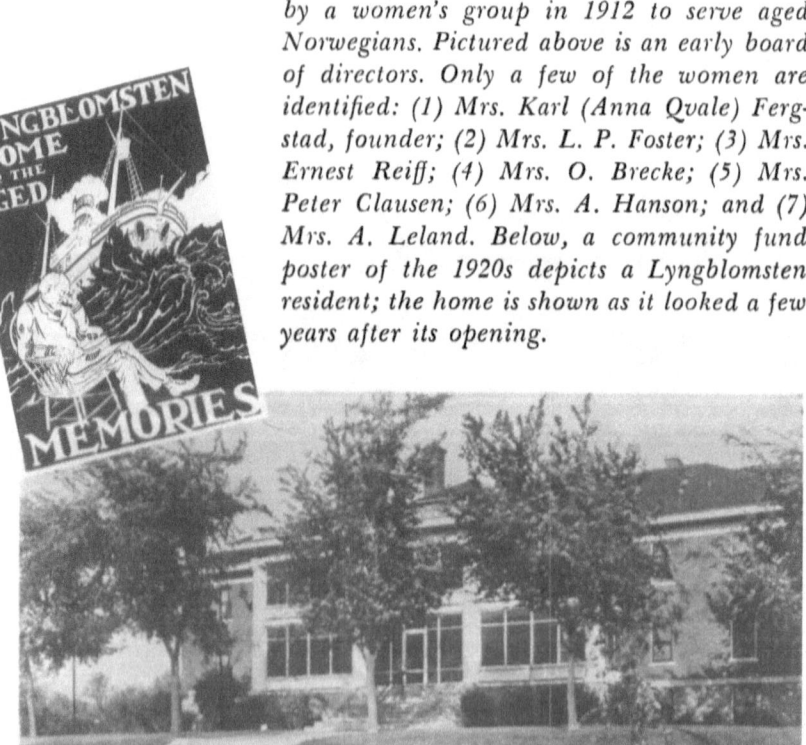

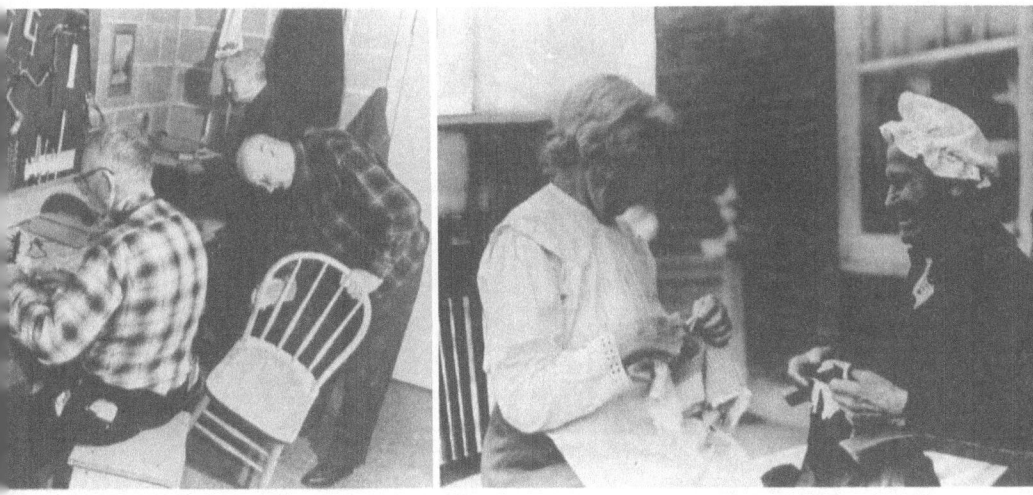

THE LARGEST *Norwegian Lutheran residence for the aged in the United States is Ebenezer Home, Minneapolis. Launched by business and professional men and the pastors of six churches, the home was opened in 1917. At left male residents are shown engaged in craftwork; at right women of the home are sewing. Photographs, 1920s.*

THE GLENWOOD *Old People's Home was opened by the Norwegian Lutheran Church of America in a building formerly used as a school. Glenwood was the only Minnesota home for the aged to close during the depression of the 1930s. Photograph from* Fire Hundred Yars Reformationfest. *Dr. Johan A. Aasgaard (inset) was one of the leaders in the Norwegian Lutheran church's program for the aged. Photograph taken in 1925, courtesy Luther Theological Seminary.*

ANOTHER RELIGIOUS *group was cared for in the Jewish Home for the Aged, established in 1908 in a house (inset) built by William L. Banning of St. Paul. Photograph from the home's* First Annual Report, *1909. A second Jewish home was built on St. Paul's Midway Parkway in 1923. Photograph about 1960, courtesy of the home. Rules prescribed the behavior and dress of its residents. A 1909 regulation requiring the women to wear white aprons "each day except while at work" was still in force when the photograph below was taken in the 1920s.*

THE FIRST *Minnesota home for aged Negroes was founded and named for Crispus Attucks by the Reverend J. Will King and his wife Fannie about 1908. In 1916 it was moved to a building formerly occupied by the Home for the Friendless, where it operated until closing in 1966. Pictures from a broadside published about 1910.*

THE INTERIOR *of a shop at the Colored Orphanage and Old People's Home, forerunner of Crispus Attucks, where boys learned to make paint brushes. Broadside published about 1910.*

FRATERNAL GROUPS *also provided homes for their aged members. At the urging of former lieutenant governor Gideon S. Ives, the Minnesota Odd Fellows raised funds for a home at Northfield, and a large crowd attended the laying of the cornerstone in 1899.*

THE MINNESOTA MASONIC HOME, *with which Ives was also associated, opened in 1920 in the former Marion W. Savage mansion at Bloomington pictured (top below) as it looked at that time. Over the years the Masons erected additional buildings. The lower photograph shows the attendants' quarters as they looked in 1937.*

STATE SENATOR *George H. Nordlin of St. Paul headed an interim committee of the legislature organized in 1927 to study poorhouses and pension plans. The committee's findings led in 1929 to the passage of a limited state old age pension law. Nordlin later served on a national advisory council on economic security. Photograph taken in 1933.*

MANY *proprietary — profit-making — homes for the aged appeared after the advent of social security. Highland Chateau at 2319 West Seventh Street, St. Paul, is an example of those built recently. Photograph taken by Becker, 1968.*

VOTERS *in Traverse County passed a bond issue to construct a modern, one-story, forty-bed nursing home at Wheaton in 1959. It was the first all new county nursing home in the state. Photograph taken in 1968, courtesy Traverse County Welfare Department.*

BY THE CLOSE *of the 1950s homes for the aged offered their inhabitants a variety of activities and services. Wilder Residences of St. Paul is a multifunction campus complex with facilities including lounges like that shown at right. Photographs by Becker, 1968.*

1928 by the United States department of labor as part of its larger investigation of the general care of the aged. The only earlier inquiries on a national scale had been made by the United States census bureau. Its findings of 1904 and 1910, published in separate documents referred to as "statistical directories," had given a general picture of the ownership, location, and purposes of benevolent institutions, the number of persons cared for, the costs of care, and the sources of funds.[15]

The 1928 study by the labor department was more extensive, delving into the qualifications of personnel, the interest of governing boards, the kinds of accommodations, the facilities for the care of the sick, the daily programs of the homes, and the efforts to provide recreation. In response to a questionnaire, 1,037 of a reported 1,268 benevolent institutions furnished data on their staffs, facilities, and programs. In addition labor department employees visited some 150 homes, most of them on the east coast. The findings, published in 1929, presented a picture of the inner workings of homes not previously available.

The department's investigators were impressed with the wide variety of institutions, ranging from the most luxurious to "homes which usually have no requirements except age and destitution" and which furnished "only cleanliness and the barest necessaries of existence — the plainest food, and sleeping accommodations in large dormitories holding as many as 30 or 35 beds." In the latter homes, they reported, there was practically no privacy and little in the way of comforts — even a splint rocker was regarded as a luxury. The average home, however, stood midway between these extremes, with comfortable if well-worn furniture and individual bedrooms.[16]

The appearance of the residents also varied. In some homes they looked sprightly and cheerful. In others the old people appeared to be resigned to their lot, and in a few homes they seemed actually forlorn. The investigators also observed: "Blank faces and vacantly staring eyes show the inert minds of the residents. This was especially evident in the homes in which no effort was made to arouse their interest." Because the "problem of idleness," as it was called, was so apparent on many of the visits, the investigators inquired diligently into what the managements of old people's homes were doing "to keep the minds and hands of the residents occupied."[17]

The visitors concluded that the degree of activity or idleness depended largely on two factors: the attitude of the management, particularly the person directly in charge of the home; and the physical and mental conditions of the residents, as well as their previous interests and abilities. The matron was considered to hold the key position because, from the residents' point of view, she was the "all-important part of the home." The happiness and well-being of the old people rested to a large extent in her hands. On the whole, the visitors agreed, the matrons were a "most remarkable group of women"; their success was all the more noteworthy when one considered that the old people entered the homes with fixed habits and attitudes. But the matrons had one fault in common: they took pride in the fact that the residents had to do nothing except eat and sleep, failing to realize that such inactivity was very harmful to vigorous old people.[18]

The report also indicated that the "guests in residence" varied greatly. While intake policies tended to restrict admission to persons of good character, temperate habits, and reasonably good health, the occupational and professional backgrounds represented were as dissimilar as those to be found in the general community. "Inmates in the homes for the aged represent all walks of life," the report pointed out. "Some had been domestic servants whose entrance fee was paid by their mistresses, some had been farmers, some actors, some school-teachers, some music teachers, some had been in business or professional lines, some had been housewives, some sailors, some common laborers."[19]

The investigators also reviewed the rules and regulations under which the homes operated, noting that even a capable matron with a houseful of reasonably healthy and intelligent guests could not perform wonders under restrictive regulations which covered all possible contingencies and served only to frustrate efforts to initiate activities. Some rules, of course, were to be expected. In the interests of smooth operation, homes planned their programs around fixed hours for eating, sleeping, attending devotions, and performing certain household tasks. Residents were expected to be in their places at mealtimes and to be quiet — even if they did not sleep — during rest periods. They might not leave the grounds without first notifying the person in charge. Anticipated guests were asked to come only during regular visiting hours so as not to disrupt the home's routine. And, although this was not generally covered by the regulations, raiding the refrigerator in search of a midnight snack simply was not done in a home for the aged. Even the most independent-minded came to accept these facts of institutional life.[20]

THE QUESTING TWENTIES 147

As to the residents' attitudes toward the home, the reporters found that newcomers were at first happy because their anxieties concerning food, shelter, and care were at an end. The department noted that "it is a common experience that the new guest is most grateful and is pleased with everything." As time went on, this new and luxurious sense of having all wants taken care of wore off. "Then comes the time, when, unless something is supplied to occupy the time and attention of the inmate, his mind begins to center on himself, and little things begin to annoy and become magnified out of all proportion to their importance. The result, for a person of active mind, is an increasing discontent and unhappiness. The idle person whose mental processes are not so alert gradually becomes more and more apathetic, sinking perhaps into senility." Ample evidence of this process had been found during the personal visits to homes. So important did the labor department consider the problem that it published a supplementary report in 1929 suggesting ways in which homes could keep their residents busy and contented.[21]

Although Minnesota homes were not among those visited by labor department representatives, some of them were studied in 1927 by Mrs. Fenlason of the University of Minnesota sociology department. She investigated nine benevolent homes in Minneapolis as well as the Masonic Home in Bloomington, the Ladies of the GAR Home in Anoka, the Minnesota Soldiers' Home, the Hennepin County Home at Hopkins, and four St. Paul institutions — Lyngblomsten, Twin City Linnea, Crispus Attucks, and the Jewish Home for the Aged — which served residents of both cities.[22]

Part of Mrs. Fenlason's study — like that of the labor department — was devoted to recreational activities. A more complete picture may be obtained by supplementing her observations with descriptions contained in the reports of other institutions. In most homes, all these sources indicate, diversions were of the spectator type, requiring relatively little effort from the old people. Some were especially designed to give them a pleasant reminder of their past.

Perhaps the most publicized form of entertainment was the special day, or fest, for which a home became noted. The Scandinavian Union Relief Home founded in Minneapolis in 1915, for example, held an annual Swedish *midsommarfest* on its lawn. Residents and visitors joined in singing patriotic songs around a Maypole decorated with the flowers and flags of various Swedish provinces. This event was always "anxiously awaited by the inmates" and was well attended by friends of the home. The Norwegian Lyngblomsten in St. Paul held its first *minnefest* in the spring of 1913, to commemorate Mrs. Fergstad's birthday. Later, because the spring mud was tracked into the building (there were no sidewalks then), the date was changed to June, and the event became a Midsummer Fest. Bethesda Homes in Willmar had an annual daylong affair, beginning with religious services in a nearby church and ending with a program on the home grounds, at which time an offering was "lifted" to provide much-needed financial aid and to stimulate interest in the work.[23]

In addition to annual events, entertainments were presented throughout the year by church choirs, Boy Scouts, Girl Scouts, community choral groups, and many other organizations. One program which the old ladies in a Minneapolis home especially enjoyed was a cabaret performance by high school girls. Important to all festivities, of course, were the refreshments, especially at Christmas when the aroma of lutefisk and sausages filled the air and the sight of julekake, lingonberries, and Christmas cookies brought memories of holidays in the old country.[24]

Much less frequent were activities in which the home residents could participate. They might join in singing, and a few of the more hardy took part in old-time dancing. Rarely did the old people assume the initiative in preparing programs, although one annual report recorded an entertainment presented by the inmates, "who very justly stated that as they had 'musicians, teachers, poets and singers' among themselves there was no reason why all their entertainment should come from outside."[25]

Some residents pleasantly occupied their time by cleaning their bedrooms, arranging cherished possessions, and reminiscing with anyone who would listen. "In most homes the dividing line between occupation and recreation is an invisible one," observed Mrs. Fenlason. "Helping with light chores around the house or in the yard is in the nature of a diversion to the aged people in the Scandinavian homes who for the most part have been active and hardworking until old age curbed their activities. The old lady in one of the homes who works hard each morning caring for her canaries by cleaning their cages, supplying their seed and water, etc., is working to be sure, but the pleasure she derives from it is her chief source of recreation."[26]

When old people were unable or disinclined to find things to do, few homes required that they be kept busy against their will. Under the prevailing philosophy, the home for the aged was a place where the elderly could at last find shelter, care, and freedom from the necessity of working. Like John Bunyan's pilgrims, they had come to the land of Beulah, where "the sun shineth night and day." As they waited to pass over the river, they tarried in a haven of rest and comfort, sustained by the presence of their fellow travelers. This concept was inherent in the very names of some homes. Bethany Covenant Home, for example, was dedicated as *en tillflyktsort för åldriga pilgrimer* — a resort for older pilgrims. Elim, by whose waters the children of Israel encamped, was the name selected by the founders of two homes. Bethel, another favorite Biblical name, recalling the spot where Jacob tarried for the night and dreamed of the ladder to heaven, signified repose and the promise of better things. And the residence called Aftenro, meaning in Norwegian "evening rest," was intended to be a place where aged people "with some savings but not enough to take care of themselves, could have . . . security, comfort and peace of mind for the rest of their lives."[27]

Governing boards in this period did make some effort to encourage residents to continue their hobbies. The Lyngblomsten board furnished yarn, thread, and rugmaking materials for the women and equipped a shop for the men. Through the courtesy of Oscar Lampland, a St. Paul lumber dealer, the shop was supplied with mill ends. "In this workshop on warm summer days," a director recalled, "one would find a strong old boat builder, Mr. Taraldsen. He would spend hours at a time making miniatures of the lofty crafts he had once commanded. Besides these, he made row boats and sail boats, launches and steamers. . . . Many a child became the proud possessor of one of these boats."[28]

For residents who liked to work outside, a number of homes provided gardens where the elderly could grow flowers and perhaps a few vegetables. "For a long time," wrote the St. Paul Little Sisters of the Poor in 1927, "we were wishing to buy the property next to us, but the price was so high, but in the spring the owner wished to sell. This gave the old folks a garden. They got so much better and stronger after they had a garden."[29]

Ordinarily most activities were carried out within the institution or on its grounds. Events which took the residents away from the home were an especially welcome break in days that held little excitement or change. The Sisters of St. Benedict, who operated

St. Ann's Home in Duluth, were well aware of the need of their people to have at least the feeling of "going places." Although the chapel was in the same building where the residents lived, each morning found the halls buzzing with excitement as the old folks, dressed in their Sunday best, put on hats, coats, and even gloves to attend Mass just around the corner, perhaps, or down a flight of stairs.

When the Woman's Christian Association Hospital of Minneapolis moved to a new location in 1925, its board members noted that the mere fact of going somewhere was an exhilarating experience for the elderly patients. "Thirty patients were moved as well as all the equipment," said the annual report. "They started moving at one o'clock and . . . at 4:45, they began serving supper to the patients in their own rooms in the new building." Far from being harmed by the trip, the old folks apparently regarded it as an adventure. Louva M. Cady, the matron, believed that "most of the patients were benefited by getting out."[80]

The directors of the Home for Children and Aged Women also observed that some of their older residents preferred to be surrounded by activity. In 1922 the board decided to provide a separate building for the old ladies who had been housed in the children's home. The change seems to have aroused mixed emotions. At first the elderly women reportedly were "enthusiastic in their praise of the comfort and luxury of the new building." It was not long, however, before the board noted that the women not only continued to mend and make quilts for the children but made frequent trips back to the children's building. At an open house held in January, 1923, a newspaper reporter observed that some residents welcomed quiet but others "miss the life of the old hallways."[81]

One of the chief stumbling blocks to providing recreational activities was the enfeebled condition of the residents, more and more of whom could be classified as ill or disabled. The problem of their care was one which every home faced sooner or later. As an institution grew older, its residents also aged. When governing boards raised age limits for admission — as some did in an effort to serve those most in need — the new residents were more elderly at the time of entrance. These factors — the aging of residents and the raising of age limits for admission — meant an increase in the number of persons with infirmities.

The problem of caring for the sick aged received considerable attention at the Deutsch Foundation conference held in March, 1930, at the University of Chicago under the auspices of its school of social work. This two-day forum, called to consider all aspects of care for the aged, brought together specialists from the fields of industry, labor, medicine, medical economics, public welfare, and private social services. Although much of the thinking at the conference was tentative and uncertain, the participants aired many new concepts in the care of the elderly.

A commitment to old age social insurance permeated the discussions, and most participants appeared to regard institutional homes — whether public or private — as a last resort for the dependent aged. The forum's director, Isaac M. Rubinow, declared that "institutionalization of [the] able-bodied aged is frequently unnecessary, cruel, and not infrequently unnecessarily expensive." He suggested that the psychological effects of life in what he harshly termed "concentration camps for the aged" offered an interesting subject for research, "but even without it, in a purely empirical way, every social worker is familiar with the stubborn resistance of most old folks against commitment to an institution."[32]

Rubinow's reference to "concentration camps for the aged" must have startled some of his listeners. At that time, a comparison was more likely to be made with another type of undesirable housing — the orphanage. For children who could not be kept at home, social workers were then advocating boarding or adoptive homes, a concept which leaders in the aged field now borrowed. "The same principle that dictated caring for children in the home rather than in an orphanage," wrote Clarke Chambers, "applied with equal force to people at the other end of life's cycle." To uproot old people from their own homes and thrust them into an unfamiliar institutional routine, these leaders believed, was particularly harmful to the elderly, affecting adversely not only their peace of mind but also their health. It will be recalled that more than seventy years earlier Thomas Hazard of Rhode Island had expressed the same idea when he said: "To separate an old person from a home that they have long been accustomed to . . . is very much like tearing an old tree from the ground. . . . they will both, in all probability, wither and die."[33]

Although private boarding homes for the aged were being tried in some areas, they did not always prove a good solution. Edna L. Foley told the conference that the plan, as attempted in Chicago "on a fairly small scale, is not very successful, for there is very little money to be made in boarding elderly people. Naturally the homes that take in the boarders wish some profit. Children who try this plan seldom can or will meet the expense, and the old parent is shunted from one private home to another."[84]

Regardless of how they felt about the institutional home for the able-bodied, most participants agreed that institutionalization was necessary for those who required medical or nursing care, and they believed that the best facility was a hospital. Michael M. Davis, director of medical services for the Julius Rosenwald Fund, suggested that it could be either a large, well-equipped hospital solely for the chronic sick and aged or a division for chronic cases operated in conjunction with a general hospital.[85]

How the home for the aged would fit into this picture was tentatively explored by several speakers. It was recognized that large numbers of elderly residents needed more care than most institutions were prepared to give. Despite policies which restricted admission to the able-bodied, private homes could not escape dealing with the problem of chronic disease. It was further pointed out that the physical conditions of older people varied a good deal; thus at one time they needed major attention and at another only custodial care. Dr. Ernst P. Boas, an eminent gerontologist, urged that opportunities be provided for a free transfer of patients from one type of institution to another. And the custodial home, he suggested, should be designed and managed so that the physically handicapped did not become "involuntary prisoners in their rooms."[86]

While there did not seem to be a clear consensus as to the ultimate role of the home for the aged in the care of the sick, it was recognized that the problem might call for the creation of new types of facilities. It was no longer possible, one speaker asserted, to view the sick elderly as a large, undifferentiated group; instead, it was imperative to recognize the existence of "a complexity of smaller groups presenting diverse medical diagnoses and diverse needs for care." In the future, types of hospitals and institutions which differed from those already in existence would have to be devised. With the development of additional resources, it was predicted, "The case workers' job will be to individualize each case, not only at the onset of dependency, but throughout dependency in order that each case will at all times be utilizing the most advisable resource that is available for its care."[87]

Along these lines, another speaker asserted that old people in need could not be classified merely on the basis of their medical conditions. "To the family agency which deals with the problem of the individual, the concept of the aged as a uniform group of dependents tends to break down," H. L. Lurie of the Chicago Jewish Social Service Bureau told the conference. "Instead, the aged take on the vivid colors of personalities, and present themselves as affected by varied problems and require varied services for their solution."[38]

Conference participants also considered the attitudes of the elderly themselves. Lurie believed that the aged looked favorably upon comfortable private homes sponsored by fraternal, ethnic, or religious groups, even though residence in such institutions represented the acceptance of charitable aid. An entirely opposite position was taken by Rubinow, who asserted that old people detested all institutions for deep-rooted psychological reasons. Aging, as he said some years later, was a "physical process which is emotionally resisted and denied." By vigorously refusing to recognize the process, the elderly found an "escape from reality" which made their "last few years worth living." From this point of view, the old people's home represented a pathetic confrontation with an unwelcome truth. It meant, said Rubinow, "giving up, cashing in, capitulating. And there are many who don't like to do it." Although social workers were familiar — as Rubinow suggested — with the "stubborn resistance" of some old folks to entering an institution, they also knew others who had no such mental reservations. It is doubtful, too, whether many residents of benevolent homes considered themselves to be recipients of charity, even though their fees seldom covered the actual cost of their support.[39]

"Preference for institutional care is an individual matter," Mrs. Fenlason noted in her study of Minneapolis homes. To some of the elderly an old people's home represented a haven; to others the very idea was unthinkable. "One old lady of my acquaintance," recounted Mrs. Fenlason, "is three years under the age limit of the home of her desires. She could have a welcome home in either of the households of her two married daughters. Instead she is doing housework as a paid employee in a stranger's home in order to keep intact the one thousand dollars she has in the bank. Until the three years elapse, she is drudging cheerfully, happy in her independence, with the home as her beacon when age qualifies her for admission, secure in the possession of the entrance fee."[40]

On the other hand, Mrs. Fenlason observed, there were many

examples of opposition to entering a home by even men and women who had no other means of care. At the 1926 state conference of social work, Mrs. Fenlason quoted the representative of an eastern agency who during the course of a year had handled the cases of 134 aged women. Not one of them wanted to enter a home. "They would rather live on next to nothing than enter one," the caseworker observed, "and rather drown themselves than enter an almshouse." Mrs. Fenlason thought it possible that the reluctance was analagous to that of the patient who is unwilling to enter a tuberculosis sanatorium, but who is appreciative of sanatorium care after entrance.

Whether they were reluctant or eager, however, many persons could not get into the home of their choice. In the late 1920s practically all Minnesota residences reported waiting lists. But there were vacancies, and Mrs. Fenlason, after studying intake policies, types of accommodations, programs offered, and other factors, concluded that the main obstacle was not an insufficiency of beds. "The kind of home and the entrance requirements," she wrote, "are more potent in obtaining or preventing entrance than the bogey of the so-called waiting list." She suggested that the lists would be reduced or nonexistent if applicants were interchangeably eligible at all of the homes.

Although Minnesota's benevolent homes usually admitted anyone who urgently needed a place to stay, they gave priority to members of their sponsoring organizations. Forty-six homes had been started by the end of 1929 (only one of them — the Church of God Home in St. Paul Park — was discontinued in this period). Twenty-nine homes, or 65 per cent of those in the state, were church-related, a high proportion compared to the national figure of 45 per cent. How many of the country's institutions were Scandinavian is not known, but here again Minnesota must have ranked high. Nineteen of its homes were operated by various Swedish, Norwegian, and Danish organizations.[41]

More than half of the forty-five residences were located in the metropolitan counties of Hennepin, Ramsey, and St. Louis; twenty-one homes were situated in eighteen counties. For homes in the Minneapolis area, Mrs. Fenlason recommended the establishment of a clearinghouse for applicants, with referral of those not accepted anywhere to a private caseworking agency which could make other arrangements. Because several Minneapolis groups were at that time considering the establishment of new institutions, she advised that they be built only to fill a definite and predetermined need.[42]

These proposals were made before the stock market crash in October, 1929. In the depression of the 1930s which followed, all questions of attitudes, waiting lists, and the establishment of new benevolent homes became more or less academic. Any kind of bed would be in demand, and the time would not be propitious for opening new institutions.

10

From Great Depression to Social Security

1930—1940

THE STOCK MARKET CRASH OF OCTOBER, 1929, marked the end of an era of relative prosperity and optimism. It was followed by the longest and most severe hard times the United States had ever known. A public welfare administrator commented in 1939 that the depression of the 1930s was "complicated and deepened in America by years of drought and flood in many sections of the country," and that "the suffering was almost universal."[1]

The mounting numbers of unemployed, the widespread distress among people who had never before known hunger or cold, the disruption of cherished plans, the expanding role of government as new alphabetical agencies were created to furnish loans, relief, and jobs, and the continuing search for formulas to prevent such suffering in the future — these developments have been described too often to need retelling here.

Less well known is the story of how homes for the aged fared in this period. In many ways the "grey, dull, terrible years of the Great Depression" were as frustrating and cheerless for the boards and managers of old people's homes, both public and private, as they were for the heads of families who wondered how long they could continue to feed and shelter members of their own households. The problem was intensified by the ever-increasing proportion of older persons in the population. For the United States, the ratio of persons sixty-five years of age and over rose from 5.4 per cent in 1930 to 6.8 per cent in 1940. In Minnesota, where the big jump had occurred in the 1920s, the 1930s saw a substantial although somewhat smaller increase — from 163,480 (6.4 per cent) in 1930 to 212,618 (7.7 per cent) in 1940. For county poorhouses, the larger number of the aged and their growing financial plight meant that there were many more persons to care for in the early years of the depression.[2]

Contrary to the expectations of its supporters, the state's old age pension law did not keep many people out of the county poor farms. As we have seen, the law's requirements were stringent. More important, however, was the fact that the law was permissive, requiring both county-board action and voter approval, and by and large the counties were unwilling or unable to adopt pension plans. Even had they done so, the majority in all likelihood would have retained their poorhouses. One reason for continuing them was suggested by G. A. Lundquist, executive secretary of the Ramsey County board, who calculated "that at least from 50 to 75 per cent of the inmates of a county home could not be taken care of by friends or relatives, because a large number need infirmary care." Lundquist's opinion was supported by events in Aitkin County. Because that area's poor fund was "greatly over drawn," the board resolved in July, 1932, that "all poor relief in Aitkin County be suspended until further notice with the exception of the care of inmates of the County Home and also all bed-ridden cases."[3]

It was in July, 1932, also, that the federal government entered the picture with the passage of the Emergency Relief and Construction Act, sometimes referred to as the Wagner-Rainey bill. Signed by President Herbert C. Hoover on July 21, 1932, the law provided for loans from the Reconstruction Finance Corporation to states and their political subdivisions to finance direct relief and work relief. By the middle of September, 1932, it had become evident that many northern Minnesota counties besides Aitkin "were in such bankrupt condition as to be unable to meet even the ordinary demands for poor relief, let alone the growing need caused by the very rapid decline in employment and decreases in prices for farm commodities." To assist the counties in preparing applications for loans, Governor Floyd B. Olson appointed a state relief administrator. He also requested that the board of control act as his agent in certifying the relief needs of counties and in establishing standards and procedures. Under the board's direction county emergency relief committees comprised of two commissioners, two child welfare board members, and a fifth person selected by the other four, were soon organized throughout the state.[4]

By 1933 Minnesota was feeling the effects of drought, high winds, and dust storms which left farmers without seed for crops or feed for their animals. Some of the misery of the time is reflected in the action of the Wilkin County board when it met in special session to consider measures to restrict the shipping in of cattle from the drought-stricken areas of the Dakotas. After reviewing the county's dwindling resources in pasture and feed, the board appealed to Governor Olson to stop the shipments, and he did so by stationing National Guard units at all roads entering the state. Probably no one who drove along the state's western and southern borders in that year could ever forget the sight of little groups of guardsmen patrolling intersections to bar the cattle of neighboring states from Minnesota's once lush pastures.[5]

In the spring of 1933 when the $300,000,000 fund of the Reconstruction Finance Corporation was nearly exhausted, Congress passed the Federal Emergency Relief Act, which provided direct grants rather than loans to the states, and created the Federal Emergency Relief Administration (FERA). President Franklin D. Roosevelt signed the bill on May 12 and immediately appointed Harry L. Hopkins as federal relief administrator. In Minnesota the board of control became the State Emergency Relief Administration (SERA), and the county relief committees already established were accepted as the new local units of administration.[6]

As the depression deepened, agitation for mandatory state old age pension laws increased throughout the country, and literally hundreds of bills were introduced in state legislatures. At Governor Olson's insistence, Minnesota's legislators in 1933 replaced the optional pension law of 1929 with a compulsory system to go into effect on January 1, 1934. Even this law did not produce a statewide system. Only some forty-five of the eighty-seven counties adopted plans, and those without funds continued to refer aged applicants to the county relief committees or to the individual's city, town, or village. In January, 1935, "Because of the difficulty on the part of eligible applicants in counties having a high rate of tax delinquency to obtain the pension justly due them," Olson recommended a state-financed, state-controlled system. A law to provide for joint state and county financing was passed by the 1935 legislature, but because of a clerical error it was later declared void. This law would have lowered the minimum age to sixty-five years.[7]

During the years from 1929 to 1935 when Minnesota had a state pension law (at first permissive, then mandatory), the number of persons who received pensions was relatively small — approximately 6,000 — as compared with more than 15,000 persons 65 years of age and over on relief. Although many destitute old folks managed to eke out an existence with the aid of relief grants and small pensions (the average monthly pension check was $9.89), others without funds continued to seek admission to the poor farms, where they could be sure at least of something to eat and a place to stay. The superintendents could not well turn them away. The almshouse, as Estelle M. Stewart once said, came "quite literally under Robert Frost's definition of home as 'a place where, when you have to go there, they have to take you in.'"[8]

Many counties, however, were hard pressed to provide that shelter. Economic conditions made new construction nearly impossible, and most poorhouses simply moved extra beds into the rooms. Although these were the same buildings which in the early 1900s had been regarded as "palaces for the poor," time had passed. The visitor of an earlier day had seen a brand new structure not yet filled, but an observer in the 1930s found the buildings showing the effects of decades of use and housing many more persons than the number for which they had been designed.

Most bedrooms, especially those for men, were long and narrow — sometimes twenty-five feet from hall to outside wall. Where the original plan had shown a row of three or at most four beds, there were now five or six, separated by only a foot or two of space. Some people had chairs, others had bedside tables; few had both a chair and a table. It was not unusual to see a feeble old man hanging over the edge of his bed, trying to eat from a tray that had been left on a chair barely within reach. Farther down the line of beds, another man might be looking over the clothing and other possessions which, for lack of closets or lockers, he kept under his mattress. Bathrooms were as inadequate as bedrooms, and the old fixtures were not always in working order. In an institution where one bathroom served some thirty men and the plumbing leaked, the matron once told a visitor that she usually found it necessary to put on rubbers before going in to clean the room in the morning.

Most counties somehow got along with their old buildings, though at least two managed to build during this trying period. In

1931 St. Louis County added a new wing and in so doing provided much-needed jobs for its unemployed. The only machine used was a hoist: all other tasks were performed by hand labor. Even the cement blocks were made on the site. The 1,600 men thus given employment received a week's work apiece and were paid with grocery orders. But even a new wing did not solve the problem of inadequate space, and in 1933 the St. Louis County board of commissioners closed the girls' industrial school on Arlington Avenue in Duluth and turned the building over to the poor commission for conversion into a women's residence and infirmary. This unit was called the Arlington Home. In 1934 the men's building was renamed in honor of A. P. Cook, long-time secretary of the St. Louis County Poor Commission, and the poor farm became the Cook and Arlington homes. By 1934 the county's poorhouse population reached 612, the highest in its history. "That was in the height of the depression," the superintendent later recalled; "some of the rooms [in the men's building] had double bunks, beds were placed in the hall ways of the 2nd and 3rd floors and men also slept in a dormitory upstairs of the laundry building."[9]

Itasca County, which also had an extremely heavy relief load, obtained a completely new building under the Public Works Administration program. This agency, which Congress created in June, 1933, was designed to provide employment and to stimulate the economy through construction projects. When it appeared that a local bond issue for a new Itasca County poorhouse would not carry, officials applied for a PWA grant. On January 17, 1934, the *Grand Rapids Herald-Review* reported that work would be started soon and completed by early summer. But government projects did not proceed that rapidly. Because "the work is being done under PWA restrictions, short hours are put in," said the paper in August, "and completion will not be announced for some little time."[10]

The building was finished and occupied late in 1934. The *Herald-Review* of December 12 reported: "Fifty-nine men and three women, inmates at the Itasca county poor farm, moved last week from the old poor house to the fine new $100,000 building just completed on the poor farm. This number includes those single men who have been cared for . . . in temporary quarters . . . about ten more men [are] to be moved here soon from state transient camps, where they have been kept while the poor house was being completed." The paper emphasized the "Great Care Taken to Assure Cleanliness," a virtue apparently not practiced in the old quarters. "All the inmates were required to bathe thoroughly and put on clean clothes before moving across the road and into the new building. All the personal effects . . . were thoroughly disinfected before any transfers were permitted. Every effort will be made to keep clean in the new building, and the construction will aid those in charge of this effort."

As the counties struggled to take care of their aged poor, reformers waged a campaign for a more comprehensive solution to America's social problems. For a long time many observers had been convinced that even mandatory state pensions would not adequately care for the aged, and that federal assistance would be necessary to assure the security which people were seeking, not only for the aged but also for the unemployed, dependent children, and the handicapped. Statistics gathered by social reformers showed that "the aged were increasingly unable to secure employment, that substantial numbers . . . had no resources and that the burden of supporting the aged was increasingly beyond the capacity of private charities, relatives and friends and local and state governments."[11]

Professional social workers and economists were not the only reformers involved. Pensions for the aged became a popular cause. One of the most widespread movements was the Townsend Plan, named for Dr. Francis E. Townsend, an elderly physician who had been practicing in Long Beach, California. Townsend wanted to restore prosperity by putting large amounts of money into circulation. He proposed that the federal government pay every person over sixty years of age an annuity of $200 a month if he would agree to retire from regular employment and spend the entire payment within thirty days. Townsend suggested that the plan be financed by levying a national sales tax. Although most economists considered it highly impractical, the proposal became immensely popular with older age groups, and Townsend clubs sprang up throughout the country. The idea of pensions for all aged persons now began to take hold. "Until the campaign for the Townsend Old Age Revolving Fund began," Grace Abbott pointed out, "most of these early proposals contemplated pensions for the needy aged only." Now many people began to argue for a national compulsory system with a fund to which the individual might contribute during his working years and from which he would draw a pension as a matter of right, rather than on the basis of need.[12]

"Striving for security is as natural as struggling for survival," a social researcher has written. On March 4, 1933, when the nation found hope in President Franklin D. Roosevelt's memorable words, "the only thing we have to fear is fear itself," Americans were struggling for survival. By 1934 the country was well launched on its quest for security. Many volumes have been written about the Social Security Act of 1935, and — although it was to have tremendous impact on homes for older persons — it does not seem necessary to give here more than the briefest outline of events leading to its passage. On June 8, 1934, President Roosevelt sent to Congress a special message calling for a broad program of security — "the security of the home, the security of livelihood, and the security of social insurance." On June 29 the president appointed a Committee on Economic Security to review the entire problem and to bring in recommendations by the end of the year. The cabinet-level committee was assisted by a technical staff and by an advisory council of citizens representing employers, employees, and the general public. Minnesota's George H. Nordlin was a member of the council, and a second Minnesotan, Dr. Albert J. Chesley, secretary of the state board of health, served on the public health advisory committee. On January 17, 1935, Roosevelt transmitted the cabinet committee's report to Congress; bills were introduced in both houses that same day. After protracted hearings and many revisions, the long-awaited Social Security Act was signed into law on August 14, 1935.[13]

The purpose of the act was to "provide for the general welfare by establishing a system of Federal old-age benefits, and by enabling the several States to make more adequate provision for aged persons, blind persons, dependent and crippled children, maternal and child welfare, public health, and the administration of their unemployment compensation laws." The act approached the problem of old age security from two directions — "immediate assistance to the indigent aged, and a pension in the future to those then and in the future employed." To carry out these purposes the law created a Social Security Board and provided for two separate programs: old age insurance and old age assistance.[14]

The *old age insurance* program provided a monthly benefit or annuity for retired workers which was related to the earnings of qualified persons irrespective of need. The benefit was, and still is, commonly referred to as an individual's "Social Security." The federal government assumed sole financial and administrative responsibility for this program. The collection of the tax on wages was not to begin until January, 1937, and the payment of regular monthly benefits was not to start until 1942. (This date was pushed forward to 1940 by an amendment approved in 1939.) Obviously, however, it would be some years before the effect of the old age insurance program reached the elderly in homes for the aged.[15]

The *old age assistance* program, on the other hand, got under way almost immediately. From the beginning its impact was felt by county poorhouses, since it provided grants on a regular monthly basis to needy individuals sixty-five years of age and over if they did *not* live in public institutions. This was a joint federal-state program: grants-in-aid were made available by the federal government, but the program was administered by the states. Those which desired federal aid were required to "take the initiative in appropriating funds and in submitting plans for the operation of the program . . . which would meet the conditions of the Federal Act and the approval of the Social Security Board." The assistance program was expected to dwindle away as more and more Americans became eligible for old age insurance. The number of recipients did gradually diminish in relation to the number receiving old age and survivors insurance, but this did not occur as rapidly as was expected at the time.[16]

The states had been following the progress of the act through Congress, and as early as December, 1935, plans began to reach the Social Security Board. Minnesota enacted the required legislation in a special session of the legislature in 1935 and designated the board of control as the agency to supervise the administration of the act in the counties. Minnesota's plan was approved on March 30, 1936, and funds were made available from March 1, 1936. The new program absorbed the state old age pension plan which had been in effect in slightly more than half the counties. By July, 1936, 42,861 Minnesotans were receiving old age assistance grants. The average monthly grant that year was $18.40.[17]

On the local level the program was administered at first by county boards of commissioners or by poor commissions if they had been established. County boards might, however, delegate the investigation of applications to a board of public welfare or to an official investigator. Copies of the application and the certificate of grant were forwarded to the state board of control, which reimbursed the county for five-sixths of the grant (two-sixths from state funds and three-sixths from federal funds), the county being responsible for one-sixth of the amount of assistance. Through its field service, the board of control worked with the local agencies on special problems. In 1937 the legislature made it mandatory for each county to establish a welfare board. Except in counties which contained a city of the first class (Hennepin, Ramsey, and St. Louis) or a Poor and Hospital Commission (Itasca), the county commissioners selected three of the five members, at least one of whom had to be a commissioner. The two remaining members, including one woman, were appointed by the board of control from a list submitted by the local board. On July 1, 1937, the new bodies took over the welfare duties formerly performed by county commissioners and child welfare boards.[18]

In the agitation for a federal social security law, as in the earlier campaign for state pensions, one of the most potent arguments was that money payments to the aged would result in the closing of the nation's poorhouses. "Underlying the public assistance provisions of the act," said the United States Social Security Board some years later, "is the concept that money payments may enable persons to live with some degree of 'freedom from want' and to have some latitude in determining their living arrangements." It was thought that anyone receiving a pension would not choose to live in a poorhouse. Older generations, said the labor department in 1925, "were brought up with 'a reverence for God, the hope of heaven, and the fear of the poorhouse.'" With old age pensions an accomplished fact, the specter of the poorhouse need no longer haunt the minds of persons who were growing old. To assure that the law would accomplish this purpose the Social Security Act of 1935 excluded old age assistance payments to inmates of public institutions. To qualify for a grant, therefore, the resident of a county home had to move out. It was believed that this restriction, plus the provision of federal old age benefits for employed workers, would "eventually take from relief rolls and poor farms all except a very few old people who have not been employed or cannot meet the residence or other requirements of the state old age assistance laws."[19]

The effect of the social security program on the country's poorhouses was closely watched by observers on the national scene, and the immediate impact in most states was less than many had anticipated. In March, 1938, the Social Security Board tentatively concluded that the "initiation and development of the old-age assistance program under the Social Security Act have not been followed by a marked reduction in the population of almshouses or in the number of almshouses except in a few States." Exceptions to this generalization, the board observed, were to be found in states where the agency administering public assistance had adopted an aggressive policy of substituting other types of care for that in almshouses. Other factors entered into the picture, however. Some states discovered that the older age group comprised only a fraction of the institutional population and that, as they moved out, younger destitute persons moved in. A number of states reported that the majority of older inmates had disabilities which made it difficult to provide other forms of care for them. A few, like Indiana, were already operating their almshouses as county infirmaries and foresaw no likelihood of closing them. Helen G. Tyson summed up the situation in 1938 when she wrote: "Governors may tell the world that they have 'abolished the poorhouse' when they sign old age assistance bills, but a small cash pension, which cannot buy medical and nursing care, does not answer the need of hundreds of aged persons today."[20]

In Minnesota, however, the public assistance program produced an immediate effect on county poor farms. The *Social Security Bulletin* of March, 1938, reported a "marked reduction in the number of almshouses" in the state "and in the number of residents 65 or more years of age." Almost as soon as the old age assistance funds became available, many of the aged moved out in order to receive their grants, or "pensions," as they preferred to call them. But not all of those over the age of sixty-five left the poor farms. Some remained because there was no other place for them, or because after weighing the advantages and disadvantages, they decided their best course was to stay. "They debate the question endlessly," said the superintendent of a county home. On the one hand was the security of bed, board, and an ordered life; on the other hand was independence — coupled, however, with the fear of the unknown. Could their pensions purchase as much as they now had? And, indeed, for many, leaving the institution was jumping from the frying pan into the fire. Certainly, the new law had not taken into consideration the fact that many persons in poorhouses were physically, mentally, and temperamentally unfit to fend for themselves. They needed more care than they could get in the boarding homes available to them, and in many "rest homes" opened by unscrupulous persons the newly created pensioners undoubtedly were exploited.[21]

County boards met the situation in several ways. Where the number of inmates was small, the farming operation unprofitable, or the building in need of expensive repairs or replacement, the board simply closed the institution and disposed of the property. Four counties — Aitkin, Anoka, Lyon, and Yellow Medicine — took this course in 1936. Kittson and Martin counties followed in 1937, as did Otter Tail and Scott in 1938 and Lake in 1939. Although Martin County discontinued its poorhouse operation in 1937, the institution was reopened some years later by the Sisters of Charity, who purchased it from the county. In 1938 Scott County put its poorhouse in Shakopee up for sale, stipulating that the buyer must guarantee to care for the poor and indigent for at least three years. The Franciscan Sisters of the Blessed Virgin Mary of the Angels purchased the building and converted it into St. Francis Hospital and Home for the Aged.[22]

Ten county boards followed a different course of action. They leased the facility to a private individual, thereby removing it from the legal category of "public institution" and making it possible for the residents to receive their old age assistance grants. Such was the intention of the Chisago County board, for example, when on February 14, 1938, it resolved that "the County cease to operate the Poor Farm and lease the Farm to some individual or individuals for periods of two years at a time, commencing on the 15th April, 1938, for the purpose of having the same operated as a private rest home." Between 1936 and 1939 at least nine other counties — Becker, Beltrami, Brown, Dodge, Hubbard, Mille Lacs, Norman, Pine, and Wabasha — leased their farms for private operation. After the institution was leased, it was no longer regarded as a poorhouse, and the population, as a rule, increased very rapidly. In Dodge County, for example, the institution housed only six persons when it was turned over; not long afterward twenty persons were in residence.[23]

In the matter of financing, the payment of a stipulated amount in assistance grants each month did not appear to be very different from the old contract plan under which the county paid the poorhouse superintendent a monthly fee for each inmate. Theoretically the manager of a leased home was free to make independent arrangements with anyone seeking admission, but in actual practice the county generally set the fee and maintained some control over admissions. Although the lessee often received residents of other counties and occasionally accepted some "private pay" cases, his own county usually had priority on the available space. Because the counties also continued to exercise some control over operations, the line between a private rest home and a public institution within the meaning of the Social Security Act was sometimes very finely drawn. To ensure that the institution was not "public," the board of control prepared a suggested form to be followed in leasing the county property.[24]

From the standpoint of the residents the new plan promised much. The aged received their grants and had the satisfaction of paying for their own care in a "private" facility. Even the name "poor farm" was eliminated; the home became so-and-so's boarding home, or "Evergreen" or "Hilltop" rest home. How much difference this could make to the residents is indicated by a story which the matron of the Dodge County home occasionally related to visitors. A woman who had lived in the institution when it was a poorhouse continued to reside there after its conversion into a private home. Of the improvements which were made, the resident liked best the removal of the big sign by the road, "Dodge County Poor Farm," and its replacement with one reading "Fairview Rest Home." In fact, the woman found that she now enjoyed writing letters, because she could use the new name in the return address.

Before long the leased homes began to experience problems similar to those long familiar to former superintendents. Most counties proved to be poor landlords, and there were many disagreements over repairs and arguments as to who would furnish certain items. The lease, which usually ran for a one- or two-year period, was often awarded to the applicant who promised to provide care at the lowest rate. When a refrigerator broke down, the water heater proved inadequate, or new beds were needed, the lessee who operated on a small margin of profit was reluctant to make a large investment in something he could not use if his lease was discontinued. Many county welfare boards, on the other hand, believed that operators were making large profits on service that was too often unsatisfactory.

Another point of contention was the rate allowed for residents who required more than average care. In most communities facilities for the care of sick persons were in short supply, and the county referred many of its most difficult cases to the leased home with little or no increase in payment. The operator was hardly in a position to refuse, even though he lacked the staff and facilities to provide proper care. Institutions were soon filled with senile and feeble old folks, many of whom were bedfast patients requiring, but not always receiving, skilled nursing care.

Even so the crowded county homes could not take all who needed a place to stay. The growing number of persons receiving old age assistance made it necessary to utilize every facility that was in any way open to the elderly. Some of these developed during the depression as older people lost their homes and livelihood. In Minnesota winters even the able-bodied homeless aged do not sleep on park benches — and many of those seeking a bed were far from able-bodied. In the large cities the old men found refuge in cheap hotels, mission centers, and flophouses. It was during the depression that the Union City Mission, a charitable organization serving homeless men in Minneapolis, expanded its program both in the city and at a newly acquired suburban farm at Medicine Lake to take care of the unending stream of the jobless. Working on a self-help basis, the men cleared land, laid out walks and driveways, and built housing for themselves. They cut logs, collected bricks and seasoned lumber from a downtown hotel which they were paid to dismantle, and removed sand from the lake shore to make mortar and plaster. Even the older men helped; one built the chapel altar and the wall behind it, "cutting and laying every stone" himself.[25]

In rural areas small-town hotels and low-cost rooming houses often accepted an old person at a reduced rate or without charge in exchange for such work as he could perform. Some homeless older men, as well as those who were younger, went into the transient camps sponsored by the Federal Emergency Relief Administration. And in the pinch of the depression, many general hospitals throughout the state accepted an occasional older person who could pay a small amount for a room, even though he might not need hospital care.[26]

Another resource, which was to assume greater importance after the advent of the social security program, was the proprietary rest home — a home operated for profit. "Rest home" has come to be a wastebasket term, loosely applied to almost any privately operated place which receives aged, infirm, or chronically ill persons. Although the term did not come into general use until the twentieth century, proprietary rest homes had existed in Minnesota from the earliest days. Even after a county acquired a poor farm, the board might continue to send some of its dependents to a home which catered to county charges. "In counties where there are no poorhouses, and sometimes where there are . . . ," the board of corrections and charities reported in the 1880s, "homeless paupers are boarded in private families at county expense, at so much per week."[27]

When the Social Security Act went into effect in 1935, proprietary homes were already developing in considerable numbers in both urban and rural areas. "I believe the public is not generally aware of the mushroom growth of so-called homes for convalescents," the secretary of the Women's Welfare League of Minneapolis wrote in 1933. "Nurses unable to get employment have banded together in twos and threes, sometimes in a none too commodious apartment, and taken patients for convalescent care. Whether such places are inspected by health authorities is a question. I understand the same condition exists in St. Paul." By 1935 Minneapolis had at least thirty-six rest homes.[28]

The state board of control also noted an increase in the number of proprietary homes in rural counties, and in the mid-1930s one of its inspectors remarked on the problem of classification which was to plague health and welfare authorities for many years. "Homes of different kinds are being opened in country districts to take care of old people," wrote the institutional inspector. "It is a question how these homes will be classified as some have only from four to ten persons. We also have throughout the State convalescent or rest homes."[29]

The development of rest homes was not limited to Minnesota. Nancy L. Austin, a Kansas social worker, described their ubiquity in 1939. "In many states where almshouses, poor farms or county homes have closed their doors, decentralized and uncontrolled methods of private care for these aged have developed," she wrote. It was "not unusual to find county home buildings rented by individuals, a man and his wife or even a man alone, and run as boarding houses for a varying number of old people of both sexes and differing physical conditions. . . . In addition to these small unsupervised institutions, there are in every state hundreds of private homes in which old people are boarding."[30]

In Minnesota proprietary homes developed in a number of ways. Fairly typical of the 1930s was a home begun on a small scale to meet the needs of one or two persons known to the owner. During the depression a man and his wife, or a woman living alone, might take in a few old friends who needed a place to stay, and who were perhaps quite feeble from lack of proper food. Sooner or later one of these aged boarders became ill or disabled. The woman gave such care as was within her skill, and if it was satisfactory, a physician, a social worker, a public health nurse, or the relatives of another old person would ask her to accept more patients. Before long the man and his wife (or the woman alone) began looking for a larger house, possibly one of the mansions distinguished by spacious rooms, elegant woodwork, and ten-foot ceilings which were then practically unsalable. By this time the owner had a full-fledged rest home on his or her hands; soon every nook and cranny, including the bay windows, was filled with homeless and helpless old persons.

As additional homes were established and they became larger and more crowded, observers began to realize that there was something drastically wrong with the system. The buildings were unsafe, the accommodations unpleasant, and the care not always directed toward the patient's needs. The most usual treatment was "rest," but to the person in the bed "rest" might mean lying on a cot only two feet from his neighbor, staring at the bare walls or ceiling. His medication was a pill out of a box containing many varieties, selected according to the operator's diagnosis of what ailed him. A refractory or mentally confused patient might be tied to a bed or a chair, or confined in a locked room on the top floor where he was out of mind and out of hearing. Of course, not all such homes were so unsatisfactory. Too much cannot be said for the kind and capable women of this period who not only provided a comfortable and pleasant place to live, but also showed considerable skill in nursing procedures.

The public had no way of distinguishing between good and bad facilities, however, or even between a proprietary home and a bona fide hospital. Many homes chose to call themselves "rest hospitals," "convalescent hospitals," or "sanitariums." They were listed under these designations in telephone directories, along with the small institutions which reputable physicians operated for the treatment of nervous and mental patients, and the places which offered "liquor cures" for alcoholics, cancer remedies, and various other unorthodox therapies.

Medical and hospital authorities began to work for some form of regulation of rest homes. As early as November 19, 1935, the Minnesota State Board of Medical Examiners stated its anxiety about current conditions: "This Board has been requested on several occasions to investigate the ever increasing number of so-called rest homes. These places are springing up in St. Paul, Minneapolis, and in other localities. Some are under the supervision of a physician, others are not. Some, undoubtedly, are places of high repute, others are not. Under the laws of this State, no license is necessary to maintain a hospital or a rest home unless maternity cases are taken in, in which event a maternity hospital license must be secured from the State Board of Control."[81]

Concerned about these unregulated homes, the medical examiners posed a number of questions: "Should these places be regulated by law? If so, what regulations are necessary and desirable to adequately protect the public and to prevent the practice of medicine by those who are neither licensed nor responsible for their action? If these places are to be regulated by law, under what state agency should they be placed?"

In seeking answers to its questions, the examiners' board sought the assistance and co-operation of the Minnesota State Medical Association. That group, convinced that some sort of regulation was necessary, in turn enlisted the support of the Minnesota Hospital Association, since the problem involved hospitals as well as physicians.[82]

During the next few years, a joint committee of the two associations began to work for a comprehensive licensing law that would cover all types of hospitals and rest homes. Before a bill could be introduced, however, the legislature passed the Reorganization Act of 1939, which abolished the state board of control and created a department of social security. The new department was comprised of three autonomous divisions: social welfare, public institutions, and employment security. To the director of the division of social welfare went the responsibility of enforcing both the maternity hospital licensing law and the general law under which charitable and correctional institutions were inspected but not licensed. At the end of 1939 the regulation of rest homes by means of a licensing law was still several years in the future.[83]

The 1930s had been momentous years for all Americans, but for the dependent aged the period was one of special significance. Many had lost their homes as well as their savings in the depression; they had, in truth, become displaced persons. For them the poorhouse was more than a threat; too often it was a grim reality. With social security came the hope of something better than living out their days at the county poor farm, but the substitutes that were offered proved disappointing. As the decade ended, people began to realize that it would take more than pensions to solve the problems of housing and caring for the aged.

11

Red Ink and Midnight Oil

1930—1940

IN SPITE OF THE DEMAND FOR BEDS during the depression, benevolent homes were not as crowded as poorhouses. In most private institutions the rooms had been designed for one or two persons and could not easily be arranged for additional occupants. Moreover, if a resident had entered the home on a life contract, expecting to retain his quarters for as long as he lived, he was not likely to welcome a roommate. When all beds were filled, therefore, boards had little alternative but to tell new applicants regretfully that their names would be placed on ever-lengthening waiting lists.

Although more facilities were urgently needed, the 1930s were not notable in Minnesota for the number of benevolent homes which were started or expanded. The decade, which began with a devastating depression and closed with the country on the verge of war, saw the opening of only nine nonprofit homes, including one formerly operated by a municipality. Three of these got under way in the first two years, the others from 1936 through 1939. Several might never have been started if the sponsors had not begun to make plans before the depression. For the most part, the homes were small and widely scattered, serving a rather limited group. All were sponsored by churches, most of which had some previous experience in caring for the aged. Four were housed in buildings originally constructed for some other purpose.

Two of the nine new facilities were sponsored by the Minnesota

Conference of the Augustana Lutheran Church, which was already operating homes at Chisago City and St. Paul. In August, 1928, the conference commenced an intensive fund drive for its charitable institutions. Part of the money was earmarked for new homes in Duluth and Mankato. All went well at first. During a four-month campaign, fund raisers secured some 22,800 pledges totaling more than $500,000. The contributions were to be spread over a three-year period, and generally speaking the donors were able to meet the first two installments. Then in 1930 disaster struck. "What had been a strong flowing stream became only a trickle," wrote the Reverend O. A. Henry. "The office closed, accountants for the fund [were] dismissed, and those who were in positions of responsibility settled down to a policy of watchful waiting." Although building plans were shelved, some other commitments had to be met immediately. "Driven by necessity," Henry continued, the fund raisers had "to take to the field" again at a time when banks were closing, salaries were being cut back, and farmers were losing their homes. Although the forays were not always successful, the conference somehow raised enough money to satisfy the most pressing needs.[1]

Fortunately for aged Lutherans in the Duluth area, preliminary steps to establish a home had already been taken. In 1927 the First Lutheran Church of that city (now known as Gloria Dei Lutheran) had petitioned the Minnesota Conference for an old people's home. After considerable deliberation the conference purchased the late Thomas Merritt's fifteen-acre estate on the shores of Lake Superior, including a house which had been partially completed before his death. The organization enlarged and finished the residence as the Lakeshore Lutheran Home for the Aged, which opened in June, 1930. Struck by the depression in its infancy, the home immediately faced almost overwhelming problems. The demand for beds was so great, however, that small units were added in 1932 and 1933.[2]

The Augustana conference's second project of the decade — the Mankato Lutheran Home for the Aged — had been planned long before anyone dreamed of a place in Duluth. It was not finished until 1937, however, because a completely new structure had to be erected. The question of a home in southwestern Minnesota, which had been debated for years, came to a head in 1922, when the Mankato Chamber of Commerce offered to donate twelve acres of land to the Minnesota Conference. An administrative reorganization of the church group's charitable institutions in 1923 delayed the project for some years. Hopes were high in 1928 when the memorable fund-raising campaign was inaugurated. Although ground was broken in 1931, only the basement was completed at that time. Six years elapsed before the institution was ready to receive its first guest on November 1, 1937. During the ten preceding years, there had been days when even the leaders of the campaign questioned the wisdom of their decision. As Reverend Henry pointed out: "It is conceivable that had the movement not been started at the time . . . Lake Shore Home and the Mankato Home would have been fond hopes and little more, at least for years to come."[3]

The Baptists of Minnesota also formulated plans for a home before the depression. In 1929 the state Baptist convention voted to convert a former Parker College dormitory at Winnebago into a home for the aged. Again organizational difficulties forced delays. In the meantime the Minnesotans decided to invite the Baptists of Iowa, Nebraska, and North and South Dakota to join the venture, and in June, 1930, the combined groups organized the Northwest Baptist Home Society. A year later on August 25, 1931, the Winnebago Baptist Residence was opened.[4]

In the late 1930s the Baptist society took over two existing institutions: the Czechoslovak Baptist Charitable Association Home in New Prague discussed in chapter 9, and the Red Wing Old People's Home in Red Wing. Funds to establish the latter had been provided in 1907 by Mrs. John A. (Amelia L.) Graham, who offered the city $30,000 for the purpose. The *Red Wing Republican* opined that no donation for municipal improvements during "the past five years" was "more practical and more far reaching in the beneficence of results" than Mrs. Graham's. The home, built in 1914 on land adjacent to the city hospital, was operated by a board of trustees until 1939, when it was acquired by the Northwest Baptist Home Society.[5]

The first of three Catholic institutions established during the 1930s was the Sacred Heart Home, a unit of St. Ansgar Hospital in Moorhead. The Sisters of St. Francis of the Immaculate Conception were already caring for a few elderly persons in the hospital basement when in 1930 they found it necessary to install a new boiler. A small annex, constructed to house the old people who had to be moved from the basement, was then opened to others in the community.[6]

In 1936 the Franciscan Sisters of the Blessed Virgin Mary of the

Angels began the first Catholic facility in the Twin Cities which took in persons able to pay for their care. This was St. Mary's Home, located at present-day Prior and Norfolk avenues in St. Paul. When the handsome new structure was completed, several applicants were already awaiting admission, and before long the home held thirty-five guests. The building was enlarged in 1939 to accommodate another thirty residents. In 1938, two years after the St. Paul home opened, the sisters acquired the Scott County poorhouse in Shakopee, converting it into the St. Francis Hospital and Home for the Aged. Built in the 1860s as St. Gertrude's Academy, this two-and-one-half-story limestone structure with walls some eighteen inches thick was in 1967 the oldest building still used for the care of aged persons in Minnesota.[7]

A second Catholic facility for paying residents was the McCabe Guest Home, which opened in June, 1939, in Duluth. It owed its existence to Mrs. William J. McCabe's gift of her twenty-five-room mansion to the Sisters of St. Benedict Benevolent Association. The Benedictine order now operated two old people's homes in the city: the new McCabe home on Abbotsford Avenue in east Duluth and St. Ann's, opened in 1910 in a former hospital building on the west side of town. Very different in type of structure and surroundings, the two homes complemented each other. Huge old St. Ann's, built close to the sidewalk with practically no yard, was a familiar friend to the west side inhabitants who had grown up in its shadow. The McCabe Guest Home with its beautifully landscaped grounds had perhaps more appeal to those able to pay for their care.[8]

Changing theories about children's care accounted for the opening of what is now the Tyler Lutheran Home in western Minnesota. For many years the Danish Evangelical Lutheran churches of Tyler and the surrounding area had operated a small children's home. By 1936 the need for such institutions had declined, thanks to the new emphasis on family boarding homes and mothers' pensions, which made it possible for many dependent children to remain in their own homes. The owners of the Tyler orphanage, noting the marked increase in the demand for facilities to care for the elderly, converted the large farmhouse on the edge of town into a home for the aged.[9]

While some groups were opening homes, the owners of existing institutions struggled to overcome problems arising from the depression. At first it was believed that the hard times would last only a few months. By the end of 1930, however, most boards realized that a long road lay ahead and that the end was not in sight. Many found it difficult to meet their payrolls, though these seem infinitesimal by today's standards. Hospitals could obtain registered nurses for $2 a day; homes for the aged paid their staff members far less than that. Many employees worked for little more than room and board, sustained largely by their genuine affection for the old folks. But the institutions had other expenses. Even though a home raised part of its food or received it as a donation, it usually had to buy milk, meat, and staples, as well as pay for heat, light, and other utilities. Some homes tried also to provide food for the "many unemployed who have come hungry to the doors." Thus in the first three months of 1932, for example, the Augustana Home in Minneapolis served 7,700 meals to nonresidents, and the food lines at the Little Sisters of the Poor Home in that city stretched for blocks.[10] Many hours of midnight oil were spent by board members going over accounts. Which bills were most urgent or how much could be paid this month on each one? Would some creditors be willing to wait for their money? Expenditures had been cut to the bone: was it possible to reduce them further? The fund raisers had scraped the bottom of the barrel; where could they go for new revenue?

Operating funds came from a number of sources. One, of course, was the lump-sum entrance fee, but after a few years this money was often "used up." Another was the payment by the week or month. If individuals using the latter method were not in arrears, their payments furnished a fairly steady although usually inadequate source of income. In some instances the sponsoring organization provided much of a home's support either from its general budget or through a special assessment on its membership. A number of institutions in Minneapolis and St. Paul also received some money from community chest drives. If not restricted for some other specific purpose, bequests, legacies, and similar gifts went for current expenses, as did the proceeds from benefits and other money-raising activities.

In the 1930s, however, homes for the aged saw their sources of income fail one by one, as investments proved worthless, property declined in value, and regular contributors decreased their gifts. The Ebenezer Home in Minneapolis, for example, which gave priority to persons without means, depended largely on annual contributions. Benefactors who had responded generously in the past found it necessary to curtail their donations. "The year 1931 will go down in the annals of many institutions as a year of financial difficulties," wrote the president, "and to say that Ebenezer did not feel the stress would not be recording the fact." The next year was no better. "As the trying times continue and the ability of our people to give support is diminishing, the need is increasing day by day," the president reported; "we dare not do less than we are doing and we cannot do less."[11]

Although some homes owned income-producing property, the depression often turned such real estate from an asset into a liability. Bethesda Homes at Willmar held title to several farms which it had received in lieu of life contracts. "Then came the depression with accompanied drought," wrote the homes' historian. "The income decreased, crops failed and feed had to be bought for the stock on the farm. Considerable debt was incurred. At one time the debt amounted to $24,000.00." Selling the farms was out of the question; no buyers could be found during the mid-thirties.[12]

Even the relatively well-financed Jones-Harrison Home of Minneapolis experienced difficulty in providing its residents with necessities: "half of our family are dependent upon us for clothing," said Mrs. E. B. Mount, secretary of the board of directors of the Jones-Harrison Home at the 1930 annual meeting of the Woman's Christian Association. The budget for purchasing clothing was small, and the wardrobe committee depended largely on gifts. "The store room, graciously kept full by friends of the Home, seems to be a veritable cruze of oil — supplying everything from coats, hats, dresses, or trousers as the case may need, to scissors, ornaments, and even 'green glass beads,'" said the secretary.[13]

As the depression deepened it was hard for board members to maintain their interest. "This year has been a difficult one for all organizations interested in welfare work," Mrs. Walter H. Wheeler reported in 1932. "Our duty has been to keep our courage up and our optimism alive in spite of depressing conditions on all sides." The women were determined not to let the buildings deteriorate if they could avoid it. Although 1934 was "a most trying year," the board in an effort to do its share to keep money circulating carried out needed repairs and as much decorating as it felt was consistent with its financial situation. The depression cloud had a silver lining, though. "The last five years have been hard," Mrs. Wheeler reminded the 1935 meeting of the Woman's Christian Association, "but they have shown the calibre of the women in the W.C.A. work. . . . it takes real stamina of character, real devotion to a cause to come to meetings month after month and hear the same story of vacancies, unemployment, unpaid board, increasing operating losses."

Morale within the institution was good. In 1930 almost half the Jones-Harrison family were octogenarians, and nearly all were native-born. Some of them could remember the hard times which followed the panic of 1857. Most could recall the 1873 collapse; their memories of the natural disasters which compounded the sufferings of that period were still vivid. They had seen the grasshopper hordes which swarmed out of the west; they could recall the destructive hailstorms, the prairie fires, and the great blizzard of January, 1873. Although the financial stringency of the late 1890s had been less dramatic, many an elderly resident may have remembered with bitterness a carefully built business which had been suddenly swept away. Thus the depression of the 1930s was not a new story to occupants of a home for the aged. Some of them found it a challenge and an opportunity to again prove their mettle. As the secretary of the Woman's Christian Association reported in 1932: "This year has been for Jones-Harrison Home an unusually busy and happy one in spite of the depression. . . . The Board has done everything possible to create a warm hearted, cheerful, comfortable home for the family who for their part have shown genuine appreciation and eager willingness to use what faculties are still unimpaired to aid in helping each other and in helping the Board to reduce expenses."[14]

There was a point, however, beyond which expenses could not be cut. The steadily increasing number of infirm persons required more nurses, special diets, and extra supplies and equipment. "We are sorry to close another year with our balance still in the red," stated the institution's 1935 annual report, "but when we compare our situation with that of a year ago we feel some satisfaction."[15]

While many homes suffered, a few had reserves to help them weather the depression. The Home for the Friendless in St. Paul, for example, had received many bequests during its long life and was particularly fortunate in its investments. In November, 1936, the secretary reported that the home had more than doubled its endowment in the preceding ten years. This comparative affluence was reflected in raising wages, purchasing new furniture, replenishing linens, and renovating the building. The institution had received some help from the St. Paul Community Chest, but in 1933 (one of the darkest years of the depression) the secretary was able to report that "our income . . . is so nearly adequate for our running expenses that we feel able to carry on without help from the Chest."[16]

In the United States approximately 115 homes for the aged closed during the 1930s. The only one in Minnesota which actually discontinued operations was the Glenwood Old People's Home, an institution of the Norwegian Lutheran Church of America. Located in the former academy building which had been renovated in 1914 at a cost of about $20,000, the home had deteriorated badly. Rooms were hard to heat, fire protection was inadequate, and a serious sewerage problem existed. In spite of the 1914 prediction that the fund built up from entrance fees would be forever "ample to meet all of the running expenses," the board found its finances inadequate, and the small community, hard hit by the depression, could not provide money for improvements. In March, 1934, the superintendent, the Reverend M. S. Knutson, called the plight of the institution to the attention of the Reverend Johan A. Aasgaard, who during the depression served as both church president and executive secretary of its board of charities. Knutson pointed out that some of the residents had been in the home as long as nineteen years, and the money they had paid in had long since been expended on their care.[17]

The matter came to a head in May, 1935, when the state board of control advised that the building was unsafe. The Norwegian Lutheran Church's board of charities then decided to close the institution rather than expend the funds necessary to make the building fire-resistive. The home closed in 1935, and Knutson rented a house where he cared for a few of the former residents; the others went to live in homes which were provided for them elsewhere.[18]

Whether the Glenwood institution and others which closed in the United States could have remained open if they had been able to hold on a few years longer is a matter of conjecture. Economic conditions generally improved in the last half of the decade, and the Social Security Act, which became effective in August, 1935, brought to benevolent homes the promise of new sources of income. Although both of its provisions for the aged — pensions for the needy and contributory old age insurance — were to have far-reaching implications for benevolent institutions, the old age assistance program was the first to make its impact felt. While it prohibited payments to persons in *public* institutions, the law did not specifically mention old age assistance for persons in *private* institutions. Thus it was believed that such payments would be permitted.[19]

This did not mean, of course, that every person in a home for the aged was entitled to a grant. In addition to meeting general eligibility requirements in regard to age, residence, citizenship, and need, occupants of benevolent institutions had to satisfy certain additional conditions set up by the states. By 1940 approximately half the states had established criteria for assistance which excluded many residents of benevolent homes. Some states specified that residents were ineligible if they received care under a life contract, or had purchased care, or had transferred property for this purpose. One state refused grants to residents of fraternal homes. Others required that the institution be licensed or approved. In Minnesota the board of control early obtained a ruling that persons accepted for boarding care were eligible while those on life contracts were not.[20]

Shortly before the assistance program went into operation in Minnesota, the Ebenezer Home of Minneapolis took a gloomy, but unjustified, view of the law's probable effect upon its finances. This residence, which did not have a life-contract plan and which gave priority to the most needy, was among the benevolent institutions most likely to have residents eligible for old age grants. Nevertheless, early in 1936 the home's quarterly publication discounted the idea of receiving substantial support from assistance payments: "If and when pensions are received . . . the burden of caring for them [the residents] will be lightened by just that much. *Most of our old people will not be able to qualify.* Just now *only one* old person in the Home receives such pension and the amount is $20.00 per month."[21]

Elderly Minnesotans — both residents and potential residents of benevolent homes — regarded the new law with mixed reactions. A number of them were extremely reluctant to apply for public assistance; in their view "going on the welfare" was no different from accepting the stigma of the poorhouse. On the other hand, the residents of some homes welcomed the idea of a "pension" and rather enjoyed the attention they received from old age assistance investigators.

When the social security program first got under way, few persons could foresee its ultimate effect on benevolent homes. In November, 1936, a staff correspondent for the *Christian Science Monitor,* noting that the "exodus from public homes already has begun on a moderate scale," pointed out that departures from fraternal, religious, and philanthropic institutions would depend in part on actions taken by the states to allow residents to receive grants while residing in the homes. The writer believed, however, that because of the offsetting influence of the depression which "still is sending an increased number of persons to seek care in such homes," it was too early to gauge the real effect of the act on either public or private charitable institutions.[22]

Unfortunately, there are no national statistics to measure the effects of old age assistance on the populations of benevolent homes. No count of residents in private institutions was made between 1928 and 1939. One can only concur with the conclusions reached by Marjorie Shearon in the *Social Security Bulletin* for March, 1938: "The depression undoubtedly caused some increase in the number of aged persons seeking this type of care. On the other hand, the operation of the Social Security Act has probably made it possible for many persons to avoid entering homes."[23]

If information is lacking on the consequences of social security for home populations, there is no doubt about its early impact on the finances of some institutions. In 1938 the Minneapolis Council of Social Agencies studied eight homes which received community fund support. The survey revealed that in three institutions — the Ebenezer, Augustana, and Scandinavian Union Relief homes — 96 of the 264 residents, or about 36 per cent, were paying for their care entirely from old age assistance funds. The other five homes had only six assistance recipients.[24]

As a result of its survey, the Minneapolis council made several proposals for the improvement of benevolent home operations. It recommended the standardization of admissions and of institutional and medical care, the improvement of diet, and the setting up of an experimental plan to determine the value of special occupational and recreational services. Because life-contract fees had apparently never been large enough to cover the cost of care, the report also recommended that in the future rates should be determined on an actuarial basis. Taking a wider view, the council noted a definite shift in responsibility for care of the indigent aged toward federal, state, and local governments. For this reason the homes were urged to keep in close touch with welfare officials. In view of the uncertainty over the ultimate effect of social security on homes for the aged, the council suggested that building expansion should be discouraged for the time being.[25]

How much expansion was being planned in the late 1930s is not known. Certainly several Minneapolis area institutions were giving serious thought to providing better facilities for their sick. The period of marking time was over; governing boards could now make plans with some assurance of being able to carry them out. In 1939 the Minnesota Masonic Home in Bloomington started work on a $200,000 infirmary building, which was completed the following year. The Ebenezer Home, with its large population, its policy of accepting those in greatest need (which usually meant the infirm), and its minimum age requirement of seventy years, now found that a major portion of its charges required nursing care. "There has been a very marked change in the physical condition of the new residents of the Home," Dr. Elmer O. Dahl told the board in 1939. "We are receiving more and more people who are either physically or mentally ill. If this trend continues, it will mean that Ebenezer will be more of a hospital than a Home, and, of course, will require more facilities for their care." The board began to develop the plans which several years later resulted in a new infirmary building.[26]

The period following the depression was a time of decision. The Tyler Lutheran Home was not the only institution which changed its emphasis in this decade from children's care to an intensified program for the aged. In August, 1935, the board of the Home for Children and Aged Women in Minneapolis, which at one time had as many as 109 children under its roof, resolved that since the building was not occupied to capacity and there were other facilities available, the children's department should be temporarily discontinued. Although the action had been precipitated by the economic situation, the board noted, this factor alone would not have caused the closing.[27]

The Bethesda Homes of Willmar, which had also started as a child-care institution, found it harder to maintain that work during the depression. Stricter state standards and the board of control's policy of favoring child care in private family homes led the Bethesda board to close the children's home in 1939. For more than forty years the organization had given care to children, and it was a sad day in its history when it decided to discontinue the work.[28]

Other governing boards might remember the late 1930s as a time of painful decisions about future programs, but for the residents of three Twin Cities homes — Danebo, Lyngblomsten, and Ebenezer — 1939 was the memorable year when members of the royal families of their native countries called at the homes. Crown Prince Frederik of Denmark and his wife arrived in Minneapolis in April for a two-day visit filled with meetings and entertainments. Somehow they managed to squeeze in a few minutes for a visit to Danebo. The prince chatted with the residents, practically all of whom had been born in Denmark, and planted a tree on the front lawn just a few yards from West River Road.[29]

Crown Prince Olav and Crown Princess Martha of Norway journeyed to the Twin Cities in June for three days of festivities. A day was reserved for visits to six local Norwegian institutions, starting with the Ebenezer Home. "Expectation was at a high pitch," an observer recalled. "One old lady kept on rearranging the photographs on the dresser. When one of the workers remarked to her that the dresser looked nicer without the photographs, she received this rebuff, 'Well, I should think the Prince would want to see the pictures of all my children.'" While it is unlikely that the prince had time to view the pictures, he did speak to the residents in the chapel, bringing them greetings from the people of Norway. One woman, alas, missed the visit entirely. Anxious to look her best for the royal visitors, she was still in her room getting ready when the entourage drove off.

It would be pleasant to report that all the Scandinavian homes received royal visits that year, but there were too many of them. Of Minnesota's 53 homes in operation in 1939, 22 had been started by people of Swedish, Norwegian, or Danish descent, and they were widely scattered throughout the state. The Scandinavian influence is probably one reason why Minnesota ranked ninth that year among all the states both in number of institutions and in number of beds. More significantly, it was fifth in the nation in the ratio of beds to the general population. The Scandinavian homes were also, as previously noted, largely church-related and thus contributed to the state's preponderance of homes under religious sponsorship. Of Minnesota homes for the aged, 72 per cent were church-related compared with only 40 per cent for the nation as a whole.[30]

While many of the denominational and other institutions for special groups did admit "outsiders," as they were called, the old people's homes, on the whole, still served a limited segment of the aged population — "highly selected on the basis of age, nativity, and health, and the ability to pay a fee." In a study made by the United States labor department in 1939, it was found that of the

44 Minnesota institutions which responded to a questionnaire, the majority required that applicants be mentally sound and physically able to care for themselves. Almost all took into consideration such other factors as church or lodge membership, racial or national origin, "good character," and ability to reimburse the home for care. At least 23 homes had a minimum entrance fee ranging from $750 to $2,000, though 15 of them also accepted applicants at regular boarding rates. Twenty-three required that the resident transfer part or all of his property to the institution.[81]

Except for the fact that there were more of them, private homes for the aged were much the same in 1939 as they had been in 1929. While social security had provided a new type of income, most homes still looked to their traditional sources of funds for expansion and improvements — money-raising activities, voluntary gifts, and help from the parent organization. Busy with their own problems during the depression, they still had relatively little contact with other institutions and community agencies. It would take the events of the turbulent decade that lay ahead to bring them out of their small corners into closer association with one another.

12

Standards and Shortages during World War II

1940—1950

THE DECADE OF THE 1940s WAS DOMINATED by the events of World War II. Inevitably the far-reaching war effort affected the aged and the programs for their care. Some developments, such as revived plans for expanding existing homes that had been held in abeyance during the depression, were checked once more by the war. Others, such as the lack of jobs for older persons, were relieved by the full employment brought about by the war effort. Surveys and investigations carried out during this period pinpointed unmet needs and inadequate services, making the public newly aware of the kind and magnitude of the problems associated with decent care for the elderly.

Underlying these trends of the 1940s were two factors — one an irreversible natural process, the other a consequence of the way old age assistance funds were administered. The first factor has been referred to by Isaac Hoffman as the development of the "two populations of the aging"; that is, the number of people seventy-five years and older increased more rapidly than the "younger aged," those from sixty-five to seventy-four years. As a result the population contained more infirm and chronically ill persons who had fewer financial resources but required more health services of a very expensive nature. Providing and financing the necessary nursing and medical care became a major concern of the period of World War II.¹

In 1940 Minnesota had 212,618 people who were 65 or older, nearly 50,000 more than in 1930. Only 16 of the 48 states had more aged persons. A major portion of them did not require sheltered care. In fact, many of the younger aged entered the labor market during the first part of the decade. "World War II, after the manner of all wars," observed the authors of *American Social Legislation,* "seemed to solve all forms of economic insecurity in the single task of producing war material financed from a bottomless Treasury war chest. The problem of finding jobs for men was suddenly reversed." Men and women of all ages were desperately needed not only to produce the airplanes, ships, tanks, munitions, and other materiel required for waging the war, but also to replace the clerks, farmers, factory workers, and others who had gone into the military services. Older persons who were able to work once again found something to do.²

It was not long before the effects of full employment were noted in Minnesota. In January, 1943, the *Social Welfare Review* reported that the first full year of war had produced a measurable effect on public assistance programs. A year later the state division of social welfare commented on the reduction in the number of old age assistance cases because the recipients were either employed or receiving support from other persons. It has been estimated that between 1945 and 1947 the number of employed persons over sixty-five rose 25 per cent above normal.³

The high employment rate of the younger aged was only a temporary phenomenon, of course, and even at the time it did not entirely obscure the situation of their more elderly contemporaries. While noting the drop in the number of assistance cases, the division of social welfare also called attention to the higher average age of recipients who remained on the rolls. The case load, as the division pointed out, consisted "more and more of the older continuing cases." The division emphasized that even with the high level of employment, the problems of providing medical, nursing, and general care of elderly people would continue to be major ones.⁴

Developments of the 1940s were shaped by a second factor — the workings of the old age assistance laws, particularly the provision that forbade grants to inmates of public institutions. For approximately eighty years Minnesota's county officials had relied primarily on the poorhouse for the care of destitute and infirm elderly persons. In the decade of the 1940s, however, it became clear that, except in the metropolitan counties, this was no longer the case. The number of poor farms in the state continued the decline which had started in the mid-1930s with the inception of the old age assistance program, and a relatively new facility — the proprietary home operated for profit — took the spotlight. The previous decade had seen the number of publicly operated homes drop by nearly 50 per cent, and a similar decrease occurred in the 1940s — from 44 homes in 1930 to 24 in 1940 to 11 in 1949.[5]

Although the poor farm was clearly declining as an important resource for the care of the elderly, nevertheless in 1942 approximately half the inmates of Minnesota's county homes were over sixty-five years of age. For most of them old age pensions had not supplied an alternative. Some had applied for assistance and were in the homes pending receipt of necessary verifications. Others could not meet residential or other requirements for grants. In at least one county several recipients had relinquished their allotments and returned to the institution because the amount allowed was not sufficient to provide for their needs.[6]

Younger persons in the county homes included nonresidents received for temporary care and destitute persons for whom no other help was available. Many of them had what one superintendent described as "institutional disabilities." They could not keep jobs, were alcoholics, or simply could not get along with others. The superintendent of a poor farm in southern Minnesota observed that his charges could not compete successfully for jobs, but he believed that during a labor shortage "many of the able-bodied or those with slight incapacities could again get farm work in the community."

By the 1940s children were seldom found in poorhouses. An exception was a seven-year-old girl who had been removed from the custody of her parents and placed in the county home, because it was believed that her parents would have interfered in a foster home. The child was kept in the matron's apartment, but the adult residents "competed for her attention, and it was difficult to keep her out of their rooms."[7]

In 1942 twenty-one counties still ran their own poorhouses. A study made by Sarah Riley, a graduate student at the University of Minnesota, showed that in July, 1942, nineteen of the county-operated institutions (two did not respond to a questionnaire) cared for a total of 1,220 people. More than three-fourths of Minnesota's poorhouse population resided in the state's three metropolitan counties. The Hennepin County home held 123 persons, the Ramsey County home, 296, and the St. Louis County home, 525.

These three populous areas employed various arrangements for the care of their ill and feeble aged. Hennepin County's facility at Hopkins was operated primarily as a boarding-care home. Indigent Minneapolis residents who needed nursing care were sent either to Parkview Hospital, a large municipally operated chronic disease facility closely associated with what is now Hennepin County General Hospital, or to one of the city's many proprietary homes. St. Paul did not have a separate chronic disease hospital. Although a large number of long-term patients were cared for in Ancker Hospital, which was operated by the city and county, many were transferred to the Ramsey County home at 2000 White Bear Avenue, where they remained under the supervision of physicians associated with the city hospital. In 1940 the St. Louis County welfare board entered into a contract with Duluth's city-owned general hospital, Miller Memorial, guaranteeing that a specified number of beds be made available for needy clients. Because of the extensive nursing load in this county, however, both the Cook and Arlington buildings of the St. Louis County home maintained large infirmaries.[8]

By the 1940s commissioners in a majority of the twenty-one counties had delegated to welfare boards at least part of their responsibilities for overseeing the county institutions. This was particularly true in the matter of determining eligibility for admission, although in some cases the commissioners, acting on the recommendations of welfare workers, still issued the actual orders to admit individuals.[9]

The administration of county-operated homes, however, remained virtually unchanged. Overseers still worked under a variety of financial arrangements. Some superintendents were employed on a salary basis; others received a per capita fee. A few counties used a combination of these two arrangements. In most areas the farm operation was still deemed important, and the county board tried to assure that a new superintendent would be a competent farmer. In at least two-thirds of the institutions the superintendent's wife acted as matron without compensation separate from that of her husband. In Hennepin County the wife received a salary. In Ramsey and St. Louis counties the matron was unrelated to the superintendent. In Washington and Itasca counties the matrons were in effect the superintendents. While the county commissioners seemed to emphasize successful farming operations, they were not entirely unmindful of the needs of their charges. According to one overseer's wife, the board told her it was looking for a "matron who would give good care to inmates, provide good, nourishing food, keep the home clean, and who would, in addition, be kindly and considerate with inmates."[10]

How to keep their charges busy and happy was as great a problem for matrons of county homes in the 1940s as it had been in the early 1900s, when James Jackson urged that community groups help brighten the lives of poor farm inmates. While most of the supervisors were used to old people and some had interests and hobbies which they could pass on to their patients, many had to learn the hard way — by trial and error. The matron of a county home, who looked back on her first years in that position as a sort of nightmare, reported that she found her biggest problem was handling people. Thrust into the job with no previous experience and practically no information about the inmates, she was told to work out her own plans. An interviewer wrote that the matron found many of her charges "dissatisfied, many quarrelsome, some with feuds against others, some with real grievances, and in the press of other work she had insufficient time to get acquainted with them. She often wished for help in knowing what to do for and with inmates."[11]

Superintendents of several institutions reported that older people did not enjoy such social activities as card games, dominoes, and checkers. They much preferred following their own pursuits. On one poor farm the overseer noted that a man who was permitted to grow vegetables and sell the surplus used his first cash proceeds to buy a padlock to keep others from working in his garden. The matron of an institution which had no radios for inmates believed that individually owned ones might be desirable, but that a "communal one would not be satisfactory."[12]

During the decade the number of counties operating their own institutions dropped from twenty-four to eleven.[13] Welfare workers therefore turned more and more to proprietary homes when a place was needed for a sick old person. These private, profit-making "rest homes" were opening everywhere, in both urban and rural areas. As they had been in the 1930s, many of the new homes were small private dwellings — farmhouses, often without plumbing, electricity, or telephone — or mansions which the original owners no longer needed or could maintain. By the 1940s men and women who looked on the operation of a rest home as a business were joining the housewives and practical nurses who had started because they felt compelled to care for a needy neighbor or found the work a means of holding on to their own homes. More large buildings came into use as prospective operators took over the discontinued hospitals, schools, hotels, and other structures which could often be obtained for a song.

Despite the fact that commercial rest homes were springing up everywhere, the problem of finding beds for sick persons was growing more difficult. The acuteness of the situation is illustrated by the experience of one social worker who in desperation bundled a homeless arthritic old man into her car and set out in search of a rest home. After traveling nearly a hundred miles through four counties and calling at every facility suggested to her, she at last found a remote farm home willing to take the patient. While this was perhaps an extreme case, many workers spent most of their time (or so it seemed) trying to locate beds for elderly people. But finding one often did not end the matter. Many homes proved unsatisfactory, and the whole dreary search had to be started again.[14]

In 1940 there were no standards which homes were required to meet, and reports of abuses were widespread. The state medical and hospital associations renewed their efforts to get a licensing law that would control the development and operation of all places caring for the sick and the aged. In the meantime the inspector of institutions for the state division of social welfare continued to visit county homes and general hospitals.

For a time he also inspected the privately owned homes which were brought to his attention, but as their numbers increased they presented more and more problems. Walter W. Finke, the division's director, questioned whether the agency should any longer try to inspect private nursing and boarding homes under the vague powers of the existing law. In April, 1941, Morris Hursh, who was then the attorney for the division, advised that it was doubtful whether the law conferred any authority to inspect privately operated facilities. Moreover, as a matter of policy, it seemed impractical for the division to inspect them when it had no legal right to enforce the correction of unsatisfactory conditions.[15]

This gap was soon closed. On April 28, 1941, the governor approved the first comprehensive licensing law in the nation, providing controls over all hospitals and related institutions in the state. Much of the credit for the bill was due to three persons: Ray M. Amberg, director of the University of Minnesota Hospitals, Alfred G. Stasel, attorney-administrator of Eitel Hospital in Minneapolis, and F. Manley Brist, legal counsel for the Minnesota State Medical Association. In formulating the bill these three, with additional representatives of the hospital and medical associations, reviewed the laws of other states and considered the situation in Minnesota. A primary difficulty was the description of what institutions the law should cover. Amberg later recalled that "there were no definitions that were puncture proof — the very definition of a hospital itself was one of our hardest handicaps. . . . Who should be taken in and who should be excluded? Who should be entitled to apply for licensure?"[16]

In respect to facilities for the aged, the laws of other states provided few answers. Most state welfare departments had the right to inspect county almshouses but no power to enforce their recommendations. A few states were beginning to require some form of approval for homes caring for old age assistance recipients, the mentally ill, and other special groups. But nowhere did the authority for supervision have a firm legal base. The committee writing the Minnesota bill decided on the broadest possible coverage, including both public and private institutions. The law, therefore, embraced all places which provided "hospitalization" and "chronic or convalescent care," but left to the administrative agency the task of defining these terms more precisely.[17]

Responsibility for enforcing the law was given to the Minnesota department of health. There the program was placed in the division of child hygiene under the supervision of its director, Dr. Viktor O. Wilson. The institutional inspector and the maternity hospital supervisor (who became the licensing supervisor under the new program) were transferred from the division of social welfare to the health department.[18]

Before the law went into effect on January 1, 1942, it was necessary to set up detailed regulations. One of the first steps was to classify institutions and prepare licensing standards for each classification. Because so many homes cared for old age assistance recipients, the health department decided to submit tentative standards to county welfare boards for their suggestions. This was done through the division of social welfare's field representatives, who worked closely with the local boards in their respective districts. During the summer of 1941 the fieldworkers discussed the implications of the new program with the local agencies, and in October they brought their recommendations to a meeting of the licensing staff.

In view of the difficulty of finding places for elderly people, it is not surprising that the principal recommendation was a negative one — not to make the requirements so strict as to shut off the supply of homes. "It is not too easy a job to find boarding homes for old age assistance recipients," reported a field representative, "and to make the requirements stringent would certainly be a mistake." Welfare workers believed that even a modest licensing fee might eliminate some homes. One representative reported that "Many of these homes would find the license fee a hardship, operating as they are on the low board and room pay basis." Among the "more difficult" of the proposed standards, one worker listed a telephone in the building, a uniform temperature of seventy degrees, and a constant supply of hot water.

While expressing themselves in favor of licensing in general, the fieldworkers asked that the law be interpreted to exempt extremely small places and homes receiving only ambulatory persons. "It is my feeling that only those homes caring for bedfast persons should be licensed," said one worker. "I feel that it would be extremely difficult to license homes caring for ambulant recipients. Many of them move about quite a bit and it might be a tremendous job to keep the homes licensed into which they move." (Under an opinion later received from the attorney general, homes having only one person who required "chronic or convalescent care" were exempted from licensure.)

The term "chronic or convalescent care" was interpreted to mean nursing care which extended or was likely to extend over a considerable period of time, but what constituted nursing care was frequently a moot question. The rather narrow definition adopted in the 1941 standards did not take into account the fact that many mentally confused and handicapped persons required a considerable amount of competent personal care. Ten years later the law was revised to cover institutions offering custodial care, thus bringing many more rest homes under its scope.[19]

In December, 1941, the health department mailed tentative standards and application forms to all institutions believed to be subject to licensure. Facilities were inspected as rapidly as possible, and in September, 1942, the health department issued its first annual directory of licensed hospitals and related institutions. Ninety proprietary homes and forty-seven benevolent homes were licensed the first year.[20]

Under a ruling of the attorney general, county-operated homes were not licensed during the first two years of the program, although leased homes were covered. In 1943 the legislature amended the licensing law to make inclusion of public institutions more specific, and under the revised standards of 1944 county-operated homes were licensed if they provided "chronic or convalescent care," that is, if they had as many as two nursing cases at one time. Because of the closing or leasing of a number of institutions, only fifteen counties still operated their own homes in 1944; of these only six were licensed as "care facilities."[21]

As the licensing program developed, it soon became apparent that wartime scarcities and restrictions would prevent many institutions from meeting all the requirements pertaining to physical plant and personnel. The provision of adequate bathing and toilet facilities, for example, usually necessitated remodeling which was impossible under existing conditions. Sanitation surveys revealed faulty plumbing installations; plumbers, however, were scarce and the materials required a high priority. Nor could some of the equipment which would facilitate dishwashing by approved methods always be obtained. Similar problems arose in meeting the standards established by the state fire marshal, whose approval was required for licensure. Quite early in the program, the marshal began to prohibit the housing of bedfast patients above the first floor in frame buildings which were not protected by automatic sprinkler systems. Although many homes made adjustments to transfer bedfast patients to first-floor quarters, others without such rooms available had no alternative but to ask for the removal of these patients.[22]

As the decade progressed, the need for beds for the increasing number of sick and incapacitated older persons became even more acute. Because of the obvious inadvisability of closing homes for aged and ill persons who had no other place to go (and who disliked being uprooted anyway), the emphasis of the health department's program during the first years was on correcting the most flagrant violations and preventing the opening of undesirable places. The department also promoted measures to improve services in existing homes and sponsored studies to determine needs in an attempt to acquaint the public with the problem.

The wartime labor shortage made it difficult for institutions to obtain personnel, especially nurses. Experience was lacking on which to base requirements for the number and qualifications of staff needed for a given institution. The standards adopted in 1944 required only that one person with "sufficient experience to qualify her for responsibility for the care of the patients" be in charge of nursing. Except for information obtained by interviewing physicians and others and observations made at the time of an inspection, the licensing staff had little basis for judging the sufficiency of the supervising nurse's experience in individual situations. Registered nurses were almost nonexistent even in very large institutions, and practical nurses were not licensed until 1949. As for other personnel, most institutions in this period were glad to get anyone who seemed reasonably capable and interested in elderly people even if he or she did not have previous experience in caring for the sick.[23]

Because of the extreme shortage of qualified personnel, the department of health as early as May, 1943, initiated training classes for rest home employees. The owners of homes in the Twin Cities area had recently formed an association to discuss their mutual problems, particularly that of feeding patients under the wartime rationing system. Members of this organization responded eagerly to the health department's offer to provide training sessions on patient care.[24]

Four classes were devoted to simple procedures of the kind taught in home nursing courses. The fifth session of this pioneering course was conducted by a physical therapist who had been invited to demonstrate techniques of massage. The therapist was so fearful of taking the group beyond its depth that she spent virtually an entire evening demonstrating a soothing back rub. (It was almost too soothing for the weary workers in attendance.) Some seven years later instructors from the University of Minnesota Hospitals were teaching almost the same group procedures for cardiac, cancer, and diabetic patient care, with special emphasis on diet, mental health, and the observation and recording of symptoms. "Teach the patient to do for himself," advised the physical therapist in 1950. Instead of demonstrating a simple back rub, she showed the workers how to get handicapped patients into and out of bed and instructed them in the use of such self-help devices as crutches.

Until the late 1940s little was done to get feeble and handicapped elderly patients out of bed, but this decade witnessed the blossoming of the idea of rehabilitating older people. Before that time many homes, in fact, frankly preferred bed patients. The operators not only found the bedfast less troublesome than the ambulatory old folks who wandered all over the place, but they also generally received more money for their care. Under the terms of legislation enacted in 1945, old age assistance recipients in licensed homes were allowed monthly payments higher than the prevailing maximum maintenance grant of $40 a month. Classification schedules adopted by the division of social welfare provided the highest rates for bedfast patients. It was generally recognized that placing a premium on this type of care tended to keep in bed many persons who with a little help could sit up in a chair or walk, but at the time it was difficult to devise a more satisfactory method of payment. The net effect of these factors, however, was to discourage activity, and rest homes became known as places filled with old people who were simply waiting to die.[25]

Certainly the problem of idleness, so apparent to labor department investigators in the late 1920s, had not been solved by the 1940s. But there were stirrings of activity which bore fruit late in the decade. A study conducted in 1948 furnished much-needed data on the interests of the aged and on the types of activities which were being carried out in nursing homes. C. Stanley Clifton, a graduate student at the University of Minnesota, surveyed the leisure-time interests and activities of 914 old age assistance recipients in 111 commercial homes in Minnesota. By this date all but 9 of the state's 120 licensed proprietary homes had at least one person receiving public assistance.[26]

Clifton found the residents he interviewed suffering from ill-health, poor memories, hearing difficulties, and depressed moods. He concluded that many patients, lacking the stimulation of former status-giving associations and memberships, had for years lived an existence that was "close to vegetative." The major portion of the time of both men and women was occupied by visiting among themselves, reading, listening to the radio, and just sitting. Watching traffic was a favorite pastime for 4 per cent of the men. (Visiting a county home in that period, the author still recalls the satisfied expression on the face of an old man as he turned from his window to exclaim elatedly: "I counted 123 cars today!")

Despite the fact that many patients favored passive activities, they recalled and talked about excursions outside the home. Proprietors frequently did not like to take patients out of the home,

Clifton noted, not only because of fear of accidents but also because the old people needed frequent toilet stops. One matron, who had taken several women for an afternoon's ride, told of four visits at service stations during the trip. Another problem, of course, was the patient who had difficulty getting into an ordinary car. The author clearly remembers a rest home patient who was "not able to bend." In order to take her on a much longed-for journey, the owner had to hire a hearse. The conveyance may have been a little gruesome, but the invalid greatly enjoyed the trip. Clifton's investigations showed that a successful recreation program depended on many factors, including the physical and mental conditions of the patients, their abilities and interests, the attitudes of the operators and their staff members, the space available, and the presence in the community of actively interested relatives, friends, and organizations.

By the end of the decade social workers and others had become actively concerned about the problem of furnishing old people with something more than the board, room, and physical care necessary to make them comfortable. "Too many persons enter the period of old age without a leisure time plan," the state division of social welfare noted in its annual report of 1949. The following year the division employed an occupational therapist to assist welfare workers and homes in setting up programs of hobbies and crafts and in planning games, parties, and other forms of entertainment. The Hennepin County welfare board also employed a worker to organize service programs and to provide leadership in developing activities.[27]

In a series of radio talks designed to interest the public in the plight of the aged, Dr. Robert N. Barr, the state health department's executive officer, also stressed the importance of leisure-time programs. On June 6, 1949, he said that "the homes provided for elderly people should be really *homes*. . . . They should be equipped to give the old people some occupation — to teach them how to do something, if they have never learned how to occupy their time. Homes for old people should also furnish recreation. They should never be places where groups of bored old people just sit around waiting to die."[28]

In April, 1948, the health department began the publication of *Nursing Home News,* a mimeographed quarterly intended to provide a medium for the exchange of ideas among licensed institutions and to bring their work and needs to the attention of others.

A considerable portion of its space was devoted to the institutions' own accounts of enjoyable patient activities. In view of the separation of many elderly residents from their former associations and membership organizations, it is not surprising that they especially welcomed events which brought outsiders into the homes. Unfortunately most entertainments were carried out during the Christmas season when it was not unusual to find five or six organizations in a single home on the same day. Throughout the rest of the year many patients did not have any visitors. Others could only wonder when the caller who had promised to come back "real soon" would show up again.

In 1949 three organizations cosponsored in Minneapolis the activity which came to be known as the Volunteer Visitors Program. The Minnesota Council of Church Women provided carefully selected visitors, the social service department of the University of Minnesota Hospitals arranged for their training, and the Minnesota Association of Nursing Homes enlisted the co-operation of its members. Under the program a unit of from three to five women visited every patient in an assigned home on a regular day each week. All plans were cleared with the person in charge of the home, and the results were carefully evaluated. So successful was the project that other communities soon began to request copies of the visitors' manuals and other information. County welfare workers, the Gray Ladies of the American Red Cross, and hospital auxiliaries were instrumental in establishing similar programs in other parts of the state. As a result a large group of women came to know at firsthand the homes for the aged in their respective localities.[29]

It was not only through the volunteer visitor programs, however, that the public became aware of the tremendous problems involved in caring for the elderly. Nearly every family, it seemed, had an aged relative or friend for whom a place must be found. Frequently the search was a long and discouraging one, often taking people to distant communities and into homes which were a far cry from the immaculate little rest hospitals they had pictured. Surveys and investigations made in this period also emphasized the need for more and better facilities. One of the earliest and most extensive was sponsored by the Commission on Hospital Care, a national nongovernmental public service body. In Minnesota the survey, which was started in 1946, was conducted by the state health department under the general direction of a committee. (This body later became the advisory council to implement the Federal Hospital Survey and Construction Act, better known as the Hill-Burton Law.) In addition to physical plants and operations, the study covered patient services and geographic, population, social, and economic factors related to the need for additional facilities. The findings pointed up inadequacies both in general hospitals and in homes for chronically ill patients.[80]

In 1948 a disastrous fire in an unlicensed Minneapolis boarding home touched off a flurry of activity in Hennepin County. About one-fifth of Minnesota's old age assistance recipients lived in this heavily populated county, and the county welfare board wished to know more about the care its clients were receiving. Late in 1948 the board released a report describing "shocking conditions" in proprietary homes. The use of restraints, insufficient food, understaffing, and poor housekeeping were the leading targets of its criticisms.[81]

The Minneapolis health department also began a survey of the city's proprietary homes. Its report, released in March, 1949, contained twelve recommendations, including one for the strengthening of local ordinances pertaining to these institutions. The city's commissioner of public health said, however, that in his opinion the "over-all picture is pretty good," and that "these private institutions are filling a need that cannot be met by public agencies."[82]

Increased public concern over conditions in commercial homes was mirrored in several other developments of the late 1940s. On March 14, 1949, the Hennepin County welfare board met with interested individuals and groups to discuss the question of transferring the licensing of proprietary homes from the health department to the state division of social welfare. The proposed change would have brought county welfare boards into the picture. It was expected that under this arrangement local welfare workers would visit the homes fairly frequently and thus exert a useful degree of control over them. Commenting on the proposal, an editorial in the *Minneapolis Star* stated: "The plight of old people in nursing homes leaves much to be desired. . . . The state health department, which licenses nursing homes, admits that some are substandard. But . . . there just aren't enough nursing homes to go around. . . . A change in the licensing agency wouldn't create more nursing homes. It would only bring the welfare department up against the same frustrating problem that now faces the health department." A bill to transfer the licensing function was introduced in the Minnesota legislature on March 24, 1949, but died in committee.[33]

The newspaper also pointed to another remedy which was then being discussed in Hennepin County — the construction of a new county home for the aged. Although the old one was still in operation (it closed in 1953), its services were largely restricted to ambulatory persons who required little more than personal care. The facility now suggested would be staffed and equipped to accommodate bedfast patients and others who needed nursing care.

While there were many objections to it, the proposal for a new public facility in Hennepin County was in line with recommendations then being made throughout the nation to restore the public institution as a resource for old age assistance recipients. But this movement faced several obstacles. One was the old age assistance law which prohibited payments to residents of public institutions; a second was the condition of existing county buildings, most of which were unsuitable for conversion into nursing homes. Since 1945 Minnesota had allowed extra grants for nursing care to old age assistance recipients in licensed private homes. If extended to public institutions, such a provision would ease the financial costs of operation. In 1949 both houses of the Minnesota legislature joined the movement by memorializing Congress to make the needed changes, and Congress did so in 1950.[84]

But the question of suitable buildings remained. By December, 1949, Minnesota had thirteen leased county homes (one more than in July, 1942) and eleven which were still operated by the counties. Only a few of these structures could be satisfactorily converted into nursing homes. A more promising possibility — unique to Minnesota — was to be found in the county tuberculosis sanatoriums. Improved medical and surgical techniques had sharply lowered the tuberculosis death rate, and as early as 1945 the division of social welfare had reported an increasing number of vacant beds in the state's sanatoriums. Observing that the vacancies were to be found chiefly in the smaller facilities, the division suggested that they be diverted to other uses, such as nursing homes for the aged. In 1949 the legislature authorized the closing of sanatoriums no longer needed for the treatment of tuberculosis patients. Further action would be necessary, however, before the structures would become resources for the aged.[85]

While the number of licensed proprietary homes had increased from 90 in 1942 to 166 in 1949, and 60 of the 68 existing benevolent homes were licensed to provide chronic and convalescent care, the state was still woefully short of beds. In its 1949 report the division of social welfare noted: "A most pressing problem is that of the aged person who needs nursing care and who lives alone or with relatives no longer able to take care of him. The services this person should have can normally be secured in either a hospital or a nursing home. Even there in many instances the quality of care and the service offered does not match the minimum requirements of the aged person because of overcrowding." Addressing himself to the shortage, Dr. Barr said in 1949: "We have with us right now a large number of elderly people who need better health care than they are getting. We need more hospital beds for older people who are actually ill. We need many more convalescent homes for those who are recovering from operations or illnesses. . . . More than anything else," Dr. Barr continued, "we need a large number of comfortable, intelligently-run rest homes or residential homes, where old people can retire to live." In conclusion Dr. Barr told his radio listeners: "When we criticize a home, we are criticizing ourselves because we are getting all that we are paying for from the vast majority of these homes. We must recognize that it is our responsibility individually and collectively to provide better facilities and services for old people."[86]

During the 1940s the general public had at last become aware of the magnitude of the aging problem. Against the backdrop of World War II and the postwar period, studies were undertaken, and organizations and individuals began to perfect plans for new buildings and services, ready to spring into action when the country returned to normal. The next decade would see a tremendous increase in facilities and services for the elderly, and a new version of the county home would take a small but important place in the constellation of benevolent, proprietary, and public institutions for the care of the aged and the infirm.

13

Regulations and Ration Books

1940—1950

IT WAS VIRTUALLY IMPOSSIBLE to erect new structures under the war and postwar conditions of the 1940s. All the new benevolent homes opened in this decade therefore began in buildings that had been planned for some other purpose. Frequently when another type of institution ceased to operate, someone proposed that the structure be converted into a home for the aged. A normal school stood vacant: why not use the dormitory for the elderly? A home for unmarried mothers was closing: could not the building shelter people of advanced years and still serve the philanthropic intent of the founders? A discontinued telephone office, an unprosperous hotel, a vacant poor farm, as well as apartment houses and private residences, furnished structures for benevolent homes started in this period, largely by organizations already in the field. Even these experienced groups, however, did not find it easy to establish institutions during the 1940s.

Our Lady of Good Counsel Home in St. Paul opened on December 7, 1941 — the day of the Japanese attack on Pearl Harbor — in a former telephone office building, which had been remodeled while materials were still relatively easy to obtain. This home was the sixth foundation in the United States undertaken by the Sisters of St. Dominic Servants of Relief for Incurable Cancer, who were invited to St. Paul by Archbishop John G. Murray. If the Good Counsel Home had not opened in 1941, it might have been several years before the required remodeling and renovation could have been carried out. Even before Pearl Harbor, the nation's manpower and money were going into the ships, planes, tanks, and antiaircraft guns that were needed to make the United States an "arsenal of democracy." As materials became scarcer and prices continued to rise, additional controls were imposed, and various federal agencies were set up to develop priorities. One of the earliest was the War Production Board, created in January, 1942. Any organization which undertook even the simplest remodeling soon found that it had to surmount hurdles in the form of federal regulations.[1]

The Norwegian Lutheran Church of America quickly became entangled in regulations and priorities when it attempted to convert a dormitory of the former Lutheran Normal School at Madison into a home for the aged. After obtaining the preliminary approval of pastors in the Lac qui Parle, Montevideo, Rock Valley, and Willmar circuits, Reverend Aasgaard, president of the church's executive board, called a meeting for August 2, 1943, at which time a committee was appointed to draw up articles of incorporation and a constitution. The project received final approval on September 28, and an organization was set up to establish the Lutheran Old People's Home at Madison. There is no doubt that the prospect of a steady income from old age assistance recipients brightened the home's outlook. Aasgaard wrote that "the old people coming in would be receiving possibly $30.00 a month each. . . . This would almost take care of the maintenance."[2]

The board then took up the problem of converting the dormitory building. The structure was in generally good repair, but it needed a new heating plant. This could not be procured without approval from the War Production Board. On September 21 Aasgaard transmitted an application to the Minneapolis office, together with "three copies of form WPB-617 and supplementary sheets, and five copies of form WPB-1612." The cost of the work was estimated at $10,300. Only then did Aasgaard learn that the local office could not handle applications involving more than $10,000. He resubmitted the application and, by eliminating labor costs which had been erroneously included in the original estimate, adjusted the amount to $9,850.[3]

The church's need for high-priority materials had to be balanced against the demands of the war effort. The War Production Board raised various questions: "Why had the necessity arisen at just this time? How are these old people taken care of at present and how were they taken care of before this time? Cannot they get along the way they are getting along until after the war is over?" Pastors who visited their elderly parishioners in overcrowded rest homes and in the cramped quarters of relatives were well aware of the need; nevertheless, Aasgaard considered the questions reasonable. "You realize," he wrote to one clergyman, "this is a very pointed and very smart analysis of our situation." Apparently the home's sponsors were able to convince the production board that the project was worthy, for the application was approved in November, 1943. By the spring of 1944 the Lutheran Old People's Home was in full operation with twenty-five persons in residence.[4]

The Norwegian Lutheran Church opened three other homes during this decade. Though small at first, they were destined to become much larger institutions. In 1943, while the Madison pastors grappled with their problems, the former president's house of a closed seminary at Red Wing became the Red Wing Seminary Memorial Home. In 1949 the church opened a second facility in Goodhue County which was called the Kenyon Sunset Home. Since these two institutions were geographically close together, they were eventually served by one superintendent who divided his time between them.[5]

A third facility, the Knute Nelson–Glenwood Memorial Home in Alexandria, became possible when the residence of the former United States senator and governor of Minnesota came into the possession of the Norwegian Lutherans in 1942. The time was not propitious for opening new homes. Not until 1946 did the religious body, which was that year renamed the Evangelical Lutheran Church, decide at least to explore the possibility. At a meeting called in 1947 by the Reverend Magnus A. Dahlen, executive secretary of the church's board of charities, pastors and laymen of the Fergus Falls and Alexandria areas decided to begin operations on a limited scale. When the building was renovated, the study and living room were preserved intact as memorials to Senator Nelson. The home, which admitted its first resident in April, 1948, provided boarding care for twelve men.[6]

In 1945 the Evangelical Lutheran Good Samaritan Society, a national charitable organization which operates homes and hospitals of various kinds, opened in the town of Bagley its first Minnesota residence. The society's work had been started in 1923 by the Reverend August J. Hoeger at Arthur, North Dakota, where he began a home for crippled children. When an elderly man appeared one day appealing for a place to stay, Hoeger recognized the need for homes for the aged. Since that time such homes have become the society's major concern. In 1967 it operated 110 such projects in 15 central and western states. Its first homes were started in old structures under what was decidedly a shoestring policy, but in recent years it has erected well-designed facilities.[7]

Finding an available building was probably the only way in which Bagley could have obtained a home for its aged citizens and those of surrounding Clearwater County in 1945. Although the war ended that year, shortages persisted. Under the general direction of the Good Samaritan Society, a local organization was set up, with the Reverend Fred A. Sommars in charge. The group acquired a small, plain, two-story house in May, 1945, and then appealed for donations. "The goal of the initial drive will be $2,000," the *Farmers Independent* of Bagley announced in June, "which is expected to get the Home under operation. They also ask those having dishes, cooking utensils, and other household equipment which they wish to donate or sell to contact Rev. Sommars." At that time it was impossible to obtain many necessary housekeeping items in any other way. The Clearwater Sunset Home opened on September 1, 1945, and is still in operation.[8]

The Walker Methodist Residence and Nursing Home in Minneapolis, which also opened in 1945, began life under somewhat more favorable circumstances. The Methodists were already operating the Elim Home, which had been established in the city by the Norwegian-Danish Conference in 1914, but a much larger facility was needed to serve the Minnesota and Northern Minnesota conferences. The opportunity came in 1945 when the board of the Harriet Walker Home and Hospital decided to close the seventy-year-old institution for unmarried mothers. The property was given to the Methodist Conference of Minnesota for use as a home for aged Methodists. The three-story brick building required relatively little remodeling to make it suitable for the new purpose. On November 6, 1945, the Elim Home was closed, and its twenty-two residents were transferred to the new facility.[9]

In addition to the seven benevolent institutions which have been described, ten others were started in this period. All were located in existing buildings. Three were nursing homes; the other seven were boarding homes, which made very little provision for care of the ill or disabled. Only one facility ceased operations in the 1940s.

The Northwest Baptist Home Society closed its New Prague institution for the aged in 1947 and transferred the residents to the newly opened Blaisdell Avenue Baptist Home in Minneapolis.[10]

Hard as it was to remodel buildings in the 1940s, it was still more difficult to operate the homes. Although money was more plentiful than it had been during the 1930s, both new and old institutions had to cope with skyrocketing prices, scarcities of supplies, and employees who left for better-paying jobs in shipyards and aircraft plants. The greater involvement in government programs — old age assistance, food rationing, licensing, old age and survivors insurance, withholding of income taxes from salaries and wages — created new problems in administration. Every mail produced fresh regulations to study, questionnaires to fill out, and letters to answer. Running an institution was no longer a simple matter of seeing that the old folks were housed, fed, and made comfortable. Matrons, nurses, and aides now found their off-duty hours filled with unaccustomed and unwelcome paper work.

Yet morale, on the whole, was high. A typical reaction was that of the secretary of the Twin City Linnea Home who, shortly after the United States entered the war, wrote: "No matter what happens tho along the war front, we must not forget or lose sight of our obligations to the old folks who are in our care . . . war has caused a rise in prices of everything we need and the [community] chests of both cities have cut their help to us drastically." She concluded confidently, however, that rising costs and budget cuts were "not going to dismay us, but push [us] on to greater efforts." By January, 1943, it was becoming a little harder to keep a stiff upper lip. "The war is closer to us than it was a year ago and even our folks in the Linnea Home feel the pinch a little, what with rationing of coffee and sugar. The shortage of meat sometimes puts the ingenuity of our cooks to the test."[11]

In less than three months meat also was rationed, along with most other foods in general use. Although wartime restrictions and controls of various kinds touched the lives of all Americans, the food rationing program especially affected the small but important fraction who lived or worked in homes for the aged. To understand the difficulties homes encountered, it is necessary to review some of the events of that trying period. Of the need for rationing, President Roosevelt in a message to Congress on April 27, 1942, said: "it is obviously fair that where there is not enough of any essential commodity to meet all civilian demands, those who can afford to pay more for the commodity should not be privileged over others who cannot. . . . where any important article becomes scarce, rationing is the democratic, equitable solution." Responsibility for the program was placed in the Office of Price Administration (OPA), which was authorized not only to ration scarce supplies but also to set price ceilings on nearly everything Americans ate, wore, and used. On the local level the program was administered by ration boards of volunteers.[12]

During the first two years of the war, the government established four food rationing programs: sugar (May 5, 1942); coffee (November 29, 1942); processed foods (March 1, 1943); and meat, edible fats and oils, canned fish, and cheese (March 29, 1943). To purchase rationed items the consumer had to surrender the required number of stamps from ration books, which were issued to every man, woman, and child in the country. Both sugar and coffee were distributed under a relatively simple unit system: each stamp represented a specific amount of the commodity, say a pound of sugar, and was redeemable during a fixed period of time. When it came to processed foods, with literally "hundreds of different products of an almost unlimited number of sizes, grades, and types of containers," it was obvious that the unit method would not work. The Office of Price Administration therefore devised a system under which a "point value" was assigned to each grocery store item, and the consumer was allowed a specified number of points to "spend" on whatever products he chose during a given period. Meat and cooking fats were rationed in much the same way. Persons whose health required special diets could obtain extra points from their ration boards by submitting certificates from a physician.[13]

Institutional users, including the larger homes for the aged, received allotment or purchase certificates for processed foods which were issued every two months on the basis of previous usage, that is, the number of meals and the amounts consumed. When the processed foods program went into effect in 1943, the homes had already gained some experience under the coffee and sugar programs in the techniques of registering with their ration boards and reporting inventories, food consumption, and the names of suppliers. Except for receipted bills and records of meals served, however, few institutions kept the kind of detailed records needed in the processed foods program. A request from the Office of Price Administration for a report listing all foods used during December, 1942, therefore, caused considerable consternation. The difficulties of compliance are suggested by the minutes of the Women's Welfare League for December 4: "The secretary had received a communication requesting a record of the amount used [in the Home for Convalescents] during December, in pounds and gallons fo[r] 25 different foods. Also what is on hand at the close of business on December 31st. She felt extra help would have to be provided for this job as Miss [Marie] Hansen [the superintendent] already has her hands full." The board voted that the secretary "take on this extra clerical work on an hourly basis."[14]

Small nursing and boarding homes, which the OPA believed would have trouble operating under the bimonthly institutional allotment plan, were treated as large households, and the ration books of lodgers and patients were pooled to buy processed foods. Many patients, however, came to the homes without books or had already used up some of the most important stamps. Others refused to allow home administrators to deduct their coupons. Many small facilities with inadequate medical supervision found it inconvenient to obtain physicians' orders for the foods needed in special diets. To alleviate these difficulties, the OPA later classified many rest homes as institutional users rather than as households.[15]

In the minds of some administrators, the complexities and added work of the food rationing programs were secondary to the problems encountered in obtaining competent help. In a 1943 report the superintendent of the Augustana Home in Minneapolis commented on the "large turnover of staff during the year. This we have had in common with many institutions. It was impossible to find replacement at the same salaries. Our payroll had to be increased." By the year's end employment had eased and most of the staff positions were again filled. The superintendent expressed her gratitude to "those who remained in service, willing to carry the extra load. To our women from the Church, who came and helped with cooking, canning, etc. . . . when help was scarce, we are indebted much."[16]

The personnel problem was further complicated in 1943 by the inauguration of federal income tax withholding, which required employers to make deductions from salaries and wages. This not only meant added clerical work, but also caused some discord in homes where employees did not at first understand that the action was taken by federal order.[17]

One happy result of all these problems was increased communication among home administrators. With the exception of a few fraternal and church homes under national organizations, not many superintendents outside the larger cities had an opportunity to discuss their work with people in the same field. In Minneapolis the administrators of a few homes had been meeting informally since 1938 to discuss administrative problems. They were "interested in knowing 'how to get along with old people' and in the problems of employing labor and marketing for an institution."[18]

Several events now occurred to bring the superintendents of rural as well as urban Minnesota homes together. The state health department, for example, called a meeting of administrators of homes for the aged on January 13, 1944, to discuss the proposed revision of licensing standards. As various participants outlined their problems in meeting certain requirements, those present had an opportunity to become better acquainted with each other. In 1946 representatives of benevolent homes throughout the state were invited to a conference at the newly opened Walker Methodist Home in Minneapolis, where they began to explore the possibility of establishing an association. The superintendents of institutions located in the Twin Cities area later formed a local organization which became the nucleus of a state-wide association in 1951.[19]

In May, 1943, an institute at the University of Minnesota Center for Continuation Study introduced the home administrators to an educational facility which was to become extremely important to them. The idea for the three-day course originated with William A. O'Brien, director of postgraduate medical education at the university. Although the gathering was held on only ten days' notice during a particularly trying year, the large attendance showed the need for a conference of this kind. The faculty, drawn largely from the medical school, lectured chiefly on diseases; the one session devoted to administrative problems, however, provoked a lively discussion.[20]

In 1949 the institute was revived on an annual basis under the cosponsorship of the state health department and the division of social welfare. That year representatives from key institutions served on the planning committee, and the three-day program focused on the special problems and interests of benevolent homes. By coincidence the Evangelical Lutheran Church scheduled a conference in Minneapolis at the same time, and administrators of the church's homes for the aged from as far away as California and Washington attended the institute. Many of the Lutheran administrators and others from outside Minnesota were to return again and again. Over the years the institutes were noteworthy not only for the large out-of-state delegations they attracted but also for the new concepts and speakers of national prominence they introduced.[21]

At the 1949 institute, for example, an architect lectured on "Points to Consider in Building a New Home." He described the future home for the aged in terms of the person who was to live in it, rather than as an imposing edifice designed to impress the public. At the time, many sponsors were planning additions, replacements, and new institutions. The then revolutionary concept of a one-story building with grade-level entrances was debated vigorously during luncheons and coffee recesses, and the lecture set the pattern for many new homes in Minnesota and nearby states.

At the 1949 annual institute, too, Dr. Frank H. Krusen, who was then on the staff of the University of Minnesota's Mayo Foundation, discussed the use of physical medicine in geriatrics. The effectiveness of rehabilitation techniques for wounded soldiers had been well demonstrated during World War II, but the idea of employing these methods in the care of elderly handicapped persons was quite new. Less than two years earlier, when Minneapolis entertained the convention of the American Congress of Physical Medicine, two Pittsburgh physicians — Drs. Murray B. Ferderber and Gerald P. Hammill — had stirred great interest with their report of an experiment, the first of its kind, conducted at the Allegheny County Home in Pennsylvania. They reported that in a program begun only a year before, "old men and women inactive for years have been helped to resume normal activities." Life for the elderly, the doctors said, "need not be living death — IF modern rehabilitation techniques are used to change 'despair and helplessness' into 'optimism and self dignity.'" A writer for the *Minneapolis Tribune* predicted that the report might "set off a shake-up in America's old-age homes."[22]

In 1949 when Dr. Krusen described the use of heat, massage, exercise, and other types of treatment which could be carried out in an old people's home, many superintendents learned for the first time that something could be done to improve the physical condition of their arthritic and other disabled patients. Keenly interested, they were eager to use the new techniques in their homes. To do so, however, required the co-operation of physicians, and at that time there were many gaps in the medical supervision of most homes.

A study made by the state health department in 1944 showed that the preadmission examination of applicants for homes for the aged was frequently regarded more as a screening measure to rule out undesirable applicants than as a positive health measure for planning the regime of the individual. Sometimes the applicant's physician, who perhaps lived in a distant town or state, failed to transmit pertinent information to the home. Even when he sent instructions, the management did not always relay them to the staff members who were in closest contact with the resident. Because of a long waiting list, the entrance examination was sometimes given months or even years before the person was actually admitted. By that time a disability might have developed which the institution did not know about. The amount of medical attention after admission also varied widely. A few institutions employed staff physicians who routinely saw all residents. The majority, however, arranged for examinations only when the individual was obviously ill or requested medical attention. By then the disability was usually less amenable to treatment. While it would be some years before these gaps in medical services were closed and institutions obtained trained therapists and other personnel, the administrators' interest in rehabilitation was aroused at this institute — an important step forward.[23]

Advances in patient care and new architectural designs for buildings were not the only topics presented in the university courses. Recent studies in nutrition, fresh approaches to recreation, and new insights into the care of the mentally ill were also discussed. To the superintendents of many homes for the aged, the appearance of a mental aberration in a previously well-balanced resident was a perplexing problem. Most homes were inclined to keep the disturbed person as long as possible, even though his care became a considerable burden. In addition to their personal attachment to the patient, board members and managers were reluctant to ask for the removal of a resident who had been accepted for life care. Many believed, too, that the mentally ill person was better off in familiar surroundings than he would be in a state institution, which at that time was generally considered only as a last resort. Superintendents were therefore eager for any suggestions which might help them provide better care for mentally ill patients.[24]

The registrants also welcomed the opportunity to discuss with government supervisors the relatively new old age assistance program. As this resource came into greater use, life-care plans in benevolent homes were losing favor. In its 1944 study the state health department had noted a distinct trend toward abolishing the lump-sum method of payment. Although many homes still sheltered persons who had entered under life contracts, most of them no longer accepted applicants on this basis. Persons who paid lump-sum fees occasionally felt that they were not receiving all the services to which they were entitled. Others preferred the independence of old age assistance grants, which under state regulations could not be paid to occupants receiving lifetime care.[25]

As institutions examined their financial arrangements more closely, they began to question not only life payments but also the adequacy of monthly charges for board. "A large number of residents now receive Old Age Assistance," the Ebenezer Home reported in 1944; "a few pay for themselves or are being paid for by relatives. But in only a few cases is enough paid to cover expenses of care and keep." Almost all benevolent homes kept records of expenditures and knew what their costs were in a general way, but not many calculated their expense per resident per day or attempted to relate this figure to the rates they charged. Because of the lack of uniform accounting procedures, cost statistics varied greatly from institution to institution. For example, some included such items as the value of contributed food while others did not. Ascertaining the costs of various types of care was still very much in the future. An exception was the Walker Methodist Home in Minneapolis which inaugurated a flat monthly rate with special charges for specified additional services based on the time involved and other factors. Fluctuating institutional populations and difficulties in determining staff time expended for personal services made such figures troublesome to compile. Yet until the homes could produce uniform cost data, it would be hard to convince legislatures that the rates allowed for the care of old age assistance recipients did not cover expenses.[26]

Sponsoring organizations planning new homes were also interested in operating expenses. Before they plunged into fund-raising campaigns, they wanted to know what to expect in the way of income and how to budget for salaries, food, utilities, and other costs. It was no longer feasible to start a home on a sudden impulse, and sponsors spent years assembling information, visiting other institutions, setting up committees, holding mass meetings, conferring with architects, lawyers, prospective donors, government authorities, and representatives of financial institutions, and attending to a thousand and one other details. Once established, nonprofit homes showed remarkable stability. Of the seventy-two benevolent homes opened in Minnesota between 1867 and 1950, only four had closed their doors. Approximately two-thirds of those in operation were church-related.[27]

While the sponsors of both existing and prospective institutions set their sights in the 1940s on new buildings designed expressly for the aged, rising construction costs and other factors would keep them from proceeding immediately. For a time buildings erected for other purposes would continue to furnish the structures for new proprietary and nonprofit homes alike. As the 1940s ended, homes for the aged — both public and private — still offered primarily boarding care for people in relatively good health when they entered, with infirmary care for those who became incapacitated after admission. Succeeding years would revolutionize not only the homes themselves but also the types of care they offered.

14

Progress in the Fifties

1950—1960

FROM 1849, WHEN MINNESOTA TERRITORY WAS ESTABLISHED, to the mid-twentieth century, care of the aged had developed in the two roughly parallel but distinct channels we have been tracing in this volume — the public segment from the county poor farm to social security, and the private nonprofit sector with its varied homes of philanthropic sponsorship. In the 1950s these two streams began to merge as the federal government assumed greater responsibility in the field. Through its old age assistance and insurance programs the Social Security Administration had encountered some problems of retired workers which were not related to income and had also become "deeply concerned with the implications for the total economy of a large nonproductive population."[1] Moreover, mounting interest in health, social adjustment, and other phases of aging inevitably led to requests for a facility through which groups around the country could become acquainted with the programs being conducted.

As a result, in August, 1950, the first National Conference on Aging was held in Washington, D.C. Sponsored by the Federal Security Agency at the request of President Harry S Truman, the meeting was attended by more than 800 people from all parts of the country. "The Conference was called," wrote Oscar R. Ewing, federal security administrator, "because the American people are growing up, in the most literal sense. The average age level is rising steadily, and the proportion of older people is increasing with equal constancy." In the past fifty years, Ewing pointed out, the number of old people had quadrupled, while the total population had only doubled. It had become necessary to find ways "of keeping people young as they grow old — not young in years but young in the sense that we associate energy, usefulness, and creativity with youth." The conference proposed to "focus attention on the problem and the needs," to explore ways of meeting them, and to "stimulate community action that would work a change in our whole pattern of behavior toward our older neighbors and friends."[2]

Housing for the aged was one of the many topics considered. It is significant that, in the discussion of congregate care facilities, the county poor farm was conspicuous by its absence. The old county home was of scant interest to this essentially forward-looking body. Those attending wanted new knowledge, fresh ideas, and guidelines for action which they could carry back to their respective communities. The old poor farm had no place in future plans for the country's aged.

The benevolent home, on the contrary, was still deemed a valuable resource, provided it was closely related to the community's social program and met the needs of its residents. These, it was pointed out, were the same as the needs of a family unit — good health, affection, emotional security, education, spiritual development, social contacts, and opportunities for self-direction and expression in work and creative activity. And because even a good home for the aged might not be the answer to every person's problem, the institution should be prepared to offer counseling and referral services which would help the applicant make his decision.[8]

The National Conference on Aging was followed in Minnesota by commissions which further explored the subject at the state level. The new Minnesota Commission on Aging was created by the legislature in 1951 to study the aging "with respect to their social and economic welfare, rehabilitation, health, recreation and family relationships, and to recommend methods of effectively meeting the problems of aging in a constructive manner." It was composed of five senators, five representatives, and ten persons drawn from fields closely concerned with older persons. Four committees were set up, which included numerous specialists and various interested lay persons. Teman Thompson, state representative from the First District, was the chairman of the commission, which was renewed by executive order in 1953. (Its activities are carried on by the present Minnesota Governor's Citizens Council on Aging.)[4]

Although only about 5 per cent of people sixty-five years of age and over lived in congregate facilities, the commission considered this group an important one. "The problem of sheltered care for older persons," its report stated, "will be with the State of Minnesota for a long time and will involve major expenditures." To facilitate the orderly development of such a program, the commission recommended "long-term planning based upon studies of the areas to be covered by existing or new institutions"; consideration of the "most effective size, the best locations, and the most desirable plan of administration; and studies of the methods of improving educational and social facilities in institutions."[5]

In 1950 Minnesota's public and private benevolent homes stood on the threshold of a new and exciting era. So numerous and varied were developments in the following ten years that they cannot be discussed in detail. Progress was made along the fronts suggested by both the national conference and the state commissions. The decade saw the adoption of a state-wide plan for the location of nursing home beds and a marked expansion in the number of new facilities. In the area of services, perhaps the most striking developments were the accent on medical rehabilitation and the emphasis on the individual, with his varied and changing needs. As the decade closed, diversified living arrangements and new programs were on the horizon, designed to assure the aged person the specific service he needed, at the time he needed it.

A long-range plan for locating new institutions was prepared by the state health department as part of its administration of the Hill-Burton hospital construction law, which was amended in 1954 to extend financial aid for building nursing homes. The Minnesota plan designated the number of hospital and nursing home beds that were needed for each region of the state, and classified beds in existing institutions for the purpose of planning construction under the law.[6]

During the early 1950s, however, the location of new facilities was governed more by the presence in the community of an interested sponsor and an available building than by a formal state plan. The postwar years were not favorable for new construction. Materials were still scarce, and it was often necessary to accept inferior substitutes, some of them very shoddy. As building costs soared, sponsors were forced to revise previous cost estimates and to seek additional funds. In many communities the effort to provide a much-needed modern hospital precluded any drive to raise funds to build a completely new home for elderly and long-term patients. Thus most public and private sponsors opened homes in remodeled buildings.

Emphasis in the 1950s was placed on institutions which could provide nursing care. The number of persons over seventy-five continued to increase at a faster rate than did the younger aged. This trend meant that more aged persons who were chronically ill or disabled were likely to require institutionalization. Several other developments helped to emphasize the importance of planning a new facility so that it could be used wholly or in part for the care of the sick. Under a 1951 law all Minnesota homes offering personal and custodial care as well as nursing care were required to be licensed. The following year institutions were classified by the state health department as either boarding care homes or nursing homes. Although the 1953 legislature began to allow some extra payments for old age assistance recipients in boarding care homes (and subsequent legislatures increased the amount), the maximum was always considerably lower than the top rate allowed for care in a licensed nursing home. A nursing home, therefore, not only was permitted to accept bedfast or other ill or disabled persons but also was entitled to a higher rate for an old age assistance recipient who needed such care. For these reasons the sponsors of virtually all new public and private nonprofit institutions planned their facilities to meet licensing requirements for the nursing home classification.[7]

One obvious source of structures for public homes, as mentioned earlier, was the small county tuberculosis sanatorium. Already owned by one or more counties, these buildings were either fire-resistive or substantial enough to warrant the installation of sprinkler systems. Their use would bring the county back into institutional care of the aged in a way quite different from the old poor farm. It was intended that the new facilities should be operated as nursing homes. The 1949 legislature had already enacted a law permitting the sale or lease of sanatoriums no longer needed for the treatment of tuberculosis, and further legislation in 1951 enabled the counties to establish nursing homes. Financing was solved, in part, by the 1950 amendment to the Social Security Act which permitted old age assistance payments to persons in public institutions.[8]

The way was now open for the conversion of the former tuberculosis sanatoriums into nursing facilities for the elderly. Built some thirty-five years earlier, the sanatoriums had been designed to allow for a method of treatment which consisted largely of rest, good food, and fresh air. Some features, such as the long sun porches on which patients received their daily "airings," would require substantial remodeling to convert them to bedrooms. On the whole, however, the structures were superior to most of the county homes then in use, and they already contained some facilities for nursing care. Moreover, they were not associated in the public mind with poor farms and were readily accepted by both patients and public. Community groups took an active part in supplying furnishings and recreation programs. The first Minnesota sanatorium to be converted under the county nursing home law was Sand Beach at Lake Park, owned jointly by Clay and Becker counties. In July, 1951, this facility was opened as the Sunnyside Rest Home. During the 1950s eight more sanatoriums were converted.[9]

A few substantial existing county homes were also available for use as public nursing facilities. These structures were enlarged and remodeled, and some which had been leased were returned to the county for operation. Following renovations and improvements in services, these homes too were usually so well accepted that expansion soon became necessary. In Chisago County, for example, the county reassumed the operation of the old leased poor farm near North Branch in 1954. Renamed Green Acres Nursing Home, the enlarged building and two substantial additions erected in 1956 and 1959 still did not provide sufficient space to meet the demand.[10]

Dodge and Koochiching counties, which had also leased their poor farms, resumed control after the county nursing home law went into effect. Five other counties — Itasca, Redwood, St. Louis, Steele, and Washington — which were still operating poor farms converted them to nursing homes. In 1954 the Pioneer Nursing Home at Baudette became the responsibility of the Lake of the Woods County board, and in 1959 the Kittson War Veterans Memorial Hospital at Hallock became a county nursing home.[11]

A notable exception to the usual practice of conversion and remodeling was the modern forty-bed facility which Traverse County completed at Wheaton in January, 1959. Officials decided to construct a new building after making an extensive survey that included visits to sixty homes in three states. "When the study was completed," commented Ray Johnson, the county auditor, "it was apparent that no conversion of present facilities would be accepted. New construction of top quality was recommended." The slogan "They helped us, now it's our turn," was adopted as the theme of an educational campaign designed to assure the voters' support for the necessary bond issue. The entire county then united to sponsor furnishings and entertainment for the home.[12]

A unique plan was carried out in St. Louis County, where there had been for many years a heavy load of nursing cases. After an intensive study of needs, the board of commissioners decided to provide buildings but to turn operations over to a hospital or some other nonprofit group. The first facility to be completed was the Pioneers' Infirmary at Virginia. It was physically connected to that city's municipal hospital but was operated by the Range Hospital Corporation, a nonprofit group which later conducted the Mesabi Home in nearby Buhl. Following the opening of the infirmary in September, 1950, twenty patients were transferred to it from the Cook and Arlington buildings of the St. Louis County home. In 1951 the county constructed a second infirmary which was operated by St. Luke's Hospital in Duluth, and that fall eighty-five patients were transferred from the county home to the new facility. Later in the decade a third infirmary unit was attached to St. Mary's Hospital in Duluth and operated by it.[13]

Despite the provision of 372 additional beds, it became necessary for St. Louis County to reopen the closed infirmary departments in both the Cook and Arlington buildings. The county did not stop there, however, but began a three-year program to improve the county home's entire physical plant, which had deteriorated badly during World War II. In the dining room colorful china and new tables seating four persons replaced the plank benches, picnic tables, and battered tin dishes of the old poor farm. The institutional grays and browns also disappeared as recreation rooms and other areas were redecorated in pleasant pastel colors.[14]

It was not expected that county governments would carry all or even a major portion of the load. Benevolent institutions, or nonprofit homes, as they were now called, were caring for more and more recipients of old age assistance. Moreover, old age and survivors insurance as well as a growing number of private retirement plans gave promise of more assured sources of future income for nonprofit institutions and proprietary homes.

Little change occurred in the types of owners responsible for the establishment of nonprofit homes during the 1950s. Approximately three-fourths of the forty-nine new homes started in the 1950s were operated by, or were closely related to, church organizations. While surveys and long-range planning now received more emphasis, the decision to locate an institution at a particular place or time was often, as it had been in earliest days, the result of a gift of land or money, the need of an individual for a home, or the availability of a building which could be used for the purpose. An early settler at Hills left property and funds to a church with the request that it start a home for the aged in the small community where he had lived for more than seventy-eight years. The Tuff Memorial Home was the result. The large mansion of Paul Watkins, a wealthy manufacturer in Winona, was donated after his death for conversion into a home for the elderly. A Catholic priest who needed a home for his mother and noted that there were other homeless old people in the community purchased on behalf of the parish two adjacent apartment houses and appealed to the women of Staples to contribute their services in caring for their aged friends and neighbors in the Mary Rondorf Home. (The facility was later staffed by the Sisters of St. Benedict.) And in Polk County a registered nurse, faced with the problem of caring for a mentally confused mother, prevailed upon the community of Erskine to establish the Pioneer Memorial Home for so-called senile patients.[15]

By far the most usual precipitating factor, however, was the availability of a building no longer used for its previous purpose. With relatively few exceptions, these structures were hospitals which had been replaced by new buildings under the stimulus of the Hill-Burton Act. Nineteen of the new homes of this decade were opened in hospital buildings. These varied considerably in the amount of renovation and remodeling needed to provide the dayrooms, dining rooms, extra toilets, and other facilities for long-term bedfast and ambulatory older persons. They shared many of the same defects to be found in existing older homes for the aged. In 1953 the Minnesota Commission on Aging noted that "many traditional institutions and homes for congregate care are poorly planned and constructed for their particular purposes. They have high ceilings, endless corridors, many stories, many staircases, and dining rooms and bathrooms in remote or inconvenient places."[16]

As the advantages of new buildings designed for special purposes became apparent, sponsors were becoming less satisfied with the old plants. For the hospital construction program the United States Public Health Service had prepared model plans incorporating wide halls, grade-level entrances, bedrooms arranged to facilitate nursing care, utility rooms, nurses' stations, large and small dayrooms, areas for occupational and physical therapy, administrative units, and a host of other features that would make the work easier for the staff and the environment more pleasant for patients. The University of Minnesota's School of Architecture also devoted considerable time to institutional pilot studies and exhibits. The efforts of individual architects in Minnesota and adjoining states as well as the state health department's plan-reviewing conferences with sponsors were helpful in influencing organizations to aim at new construction rather than the conversion of old buildings. Every newly completed institution became an object of interest, visited by prospective sponsors from all over the state.[17]

But such modern facilities were expensive to build, and questions about how to finance the ever-greater need for beds loomed large. In January, 1955, the Minnesota Commission on Aging stated that even though government and nonprofit agencies and private enterprise extended themselves "to the limit" the need for nursing homes would not be met for many years: "So far we have not even managed to 'bail out the boat,' so to speak, in keeping up with the increasing demands for beds." The commission recommended that municipalities, counties, and nonprofit associations be given state assistance in the construction of nursing homes and drafted a bill to this effect which was submitted to the legislature on January 17, 1957. The principles of the program were endorsed by a majority of the counties and their welfare boards, the state medical association, and numerous citizens' groups. The proposed legislation was opposed by the proprietary homes, whose owners urged that private enterprise first be allowed to try to meet the need. Although the bill failed to pass, it pointed up the shortage of beds and spurred benevolent groups and private individuals to plan new homes. The promise of more favorable financing under the Federal Housing Act and the greater interest shown by conventional lending agencies were also helpful in starting communities on their way to building. These and other developments bore fruit late in the decade. Seven of the eight benevolent homes which opened in 1959 inaugurated their services in new buildings.[18]

The new facilities of the late 1950s were generally one-story structures planned initially for thirty to sixty-five residents, with future expansion in mind. Although they had separate infirmaries, most of them were designed so that every room could, if necessary, be used for nursing care. This was made possible by placing nurses' stations and other facilities in central locations. And no longer were the physically handicapped "involuntary prisoners in their rooms," for the new homes were designed to encourage patients' mobility.

How even a small institution could provide a full program of activities through the use of multipurpose areas is indicated in the following description of a typical home of the period. *"The resident's room* becomes his home," wrote the sponsor. *"The halls,* which will be 7½ feet wide, with dome lights in the ceiling, become the streets. There will be room enough to walk, and to sit down and visit; and to be taken in a wheel chair or a walker; yes, even in a bed to any place in the building. *The dining room* becomes the place for physical nourishment and fellowship — family style. As many residents as possible will come, or be brought, to the dining room. . . . *The living room area* will be a place of fellowship, games, programs, slides and films. But above all, by opening a folding door to the Altar and arranging the chairs, the living room becomes *the chapel.* . . . Then . . . there is the *multi-purpose room* for hobbies and crafts, for family gatherings and for many other activities. In the future this could even serve as a physical therapy room. *The lounge room* in each wing will provide a smaller gathering place for more privacy and withdrawal from the larger group." The basement had space for bowling lanes, shuffleboard courts, and a shop.[19]

Public and nonprofit agencies did not have a monopoly on new facilities. Proprietary owners, eager to show what private enterprise could do, intensified their efforts to put up buildings. One favorable influence was the loan program of the Small Business Administration. Created by Congress in 1953 to advise and assist the nation's small business enterprises, this agency offered two types of financing — participation loans made jointly with banks or other private lending institutions, and direct loans made by the agency alone. Privately owned nursing homes were eligible to receive small business loans, and between June, 1957, and May, 1959, $715,500 was approved for such projects in Minnesota.[20]

Progress during the 1950s was not concentrated solely on construction. The problems of administration were also considered. The diversity of services which homes for the aged were now called upon to render and the increasing complexity of their operation had made their administration not only a full-time job, but also a highly specialized one, for which — unfortunately — there were few formal training opportunities. At the annual institutes held in the University of Minnesota Center for Continuation Study, the administrators of nonprofit homes discussed such topics as staff organization, cost accounting, building maintenance, public relations, and liaison with governing boards. Recognizing the "advantages of a close alliance" with state and local health and welfare agencies as well as the need for a forum to discuss mutual problems, benevolent home managers in 1951 organized the Minnesota Association of Administrators of Homes for the Aged. In 1958 the organization's name was changed to the Minnesota Association of Geriatric Homes.[21]

The superintendents of county nursing homes were members of the benevolent home association, but they also belonged to a group which met periodically with the state welfare department. In 1953 the new Department of Public Welfare, created by consolidating the divisions of social welfare and public institutions, took over from the health department the licensing of county nursing homes.[22]

Proprietary homes also had an active organization, the Minnesota Association of Nursing Homes, which was the outgrowth of a Twin Cities group started in 1943.[23] Although the organization was open to all types of sponsors, most of its members represented proprietary homes. Generally speaking, the latter were smaller (though more numerous) than the public and nonprofit institutions, and their administration was thus less complex. While they had their own special management and financing problems, they were not usually concerned with board and committee relationships, fund-raising activities, or the formulation of elaborate admission policies and procedures.

All types of owners shared certain problems, however, and one of the most urgent at this time was the increasing number of residents who — because of accidents, extreme age, or disabling illnesses such as arthritis and strokes — were unable to care for themselves. The large number of handicapped old people to be found in homes was dramatically revealed in the findings of a 1954 study conducted by the Commission on Chronic Illness, an independent, national agency sponsored by four groups — the American Hospital Association, the American Medical Association, the American Public

Health Association, and the American Public Welfare Association. In its Minnesota survey, the commission found that nearly half the patients in proprietary, public, and nonprofit nursing facilities were totally or partially confined to bed. About one-sixth of the 3,706 persons in residental homes for the aged were also found to be limited in their ability to move around freely.[24]

As we have seen, the concept of helping residents to become more self-sufficient was not new, but in the 1950s there were promising developments not only in Minnesota but elsewhere in the United States. In 1953 the Minnesota Commission on Aging observed that "rehabilitated older persons can assume responsibility for their own care and possibly become productive again." Interest in providing the needed therapies was keen, and the decade became strongly oriented toward rehabilitation. The department of public welfare employed an occupational therapist who advised both public and private homes on setting up such programs. The nursing rehabilitation consultant of the state health department conducted classes throughout the state for the purpose of demonstrating simple equipment and techniques to nursing home personnel. Physicians, hospital staffs, public health nurses, and others joined in the movement to release incapacitated old people from what a newspaper reporter a few short years earlier had termed a "living death."[25]

One of the first institutions to start a comprehensive rehabilitation program was Oak Ridge, a proprietary nursing home in Minneapolis operated by Mr. and Mrs. H. Stanley Wessin. The home opened in a converted Jewish parochial school in November, 1951, "with a cook, a nurse, and 90 empty beds." To fill those beds, Mrs. Wessin, a registered nurse, knew she would have to rely on service rather than on deluxe accommodations. The large classrooms could not be made into desirable single or even double rooms. "We have fairly large wards," Mrs. Wessin explained later. "We prefer to spend what money we have on rehabilitation services rather than on private rooms." The owners decided to admit only patients whose physicians gave specific orders for rehabilitative treatment. A realistic goal was set for each patient, which might vary from reduced nursing care to complete independence. Goals were reevaluated at frequent intervals. The original staff of a cook and a nurse was expanded to include physical and occupational therapists and other specialists, additional registered nurses, licensed practical nurses, and nurses aides, all of whom participated in the rehabilitation program through a team approach. This was made possible through classes and demonstrations, conferences on individual patients, and progress reports to all personnel involved in the care of a particular patient.[26]

The national conference of 1950 had called for a "change in our whole pattern of behavior" toward the elderly, and compared to earlier decades a remarkable shift in attitudes was indeed perceptible among administrators of Minnesota's public and private facilities. Care was becoming far more personal, directed toward supplying specific needs, relieving anxieties, and sustaining the self-respect of old people as individuals.

Mrs. Hendry, the Ramsey County matron who in 1900 had stressed the importance of strict regulations, would doubtless have been startled by the views of a colleague in the 1950s. "Human beings at any age, condition, or place do not like regimentation," declared May Morrow, supervisor of St. Louis County's Arlington Home. "We have helped somewhat by not dressing them alike." The home purchased bright, flowered fabrics and had smocks made up in a variety of styles for its old ladies.[27]

In the benevolent homes, too, there was a greater effort to individualize care. Recognizing that group living usually required a radical change in habits and attitudes among persons whose age made them particularly inflexible, administrators took various measures to make the adjustment as easy as possible. As the social service director of a Minnesota institution pointed out in 1955, the residents of a home for the aged are a captive audience. Most would have preferred to live in their own homes, and many entered the institution with a great deal of trepidation. The director suggested the need for more information about the applicant. "We ought to be able to make some kind of appraisal about his strengths and weaknesses in our task of helping him make the best possible adjustment. What do we know of his background, his family life, his vocational and avocational interests — is he a dependent person leaning on others or just the opposite — the kind of person who wants to do things for himself — disdaining help."[28]

Under some circumstances, the speaker pointed out, the administrator or social worker does not see the new resident until he arrives, ready to stay. "So here then is Mr. or Mrs. B. He has come himself or has been 'delivered' so to speak, on our threshold. His baggage is in the hallway and we can think of those few or many suit cases as representing to him all that he has salvaged from his previous life." A few tactful comments on the difficulty of choosing what to bring and what to discard would help establish rapport. The resident's response might also provide information on his interests which could be useful later in helping to meet his recreational needs.

The interest in leisuretime activities which had been generated in the 1940s carried over into the 1950s. Benevolent homes had always attempted to give their people care, comfort, affection, the opportunity to participate in religious services, and as many pleasures as they could. The residents felt cherished, and for some this was probably enough. But a speaker reminded participants in a conference on the aging: "What a person lives by is not only a sense of belonging but also a sense of indebtedness. . . . Getting older must not be taken to mean a process of suspending the requirements and commitments under which a person lives."[29]

How might a home for the aged help its residents fulfill a meaningful role in society? "The most satisfying activity," wrote Morton Leeds, "is built around the individual needs of the residents and is tied to the reality of everyday living." Leeds suggested that helping himself or his institution develops in the resident a sense of purpose and belonging that can replace, in part, his former role in society.[30]

The satisfactions of participating in the operation of an institution were discovered by residents of the St. Francis Home for the Aged in Breckenridge. In response to a suggestion by Sister Mary Laurice, the administrator, that better communication should be established between management and residents, the latter organized the Busy Bee Club, complete with constitution, officers, and a weekly newsletter, *The Latest Buzz*. Through very active committees, club members performed such services as welcoming new residents. With the proceeds of various club-sponsored entertainments, the members not only made substantial contributions to the home's building fund but also purchased for their common enjoyment slide and movie projectors, a coffee urn, a popcorn popper, a television set, and other articles. A suggestion box in the lounge proved an effective channel of communication between the staff and the residents and led to such innovations as a garden "of their own" and a pancake breakfast served by the Busy Bees.[31]

The residents' activities were not confined to the institution. As Sister Mary Laurice pointed out to a group of administrators, "Each of our Homes is located in a community. We can help the community if we but try, and the community will help us if we but let it." It would be difficult to say who tried harder — the 320 volunteers, who in one capacity or another served St. Francis, or the 132 residents of the home. They collected and packed boxes of clothing for the poor, including a family with eleven children who were the victims of a fire. Moved by the plight of many Indian children, they sponsored a boy and a girl in a local boarding school. They displayed their handiwork and the vegetables which they had raised at the county fair, and they took part in local talent and fashion shows. The residents also had their own weekly program over a local radio station, with a master of ceremonies who, except for the power of speech, was totally helpless. The program not only kept the public informed of the home's plans and doings, but also gave the residents an opportunity to recognize publicly the volunteers who had helped them. A thirty-minute telecast depicting activities in the home turned out to be an effective public relations tool not only for the institution but for the aged living elsewhere. One result was to stimulate interest in the program to train college students in recreational therapy for senior citizens.

Older people vary in their responses to an activities program, as the Itasca County Nursing Home near Grand Rapids learned in the mid-1950s. During the early days of this former poor farm in northern Minnesota, the men fished, worked the land, and walked to town to peddle their produce. By 1950 the home's population had changed, and the older, more infirm residents found little to do with their time. When Mrs. Alice J. Colter became superintendent in the early 1950s, she decided to introduce a program of crafts. She soon found that state and county officials were more enthusiastic than the residents. "It's a devastating time for old folks when, through illness or financial reverses, they find they have to go into a home," Mrs. Colter explained. "They are depressed and unhappy, and developing new interests is, understandably, difficult." Gradually the residents participated, and in 1957 the Blandin Foundation furnished funds to erect a separate recreational pavilion. Coffee proved to be the lure which drew the reluctant to the new facility. When they saw what others were doing, they too wanted to try their hands. Soon the home's occupants were happily weaving rugs, stuffing toys, and producing good, salable articles of metal and leather.[32]

By 1959 an expanding program made it necessary to enlarge the pavilion. At the dedication ceremonies, Governor Orville L. Freeman stressed the value of a program which would make the residents feel that they still had a "place in the sun." The elderly, he said, need "an opportunity to participate in activities which will show them that they are integrated into the community's life."[33]

This concept of the home for the aged as "an integrated element in a total community institutional and service complex" emerged in the 1950s. Many years before, the Minneapolis Council of Social Agencies had deprecated the fact that the services of a home for the aged were isolated from other community services. This was no longer true. Of the many forces which made Minnesota nonprofit institutions more aware of developments outside their own four walls, perhaps the most potent were the activities which preceded a second national conference on aging, held in January, 1961.[34]

Authorized by Congress in August, 1958, the White House Conference on Aging was held under the direction of the Department of Health, Education, and Welfare. Minnesota's fifty-two-member delegation included thirty-six persons appointed by Governor Freeman, nine representatives of national voluntary organizations, and seven consultants who had served in various capacities in preparing for the meeting. More important than the conference itself, however, were the preparatory activities, which in Minnesota extended over two and a half years and mobilized an unprecedented number of individuals, voluntary groups, and government agencies concerned with the problems of the aged. Congress made limited funds available to underwrite the work of state planning committees. Minnesota received the maximum appropriation of $15,000, but, as Arnold M. Rose, chairman of the state committee, pointed out: "If the monetary value of all the volunteer work and contributions in kind were counted, Minnesota's preparations . . . would have cost at least ten times the $15,000." Unmeasurable in dollars, of course, was the gain in understanding and interest on the part of thousands of people who participated in the surveys, institutes, demonstrations, and other projects. During the course of the planning activities, administrators and board members of homes for the aged rubbed shoulders with health department personnel, social workers, educators, recreation leaders, and others serving in programs for older persons. In the process they became more aware of the help to be obtained from community agencies and the contributions which their institutions could make. The Walker Methodist Home, for example, extended counseling and physical therapy services to older people in the community and invited them to participate in recreational events.[35]

As the homes examined their role in the community, they began to consider the possibility of offering even more varied accommodations. By mid-century it had become apparent that, as never before, elderly citizens had the means to make a choice in their living arrangements. Greater national prosperity coupled with the increasing number of people covered by the old age and survivors insurance features of the social security program meant a larger group of older persons who possessed an assured, though often inadequate, source of monthly income. The increased emphasis on the individual and his needs had also made people aware that the elderly could not be considered as a single, homogeneous group. Rather the aged population was composed of individuals "of different circumstances, preferences and backgrounds." A study carried out in greater Minneapolis by the Community Health and Welfare Council of Hennepin County observed succinctly: "It may be that no two 'senior citizens' have common circumstances except the fact of reaching age 65 — and even the fact of attaining age 65 is merely a chronological measurement with no direct relation to the unique needs of individuals."[36]

By the close of the 1950s the traditional home for the aged was still providing accommodations and services for persons who wanted companionship and a place to stay and infirmary sections for those who became ill or incapacitated. The sponsors of existing and prospective homes now began to talk about — and some to plan — more complex and costly types of facilities. Great interest was shown in the Wilder Residences of St. Paul, which were then being designed to embody the idea of locating a variety of services on one "campus." This multifunction institution included kitchenette apartments, a boarding home, and an infirmary in separate buildings, all available to the residents according to their changing needs. The elderly inhabitants could participate in the program of activities and also find within easy walking distance churches, a store, a bank, a motion picture theater, and a branch public library.[37]

During the early 1960s the construction of apartment buildings in conjunction with nursing homes became a reality for a number of institutions scattered throughout the state. Some were operated in connection with hospitals. The Bethesda Hospital Association of Crookston, for example, maintained a large nursing home as well as the Woodland Apartments for the elderly. Each apartment consisted of a bedroom, a bath, and a living room with kitchenette.

The kitchen unit was intended chiefly for preparing coffee, since residents took their three principal meals in a central dining room. "Woodland is a new building designed and constructed to meet the needs of today's older people," the sponsor said when the home opened in 1962. "It offers its residents independence, security, safety, comfort, convenience and care."[38]

Other institutions, such as the Gloria Dei Home connected with the Emmaus Lutheran Home in Litchfield, gave residents a choice in the number of meals they prepared for themselves. They were all expected to eat (or at least to pay for) the noon dinner in the home dining room but could elect to cook breakfasts and suppers in their kitchenette apartments.[39]

The Teachers Home, Inc., in Minneapolis also considered independence coupled with security important. "There is privacy when you wish it and above all, there is a feeling of security," said a brochure describing the home. Unlike most apartment accommodations for the elderly, the Teachers Home was largely planned and financed by the group from which it drew its future occupants. Like the traditional homes for the aged, however, the institution was governed by a board of directors, and applications and health certificates were required for admission. The idea for the home was originated about 1955 by active and retired teachers; membership was later extended to retired persons of other professions. Funds for the building were raised through loans, residential participation warrants (entrance fees), and donations, including a $50,000 legacy from the estate of Elizabeth L. Hall, former assistant superintendent of the Minneapolis public schools. The 109 units included efficiency and one- and two-bedroom apartments with living rooms, kitchenettes, and baths. From the beginning a small infirmary was available for residents who became ill, and several years later a dining room was opened on a limited basis.[40]

While planning went forward to expand the functions of homes for the aged, other proposals were made for services which would enable the older person to live in his own home. It was estimated that 95 per cent of the aged did not live in institutions. The situation of many of them, however, left much to be desired. What was happening to these elderly people became a matter of special concern to the Governor's Citizens Council on Aging, the county committees on aging who worked with the council, and many religious, social, health, recreational, and educational agencies on both state and local levels.[41]

To aid the feeble and disabled, various community organizations explored the possibility of initiating — if they did not already have them — housekeeping programs, visiting nurse services, classes for handicapped homemakers, loan closets which could be called upon for unusual or very expensive equipment, and the extension of hospital care into the homes of discharged patients.

To meet recreational needs, churches, libraries, service clubs, and social work agencies, as well as the county committees, provided services to ward off loneliness and enrich the lives of old people in their own homes. Activities included day centers, hobby shows, adult education classes, deliveries of library books, and various volunteer visiting programs. Car pools were often set up to furnish transportation for the infirm who could not otherwise participate in such activities. Many of these services were also extended to residents in homes for the aged. Those institutions, in turn, offered more varied programs to meet the changing needs of their residents.

The 1950s saw a new recognition of the importance of the aged citizen as an individual and as a participating and contributing member of the community according to his ability. No longer was the private institution for the aged or the county nursing home completely isolated from the surrounding community. Bridges of communication in the form of organized programs were being established, and both nonprofit and governmental homes for the aged took long strides toward becoming truly community-oriented service institutions during this decade.

15

Changes and Challenges

1850—1960s

THIS BOOK HAS ATTEMPTED TO CHART the development of public and private nonprofit homes for the aged in Minnesota over more than a century. Of the factors which created the need for "homes for the homeless" during the period from the 1850s through the 1950s, the most insistent was the lengthening life span — the sheer increase in both the number and the proportion of the aged among the American people. Other powerful influences were the changing patterns of culture in the United States: the shift from rural to urban living which saw the large farmhouse give way to the city dwelling without space for three generations of the family, the rise of an activist, youth-centered society which had little disposition to take on the burden of an enfeebled and difficult parent, the loss of income and increasing unemployment of older persons in times of economic depression and rapidly changing technology, and the evolvement of a challenging new philosophy which demanded a secure old age and led to the passage of such measures as social security and, later, medicare.[1]

While these trends affected both the public and the private sectors of aged care, the century witnessed varied responses to the changing needs. By 1960 the public almshouse or poor farm was a thing of the past, a rarely mentioned relic of a bygone era. It had been replaced in the United States by a relatively small number of publicly owned nursing homes which were divorced from un-

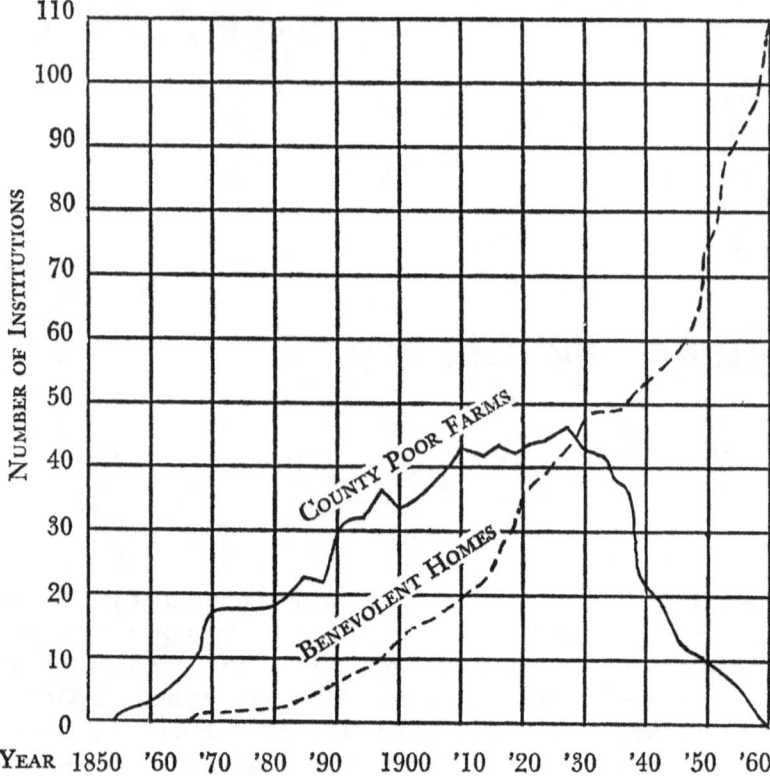

Numbers *of county poor farms and benevolent homes in Minnesota.*

pleasant associations with public relief. The private nonprofit institution, on the other hand, was in 1960 an accepted resource in a growing constellation of services for the aged. Of the 449 licensed nursing and boarding care homes in Minnesota, 117 were nonprofit facilities, while only 29 were operated by public agencies of the state, county, or municipality. Another 303 institutions in Minnesota were proprietary homes, profit-making facilities which had risen to prominence after the advent of social security.[2]

Why had the poor farm all but disappeared, while the home founded by a philanthropic organization not only had survived but was expanding? Even a cursory review of the early histories of these institutions will suggest some answers. Others can be found in the relative responsiveness of the two types of facilities to the changing needs and challenges of society.

As we have seen, the county poor farm in Minnesota was older than the state, and for many years was the chief resource of the dependent aged. From 1854 to 1926, when the last farm was acquired, fifty-five counties opened poorhouses. The peak was reached in 1910. In that year forty-four such institutions were in operation, and the number remained near this level for the next twenty years.[8]

One reason for the unpopularity and eventual demise of the poor farm was undoubtedly its connection with a poor relief system, brought to Minnesota from England via the eastern seaboard and the Northwest Territory, which put the stigma of pauper on every old person who became an inmate. Another was the inadequacy of the structures themselves. The records offer ample evidence that the poorhouse of the early days was generally crowded, unsanitary, and lacking in privacy or comfort. Even the new ones built during the first two decades of the twentieth century soon began to resemble those they had replaced, as the buildings deteriorated and were filled far beyond their intended capacities. In addition, as we have seen, overseers were hired on the basis of their farming experience and ability to save the county money, rather than for their competence and fitness to care for their ill-assorted charges. Perhaps, as Theodore Dwight had observed as early as 1869, the whole management of poorhouses was too "purely official."

The most frequent criticism of the poor farm, however, was that it herded together all ages and conditions of people. Because officials were required by law to aid all the needy in their counties, they could not be selective in their admission policies, and poor farms became human dumping grounds. Although dependent children, needy war veterans, mentally ill, deficient, blind, deaf, and other handicapped persons were gradually siphoned off to specialized state institutions, the impoverished but respectable aged in poorhouses were thrown into close daily contact with vagrants, misfits, incompetents, and "members of the drinking class."

From the beginning, Minnesota poorhouses cared for the dependent sick and disabled. On occasion it was suggested that they be turned into county hospitals, but their small size, their rural locations, and the extension of community and physician-owned hospitals into all areas of the state made this move unfeasible. A few large institutions had infirmaries, but by and large county homes were miserable places for the sick.

As the aged population continued to increase, the elderly found it harder to obtain employment. "Attention was first drawn to our older people on a recognizable scale during the 1920's and early

'30s," said a speaker at the 1950 National Conference on Aging, "when a few States discovered that families and private charity were unable to guarantee financial security to those who could no longer find a place in the industrial economy and to the survivors of older workers who had died." For many elderly persons, the only solutions were public relief or the poorhouse.[4]

Then began the search for security, first in the form of state pensions. But under the permissive laws of most states, relatively few counties adopted such plans. In 1933 the Minnesota legislature replaced the state's optional plan with a compulsory law "so that elderly persons may not be thrown upon the scrap heap of society."[5] Bankrupt counties, however, continued to give relief rather than pensions. In 1935 social security became a reality, bringing immediate assistance for the needy aged and the hope of future retirement income for workers and their dependents.

The old age assistance program, which got under way at once, had an immediate impact on county homes. Its prohibition of grants to persons in public institutions resulted in the closing of fifteen Minnesota poor farms between 1935 and 1950, and the leasing of sixteen others for private operation.[6] During the 1950s, a new version of the public facility — the county nursing home — came into being, and the poorhouse slipped out of the picture.

It is possible that larger institutions, more enlightened administration, and improved services could have saved the poor farm, but it was cast in too rigid a mold. Any real upgrading would have required drastic changes in the poor laws, a complete break with a tradition older than the nation, and more generous support from the taxpaying public. Even the extensive public and private investigations of the 1920s did not result in poorhouse reform. The revelation of its appalling conditions merely helped to further the movement for state pensions and a federal program of social security. The goal of social reformers became financial security for the aged; the only security which the poor farm could offer was the finality of "over the hill" to the end of the road. In a sense, the poor farm was the instrument of its own demise.

In Minnesota benevolent homes started later and developed more slowly than poor farms; not until 1928 did they equal the latter in number. Their progress was stable, however, and before 1960 rarely did one close.[7] The sponsors started their homes from a sense of moral duty — sometimes more compelling than the responsibility imposed by law. From the earliest years groups of philanthropic individuals were interested in helping the "friendless" — a term applied to homeless immigrants, young working girls, needy women, orphaned children, unmarried mothers, and old people who had no place to stay.

The early benevolent home for the aged was a form of charity, but to most of its residents private philanthropy was more palatable than public relief. Admission did not carry the stigma of pauperism which public opinion placed on inmates of the poor farm. Indeed, few benevolent home residents realized that their modest entrance fees did not cover the entire cost of care. In contrast to the squalor of poorhouses, the nonprofit homes on the whole were clean, comfortable, and well regulated, especially appealing to those who preferred decorum in their living arrangements and the security of life care. The assurance of a permanent home, often incorporated into the admission contracts, was in fact a real force in keeping many such institutions open. In addition, the members of the boards of directors took a personal interest in the residents; many, indeed, participated in managing the home.

A trend toward specialization was observable among benevolent homes after the turn of the century when facilities for the sole purpose of caring for the aged began to appear. The sponsors were largely church bodies, nationality groups, and fraternal societies desirous of taking care of their own people. Since some churches were set up along ethnic lines, a single home might be both national and church-related in character. The special importance of national origins in Minnesota is readily appreciated when it is recalled that as late as 1910 one-fourth of the state's population had been born outside the United States.[8] Many elderly people could read, write, and speak only their native language. They would be happier, it was believed, if they lived among persons with whom they could communicate easily, and who shared the same traditions and customs. Because of the heavy immigration from Norway, Sweden, and, to a lesser extent, Denmark — countries where homes for the aged were part of the culture — Minnesota has an especially large number of Scandinavian homes.

The population of the benevolent home was far more homogeneous than that of the poorhouse. Entrance requirements usually stipulated that the applicant be physically able, mentally sound, and of good moral character. The probationary period required by many institutions helped to sift out those who, in the opinion of the governing body, would not "fit into our home." Lump-sum entrance fees, though often waived, eliminated the truly impoverished. In church, ethnic, and fraternal homes, the policies which favored members of the sponsoring organization made for more congenial groups.

But it was their responsiveness to changing needs and conditions which made benevolent homes better able to survive than poorhouses. In their long history the nonprofit homes faced many challenges. Their resiliency and adaptability are well illustrated by their response to four major developments: (1) the unremitting pressure for more beds for the elderly; (2) the problem of caring for the growing number of sick aged; (3) the necessity of adjusting financial structures and practices to steadily increasing costs and new sources of income, notably social security in its various forms; and (4) the development of other services for the aged, which led the benevolent home to examine its role as a community agency.

In providing beds for homeless elderly persons, the philanthropic organizations had several advantages over county boards. For one thing, their potential for extension into new areas was much greater. There was nothing, for example, to prevent the establishment of more than one home in a single county, or even within a community. For another, in raising funds for a new institution, such sponsors as large church bodies, fraternal societies, or other multicounty or multistate groups, had a much broader base of support. A third advantage to the nonprofit group lay in its access to structures suitable for conversion. One cannot overlook the relationship between the establishment of a home for the aged and the discontinuance of an earlier institution or social service. Many a home was started to fill a void in an organization's program, or to make use of a building no longer needed for its original purpose. The physical plants of hospitals, orphanages, and boarding schools — often already owned by the sponsoring organization — were usually better adapted for group care than the farm dwellings in which practically all poorhouses began their existence. Moreover, after it was in operation every old people's home served as a demonstration of need, as evidenced by the long waiting lists. This fact, together with its assured position as a community asset, made it easier for philanthropic sponsors to finance necessary additions and replacements.

A second major adjustment which benevolent homes had to make was in the care of the sick. For many years it was the policy of most homes to accept only the well aged. They would, however, care for those who became ill or incapacitated after admission. The increasing number of the infirm required more facilities for care. Because of their generally larger size and greater ability to expand, the benevolent homes were able — as the poor farms were not — to set up separate nursing sections. From the late 1930s on, many of the new additions took the form of infirmary departments. Gradually the institutions amended their policies and accepted persons who needed care when they entered. In accordance with new concepts in rehabilitation the sponsors remodeled their buildings, provided additional services, and in many instances affiliated with hospitals.

Although a third major development — the passage of the Social Security Act — resulted in the closing or leasing of many Minnesota poorhouses, it had a totally different effect on the financial structures of private homes for the aged. Before the depression of the 1930s, benevolent homes generally had been able to meet operating expenses from life-care contracts, monthly boarding payments, endowments, allotments from parent organizations, aid from community funds, donations, bequests, and other gifts, including a considerable amount of contributed labor. They had been slow to raise their fees to keep pace with increasing costs, and in the mid-1930s they realized how thoroughly unrealistic their rates had become. Old age assistance represented a new source of income, but it also called for adjustments. Most institutions eventually abolished their contract plans and made other changes in admission policies in order to enable their residents to receive grants.

A fourth movement which had tremendous implications for homes for the aged was the development of other services for the elderly, including new types of facilities. The appearance of the proprietary home in the 1930s was of particular significance to both public and private nonprofit institutions. Although the proprietary rest home — or nursing home, as it came to be called — had existed for years, its growth was markedly accelerated by the Social Security Act of 1935. "So rapidly has the nursing home developed during the past 20 years," two observers noted in 1955, "that its history seems more like an eruption than an evolutionary development."[9] The proprietary home took much of the load from the poor farm. If such homes had not been available for the new recipients of old age assistance, it is doubtful whether some of the poorhouses could have been closed.

For the nonprofit home the emergence of the proprietary home, together with the development of public housing, apartment or residential hotels, foster homes, and boarding homes, led to a reappraisal of its own functions in the care of aged persons. As more of the elderly began to receive old age and survivors insurance and other forms of retirement income and as more kinds of living arrangements became available for them, they had a wider choice in selecting their dwelling places. It was not long before governing boards of homes for the aged noticed that applications were coming less frequently from the able-bodied than from the sick aged.[10]

In their efforts to meet these challenges, the nonprofit homes (which were better able than private enterprise to experiment with new construction and the use of community resources) began to plan for more varied accommodations and a wider range of programs within their institutions. New terms came into use. The "multifunction agency" or "complex," consisting of apartments, boarding care sections, nursing home units, and day centers made possible the "internal migration" of residents from one department to another in accordance with their changing needs. Under a "revolving-door policy" some older persons, after a period of rehabilitation therapy, might return to their own homes. Day care centers on the "campus" served extramural residents who came to the facility for recreation and other services designed to delay physical and mental deterioration. And, as people learned that the aged do not want to be isolated from society, the sponsors fostered programs that would keep their residents in the main stream of life.[11]

Even the names of institutions expressed the new philosophy. Those which opened in the late 1950s and early 1960s seldom incorporated "old people's home" or even "home for the aged" in their names. Instead, they designated their abodes as villas or manors (who wouldn't want to live in a manor house?), or, perhaps, simply as the Such and Such Residence, which, after all, is what most Americans call the dwelling they live in.

The 1960s have seen tremendous activity in all areas of importance to the aging, including their housing, education, income, health and medical services, recreation, and institutional care. Many of the programs can be traced to legislation enacted in 1965 by the Eighty-ninth Congress, which provided funds for medicare and dozens of programs for older Americans. Others — often joint state and federal efforts — were in operation before that landmark year. Most of them, however, were of recent development.[12]

Neither state nor federal governments had taken a leading role in providing for the country's older citizens in the nineteenth century. In early Minnesota, as we have seen, responsibility for the relief of the destitute, including the needy aged, was placed on county boards of commissioners. The state's concern was manifested in the establishment of specialized institutions for veterans and certain groups of unfortunates, and in the creation of boards to investigate the whole system of public charities. During the 1920s, when the United States labor department began its inquiry into provisions for retired workers, the Minnesota senate initiated the study which culminated in the passage of the short-lived state pension law. Then came social security and the realization that putting cash income into the hands of the elderly did not solve all their problems. The inadequacy of existing facilities for those who needed care soon became apparent. Standards were set, and institutions were licensed by the state. Additional old age assistance was allowed for licensed rest home care, and educational programs were started to aid both public and private homes in meeting the new requirements. Efforts were also made to stimulate the provision of more beds for those who could not live in their own homes.

After the passage of the Social Security Law, the federal government gradually became more active in the field of aged care. The first National Conference on Aging was held in 1950. It was followed in Minnesota by the creation of a commission to study the health, housing, recreation, employment, and welfare needs of the state's aging citizens, who were now recognizable as a large, special group. Programs for the elderly, both in and out of sheltered homes, were started in rehabilitation, recreation, nutrition, and other areas. In preparation for and following the White House Conference on Aging in 1961 the tempo quickened. It was further accelerated by federal legislation, including medicare, enacted in 1965. The speed with which events have moved since then was emphasized by Bernard E. Nash, who told a recent conference that "The future is this afternoon."[18]

In the face of this rapidly changing picture, it is impossible to predict definite trends; some current developments may serve, however, as straws in the wind. The multiplication of both public and private group-care facilities in unprecedented numbers is apparent from even a superficial reading of the accounts which appear in the daily press. Numerous nursing homes, retirement centers, apartments for the elderly, and many other forms of living arrangements are reported in the planning stages, under construction, or ready to hold dedication ceremonies. The statistics also tell the story: in Minnesota beds in licensed nursing and boarding care homes increased from 15,673 in 1960 to 26,928 in 1965 and to 34,362 in 1968.[14]

More emphasis than ever before is now being placed on hospital connections. Nursing and old people's homes not already associated with hospitals are developing co-operative relationships. Such an affiliation, the Minnesota health department observed, "allows closer medical supervision, more efficient use of existing personnel, a flexible mechanism for transfer of patients, and joint use of basic services." One of the most striking developments of the mid-1960s has been the marked increase in the number of nursing care and convalescent units in general hospitals. Hospital connections for nursing homes may become even more important in the future because of the medicare program. It provides benefits to cover the cost of short-term care in accredited nursing homes for patients who have been hospitalized and who still need skilled nursing and related services. It is difficult to foresee with any preciseness the long-range effects of medicare on homes for the aged, but if history is any guide, the provisions of the act are likely to be liberalized in the decades ahead.[15]

Another trend of the mid-1960s has been the spread of institutions throughout the state in a pattern quite different from that of the earlier rural poor farms. Almost every city, town, and village wants its own old people's home, either public or private. (The public institutions of this decade are likely to be nursing home units in municipal, county, or district hospitals.) Although to many older persons in our mobile society the kind of facility is more important than its location, many observers agree that the home for the aged is most satisfactory when it is situated within easy reach of the families and friends of its residents in a community which takes a personal interest in the facility and its occupants.

"The most encouraging trend in congregate living," wrote Ollie A. Randall in 1959, "is the recognition that the older person is a person, and has desires and yearnings that deserve attention and respect; that life in the home should allow as much gratification of these feelings as possible; and that the home should make the effort to fit its accommodations and services to the individual." Homes are attempting to provide more than a roof over the heads of their elderly occupants. The trend toward concern for the individual has already been noted. That it will become more marked in future years is apparent from the many studies now being conducted on the personal and social needs of residents of homes for the aged.[16]

At the 1962 Minnesota Governor's Conference on Aging, Governor Elmer L. Andersen charged the participants "to assist in defining the individual's role in planning for the aging." What is the older person's own responsibility, he asked, "to himself, for his community, for his state?" In establishing institutions for the aged many older persons sit on initiating committees and spearhead moves to provide homes for their contemporaries. That those who enter homes can help fellow residents was shown earlier. No longer are homes started informally as they were in the early years. Because sponsors must anticipate the future as well as the present needs and desires of those who will occupy the homes, the task is now more complex and difficult.[17]

At the 1950 national conference, participants agreed that the problems raised by the steady aging of the population could only be solved by many individuals and agencies, both public and private, but above all by the community on a local scale. "The community, the neighborhood, the home town — here lies the key to the problem," said Oscar Ewing. "Only in the home town can the final job be done. No national conference, no Federal agency, no transcontinental educational campaign can take the place of neighbors helping one another in their own community."[18]

In a sense, this was the way many of Minnesota's homes for the aged developed. "A time comes in the history of every enlightened community," the early local historian had written, "when some provision must be made for the aged and infirm poor, who have no means of support." From the time twelve women of the Evangelical churches of St. Paul met to consider the need for a "home for the homeless" and heeded the command to "Go Forward," groups of concerned men and women had banded together to provide homes for their neighbors. And while county boards often acquired poor farms as land investments or in the hope of saving the county money, they also opened homes for the "Safe Keeping of a Crazy Man," or because "the poor of the county must be provided for, their poverty is frequently their misfortune, without being their fault."

Minnesotans made provisions for their aged citizens and they adapted their institutions over the years to the challenges and needs of a changing society. The poor farm died — and no one laments its passing! — but in its place rose the county nursing home. The benevolent home became not only a resource for "other aged people in trouble," but also a refuge for elderly persons who chose it for themselves.[19]

What the future home for the aged will be like is not entirely clear. A student of geriatrics suggested in the mid-1960s that such institutions might elect "to serve the well aged or to go into low-cost housing as one aspect; to stress the care of the chronically ill, in affiliation with hospital services or, to become multipurpose centers which would serve the community as well as the institutionalized aged. These are the options, and only the future will tell which of them will become the dominant trend and solution."[20]

One thing is sure. Homes for the aged will not remain static. "The measure of our affection for our senior citizens," said Dr. Robert Morris at the 1961 White House Conference on Aging, "will be our readiness to change our agencies and our services to meet their expressed wants. In this conversion, the institutions for the aged will not be laggard."[21]

The future will bring many challenges: questions of expansion and types of service, the implications of the medicare program for the operation and financing of nonprofit homes, the present emphasis on catering to the resident's social wants as well as meeting his physical needs. All these will call for flexibility and imagination. Already some authorities are calling attention to the possibility of overbuilding in certain areas, and institutions in older, outmoded buildings are asking whether they should enlarge or improve their present physical plants or erect completely new facilities in different locations. Types of services, too, are receiving new scrutiny. How, for example, can the institutional apartment give the occupant a feeling of independence if it must also, for his own security, curtail some of his liberties? And in what ways can a hospital nursing home unit provide the homelike atmosphere which is so important to many long-term patients? These are only a few of the questions and problems facing institutional homes; they can perhaps best be solved through the sharing of collective experience.

The problems should not be insurmountable. The little band of women who founded Minnesota's first home for the friendless a hundred years ago were not dismayed by the magnitude of the undertaking, for behind them were the women of their churches. Behind today's homes are many public-spirited citizens, the men and women of churches, fraternal societies, and other organizations ready to give both moral and material support. And to guide them, today's homes have a rich heritage in the long line of able and devoted men and women who preceded them and who — when changing conditions required it — set their course in the new directions we have traced in these pages.

Appendix

TABLE 1. COUNTY POORHOUSES IN MINNESOTA

Opened	County	Comments
1854	Ramsey	Operated as county nursing home, 1967
1858	Washington	Converted to county nursing home, 1954
1864	Goodhue	Closed 1963
	Hennepin	Closed 1953
1866	Dakota	Leased 1947; closed 1952
	Rice	Closed 1953
1867	Blue Earth	Leased 1957; operated as boarding-lodging house, 1967
	Nicollet	Leased 1946; closed 1958
	Wabasha	Leased 1936; closed 1956
1868	Chisago	Leased 1938; converted to county nursing home, 1954
	Faribault	Farm only
	Fillmore	Closed 1943
	Le Sueur	Closed 1880
	Mower	Leased 1946; operated as boarding-lodging house until 1963; subsequently operated by State of Minnesota Sheriffs Association as home for boys
	Olmsted	Closed 1944
	Winona	Closed 1941
1869	Dodge	Leased 1938; converted to county nursing home, 1952
1870	Brown	Farm only. See 1903, below
	Carver	Closed 1877
	Freeborn No. 1	Closed 1875. See 1889, below
1873	St. Louis	Operated as county nursing home, 1967
1878	Houston	Leased 1944; operated as boarding-lodging house, 1967
1879	Murray	Farm only. See 1896, below
1880	Steele	Operated as county nursing home, 1967

OPENED	COUNTY	COMMENTS
1881	Otter Tail	Closed 1938
	Rock	Leased for farm operation some time prior to 1936; reopened and leased to Good Samaritan Society 1950; closed 1963
1882	Todd	Closed 1885
1883	Becker	Leased 1936; closed 1940
	Chippewa	Closed 1927
	Lyon	Closed 1936
	Marshall	Farm only
	Martin	Farm only. See 1915, below
	Swift	Farm only
1884	Redwood	Farm only. See 1889, 1909, below
1887	Cottonwood	Closed 1903
	Morrison	Closed 1889
1888	Crow Wing	Closed 1913
	Yellow Medicine	Closed 1936
1889	Freeborn No. 2	Leased 1947; sold to Good Samaritan Society, 1953
	Lac qui Parle	Leased some time in 1950s; operated as boarding-lodging house, 1967
	Redwood No. 1	Closed 1899. See 1909, below
	Scott	In 1938 transferred to Sisters of St. Francis who continued to care for county's indigent
1890	Pipestone	Closed 1944
1891	Renville	Closed 1899
1895	Big Stone	Farm only
1896	Itasca	Converted to county nursing home, 1957
	Murray	Closed 1944
	Stevens	Closed 1911
1898	Anoka	Closed 1936
1901	Beltrami	From 1909 to 1919 the Beltrami County poorhouse was operated by the city of Bemidji; the county leased it for private operation in 1936, and closed it in 1951
1903	Brown	Leased 1938; closed 1965
1904	Aitkin	Closed 1936
1906	Hubbard	Leased 1937; closed 1955
1907	Kandiyohi	Closed 1913
	Pine	Leased 1937; operated as licensed boarding-care home, 1967
1908	Koochiching	Leased 1942; converted to county nursing home, 1956. Closed 1963 when new home was built at International Falls
1909	Redwood No. 2	Operated as county nursing home, 1967
	Wilkin	Closed 1929
	Wright	Closed 1942

Opened	County	Comments
1910	Kittson	Closed 1937
	Mille Lacs	Leased 1936; closed 1949
1913	Lake	Closed 1939
1915	Martin	Closed 1937
1918	Traverse	Prior to 1918 Traverse County acquired a farm and in 1920 made the dwellings available to indigent persons but did not operate a county poorhouse
1919	Beltrami	Reopened. See 1901, above
1926	Norman	Leased 1937; closed 1943

This table was compiled from the sources cited in this book and from county files in McClure Papers.

TABLE 2. POPULATION 65 YEARS OF AGE AND OVER
1870–1960

	United States			Minnesota		
		65 Years and Over			65 Years and Over	
Year	Total	No.	%	Total	No.	%
1870	38,558,371	1,153,649	3.0	439,706	8,309	1.9
1880	50,155,783	1,723,459	3.4	780,773	19,190	2.5
1890	62,654,302	2,417,681	3.9	1,301,826	41,569	3.2
1900	76,212,168	3,083,939	4.0	1,751,394	66,771	3.8
1910	92,228,531	3,953,945	4.3	2,075,708	86,057	4.1
1920	106,021,568	4,939,737	4.7	2,387,125	110,766	4.7
1930	123,202,660	6,644,378	5.4	2,563,953	163,480	6.4
1940	132,165,129	9,036,329	6.8	2,792,300	212,618	7.7
1950	151,325,798	12,294,698	8.1	2,982,483	269,130	9.0
1960	179,323,175	16,559,580	9.2	3,413,864	354,351	10.3

Tables 2 and 3 were compiled from statistics in the following volumes of the *United States Census*: 1940, *Population*, vol. 2, part 1, p. 26; part 4, p. 21; 1960, *Population*, vol. 1, part 25, p. 49, and vol. 1, part 1, p. 153. The 1870 and 1880 statistics are from the 1940 volume; those for 1890–1960 are from the 1960 volume.

TABLE 3. GROWTH RATES OF TWO GROUPS OF
MINNESOTA'S AGED 1870–1960

YEAR	65 Years–74 Years		75 Years and Over	
	Number	Percentage of total 65 years and over	Number	Percentage of total 65 years and over
1870	6,407	77.1	1,902	22.9
1880	14,047	73.2	5,143	26.8
1890	31,136	74.9	10,433	25.1
1900	47,675	71.4	19,096	28.6
1910	58,361	67.8	27,696	32.2
1920	76,015	68.6	34,751	31.4
1930	117,335	71.8	46,145	28.2
1940	143,090	67.3	69,528	32.7
1950	178,893	66.5	90,237	33.5
1960	233,401	65.9	120,950	34.1

Reference Notes

CHAPTER I — MINNESOTA'S FIRST POORHOUSES 1849–1864

¹ J. A. Kiester, *The History of Faribault County*, 265 (Minneapolis, 1896). Portions of this chapter were previously published as "An Unlamented Era: County Poor Farms in Minnesota," in *Minnesota History*, 38: 365–377 (December, 1963).
² William Anderson and Bryce E. Lehman, *An Outline of County Government in Minnesota*, 24, 69 (Bureau for Research in Government, University of Minnesota, *Publications*, no. 7 — Minneapolis, 1927); Josephine C. Brown, *Public Relief, 1929–1939*, 3–5 (New York, 1940). See also George A. Lundberg, "Poor Relief Legislation in Minnesota," in *Summaries of Ph.D. Theses, University of Minnesota*, 1: 318–321 (Minneapolis, 1939). The author was unable to locate a copy of this thesis.
³ Alexander Johnson, *The Almshouse*, 151 (New York, 1911); for the quotations, see Robert W. Kelso, *The History of Public Poor Relief in Massachusetts*, 25 (Boston and New York, 1922).
⁴ Kelso, *Poor Relief in Massachusetts*, 27; Grace A. Brown, *The Development of Poor Relief Legislation in Kansas*, vii (Chicago, 1935).
⁵ Kelso, *Poor Relief in Massachusetts*, 29, 33, 92 (quote), 121.
⁶ Kelso, *Poor Relief in Massachusetts*, 93. See also Kirk H. Porter, *County and Township Government in the United States*, 28 (New York, 1922).
⁷ Homer Folks, *The Care of Destitute, Neglected, and Delinquent Children*, 3 (New York, 1902). Folks also mentioned a fifth method — indenture — especially applicable to children, but used also for adults. Early in the nineteenth century the law in several states provided that "idle or vagrant persons might be indentured to respectable citizens for a period of one year."
⁸ Kelso, *Poor Relief in Massachusetts*, 103–106.
⁹ Kelso, *Poor Relief in Massachusetts*, 107.
¹⁰ Kelso, *Poor Relief in Massachusetts*, 111.
¹¹ Kelso, *Poor Relief in Massachusetts*, 113. The term "almshouse," used in New England and some eastern states, was adopted by the United States Census Bureau in 1880. In the Middle West, where farming was important, the institution was usually referred to as a poor farm, although the terms poor farm and poorhouse were employed almost interchangeably. In England the institution was known as the workhouse.
¹² Kelso, *Poor Relief in Massachusetts*, 118, 121, 122, 124, 127, 138–141. On Dorothea Dix, see Grace Abbott, *From Relief to Social Security: The Develop-*

REFERENCE NOTES — CHAPTER 1 249

ment of the New Public Welfare Services and Their Administration, 13–17 (Chicago, 1941). The practice of reimbursing towns for the relief of persons without legal settlement began in 1675 during King Philip's War, when settlers sought refuge in the towns, particularly Boston. The law was never repealed, and in time there developed a class of dependents known as the "Province poor," later termed "State paupers."

[13] Folks, *Care of Children*, 3, 35, 36, 37 (quotes), 42.

[14] Folks, *Care of Children*, 38; New York Senate Select Committee on Charitable Institutions, *Report No. 8*, 2 (New York, 1857).

[15] Thomas R. Hazard, *Report on the Poor and Insane in Rhode-Island*, 87 (quote), 90 (Providence, 1851). An analysis of statistical tables in the report shows that 109 of 395 inmates in the 15 poorhouses were 60 years of age or over.

[16] Brown, *Public Relief*, 5. The poor laws of the Northwest Territory are discussed in Sophonisba P. Breckinridge, *The Illinois Poor Law and Its Administration*, 9, 10 (quote), 13 (Chicago, 1939). For the text of the 1795 law, see Theodore C. Pease, ed., *The Laws of the Northwest Territory, 1788–1800*, 216–232 *(Illinois Historical Collections*, vol. 17 — Springfield, 1925). The quoted provision relating to workhouses is on p. 217.

[17] In addition to the histories of poor relief already cited, see Aileen E. Kennedy, *The Ohio Poor Law and Its Administration*, 32–36 (Chicago, 1934); Alice Shaffer and Mary W. Keefer, *The Indiana Poor Law*, 17–21, 34–37 (Chicago, 1936); Isabel C. Bruce and Edith Eickhoff, *The Michigan Poor Law*, 12–14 (quote), (Chicago, 1936); and for Wisconsin, John L. Gillin, *History of Poor Relief Legislation in Iowa*, 39–43 (Iowa City, 1914).

[18] On the poorhouse as a catchall, see Kennedy, *Ohio Poor Law*, 36, 37 (quote).

[19] On the establishment of Minnesota Territory, see Theodore C. Blegen, *Minnesota: A History of the State*, 160–163 (Minneapolis, 1963). For the Organic Act, see Minnesota Territory, *Laws*, 1849, p. xxx–xxxvii.

[20] *Laws*, 1849, p. 128–130.

[21] *Laws*, 1849, p. 130. The expenditure of funds for the construction of workhouses was authorized by an act which permitted county boards to provide "at the common expense of the county . . . all . . . necessary buildings, for the use of the county." *Laws*, 1849, p. 114.

[22] George E. Warner and Charles M. Foote, eds., *History of Ramsey County and the City of St. Paul*, 117 (Minneapolis, 1881).

[23] *Laws*, 1849, p. 7–9, 51–55.

[24] Warner and Foote, eds., *Ramsey County*, 177, 204. The elected board took office in January, 1850, replacing two appointive commissioners, Ard Godfrey of St. Anthony and Louis Robert of St. Paul, who had been chosen by Governor Alexander Ramsey in November, 1849.

[25] Warren Upham and Rose B. Dunlap, comps., *Minnesota Biographies, 1655–1912*, 174 *(Minnesota Historical Collections*, vol. 14 — St. Paul, 1912); Thomas M. Newson, *Pen Pictures of St. Paul, Minnesota, and Biographical Sketches of Old Settlers*, 174 (quote), (St. Paul, 1886).

[26] Upham and Dunlap, *Minnesota Biographies*, 252, 646; Warner and Foote, eds., *Ramsey County*, 204, 598 (quote); Newson, *Pen Pictures*, 143.

[27] Ramsey County Board of Commissioners, "Proceedings," January 9, 10, 11 (for Goodhue's appointment), 26, April 1, 1850. The Minnesota Historical Society has transcripts of county board proceedings filed in the Works Projects Administration Papers. Except where otherwise noted, references to county board activities cited throughout this book may be found in the society's WPA transcripts file. All references to the Minnesota Historical Society are hereafter abbreviated as MHS.

[28] Ramsey County Commissioners, "Proceedings," April 1, July 15, 1850. For the commissioners' "marks," see "Proceedings," November 5, 1850.

[20] Newson, *Pen Pictures*, 464.

[30] Ramsey County Commissioners, "Proceedings," December 23, 30, 1854. On Bennett's appointment, see Warner and Foote, eds., *Ramsey County*, 204.

[31] Ramsey County Commissioners, "Proceedings," January 16, 1855. For items of expenditure, see *St. Paul Daily Pioneer*, April 16, 17, 1855. On St. Joseph's Hospital, see Helen Angela Hurley, *On Good Ground: The Story of the Sisters of St. Joseph in St. Paul*, 77 (Minneapolis, 1951). Unless otherwise noted, newspapers cited throughout this book are in the collections of the MHS.

[32] *St. Paul Daily Pioneer and Democrat*, March 31, 1856. The letter of complaint was said to have appeared in the *St. Paul Daily Free Press* of March 22, 1856; this issue is missing from the MHS files.

[33] On the handling of insane patients, see *Goodhue Volunteer* (Red Wing), January 13, 1864; *Saint Paul Daily Minnesotian*, January 17, 1859. On the "Maniac Hospital," see Ramsey County Commissioners, "Proceedings," February 1, 1856.

[34] Ramsey County Commissioners, "Proceedings," February 6, 13, 1858.

[35] Ramsey County Commissioners, "Proceedings," March 17, 1857; *Daily Pioneer and Democrat*, June 25, August 27 (quote), 1858.

[36] George E. Warner and Charles M. Foote, eds., *History of Washington County and the St. Croix Valley*, 334, 490 (Minneapolis, 1881); Washington County Board of Supervisors, "Proceedings," June 10, 1859, in the office of the county auditor, Washington County Courthouse, Stillwater. On Proctor, below, see James T. Dunn, "The Minnesota State Prison during the Stillwater Era, 1853–1914," in *Minnesota History*, 37:142 (December, 1960).

[37] Washington County Supervisors, "Proceedings," September 13, 1859; Washington County Board of Commissioners, "Proceedings," June 8, 1860; interview of the author with Mr. and Mrs. Walter Schmidt, Stillwater, June 11, 1966. The cabin was demolished in 1925.

[38] Warner and Foote, eds., *History of Washington County*, 491; Alfred T. Andreas, *An Illustrated Historical Atlas of the State of Minnesota*, 230 (Chicago, 1874); Washington County Supervisors, "Proceedings," January 11, 1860; interview with Mr. and Mrs. Schmidt, June 11, 1966.

[39] J. Fletcher Williams, *A History of the City of Saint Paul and of the County of Ramsey, Minnesota*, 380 (Minnesota Historical Collections, vol. 4 — St. Paul, 1876).

[40] *Laws*, 1858, p. 191, 193, 204. See also William W. Folwell, *A History of Minnesota*, 2:64n (Reprint edition, St. Paul, 1961).

[41] John P. Owens, "Political History of Minnesota," 479, a manuscript in the MHS; Upham and Dunlap, *Minnesota Biographies*, 572.

[42] Ramsey County Supervisors, "Proceedings," June 17, 1858.

[43] *Laws*, 1858, p. 207 (quote); *History of Goodhue County*, 273 (Red Wing, 1878).

[44] *Daily Pioneer and Democrat*, August 26, 1858.

[45] *Daily Pioneer and Democrat*, July 8, 1858.

[46] Ramsey County Supervisors, "Proceedings," August 21, 1858; *Daily Pioneer and Democrat*, August 26, 1858.

[47] Ramsey County Supervisors, "Proceedings," August 14, 21, 1858.

[48] Ramsey County Supervisors, "Proceedings," August 21, October 2, 1858.

[49] *Daily Pioneer and Democrat*, January 8, February 8, 1859.

[50] Ramsey County Supervisors, "Proceedings," February 8, June 4, 1859; *Weekly Minnesotian*, March 5, 1859.

[51] *Weekly Minnesotian*, May 17, 1859; *Daily Pioneer and Democrat*, August 20, 1859 (quote).

[52] Owens, "Political History of Minnesota," 540, 541 (quote); *Laws*, 1860, p. 114.

[53] Warner and Foote, eds., *Ramsey County*, 131; Lowry Nelson, Charles E. Ram-

sey, and Jacob Toews, *A Century of Population Growth in Minnesota*, 30, 35 (University of Minnesota, Agricultural Experiment Station, *Bulletins*, no. 423 — n.p., 1954).
⁵⁴ *Laws*, 1861, p. 276.

CHAPTER 2 — COUNTY POOR FARMS 1864–1880

¹ *Laws*, 1864, p. 48–53, especially sections 1, 4, 7, 9, 10, 11. For the old law, see *Laws*, 1849, p. 130.
² *Laws*, 1864, p. 58; Warner and Foote, eds., *Ramsey County*, 155 (quote).
³ St. Louis County Board of Commissioners, "Proceedings," April 12, September 12, 1864.
⁴ A list of counties and the dates of their establishment can be found in any edition of the *Minnesota Legislative Manual*. For accounts of early experiences in the southern counties, see *History of the Minnesota Valley* (Minneapolis, 1882). For a complete list of Minnesota poor farms and the dates of their establishment, see Appendix, Table 1, below. Files for all counties mentioned in this book may be found in the Ethel McClure Papers, MHS.
⁵ See, for example, Kiester, *Faribault County*, 266.
⁶ *Goodhue Volunteer*, January 13, 1864; *Goodhue County Republican* (Red Wing), January 15, 1864; *History of Goodhue County*, 241, 260; Joseph W. Hancock, *Goodhue County, Minnesota, Past and Present*, 159 (Red Wing, 1893).
⁷ *Volunteer*, quoted in *Republican*, February 5, 1864.
⁸ *History of Goodhue County*, 274; *Republican*, March 19, 1866, April 12, 1867, March 20, 1868. For the quotation on the inmates, see W. H. Mitchell, *Past and Present of Goodhue County*, 82 (Minneapolis, 1869).
⁹ John H. Stevens, *Personal Recollections of Minnesota and Its People and Early History of Minneapolis*, 184 (Minneapolis, 1890); *State Atlas* (Minneapolis), May 4, 1864 (quotes).
¹⁰ *State Atlas*, March 30, April 20, 1864.
¹¹ *State Atlas*, April 27, July 13, 1864; *St. Anthony Falls Democrat*, December 31, 1869 (quote). The date of opening is given in a report submitted by the Hennepin County poorhouse to the State Board of Health, as part of a survey conducted by the board in 1946 for the Commission on Hospital Care. The report is in the files of the Minnesota Department of Health, Minneapolis.
¹² See also Blegen, *Minnesota*, 287; Folwell, *Minnesota*, 2:344.
¹³ *Hastings Conserver*, July 17, 1866.
¹⁴ *Hastings Union*, September 14, 1870 (quote). Bills for medical care are reported in the *Hastings Gazette*, January 18, 1868; *Dakota County Union* (Hastings), January 15, 1868, January 12, 1869.
¹⁵ *History of the Minnesota Valley*, 642.
¹⁶ Mrs. Tyler's story is in Thomas Hughes, *Old Traverse des Sioux*, 133 (St. Peter, Minn., 1929). "Rob, the Pauper," can be found in Will Carleton, *Farm Legends*, 40–50 (New York, 1875).
¹⁷ *Saint Peter Tribune*, March 27, 1867 (quote); William G. Gresham, ed., *History of Nicollet and Le Sueur Counties, Minnesota: Their People, Industries and Institutions*, 1:91 (Indianapolis, 1916).
¹⁸ See also *Mantorville Express*, June 11, September 10, 1869.
¹⁹ *History of the Minnesota Valley*, 520; *Le Sueur Courier*, January 22, March 25, 1868.
²⁰ Olmsted County Board of Commissioners, "Proceedings," March 12, 1868; Joseph A. Leonard, *History of Olmsted County*, 101 (Chicago, 1910).
²¹ For the purchase and description of the farm, see Thomas Hughes, *A History of Blue Earth County*, 164 (Chicago, [1909?]). On other actions of the board,

see *Mankato Weekly Record,* November 30, 1867; *Garden City Herald,* January 22, 1868.

²² *Preston Republican,* May 17, 1867; January 17, June 5, 26, 1868. See also Andreas, *Illustrated Historical Atlas,* 250; *History of Fillmore County,* 290 (Minneapolis, 1882).

²³ See also *Valley Herald,* March 19, 1869, for the proceedings of the Carver County Board, March 2, 1869.

²⁴ Wabasha County Board of Commissioners, "Proceedings," January 3, March 14, 1867 (quote), September 3, 1872 (quote), March 4, 1873; Franklyn Curtiss-Wedge, *History of Wabasha County,* 45 (Winona, Minn., 1920).

²⁵ Andreas, *Illustrated Historical Atlas,* 239; *History of Freeborn County,* 418 (Minneapolis, 1882); *Evening Tribune* (Albert Lea), June 7, 1957, p. 16.

²⁶ Kiester, *Faribault County,* 265; Faribault County file, McClure Papers.

²⁷ Brown County Board of Commissioners, "Proceedings," March 11, 1868, March 9, 10, 1869.

²⁸ On Carleton, see A. Elwood Corning, *Will Carleton, A Biographical Study,* 10, 38 (New York, 1917).

²⁹ Corning, *Will Carleton,* 39.

³⁰ *United States Census,* 1870, *Population,* 181. In August, 1869, the board approved bills for "stove, Etc." and "two mattrasses," as well as a payment of $9.00 for food for hospital patients and a salary item of $63.75 to cover the services of an overseer and his assistant. See *Duluth Weekly Minnesotian,* August 14, 28, 1869. On expenditures for outdoor relief, see St. Louis County Commissioners, "Proceedings," for 1871 and 1872.

³¹ St. Louis County Commissioners, "Proceedings," January 23, February 1, 1873. For the bills, see especially "Proceedings" for June 28, July 26, August 28, September 25, 1872.

³² St. Louis County Commissioners, "Proceedings," February 11, 1873; *Duluth Minnesotian,* August 23, 1873.

³³ St. Louis County Commissioners, "Proceedings," August 16 (quote), 23, 1873.

³⁴ Olmsted County Commissioners, "Proceedings," April 23, 1868; Wabasha County Commissioners, "Proceedings," March 3, 1873.

³⁵ Warner and Foote, eds., *Washington County,* 334; *Saint Paul Daily Press,* January 23, 1872.

³⁶ *Blue Earth City Post,* March 21, 1874. On the removal order and the reaction to it, described below, see Kiester, *Faribault County,* 375.

³⁷ See Warner and Foote, eds., *Ramsey County,* 158–160, for state-wide disasters of 1871–77. For Brown County, see Board of Commissioners, "Proceedings," September 7, 1871 (quote), January 30, March 14, 1872; *History of the Minnesota Valley,* 699.

³⁸ Brown County Commissioners, "Proceedings," March 18, September 8, 1874; June 14, 1875.

³⁹ Minnesota State Board of Corrections and Charities, *Biennial Reports,* 1887–88, p. 186. On the Township Act of 1858, see p. 15, above.

⁴⁰ Between 1875 and 1891 the change to the town plan required a special enactment of the state legislature, followed in some instances by ratification of the voters. In 1889 the legislature passed a general law permitting a county to change from one system to the other at the option of its voters. Since then, the number of counties under each system has varied from time to time, although a majority has usually elected the county system. See Anderson and Lehman, *County Government in Minnesota,* 69–74; William Anderson, *Local Government and Finance in Minnesota,* 266–269 (Minneapolis, 1935); *Laws,* 1889, p. 279–284; Board of Corrections and Charities, *Biennial Reports,* 1887–88, p. 187–189.

⁴¹ The special laws did not repeal section 4 of the 1864 law, which made it mandatory for every county to provide a poorhouse or a suitable substitute.

REFERENCE NOTES – CHAPTER 3   253

⁴² Freeborn County obtained its law in 1875 and closed the poorhouse; Carver County obtained its law in 1877, closed the poorhouse, and sold the farm in 1878; Le Sueur County obtained its law in 1881 and sold the farm to Michael Sheehy, who thereafter boarded county paupers. See, respectively, Board of Corrections and Charities, *Biennial Reports,* 1883–84, p. 200; Carver County file, McClure Papers; Gresham, *Le Sueur County,* 1: 377. On Stearns County, see William B. Mitchell, *History of Stearns County,* 107, 108, 113 (Chicago, 1915); *Biennial Reports,* 1887–88, p. 188.

⁴³ For Houston County, see Board of Corrections and Charities, *Biennial Reports,* 1883–84, p. 206; *History of Houston County,* 314 (Minneapolis, 1882). For Murray County, see *Biennial Reports,* 1883–84, p. 210; 1897–98, p. 114. In addition to those already mentioned, poor farms were purchased by Rice County in 1866; by Chisago, Mower, and Winona counties in 1868. See Appendix, Table 1, below. Chisago County's first farm was located in Township 35, Range 20, section 15, near Sunrise. A second farm acquired by the county in 1903 near North Branch is now the site of Green Acres Nursing Home. Chisago County Board of Commissioners, "Proceedings," September 4, 1868; September 19, 1870; April 3, July 13, 1903.

⁴⁴ State institutions established before 1880 included the prison at Stillwater, 1853; State Reform School, St. Paul, 1867; St. Peter State Hospital for the Insane, 1866; Rochester State Hospital for the Insane, 1878; State School for the Deaf, Faribault, 1863; State School for the Blind, Faribault, 1874 (first opened in 1866 as a department of the School for the Deaf); State School for Idiots and Imbeciles, Faribault, 1879; State Soldiers Orphans Home, Winona, 1872. See Board of Corrections and Charities, *Biennial Reports,* 1883–84, p. 14–20, 24; Henry A. Castle, *Minnesota: Its Story and Biography,* 1:353–360 (Chicago, 1915).

⁴⁵ Among the institutions which had been opened by private organizations prior to 1880 were: *home for homeless men, women, and children* — Home for the Friendless, St. Paul; *children's homes* — Protestant Orphan Asylum, St. Paul, 1865; Vasa Orphans' Home, Vasa, 1865; St. Joseph's Catholic Orphan Asylum, St. Paul, 1876; Minneapolis Catholic Orphan Asylum, Minneapolis, 1878; *rescue homes for women* — House of the Good Shepherd, St. Paul, 1869; Minnesota Woman's Christian Home, St. Paul, 1873; Bethany Home, Minneapolis, 1875; *women's boarding home* — Woman's Christian Association Boarding Home for Women, Minneapolis, 1874; *hospitals* — St. Joseph's, St. Paul, 1854; Cottage (later St. Barnabas), Minneapolis, 1872; St. Luke's, St. Paul, incorporated in 1873; Stillwater, about 1875. Files on these institutions may be found in McClure Papers.

⁴⁶ For material here and below, see C. S. Watkins, "Poorhouses and Jails in the North-western States," in National Conference of Charities, *Proceedings,* 1879, p. 98.

⁴⁷ See Appendix, Table 2, below, for population statistics on the aged.

CHAPTER 3 – THE HOME FOR THE FRIENDLESS 1867–1883

¹ Bishop, *Floral Home, or First Years of Minnesota,* 340 (New York, 1857). Portions of this chapter were previously published as "The Protestant Home of St. Paul: A Pioneer Venture in Caring for the Aged," in *Minnesota History,* 38: 74–85 (June, 1962).

² Bishop, *Floral Home,* 101 (quotes), 102.

³ For accounts of women's activities, see Daniel R. Noyes, "Charities in Minnesota," in *Minnesota Historical Collections,* 12:167–182 (St. Paul, 1908); Castle, *Minnesota,* 1:335; Mary A. Livermore, *My Story of the War,* 137 (quote), (Hartford, Conn., 1888).

⁴ Christian Aid Society, Minutes, January 27, June 22, 1866, photocopy in MHS. In 1873 the organization's name was changed to the Woman's Christian Association, which owns the original minutes. For its later development, see chapter 4, below.

⁵ Ladies Christian Union of the City of St. Paul, Minute Book, May 4, 1867, in MHS. These records, cited hereafter as Minutes, include the transactions of the association under its various name changes.

⁶ For the quotations, see *St. Paul Daily Pioneer,* May 18, 1867, and Philip D. Jordan, *The People's Health: A History of Public Health in Minnesota to 1948,* 38 (St. Paul, 1953).

⁷ Henry A. Castle, *History of St. Paul and Vicinity,* 101 (Chicago, 1912).

⁸ *Daily Pioneer,* May 18, 1867.

⁹ Minutes, May 4, 11, 1867. Represented at the May 4 meeting were First, Central, and House of Hope Presbyterian churches; Jackson Street, German, Scandinavian, and Market Street Methodist churches; Christ and St. Paul's Episcopal churches; First Baptist Church; Trinity Lutheran Church; and Plymouth Congregational Church.

¹⁰ Information on early benevolent institutions, here and below, is drawn from United States Department of Commerce and Labor, Bureau of the Census, *Benevolent Institutions, 1904,* 220–265 (Washington, D.C., 1905). This report gives the founding dates of homes in operation in 1904. Some of the early homes may have been discontinued by that time and thus were omitted from the study, but it seems unlikely that there were very many of them. Benevolent institutions are noteworthy for their longevity, and relatively few homes for the aged closed in the nineteenth century.

¹¹ Minutes, May 26, 1867.

¹² Minutes, May 26 (quote), June 7, 1867.

¹³ Minutes, June 10, 1868.

¹⁴ Minutes, August 10, September 11, October [9] (quotes), 1867.

¹⁵ Minutes, October [9], 1867, June 10, 1868; *Daily Pioneer,* January 28, 1869.

¹⁶ Minutes, October 14, 1868, January 27, 1869; *Daily Pioneer,* January 28, 1869.

¹⁷ Minutes, January 27, 1869; *Daily Pioneer,* January 28, 1869.

¹⁸ Minutes, January 27, 1869; Home for the Friendless, *Annual Reports,* 1877, p. 4, in MHS.

¹⁹ Home for the Friendless, *Annual Reports,* 1877, p. 4; Minutes, April 11, May 4, 1869.

²⁰ Home for the Friendless, *Annual Reports,* 1877, p. 7; Minutes, November 2, 1869.

²¹ Minutes, February 1, 1870.

²² The quotations may be found, respectively, in Minutes, December 7, 1869, and October 3, 1871. See also entries for April 5, 1870; August 1, 1871; August 6, 1872.

²³ Minutes, October 10, 1871; July 2, 1872. See also McClure, in *Minnesota History,* 38:77.

²⁴ *Daily Pioneer,* January 12, 1869.

²⁵ *North-western Chronicle* (St. Paul), May 1, 1869; Castle, *St. Paul and Vicinity,* 1025 (quotes).

²⁶ Castle, *St. Paul and Vicinity,* 583.

²⁷ Home for the Friendless, *Annual Reports,* 1877, p. 6.

²⁸ Christopher C. Andrews, ed., *History of St. Paul,* 94 (Syracuse, N.Y., 1890); Home for the Friendless, *Annual Reports,* 1877, p. 6 (quote).

²⁹ Minutes, February 2, April 20, 1875. On orphan asylums, see chapter 2, notes 44, 45, above.

³⁰ Home for the Friendless, *Annual Reports,* 1877, p. 6.

³¹ Home for the Friendless, *Annual Reports,* 1877, p. 5; Minnesota, *Special*

REFERENCE NOTES — CHAPTER 4   255

Laws, 1877, p. 231. See also Minutes, February 1, 1876; January 24, 1877.
³² *Daily Pioneer,* January 26, 1871.
³³ Minutes, April 2, 1878, October 15, 1881; *Daily Pioneer Press* (St. Paul and Minneapolis), December 6, 1883; *St. Paul Globe,* January 24, 1884. On the Hennepin County poorhouse, see chapter 5, below.
³⁴ *Pioneer Press,* November 20, 1887. The home closed in 1966.
³⁵ The rules and the agreement below appear in the home's annual report for 1883, which was printed in the *St. Paul Globe,* January 24, 1884.
³⁶ For the later history of the Home for the Friendless, see McClure, in *Minnesota History,* 38:81–85.

CHAPTER 4 — WOMEN OF THE CHURCHES 1880–1900

¹ Van Cleve, *Three Score Years and Ten,* 161 (Minneapolis, 1888). The quotation in the following paragraph can be found in Mark Twain (pseud.), *Life on the Mississippi,* 584 (Boston, 1883).
² Van Cleve, *Three Score Years and Ten,* 162; Board of Corrections and Charities, *Biennial Reports,* 1885–86, p. 235–242; 1887–88, p. 253–261.
³ Board of Corrections and Charities, *Biennial Reports,* 1889–90, p. 236; 1894, p. 152; Mrs. C. A. Severance, "Humane Societies," in Minnesota Conference of Charities and Correction, *Proceedings,* 1898, p. 58 (quote). For a recent comment on Bergh's work, see Gerald Carson, "The Great Meddler," in *American Heritage,* December, 1967, p. 28–33, 94–97.
⁴ Amos G. Warner, *American Charities,* 318n (Boston and New York, 1894).
⁵ In 1900, for example, the population of the state's 34 poorhouses included 436 males and 90 females. For the quotation, see Noyes, in *Minnesota Historical Collections,* 12:167.
⁶ Isaac Atwater, *History of Minneapolis,* 598 (New York and Chicago, 1895); Children's Home Society, Minutes, October 28, 1881, in the possession of Stevens Square, Minneapolis; *Minneapolis Tribune,* September 10, 1885 (quote).
⁷ Undated newspaper clipping, *ca.* 1894, owned by Stevens Square. The news story was written by Mrs. James K. (Jenny G.) Hosmer, a member of the board from 1893 to 1903.
⁸ Home for Children and Aged Women, "Child History Record, 1881–86," in records of the Department of Public Welfare, Minnesota State Archives, State Records Center, St. Paul; Children's Home Society, *Annual Reports,* 1882, p. 8 (quotes), in MHS.
⁹ Children's Home Society, Minutes, October 28, 1881.
¹⁰ Minutes, November 2, 1881; *Annual Reports,* 1910, p. 11.
¹¹ Minutes, August 5, September 23, 1882; June 23, 1885.
¹² Atwater, *History of Minneapolis,* 255, 268; Minutes, May 22, 1882.
¹³ *Annual Reports,* 1884, p. 12.
¹⁴ Minutes, June 23, 1885 (quote); *Daily Pioneer Press,* June 24, 1885; *Minneapolis Tribune,* September 10, 1885.
¹⁵ *Minneapolis Tribune,* October 29, 1885; *Daily Pioneer Press,* November 23, 1887 (quote); Stevens Square, *History, Articles of Incorporation, By-Laws,* 11 (Minneapolis, 1960), in MHS.
¹⁶ Home for Children and Aged Women, Minutes, May 1, August 3, November 2, 1886, in the possession of Stevens Square; *Annual Reports,* 1899, p. 16; 1908, p. 13, in MHS.
¹⁷ *Minneapolis Tribune,* September 18, 1886.
¹⁸ Minutes, May 3, 1887; *Annual Reports,* 1908, p. 13.
¹⁹ Home for Children and Aged Women, *Annual Reports,* 1895, p. 16; 1900, p. 10.

[20] Home for Children and Aged Women, *Annual Reports*, 1886, p. 12; 1899, p. 15, 16; 1900, p. 12; Stevens Square, *History*, 4.

[21] Woman's Christian Association, *The Jones-Harrison Home*, 1, undated pamphlet in McClure Papers; Minutes, June 11, 1886, in the offices of the Woman's Christian Association, Minneapolis.

[22] United States Manuscript Census Schedules, 1870, Hennepin County, p. 591; *A Charming Retreat*, undated broadside advertising Oak Grove House — both in MHS. On Minnesota as a health resort, see Helen Clapesattle, "When Minnesota Was Florida's Rival," in *Minnesota History*, 35:214–221 (March, 1957). See also Woman's Christian Association, *Annual Reports*, 1886, p. 11. Partial files of the latter may be found in MHS and in the association's offices, Minneapolis.

[23] Atwater, *History of Minneapolis*, 249, 511; Woman's Christian Association, Minutes, June 11, 1886.

[24] Minutes, October, 1886; *Annual Reports*, 1888, p. 47; 1889, p. 11, 43; 1891, p. 36 (quote).

[25] Minutes, July 19, August, 1890; *Annual Reports*, 1891, p. 36 (quote); 1893, p. 35.

[26] Minutes, January 9, 1891; *Annual Reports*, 1891, p. 36; 1897, p. 43 (quote); 1901, p. 45. For the quotation in the next paragraph, see *Annual Reports*, 1901, p. 45.

[27] Little Sisters of the Poor, "Histoire de notre Maison de St. Paul," 1, a manuscript in French covering the years 1883–99 owned by the Little Sisters. Portions of the history were translated by Sister M. Jeanne Berchmans in interviews with the author, January 19, 30, 1962.

[28] A. Leroy, *In the Land of Charity*, 15, 16 (Abbeville, Fr., [1903]); Agnès Richomme, *Jeanne Jugan, Foundress of the Little Sisters of the Poor* (Paris, 1960). For a map showing places and dates of establishment for foundations of this order in the United States, see *Today and Tomorrow* (Boston, 1960), a brochure by the Little Sisters, in MHS.

[29] Little Sisters, "Histoire," 1; *North-western Chronicle*, June 2, August 2, 16, 1883.

[30] Henry D. Funk, *A History of Macalester College*, 33 (St. Paul, 1910); *North-western Chronicle*, January 3, 1884; *St. Paul Daily Globe*, January 8, 1888. See also Board of Corrections and Charities, *Biennial Reports*, 1885–86, p. 231.

[31] "Cahier des Vieillards de notre Maison de St. Paul (Minn.)," admissions record owned by the Little Sisters, St. Paul; *North-western Chronicle*, May 3, 1884.

[32] Benedictines of Teignemouth, *Father Ernest Le Lievre*, 18 (London, 1934); *North-western Chronicle*, January 3, 1884; Little Sisters, "Histoire," 3, 9 (quotes).

[33] Little Sisters, "Cahier"; *Daily Globe*, January 8, 1888. An inventory at the back of the "Cahier" lists the inmates' possessions.

[34] For material here and below, see Leroy, *In the Land of Charity*, 15 (quotes); Little Sisters, "Cahier."

[35] Little Sisters, "Histoire," 21.

[36] Little Sisters, "Histoire," 21 (quote). See also *Daily Globe*, January 8, 1888; *North-western Chronicle*, February 7, 1890.

[37] Little Sisters, "Histoire," 24. Other gifts by Hill are recorded in "Histoire."

[38] Little Sisters, "Histoire," 29.

[39] Little Sisters, "Histoire," 58.

[40] Information here and in the next paragraph was drawn from a manuscript history of its home owned by the Minneapolis foundation of the Little Sisters of the Poor. Portions were translated by Sister Helene De La Providence in an interview with the author on February 10, 1964. See also *North-western Chronicle*, February 15, 1889; *Minneapolis Tribune*, April 1, 1896.

[41] Material on St. Otto's here and below may be found in the home's file, McClure Papers.

⁴² *Little Falls Transcript*, March 6, 1891; Sister Mary Assumpta to the author, November 5, 1963, McClure Papers. The *Transcript* incorrectly gives the date of official recognition as March 2.

⁴³ *Transcript*, January 16, 1891; *Morrison County Democrat* (Little Falls), November 28, 1891.

⁴⁴ *Transcript*, March 6, August 21, 28, 1891.

⁴⁵ *Transcript*, January 15, 1892; January 1, 1894; February 8, June 7, July 9, 14, 1895.

⁴⁶ This home for the aged was not included in Bureau of the Census, *Benevolent Institutions, 1904*, although both St. Gabriel Hospital and St. Otto's Orphanage were listed. It was not until after the transfer of the children's program to St. Cloud in 1924 that the old people's home had its own name and building. A new St. Gabriel Hospital was built in 1916.

⁴⁷ George C. Tanner, *Fifty Years of Church Work in the Diocese of Minnesota 1857–1907*, 242, 245, 262 (St. Paul, 1909). The quotation is from "Sister Annette and Her Work," an unsigned typescript, ca. 1915, in the Church Home of Minnesota file, McClure Papers.

⁴⁸ Board of Corrections and Charities, *Biennial Reports*, 1885–86, p. 226; "Sister Annette," McClure Papers.

⁴⁹ *The Church Home of Minnesota*, 2, a pamphlet in MHS; for the addresses, see *St. Paul City Directories*, 1895, 1897.

⁵⁰ Undated mimeographed history, McClure Papers; *Church Home of Minnesota*, 3; *St. Paul City Directories*, 1898, 1899, 1905.

⁵¹ Information here and below on the Augustana home has been taken from two pamphlets entitled *Fifty Years of Service* and *Our Heritage* in the home's file, McClure Papers.

⁵² *Belle Plaine Herald*, June 8, July 13, 1898.

⁵³ *Herald*, November 2, 9, 1898. Although the Lutheran Home cared for some children, it was from the beginning primarily a home for the aged. According to Hiram W. Slack, comp., *Directory of Charitable and Benevolent Organizations*, 306 (St. Paul, 1913): "Children are taken into this Home if there is room for them but only for a short time, and with the purpose to place them later in family homes through the Kinderfreund Society."

⁵⁴ Ladies of the Grand Army of the Republic, Department of Minnesota, *Proceedings*, 1893, p. 5, 6; 1895, p. 45, 49, 50, in MHS.

⁵⁵ *Proceedings*, 1896, p. 89; 1927, p. 53 (quote). For the quotation in the next paragraph, see *Proceedings*, 1900, p. 37. On the Minnesota Soldiers' Home, see chapter 5, below.

⁵⁶ *Proceedings*, 1901, p. 51; 1927, p. 54 (quote); 1940, p. 52; *Minneapolis Star*, January 21, 1960, p. 21.

⁵⁷ Warner, *American Charities*, 293.

CHAPTER 5 – THE STATE EXPANDS ITS ROLE 1880–1900

¹ Frank B. Sanborn, "The Supervision of Public Charities," in *Journal of Social Science*, 1:77–80 (American Social Science Association, *Transactions*, 1869); Kelso, *Poor Relief in Massachusetts*, 143–150.

² Sanborn, "The Year's Work in Administration and Legislation," in National Conference of Charities, *Proceedings*, 1879, p. 26.

³ For the 1856 investigation, see chapter 1, note 14, above; Dwight, "The Public Charities of the State of New York," in *Journal of Social Science*, 2:84, 85 (quote), (American Social Science Association, *Transactions*, 1870), a report presented on October 26, 1869.

MORE THAN A ROOF

[4] Sanborn, in National Conference of Charities, *Proceedings,* 1879, p. 27.

[5] "Conference of Boards of Public Charities," in *Journal of Social Science,* 6:60, 87 (*Transactions,* 1874); National Conference of Charities, *Proceedings,* 1877, p. viii, 20.

[6] Board of Corrections and Charities, *Biennial Reports,* 1883–84, p. 247.

[7] *Laws,* 1883, p. 171 (quote); Board of Corrections and Charities, *Biennial Reports,* 1883–84, p. 13, 248.

[8] Folwell, *History of Minnesota,* 4:409 (St. Paul, 1920); Upham and Dunlap, *Minnesota Biographies,* 305; *Worthington Advance,* May 31, July 26, 1883; *St. Paul Globe,* July 11, 1883.

[9] Folwell, *Minnesota,* 4:409, 412.

[10] For Hart's survey, see Board of Corrections and Charities, *Biennial Reports,* 1883–84, p. 189–236. The quotation is on p. 175. His comment on the Lyon County poorhouse, below, is in *Reports,* 1889–90, p. 215. The following counties opened poorhouses between 1880 and 1884: Steele (1880); Rock and Otter Tail (1881); Todd (1882); Chippewa, Lyon, and Becker (1883). Four other counties — Martin, Marshall, Swift, and Redwood — acquired farms but did not open poorhouses during these years. See Appendix, Table 1, below.

[11] For the quotations here and in the next two paragraphs, see Board of Corrections and Charities, *Biennial Reports,* 1883–84, p. 188, 194, 206, 224. See also p. 178, 184.

[12] See Board of Corrections and Charities, *Biennial Reports,* 1883–84, p. 187, 195, 199, 231, 235; 1893–94, p. 130. For the description of the Hennepin County poorhouse quoted below, see *Reports,* 1883–84, p. 203–205. Disbursements for building are recorded in Hennepin County, *Financial Statements,* 1884, p. 6; 1885, p. 8.

[13] Board of Corrections and Charities, *Biennial Reports,* 1883–84, p. 188, 199 (quote), 202, 211 (quote). On separation of the sexes, below, see *Reports,* 1883–84, p. 235; 1891–92, p. 199.

[14] For the examples cited, see *Biennial Reports,* 1883–84, p. 188, 197, 202. On the gathering of statistics, in the next paragraph, see 30, 145–164.

[15] *Biennial Reports,* 1883–84, p. 165–169 (quote).

[16] For Hart's observations here and in the next paragraph, see *Biennial Reports,* 1883–84, p. 182, 184, 185. See also p. 208, 227.

[17] The quotations are in *Biennial Reports,* 1883–84, p. 187, 236; 1899–1900, p. 37. See also *Laws,* 1899, p. 295.

[18] On the purchase of farms here and in the next paragraph, see *Biennial Reports,* 1883–84, p. 181–183. Of the thirty-one counties owning such land in September, 1884, only nine held less than 160 acres. See *Reports,* 1883–84, p. 177.

[19] *Biennial Reports,* 1883–84, p. 176, 181 (quote).

[20] Warner, *American Charities,* 142, 228; Miriam Z. Langsam, *Children West: A History of the Placing-Out System of the New York Children's Aid Society, 1853–1890,* 61–65 (Madison, Wis., 1964).

[21] Langsam, *Children West,* 45–67; Hart, "Placing Out Children in the West," in National Conference of Charities and Correction, *Proceedings,* 1884, p. 143–150; 1879, p. 158 (quote). The comment on juvenile crime was offered by A. G. Byers.

[22] Board of Corrections and Charities, *Biennial Reports,* 1883–84, p. 33 (quote), 138–140; 1897–98, p. 38–40; 1899–1900, p. 41. See also *Laws,* 1899, p. 138.

[23] Folks, *Care of Children,* 72 (quote); Board of Corrections and Charities, *Biennial Reports,* 1883–84, p. 259.

[24] Minnesota's first venture in state care of dependent children had been the State Soldiers Orphans Home at Winona. It opened in a rented building in 1872 and closed six years later, when the number of children had dwindled to the point where a large institution was no longer necessary. Castle, *Minnesota,* 360;

REFERENCE NOTES — CHAPTER 5   259

Board of Corrections and Charities, *Biennial Reports*, 1883–84, p. 259; 1885–86, p. 30, 61.

²⁵ Board of Corrections and Charities, *Biennial Reports*, 1885–86, p. 30, 186 (quote); 1899–1900, p. 108. Perhaps not all of the decrease in the number of children in poorhouses should be attributed to the state public school, for the 1880s also saw the opening of several children's homes under private auspices. Among them were the Children's Home (which later became the Home for Children and Aged Women), Minneapolis, opened in 1881; Sheltering Arms, Minneapolis, and the St. Paul Catholic Orphan Asylum, St. Paul, both opened in 1883; and the Washburn Memorial Orphan Asylum, Minneapolis, opened in 1886.

²⁶ Castle, *Minnesota*, 387; Brown, *Public Relief*, 20.

²⁷ Castle, *Minnesota*, 389. See also *Laws*, 1887, p. 249–257; Board of Corrections and Charities, *Biennial Reports*, 1891–92, p. 28. The soldiers' home apparently admitted at least a few veterans, perhaps those who were ill or disabled, who had dependents at home. See *Reports*, 1889–90, p. 26, for a discussion of policy concerning this category of residents. Some years later provision was made at the home for the admission of female dependents; the first woman was admitted in 1906. See Castle, *Minnesota*, 386.

²⁸ Board of Corrections and Charities, *Biennial Reports*, 1887–88, p. 21; 1889–90, p. 25; Castle, *Minnesota*, 387, 388 (quotes).

²⁹ Board of Corrections and Charities, *Biennial Reports*, 1887–88, p. 22; 1899–1900, p. 13 (quote), 26.

³⁰ Board of Corrections and Charities, *Biennial Reports*, 1889–90, p. 25; 1891–92, p. 25; 1893–94, p. 15 (quote); 1897–98, p. 14. For the quotations in the following paragraph, see 1895–96, p. 18.

³¹ *Biennial Reports*, 1897–98, p. 14.

³² *Biennial Reports*, 1893–94, p. 41; 1899–1900, p. 108.

³³ *Biennial Reports*, 1883–84, p. 112; *Laws*, 1883, p. 17. On the Goodhue County home, see *Biennial Reports*, 1889–90, p. 208, 212; *Red Wing Argus*, October 10, 1889. For the quotation in the paragraph below, see *Biennial Reports*, 1891–92, p. 197.

³⁴ Board of Corrections and Charities, *Biennial Reports*, 1897–98, p. 41; 1899–1900, p. 36, 37 (quote); *Minnesota Bulletin of Charities and Correction*, March, 1898, p. 1, a quarterly periodical issued by the state board. Jackson remained in this post for only three years, leaving in June, 1901, to become assistant secretary of the Charity Organization Society of New York City.

³⁵ The pamphlet entitled *Poorhouses: Their Location, Construction and Management* was issued as a supplement to the June, 1900, issue of the *Minnesota Bulletin of Charities and Correction*. No evidence has been found to indicate that the volunteer committees were ever set up. For the quotation, see *Minnesota Bulletin*, December, 1900, p. 40.

³⁶ Board of Corrections and Charities, *Biennial Reports*, 1899–1900, p. 37 (quote), 46; *Laws*, 1901, p. 128, 147. For a sketch and floor plan of the Becker County poorhouse, see *Reports*, 1899–1900, p. 38.

³⁷ Board of Corrections and Charities, *Biennial Reports*, 1895–96, p. 55; 1899–1900, p. 41, 42 (quotes).

³⁸ Board of Corrections and Charities, *Biennial Reports*, 1883–84, p. 176; 1899–1900, p. 107. The following counties opened poorhouses between 1885 and 1900: Anoka, Cottonwood, Crow Wing, Itasca, Lac qui Parle, Morrison, Murray, Pipestone, Redwood, Renville, Scott, Stevens, and Yellow Medicine. Big Stone acquired a farm in 1895 but never opened a poorhouse. Freeborn reopened its poorhouse in 1889. See Appendix, Table 1, below.

³⁹ For the state institutions, see Board of Corrections and Charities, *Biennial Reports*, 1899–1900, p. 9, 32. See also Appendix, Table 2, below.

40 Warner, *American Charities*, 143; Board of Corrections and Charities, *Biennial Reports*, 1899–1900, p. 108.

CHAPTER 6 – IMPROVING COUNTY POOR FARMS
1900–1920

1 Dwight L. Dumond, *America in Our Times, 1896–1946*, 39 (New York, 1947).
2 Blegen, *Minnesota*, 461.
3 Board of Corrections and Charities, *Biennial Reports*, 1899–1900, p. 107, lists poorhouses in operation on December 31, 1899. Although Pipestone County did not report any inmates, it still owned a farm. For the session on poorhouses, see Minnesota Conference of Charities and Correction, *Proceedings*, 1900, p. 23–31. See also Appendix, Tables 1, 2, below.
4 For Mrs. Hendry's paper quoted here and below, see *Proceedings*, 1900, p. 23–25.
5 For the discussion of management practices here and in the next four paragraphs, see *Proceedings*, 1900, p. 25–30.
6 Folwell, *History of Minnesota*, 3:262 (St. Paul, 1926). The first members of the new board were Silas W. Leavitt of Litchfield, chairman; William E. Lee, Long Prairie; and Charles A. Morey, Winona. Morey soon resigned and was replaced by Ozro B. Gould, Winona. For Governor Samuel R. Van Sant's recollections concerning the passage of the "State Board of Control Law," see Board of Control, *Quarterly*, November 20, 1932, p. 7–11. See also S. W. Leavitt, "Organization of the State Board of Control and Something of Its Early History," in the same issue, p. 12–23.
7 Minnesota Conference of Charities and Correction, *Proceedings*, 1902, p. 89. Commissioners gave many papers at conference sessions and participated freely in the discussion periods. Minutes of their association's meetings were published in the conference *Proceedings*.
8 Conference of Charities and Correction, *Proceedings*, 1908, p. 115–118.
9 *Proceedings*, 1910, p. 109, 168.
10 See, for example, transcripts of the "Proceedings" of the Hubbard, Kittson, and Wilkin boards of county commissioners for 1909. The twelve counties which acquired poor farms between 1900 and 1919 were: Beltrami (1901), Aitkin (1904), Hubbard (1906), Pine and Kandiyohi (1907), Koochiching (1908), Wilkin and Wright (1909), Kittson and Mille Lacs (1910), Lake (1913), and Traverse (sometime before 1920). Two counties – Brown and Martin – which had earlier purchased land opened poorhouses in 1903 and 1915, respectively. Redwood County, which closed its old poorhouse in 1899, opened one in a new building in 1909. Four poorhouses were closed: Cottonwood (1903), Stevens (1911), and Crow Wing and Kandiyohi (1913). Traverse County did not operate a poorhouse but made the facilities available to indigents who needed a place to stay. Robert Braseth, Traverse County attorney, to the author, March 13, 1968, and other material in Traverse County file, McClure Papers.
11 For a general discussion of pesthouses, see Johnson, *The Almshouse*, 117.
12 See Williams, *History of Saint Paul*, 263, and the files for St. Louis, Aitkin, and Koochiching counties, McClure Papers.
13 Folwell, *Minnesota*, 3:262; State Board of Control, *Biennial Reports*, 1907–08, p. 14 (quote).
14 *Revised Laws of Minnesota, 1905, as Reported by the Commission Appointed . . . to Revise and Codify the General Laws*, 356 (St. Paul, 1905); *Report of the Statute Revision Commission to Accompany its Draft of a Proposed Revision of*

the General Laws . . . 1905, 16 (St. Paul, 1905); Revised Laws, 1905, p. 379. For the quotations here and below, see Biennial Reports, 1907–08, p. 14, 15.

[15] *Biennial Reports,* 1907–08, p. 14. Correspondence and inspection reports prior to 1925 have not been located. It seems likely, however, that the forms remained practically unchanged from the first years.

[16] *Biennial Reports,* 1915–16, p. 290; 1917–18, p. 47.

[17] On the plans, see p. 88, above.

[18] *Faribault Republican,* July 15, 1903.

[19] On unpublicized moves, see, for example, *Mower County Transcript Republican* (Austin), February 8, 1917. On Brown County, see *Brown County Journal* (New Ulm), January 25, 1908, and, for the Eckstein quotation, Brown County file, McClure Papers.

[20] *Martin County Independent* (Fairmont), November 24, 1915.

[21] *Hinckley Enterprise,* November 16, 1921.

[22] *Houston Signal,* January 30, 1902.

[23] State Board of Control, *Biennial Reports,* 1915–16, p. 290.

[24] Minnesota State Conference of Charities and Correction, *Proceedings,* 1905, p. 40 (quote), 52. See also *Proceedings,* 1903, p. 79.

[25] State Conference of Charities and Correction, *Proceedings,* 1911, p. 137 (quote); 1914, p. 80, 86; *Biennial Reports,* 1913–14, p. 8 (quote).

[26] State Conference of Charities and Correction, *Proceedings,* 1901, p. 31.

[27] J. Arthur Myers, *Invited and Conquered: Historical Sketch of Tuberculosis in Minnesota,* 408 (St. Paul, 1949).

[28] *Laws,* 1909, p. 398–400; 1913, p. 731; editorial in *Modern Hospital,* March, 1917, p. 200 (quote). In 1918 Minnesota had one state, fourteen county, one city, and two private tuberculosis sanatoriums. The county sanatoriums were opened in the following years: Nopeming, 1912; Otter Tail, 1913; Ramsey, 1914; Mineral Springs, 1915; Glen Lake, Sunnyrest, Lake Julia, and Sand Beach, 1916; Riverside, Buena Vista, and Southwestern Minnesota, 1917; Oakland Park, Fair Oaks Lodge, and Deerwood, 1918. All but Nopeming, Otter Tail, Ramsey, and Glen Lake were owned by two or more counties. See Myers, *Invited and Conquered,* 79a, 397, 415, 436–438, 440–444.

[29] See Chapter 14, below.

[30] Minnesota Conference of Charities and Correction, *Proceedings,* 1914, p. 72. For the Bullis quotations here and below, see p. 75–77.

[31] *Minnesota Bulletin of Corrections and Charities,* June, 1901, p. 2.

[32] Minnesota Conference of Charities and Correction, *Proceedings,* 1914, p. 72, 82 (quote).

[33] Conference of Charities and Correction, *Proceedings,* 1914, p. 81.

[34] Clark, "The Passing of the County Farm," in *The Survey,* 42:624 (July 26, 1919).

[35] The main portion of the code is in Minnesota, *General Statutes,* 1917 Supplement, p. 658–670. See also p. 370–373 for laws implementing the board's administration of this act.

CHAPTER 7 — ETHNIC GROUPS PROVIDE FOR THEIR AGED 1900–1920

[1] The material here and below is drawn from Sister M. Grace McDonald, *With Lamps Burning,* 253, 256–258, 262 (quote), (St. Joseph, Minn., 1957); St. Joseph's Home file, McClure Papers.

[2] *Springfield Advance,* January 11, 25, March 29 (quote), 1901, January 22, 1903; St. John Lutheran Home file, McClure Papers.

[3] St. John's Hospital was closed in 1958, and the institution is now known as St. John Lutheran Home. It is sponsored by the American Lutheran Church. St. Alexander Home, New Ulm, still operated under that name in 1967. See James M. Reardon, *The Catholic Church in the Diocese of St. Paul*, 675 (St. Paul, 1952); Loretto Hospital, *Loves' Service, 1884–1959*, 25 (New Ulm, 1959); Bethel Home for the Aged file, McClure Papers; John A. Brown, *History of Cottonwood and Watonwan Counties*, 1:161 (Indianapolis, 1916). St. Ann's Home closed on November 23, 1956. See St. Ann's Home file, McClure Papers.

[4] On care of the aged in Scandinavia, see B. J. Hovde, *The Scandinavian Countries, 1720–1865*, 623, 642 (New York, 1948); William E. Curtis, *Denmark, Norway and Sweden*, 40, 339, 406 (Akron, 1903); Mrs. Woods Baker, *Pictures of Swedish Life*, 187–192 (New York, 1894).

[5] Nelson, et al., *Population Growth*, 13; *Republican Gazette* (Willmar), October 23, 1902; Bethesda Hospital, St. Paul, *Annual Reports*, 1931, p. 47; *Minnesota Conference Charities*, September, 1944, an unpaged quarterly publication of the Board of Christian Service. The file consulted by the author is in the superintendent's office, Bethesda Hospital, St. Paul.

[6] Emeroy Johnson, *God Gave the Growth: The Story of the Lutheran Minnesota Conference, 1876–1958*, 78, 235 (Minneapolis, 1958); June D. Holmquist, "Swedeland, U.S.A.," in *Gopher Historian*, Spring, 1959, p. 19–21; Chisago Lutheran Home file, McClure Papers.

[7] Paul A. Bergquist, "A complete write-up on the Bethesda Old People's Home" (quote), in Writers' Project, Works Project Administration Papers, MHS; Bethesda Hospital, *Annual Reports*, 1931, p. 47.

[8] *St. Paul Pioneer Press*, October 24, 1906, p. 9 (quote); interview of the author with Mrs. E. M. Rystrom, St. Paul, January 28, 1964.

[9] *Pioneer Press*, October 24, 1906, p. 9; St. Paul Linnea Society, Minutes, December 6, 1904, owned by the Twin City Linnea Home for the Aged, St. Paul (photocopy in McClure Papers); interviews with Mrs. Rystrom, January 28, 1964, February 26, 1968. The early Minutes are in Swedish; the portion here cited was translated by the late Helene M. Thomson. See Linnea Home file, McClure Papers. Mrs. Kindwall's name was also spelled Kjindvall and Kindvall.

[10] On the society's name and finances, see St. Paul Linnea Society, Minutes, December 6, 1904. The articles of incorporation for the St. Paul group, dated October 23, 1906, are in the office of the Minnesota Secretary of State, St. Paul.

[11] Twin City Linnea Society, Articles of Incorporation, May 6, 1909 (quotes), Secretary of State's office; *Pioneer Press*, October 24, 1906. See also St. Paul Linnea Society, Minutes, January–July, 1908. This portion was translated in 1964 by a committee of the Linnea Home's board of directors; see Linnea Home file, McClure Papers.

[12] Twin City Linnea Society, Minutes, September 18, 1915; May 11, 1916; November 6, 1917; February 22, October 1, 1918; February 22, 1919, owned by the Twin City Linnea Home, St. Paul. These records are in English.

Other Swedish homes established between 1900 and 1920 were the Scandinavian Union Relief Home, Minneapolis (1915); Bethany Home, Alexandria (1917); Ebenezer Home, Buffalo (1918); and Bethesda Lutheran Home for Invalids, St. Paul (1914), described on p. 120, below. See files in McClure Papers; Ethel McClure, *A Historical Directory of Minnesota Homes for the Aged* (St. Paul, 1968).

[13] Nelson, et al., *Population Growth*, 13. For material here and in the next three paragraphs, see *Lyngblomsten Souvenir Book Covering a Thirty Year Period*, [5]–9, 14–18, 30 (n.p., 1933), a pamphlet in MHS. The quotations are on p. [5] and 7. The opening date is given in *Lyngblomsten*, May 17, 1914, p. 1, a periodical in the possession of the home. For the later history of Lyngblomsten, see p. 148, 182, below.

REFERENCE NOTES — CHAPTER 7   263

¹⁴ Glenwood Old People's Home, "Articles of Incorporation, History, and Minutes of Board Meetings," July 16, 1911, p. 11, 12; January 10, 1913, p. 13ff, in the offices of the American Lutheran Church, Minneapolis (photocopy in McClure Papers). Through a series of mergers, the Norwegian Synod became a part of the present American Lutheran Church. In 1967 the American Lutheran Church operated 108 old people's homes in nineteen states. See *Guide to the Social Services of the American Lutheran Church*, 8–12 ([Minneapolis, 1967]).

¹⁵ On the closing of the academy, see E. Clifford Nelson, *The Lutheran Church Among Norwegian-Americans: A History of the Evangelical Lutheran Church*, 2:117 (Minneapolis, 1960). See also *Prospectus: The Glenwood Old People's Home* (Glenwood, 1915), a pamphlet in the files of Luther Theological Seminary, St. Paul (photocopy in McClure Papers); *Glenwood Herald*, October 10, December 12, 1913; December 2, 3, 10, 1914.

¹⁶ *Glenwood Herald*, October 3, 1913, December 10, 1914 (quote). For the later history of this home, see chapter 11, below.

¹⁷ "A History of Ebenezer Home for Old People," in *Ebenezer*, May, 1942, p. 3, a quarterly publication of the Ebenezer Home Society, Minneapolis, which has a complete file (photocopy in McClure Papers).

¹⁸ *Ebenezer*, May, 1942, p. 10; August, 1957, p. 5 (quote). For the later history of this home, see chapter 11, below.

¹⁹ *Bethesda Homes, Willmar, Minnesota, 1897–1953*, [2]–5, in Bethesda Homes file, McClure Papers. See also Clarence J. Carlsen, *The Years of Our Church*, 187 (Minneapolis, 1942).

Other Norwegian institutions of this period were the Sarepta Home, Sauk Centre, started about 1910 by the Church of the Lutheran Brethren, and the Elim Home, Minneapolis, opened in 1914 by the Norwegian-Danish Conference of the Methodist Church. See Charles N. Pace, *Our Fathers Built: A Century of Minnesota Methodism*, 129 ([Minneapolis, 1952]); files in McClure Papers.

²⁰ Jewish Home for the Aged, *First Annual Report*, 1909, p. 2, in Hiram D. Frankel Papers, MHS.

²¹ W. Gunther Plaut, *The Jews in Minnesota: The First Seventy-five Years*, 227 (New York, 1959); *Daily Minnesota Pioneer* (St. Paul), April 13, 1855; Jewish Home, *First Annual Report*, 1909, p. 2, 3 (quote). See also *Pioneer Press*, June 15, 1908, p. 4.

²² The rules may be found in *First Annual Report*, 1909, p. 2, 10. See also Plaut, *Jews in Minnesota*, 227.

²³ Plaut, *Jews in Minnesota*, 228. The Jewish Home for the Aged of the Northwest is located at 1554 Midway Parkway, St. Paul.

²⁴ Nelson, et al., *Population Growth*, 30; *Colored Orphanage and Old People's Home* (quote), broadside in MHS. See also *Pioneer Press*, February 9, 1964, p. 8. On Attucks, see *Webster's Biographical Dictionary*, 75 (Springfield, Mass., 1943).

²⁵ *Colored Orphanage and Old People's Home*; *St. Paul City Directories*, 1904, 1905, 1906.

²⁶ *Appeal* (St. Paul and Minneapolis), December 7, p. 3, December 14, p. 3, 1907; December 12, p. 3, 1908; July 10, p. 3, November 13, p. 3, December 4, p. 3, 1909.

²⁷ *Appeal*, November 13, 1915, p. 4; April 8, p. 3, April 15, p. 2, November 25, 1916, p. 3; State Board of Control file on Crispus Attucks Home, in records of the Department of Public Welfare, Minnesota State Archives. The home remained at 469 Collins Street until it closed in 1966. See *St. Paul Dispatch*, November 16, 1966, p. 21.

²⁸ United States Department of Commerce and Labor, Bureau of the Census, *Benevolent Institutions, 1910*, Table III (Washington, D.C., 1913); *An Outline . . . of the Progress of the Movement for an Odd Fellows Home in Minnesota*, 11–13, 38, 40, 43 (Northfield, 1899).

[29] *Northfield Independent*, June 15, 21 (quote), 28 (quote), 1900.
[30] Bureau of the Census, *Benevolent Institutions, 1904*, 13.
[31] Board of Corrections and Charities, *Biennial Reports*, 1889–90, p. 228.
[32] Bethesda Hospital, *Annual Reports*, 1931, p. 56.
[33] Johnson, *God Gave the Growth*, 235. For the Hultkrans quotation, see Bethesda Invalid Home file, McClure Papers.
[34] Bethesda Hospital, *Annual Reports*, 1931, p. 55, 56. The Bethesda Invalid Home moved in 1932 from Lake Gervais to the Bethesda Hospital building at 249 East Ninth Street, St. Paul. In 1957 the name was changed to Bethesda Lutheran Home for Invalids. The institution closed in 1964 after a new nursing unit in Bethesda Hospital was opened. See Bethesda Invalid Home file, McClure Papers.
[35] Marion D. Shutter, ed., *History of Minneapolis*, 1:209 (Chicago and Minneapolis, 1923); Women's Welfare League of Minneapolis, Minutes, May 4, 1913, in MHS.
[36] Minutes, December 5, 1913; November 3, 1916.
[37] Minutes, January 18, December 6, 1918; April 11, September 12, October 10, 1919; January 21, April 9, May 28, June 11, 1920; September 9, 1921 (quote); *Rest Home for Convalescent Women* ([Minneapolis, 1918]) and other brochures among the Women's Welfare League Papers, in MHS. The Home for Convalescents moved to 100 Clifton Avenue on October 1, 1924, and closed on October 31, 1961. See McClure Papers.
[38] *Woman's Christian Association of Minneapolis*, 14, 22 (Minneapolis, 1960); *Annual Reports*, 1922, p. 8, 9.
[39] *Annual Reports*, 1926, p. 8 (quote); *Woman's Christian Association of Minneapolis*, 14. In 1958 the sponsorship of the Vocational Nursing Home was transferred to Mount Olivet Lutheran Church, Minneapolis. See McClure Papers.
[40] Stevens Square, *History*, 12; Bureau of the Census, *Benevolent Institutions, 1904*, 240; Slack, *Directory of Charitable Organizations*, 328.
[41] *Lyngblomsten Souvenir Book*, 23, 26 (quote). For the material in the next paragraph, see *Souvenir Book*, 26–28.
[42] Frank J. Bruno, *Trends in Social Work 1874–1956: A History Based on the Proceedings of the National Conference of Social Work*, 199 (quote), 200–206 (New York, 1957); Minneapolis Council of Social Agencies, *Agency Report: Care of the Aged*, 7 (Community Survey of Social and Health Work in Minneapolis, 1938); Joint Committee on Community Chest, *The Community Chest*, [i] (St. Paul, 1920).
[43] *Community Chest*, 1; Bruno, *Trends in Social Work*, 203.
[44] *Lyngblomsten Souvenir Book*, 30.

CHAPTER 8 – THE POORHOUSE UNDER SCRUTINY
1920–1930

[1] Clarke A. Chambers, *Seedtime of Reform: American Social Service and Social Action, 1918–1933*, ix, 126, 127 (Minneapolis, 1963); Bruno, *Trends in Social Work*, 156–168, 291; Abbott, *From Relief to Social Security*, 182, 183. The joint committee on delinquency was organized under the auspices of the Commonwealth Fund of New York and included the New York School of Social Work, the National Committee on Visiting Teachers of the Public Education Association of New York, and the National Committee for Mental Hygiene.
[2] Bruno, *Trends in Social Work*, 153, 298 (quote); Chambers, *Seedtime of Re-*

REFERENCE NOTES — CHAPTER 8   265

form, 49; Samuel E. Morison, *Oxford History of the American People*, 889, 890, 897–900 (New York, 1965); Blegen, *Minnesota*, 481.

³ See Appendix, Table 2, below, and Louis I. Dublin, "Old Age: An Increasing Problem," in *Survey Midmonthly*, 56:545 (August 15, 1926).

⁴ Isaac L. Hoffman, "An Inventory of Our Older Residents," in Arnold M. Rose, ed., *Aging in Minnesota*, 35 (Minneapolis, 1963). See also Appendix, Table 2, below.

⁵ John A. Lapp, "Why Are There Poor?" in Minnesota Conference of Social Work, *Proceedings*, 1926, p. 17.

⁶ Minnesota Senate Interim Committee on Old Age Pensions, *Report*, 3 (n.p., [1929]); Blegen, *Minnesota*, 453.

⁷ Senate Interim Committee, *Report*, 3.

⁸ For the quotations here and below, see Anne F. Fenlason, "The Problem of the Aged," in Minnesota Conference of Social Work, *Proceedings*, 1926, p. 32, 33.

⁹ Minnesota Conference of Social Work, *Proceedings*, 1920, p. 15; 1924, p. 11.

¹⁰ Minnesota Conference of Social Work, *Proceedings*, 1924, p. i; Minnesota Association of County Commissioners, *Proceedings*, 1925, p. 35 (quote), 40; 1929, p. 37–39, 41–45; 1930, p. 171.

¹¹ United States Department of Commerce, Bureau of the Census, *Paupers in Almshouses, 1923* (Washington, D.C., 1925).

¹² Estelle M. Stewart, *The Cost of American Almshouses*, 7 (United States Department of Labor, Bureau of Labor Statistics, *Bulletins*, no. 386 — Washington, D.C., 1925). The labor department continued its inquiry into all types of institutional care for the dependent aged and made an exhaustive study of retirement systems and pension plans. Four years later it issued a greatly expanded report by Florence E. Parker, *Care of Aged Persons in the United States* (Bureau of Labor Statistics, *Bulletins*, no. 489 — Washington, D.C., 1929).

¹³ Evans' report was published at Des Moines, Iowa. Its importance is suggested by the comment of two later social historians, who called its publication "the turning point in the movement for old-age pensions. . . . Where public investigations pointing to excessive costs and inhumanity had failed to awaken an indifferent public, this study succeeded." John D. Hogan and Francis A. J. Ianni, *American Social Legislation*, 492 (New York, 1956).

¹⁴ Senate Interim Committee, *Report*, 1. In addition to Nordlin, the committee included Senators William C. Zamboni, Owatonna, Henry L. Morin, Duluth, K. K. Solberg, Clarkfield, and A. L. Lennon, Minneapolis.

¹⁵ Bureau of the Census, *Paupers in Almshouses*, 5, 7; Senate Interim Committee, *Report*, Table.

¹⁶ Bureau of the Census, *Paupers in Almshouses*, 10, 11, 50; Parker, *Care of Aged Persons*, 6, 15.

¹⁷ Stewart, *Cost of American Almshouses*, 5.

¹⁸ Minnesota Conference of Social Work, *Proceedings*, 1924, p. 11; State Board of Control, *Biennial Reports*, 1925–26, p. 52.

¹⁹ Stewart, *Cost of American Almshouses*, 10, 11, 12.

²⁰ Stewart, *Cost of American Almshouses*, 16, 25, 42–48. The quotation is on p. 42.

²¹ Stewart, *Cost of American Almshouses*, 29–37 (quote, p. 36); Evans, *American Poorfarm*, 2, 55. Evans' Minnesota sampling included poorhouses in Aitkin, Anoka, Blue Earth, Dakota, Hubbard, Koochiching, Mower, Murray, St. Louis, and Wilkin counties. Only one — Mower County — had a new building. Evans' criticism of that institution (p. 55 — "sexes not segregated; sleep on same floor") hardly seems valid, in view of the fact that the quarters for men and women were at opposite ends of the building separated by the superintendent's apartment.

²² Stewart, *Cost of American Almshouses*, 35. Evans, *American Poorfarm*, de-

scribes numerous institutions for the poor combined with, or in close proximity to, convict farms. See, for example, p. 56, 63, 76.

²³ Stewart, *Cost of American Almshouses*, 41; Evans, *American Poorfarm*, [i] (quote), 9-11.

²⁴ Stewart, *Cost of American Almshouses*, 49; Evans, *American Poorfarm*, 3.

²⁵ Senate Interim Committee, *Report*, 4.

²⁶ Stewart, *Cost of American Almshouses*, 11; Bureau of the Census, *Paupers in Almshouses*, 3.

²⁷ Stewart, *Cost of American Almshouses*, 49, 52.

²⁸ Clark, in *The Survey*, 42:624; National Conference of Social Work, *Proceedings*, 1926, p. 528, 564.

²⁹ Stewart, *Cost of American Almshouses*, 52.

³⁰ Norman County Board of Commissioners, "Proceedings," March 18, 1926.

³¹ *Laws*, 1899, p. 295; Stewart, *Cost of American Almshouses*, 22.

³² See pages 85 and 103, above.

³³ E. C. Teachout, "Homes for the Aged," in Minnesota Conference of Social Work, *Proceedings*, 1920, p. 66; Isaac M. Rubinow, *The Quest for Security*, 262 (New York, 1934); Minnesota Sunset Homes Committee, *A Practical Plan for the Care of the Aged under Honorable Conditions* (n.d., n.p.), a brochure in Elmer E. Adams and Family Papers, MHS.

³⁴ On Teachout and the commission here and below, see Minnesota Conference of Social Work, *Proceedings*, 1920, p. 66-69. The quotation below is on p. 68.

³⁵ A copy of the circular is in Governor's Correspondence, 1920, Minnesota State Archives. A revised but essentially similar version of the proposals may be found in Minnesota Conference of Social Work, *Proceedings*, 1928, p. 76. See also *Proceedings*, 1920, p. 67, for the Teachout quotation.

³⁶ A copy of the Sunset Homes Bill may be found among those preserved by the MHS for the 42 session, 1921, Senate File 175. See also *Senate Journal*, 1921, p. 86, 219, 221, 294, 367, 402; *House Journal*, 1921, p. 359, 363, 367, 383, 405, 415; Minnesota Conference of Social Work, *Proceedings*, 1928, p. 76; Anne F. Fenlason, "The Problem of Old Age Particularly with Reference to the Institutional Facilities in Minneapolis," 68, 69, 83 (Master's thesis, University of Minnesota, 1927). For Mrs. Fenlason's comments, see Minnesota Conference of Social Work, *Proceedings*, 1926, p. 34 (quote).

³⁷ Thomas Paine, *Agrarian Justice, Opposed to Agrarian Law, and to Agrarian Monopoly*, 11 (Philadelphia, 1797); Chambers, *Seedtime of Reform*, 154; Parker, *Care of Aged Persons*, 86, 110, 113, 158, 287, 296.

³⁸ Amelia Sears, in Minnesota Conference of Social Work, *Proceedings*, 1926, p. 43. For Mrs. Fenlason's remarks quoted in the next paragraph, see p. 34; on the Senate Interim Committee, see p. 129, above.

³⁹ Chambers, *Seedtime of Reform*, 164; Senate Interim Committee, *Report*, 1 (quote). In 1933 the name of the national organization was changed to the American Association for Social Security.

⁴⁰ Minnesota Conference of Social Work, *Proceedings*, 1928, p. 79.

⁴¹ Senate Interim Committee, *Report*, 1, 2 (quote); *Laws*, 1929, p. 42-48.

⁴² Parker, *Care of Aged Persons*, 69, 70, 73, 79; Chambers, *Seedtime of Reform*, 162. Minnesota, Utah, and California obtained pension laws in 1929 and were not included in the bureau's study. For a comparison of the Minnesota law with those of other states, see "Operation of Public Old-Age Pension Systems in the United States, 1930," in *Monthly Labor Review*, 6:1267-1280 (June, 1931).

⁴³ Complete population figures for Minnesota poorhouses in 1930 are not available, although it is known that those in Hennepin, Ramsey, and St. Louis counties contained 856 inmates in that year. See Glenn Steele, "Number of Aged in Public and in Private Institutions, 1930," in *Monthly Labor Review*, 34:256 (February, 1932).

On Pine County, see p. 101, above. Chippewa County discontinued its poorhouse in December, 1927, and leased the property for farm operation only. Wilkin County closed its poorhouse near Breckenridge in January, 1929. See Sarah Riley, "County Poor Farms in Minnesota," 47 (Master's thesis, University of Minnesota, 1943), and files of the counties mentioned, McClure Papers.

CHAPTER 9 — THE QUESTING TWENTIES 1920-1930

[1] See Appendix, Table 2, below.

[2] See, for example, the discussion of the Evangelical Lutheran Church's development in Edwin L. Lueker, ed., *Lutheran Cyclopedia*, 351–353 (St. Louis, 1954).

[3] McDonald, *With Lamps Burning*, 263; St. Elizabeth's Nursing Home file, McClure Papers.

[4] *St. James Plaindealer*, October 5, 1922.

[5] *St. Paul City Directories*, 1922, 1925; *St. Paul Dispatch*, August 16, 1962, p. 8. The home, which is now affiliated with the United Church of Christ, still operates at 494 Ashland; a new wing was added in 1962. See *The St. Paul's Church Home*, a pamphlet in MHS.

[6] See Bethany Covenant Home file, McClure Papers; *Princeton Union*, May 19, 1927; *Elim Home Dedication*, a leaflet dated May 17, 1961, in MHS; Gunnar A. Bloom, *The Svithiod Singing Club*, 33 (Chicago, [1957?]); and Svithiod Home file, McClure Papers. The Svithiod Home closed in 1967. The Swedish Evangelical Covenant Church's first home was Ebenezer Home at Buffalo, established in 1918.

[7] Aftenro Home file, McClure Papers; *Duluth News-Tribune*, June 3, 1956, Women's Activities Section, p. 4.

[8] Pioneer Memorial Home file, McClure Papers; *Fergus Falls Tribune*, April 26, May 10, December 6, 1928; *Fergus Falls Daily Journal*, December 9, 1928.

[9] Interview of the author with Mrs. Irene Zerahn, Minneapolis, March 12, 1964; "Admission Register," 1925–28, in the possession of Danebo Home, Minneapolis.

[10] Vaclav Vojta, *Czechoslovak Baptists*, 216 (Minneapolis, 1941).

[11] Estella L. Elke, "The Moravians in Carver County, Minnesota," 14, a typewritten manuscript, and *The Lake Auburn Home*, an undated brochure, both in MHS; *Weekly Valley Herald* (Chaska), November 15, 1928.

[12] Minnesota Masonic Home file, McClure Papers; John B. Tomhave, "The Minnesota Masonic Home," in Educational Lodge no. 1002, *Bulletins*, December 1, 1957, p. 1, 2 (quote).

[13] Robert Morris, "The Future Institution for the Aged," in *Aging with a Future: Reports and Guidelines from the White House Conference on Aging*, 100 (Washington, D.C., 1961).

[14] Chambers, *Seedtime of Reform*, 160.

[15] For the labor department study here and in the next paragraph, see Parker, *Care of Aged Persons*, 3, 4, 13, 34. The two census bureau studies were entitled *Benevolent Institutions, 1904* and *Benevolent Institutions, 1910*.

[16] Florence E. Parker, "Institutional Care of the Aged in the United States," in Isaac M. Rubinow, ed., *The Care of the Aged: Proceedings of the Deutsch Foundation Conference*, 36 (Chicago, 1931).

[17] Parker, *Care of Aged Persons*, 23, 25 (quote); "Problem of Idleness in Old People's Homes," in *Monthly Labor Review*, 29:1233 (December, 1929).

[18] Parker, *Care of Aged Persons*, 38, 39 (quotes); "Problem of Idleness," in *Monthly Labor Review*, 29:1233.

[19] Parker, *Care of Aged Persons*, 23.

[20] Parker, *Care of Aged Persons*, 26, 30.

268 MORE THAN A ROOF

²¹ "Problem of Idleness," in *Monthly Labor Review*, 29:1233. This issue carried the labor department's supplementary report.
²² Fenlason, "Problem of Old Age," 19.
²³ Woman's Union Relief Society, *Scandinavian Union Relief Home, Twenty-fifth Anniversary Souvenir*, 6 (Minneapolis, 1931); *Bethesda Homes*, 11 — both in McClure Papers; *Lyngblomsten Souvenir Book*, 33.
²⁴ On the cabaret, see Fenlason, "Problem of Old Age," 49.
²⁵ Home for the Friendless, *Annual Reports*, 1899, p. 4.
²⁶ Fenlason, "Problem of Old Age," 49.
²⁷ E. W. Walters, ed., John Bunyan, *The Pilgrim's Progress*, 153 (quote), 317, 318 (Nashville, Tenn., [1939]); *Våra ålderdomshem*, 5, an undated brochure owned by Bethany Covenant Home, Minneapolis; Aftenro Home file (quote), McClure Papers. For the Biblical references, see Exodus 15:27 and Genesis 28:19.
²⁸ *Lyngblomsten Souvenir Book*, 28.
²⁹ Little Sisters of the Poor, "Histoire," Book 2, covering the years 1900–36, owned by the St. Paul Little Sisters. The quotation was translated by Sister M. Jeanne Berchmans.
³⁰ Woman's Christian Association, *Annual Reports*, 1926, p. 8, 9.
³¹ Home for Children and Aged Women, Minutes, January 9, 1922; *Annual Reports*, 1922, p. 8 (quote); *Minneapolis Journal*, January 14, 1923, Women's Section, p. 4.
³² On the conference, see Isaac M. Rubinow, "The Modern Problem of the Care of the Aged," in Rubinow, ed., *Care of the Aged*, 10 (quote).
³³ Chambers, *Seedtime of Reform*, 161. On Hazard, see p. 5, above.
³⁴ Edna L. Foley, in Rubinow, ed., *Care of the Aged*, 51.
³⁵ Michael M. Davis, "Some Medical Aspects of the Care of the Aged," in Rubinow, ed., *Care of the Aged*, 48.
³⁶ Ernst P. Boas, "The Care of the Aged Sick," in Rubinow, ed., *Care of the Aged*, 44.
³⁷ Frank Z. Glick, in Rubinow, ed., *Care of the Aged*, 53.
³⁸ H. L. Lurie, "The Relation of the Family Service Agency to the Care of the Aged," in Rubinow, ed., *Care of the Aged*, 66.
³⁹ Lurie, in Rubinow, ed., *Care of the Aged*, 71; Rubinow, *Quest for Security*, 240.
⁴⁰ Quotations from Mrs. Fenlason, here and below, are in her thesis, "Problem of Old Age," 15, 24, 26. On the eastern caseworker, see Minnesota Conference of Social Work, *Proceedings*, 1926, p. 23.
⁴¹ Parker, *Care of Aged Persons*, 13, 14, 128. The Bureau of Labor Statistics included 55 homes operated by federal and state governments and 43 sponsored by labor unions. If these are excluded in order to conform to the type of institutions included for Minnesota, the national total was 1,172. Of these, 526, or 45 per cent, were church-owned.
The Church of God Home was opened in 1908. For information on its development, see the home's file, McClure Papers.
⁴² Fenlason, "Problem of Old Age," 83.

CHAPTER 10 – FROM GREAT DEPRESSION TO SOCIAL SECURITY 1930–1940

¹ Abbott, *From Relief to Social Security*, 3 (quote). See also David A. Shannon, *The Great Depression*, especially chapters 2, 5, 6 (Englewood Cliffs, N.J., 1960).
² Donald Anderson, "Unemployment Insurance," in Minnesota Governor's

Conference on Aging, *Reports,* 1962, p. 40 (quote). See also Appendix, Table 2.

³ *Laws,* 1929, p. 42. The law was amended in 1931 to transfer to county boards the duties previously assigned to the district judges, but no change was made in pension requirements. See *Laws,* 1931, p. 157–161. See also G. A. Lundquist, in Minnesota Association of County Commissioners, *Proceedings,* 1931, p. 135; Aitkin County Board of Commissioners, "Proceedings," July, 1932.

⁴ Brown, *Public Relief,* 124, 125; Frank M. Rarig, ed., *A Report of the Minnesota State Board of Control as the State Emergency Relief Administration, 1932-34,* p. 9 (quote), 13 (St. Paul, 1934).

⁵ Blegen, *Minnesota,* 526; Wilkin County Commissioners, "Proceedings," May 22, 1934.

⁶ Brown, *Public Relief,* 142; Rarig, ed., *Report of State Emergency Relief Administration,* 31, 33.

⁷ *Old Age Security Herald,* March, 1933, p. 1, published by the American Association for Social Security; *Laws,* 1933, p. 569, 1935, p. 643–652; Karleen Fawcett, *Old Age Pensions as a Minnesota Problem,* 16n (Minneapolis, 1935). On Olson, see John S. McGrath and James J. Delmont, *Floyd Björnsterne Olson, Minnesota's Greatest Liberal Governor: A Memorial Volume,* 182, 229, 269 (quote), ([St. Paul], 1937). On the effects of state pension laws, see McGrath and Delmont, *Olson,* 292, and Boards of Commissioners, "Proceedings" for the following counties: Norman, January 4, 1934; Pine, February 6, 1934; Becker, April 2, 1934; Wilkin, September 14, 1933, November 1, 1934.

⁸ McGrath and Delmont, *Olson,* 292; Minnesota Emergency Relief Administration, *Analysis & Report on Old Age Pension and Mothers' Allowance by Counties,* 9 (St. Paul, 1935); Stewart, *Cost of American Almshouses,* 5.

⁹ "History," 1, 2, in St. Louis County Home file, McClure Papers.

¹⁰ United States Public Works Administration, *America Builds: The Record of PWA,* 7 (Washington, D.C., 1939); *Grand Rapids Herald-Review,* September 6, October 4, 1933, January 17, August 22 (quote), 1934.

¹¹ Chambers, *Seedtime of Reform,* 167–170, 177–181; National Association of Manufacturers, *Retirement Security in a Free Society,* 12 (quote), (Research Department, *Economic Policy Division Series,* no. 67 – New York, 1954).

¹² Abraham Holtzman, *The Townsend Movement, A Political Study,* 36 (New York, 1963); Abbott, *From Relief to Social Security,* 236.

¹³ Poyntz Tyler, ed., *Social Welfare in the United States,* 12 (quote), (*Reference Shelf,* vol. 27, no. 3 – New York, 1955); Edwin E. Witte, *The Development of the Social Security Act,* 7–9, 49, 75, 108, 201 (Madison, Wis., 1962); Samuel I. Rosenman, comp., *The Public Papers and Addresses of Franklin D. Roosevelt,* 2:11, 3:292 (New York, 1938); United States Committee on Economic Security, *Report to the President,* 52 (Washington, D.C., 1935).

¹⁴ United States, *Statutes at Large,* vol. 49, part 1, p. 620 (quote), 648; National Association of Manufacturers, *Retirement Security in a Free Society,* 12 (quote). Under the Reorganization Act of 1939, the Social Security Board became part of the Federal Security Agency.

¹⁵ Social Security Board, *Annual Reports,* 1936, p. 19, 20; *Social Security Bulletin,* August, 1938, p. 1. See also Tyler, ed., *Social Welfare in the United States,* 25.

¹⁶ Brown, *Public Relief,* 328 (quote); Tyler, ed., *Social Welfare in the United States,* 51. Not until February, 1951, did the number of aged persons receiving old age and survivors insurance benefits first exceed the number on old age assistance, according to United States Department of Health, Education, and Welfare, *Annual Reports,* 1953, p. 10, 30.

¹⁷ Brown, *Public Relief,* 328; Minnesota, *Laws, Extra Session,* 1935, p. 122–137. Minnesota Board of Control, *Biennial Reports,* 1935-36, p. 8, 82; Minnesota Department of Social Security, Division of Social Welfare, *Annual Report on Old Age Assistance, 1939,* 5.

¹⁸ Minnesota, *Laws, Extra Session*, 1935, p. 132; *Laws*, 1937, p. 466, 468.

¹⁹ For the quotations, see Social Security Board, Bureau of Public Assistance, *Sheltered Care and Home Services for Public Assistance Recipients*, 1 (*Public Assistance Reports*, no. 5 — Washington, D.C., 1944); Stewart, *Cost of American Almshouses*, iii; Abbott, *From Relief to Social Security*, 238. On the Social Security Act, see note 14, above.

²⁰ *Social Security Bulletin*, March, 1938, p. 42 (quote); *Monthly Labor Review*, 47:522, 523 (September, 1938); Helen G. Tyson, "The Poorhouse Persists," in *Survey Midmonthly*, 74:76 (March, 1938).

²¹ *Social Security Bulletin*, March, 1938, p. 42.

²² On county poor farms closed during the 1930s, see Riley, "County Poor Farms in Minnesota," 48, and a consolidated list prepared by the author, McClure Papers. See also *Fairmont Daily Sentinel*, January 29, 1937; *Shakopee Argus-Tribune*, September 29, October 27, 1938; and p. 175, below.

²³ For the counties which leased their facilities during the 1930s, see Riley, "County Poor Farms in Minnesota," 64, 95, 100, and Appendix, Table 1, below. See also Chisago County Board of Commissioners, "Proceedings," February 14, 1938 (quote). In some areas the increased population of leased county facilities was probably due also to the fact that the counties now received both state and federal funds and could provide help to more persons.

²⁴ Riley, "County Poor Farms in Minnesota," 41; for the anecdote in the next paragraph, see Riley, 97.

²⁵ *The Mission Farms*, an unpaged brochure published by the Union City Mission, 1966. The MHS has a copy. For the early history of this institution, see Union City Mission, *Annual Reports*, 1922, p. 3, in MHS.

²⁶ Rarig, ed., *Report of State Emergency Relief Administration*, 35–38.

²⁷ Board of Corrections and Charities, *Biennial Reports*, 1883–84, p. 173.

²⁸ Women's Welfare League of Minneapolis, "Secretary's Report, 1933," p. 4, a manuscript in MHS; Ethel McClure, *Homes for Aged and Chronically Ill Persons in Minnesota: Their Development and Licensure, 1959*, 18 (Minnesota Department of Health, Division of Hospital Services — Minneapolis, 1959).

²⁹ Board of Control, *Biennial Reports*, 1935–36, p. 137.

³⁰ Nancy L. Austin, "Old Folks Without Homes," in *Survey Midmonthly*, 75:9 (January, 1939).

³¹ For the quotations here and in the next paragraph, see Julian F. DuBois to H. M. Workman, November 19, 1935, in the files of the Minnesota Department of Health, quoted in McClure, *Homes for Aged and Chronically Ill Persons, 1959*, 27.

³² See E. A. Meyerding to Arthur M. Calvin, November 26, 1935, in the files of the Minnesota Department of Health, quoted in part in McClure, *Homes for Aged and Chronically Ill Persons, 1959*, 28.

³³ *Laws*, 1939, p. 943–947.

CHAPTER 11 – RED INK AND MIDNIGHT OIL 1930–1940

¹ *Minnesota Lutheran* (Clear Lake, Wis.), December 13, 1939, p. 2, a weekly newspaper carrying official announcements of the Lutheran Minnesota Conference. On earlier Augustana homes at Chisago City and St. Paul, see chapter 7, above.

² *Minnesota Conference Charities*, August, 1940, p. 1; February, 1954, p. 3. See also Bethesda Hospital, *Annual Reports*, 1931, p. 52.

³ *Minnesota Lutheran*, December 13, 1939, p. 1, 2 (quote); Mankato Lutheran Home file, McClure Papers.

⁴ *Blue Earth Post,* August 20, 1931; *Winnebago City Press-News,* October 19, 1929, January 18, 1930; Pace, *Our Fathers Built,* 147; Winnebago Baptist Residence file, McClure Papers. The residence is still in operation.

⁵ Regarding plans to take over the New Prague home, see circular letter, March 28, 1939, in files of Northwest Baptist Home Society, 122 West Franklin Avenue, Minneapolis. See also p. 143, above, and p. 205, below.

On the Red Wing home, see *Republican,* July 24, 1907; Christian A. Rasmussen, *A History of the City of Red Wing, Minnesota,* 176 ([Red Wing], 1933); Northwest Baptist Home Society, Minutes, October 6, 20, November 28, 1939, March 5, 1959, October 25, 1960, in the society's files. The Red Wing home closed in 1961.

⁶ See Sacred Heart Home file, McClure Papers. The home was discontinued in 1952.

⁷ St. Mary's Home and St. Francis Home files, McClure Papers; *Pioneer Press,* October 4, 1936, Section 1, p. 9; Reardon, *Catholic Church in the Diocese of St. Paul,* 609, 663, 672, 676; McDonald, *With Lamps Burning,* 95; Julius A. Coller II, *The Shakopee Story,* 66, 68, 156 (Shakopee, 1960); *Shakopee Argus-Tribune,* September 29, October 21, 1938. There is some discrepancy among these sources on the date St. Gertrude's Academy was built.

⁸ McCabe Guest Home file, McClure Papers; *Duluth City Directories,* 1939, 1940, 1941. St. Ann's closed in 1956; the few remaining residents were transferred to St. Mary's Hospital, Duluth. The McCabe home closed in 1963; its residents were transferred to the new St. Ann's Home.

⁹ Tyler Lutheran Home file, McClure Papers. The name of the institution until 1960 was the Tyler Old People's Home. It is still in operation.

¹⁰ Ida A. Johnson, "Augustana Home History," 27 (quote), a typed manuscript in the possession of the home. Excerpts from this manuscript are in Augustana Home file, McClure Papers.

¹¹ On sponsors' financial support, see Parker, *Care of Aged Persons,* 32. See also *Ebenezer,* May, 1942, p. 12 (quotes).

¹² *Bethesda Homes,* 11.

¹³ For quotations on the Jones-Harrison Home here and in the next paragraph, see Woman's Christian Association, *Annual Reports,* 1930, p. 31; 1932, p. 2; 1935, p. 9, 14.

¹⁴ Minneapolis Council of Social Agencies, *Agency Report: Care of the Aged,* 42, 43; Woman's Christian Association, *Annual Reports,* 1930, p. 30; 1932, p. 4 (quote).

¹⁵ Woman's Christian Association, *Annual Reports,* 1935, p. 22.

¹⁶ Home for the Friendless, *Annual Reports,* 1936, p. 6; Minutes, January, 1931; November, 1933 (quote).

¹⁷ Norwegian Lutheran Church of America District Convention, *Annual Reports,* 1935, p. 19, in the files of Luther Theological Seminary, St. Paul; copies of minutes of the board and other material in Glenwood Home file, McClure Papers. For statistics on home closings, see United States Department of Labor, Bureau of Labor Statistics, *Homes for Aged in the United States,* 2 (*Bulletins,* no. 677 — Washington, D.C., 1941).

¹⁸ Norwegian Lutheran Church, *Annual Reports,* 1936, p. 129. In 1944 the assets of the Glenwood Home were transferred to the Knute Nelson Home in Alexandria, and for some years the latter was known as the Knute Nelson-Glenwood Memorial Home. The Glenwood portion of the name was dropped before 1961. Glenwood Home file, McClure Papers.

¹⁹ Bureau of Public Assistance, *Sheltered Care and Home Services,* 1.

²⁰ Bureau of Public Assistance, *Sheltered Care and Home Services,* 1, 2, 13, 20; Hogan and Ianni, *American Social Legislation,* 501; Minneapolis Council of Social Agencies, *Agency Report: Care of the Aged,* 28; Minnesota Board of Control,

A *Digest of the Old Age Assistance Act Annotated with Opinions of the Attorney General relating to the Act*, 24 ([St. Paul], 1938). See also Floyd A. Bond, et al., *A California Study of a National Problem*, 110 (New York, 1954).

[21] *Ebenezer*, February, 1936, p. [16].

[22] Unidentified clipping dated November 27, 1936, bylined "A Staff Correspondent of the *Christian Science Monitor*," in Aging—Minnesota Institutional Care file, Minneapolis Public Library, Sociology Section. A copy is in McClure Papers.

[23] Shearon, "Economic Status of the Aged," in *Social Security Bulletin*, March, 1938, p. 16.

[24] *Agency Report: Care of the Aged*, 45. There were, in addition to recipients in the eight homes studied, thirteen recipients in three of the four Minneapolis homes not associated with the Community Fund. The fourth home — the Little Sisters of the Poor — did not accept old age assistance recipients on the grounds that they were not "dependent aged" as defined by the rules of the order.

[25] *Agency Report: Care of the Aged*, 20, 28, 29, 30.

[26] Minnesota Masonic Home file, McClure Papers; *Ebenezer*, May, 1942, p. 14 (quotes).

[27] Home for Children and Aged Women, Minutes, July 9, August 13, 1935. The children's department was never reopened.

[28] *Bethesda Homes*, 12.

[29] On the royal visits, here and below, see *Minneapolis Tribune*, April 22, p. 12; June 10, p. 1; June 11, p. 11; June 14, p. 2; *Minneapolis Journal*, April 23, p. 1—all in 1939. See also *Ebenezer*, May, 1942, p. 28 (quote).

[30] Bureau of Labor Statistics, *Homes for Aged*, 6, 13.

[31] Minneapolis Council of Social Agencies, *Agency Report: Care of the Aged*, 20 (quote); Bureau of Labor Statistics, *Homes for Aged*, 64–66.

CHAPTER 12 – STANDARDS AND SHORTAGES DURING WORLD WAR II 1940–1950

[1] Hoffman, in Rose, ed., *Aging in Minnesota*, 40 (quote), 42.

[2] "Population Aging and Assistance," in *Social Welfare Review*, December, 1943, p. 13, a monthly publication of the Minnesota Division of Social Welfare; Hogan and Ianni, *American Social Legislation*, 505; William E. Leuchtenburg, et al., *New Deal and Global War*, 102, 117 *(Life History of the United States*, vol. 11 — New York, 1964).

[3] *Social Welfare Review*, January, 1943, p. 17; February, 1944, p. 14; Le Mont Crandall, "Aged Face Many Problems," in *Minnesota Welfare*, June, 1948, a monthly publication of the Minnesota Division of Social Welfare.

[4] Minnesota Division of Social Welfare, *Annual Reports*, 1945, p. 18.

[5] See Appendix, Table 1, below.

[6] For material here and in the next paragraph, see Riley, "County Poor Farms in Minnesota," 54, 70, 79 (quotes), 92.

[7] See Riley, "County Poor Farms in Minnesota," 93, and for material in the next paragraph, p. 50, 53. Redwood and Fillmore counties did not reply to the questionnaire.

[8] On Parkview Hospital, see Minneapolis Council of Social Agencies, *Agency Report: Health and Organized Care of the Sick*, 103 *(Community Survey of Social and Health Work in Minneapolis*, 1938).

On St. Paul, see Ramsey County and City of St. Paul Public Welfare Board, *Annual Reports*, 1939, p. 124. For background on Ancker Hospital, which closed in 1965, see Castle, *History of St. Paul*, 1:344; *Pioneer Press*, October 3, 1965,

REFERENCE NOTES – CHAPTER 12   273

First Section, p. 15; *St. Paul Dispatch,* October 14, 1965, p. 4.

For the arrangements with Miller Memorial Hospital, see the Commission on Hospital Care report on that institution, 1946, in the files of the Minnesota Department of Health, Minneapolis.

⁸ On county welfare boards, see chapter 10, note 18, above; on administrative responsibility for admissions, see Riley, "County Poor Farms in Minnesota," 54.

¹⁰ See Riley, "County Poor Farms in Minnesota," 55, 56, 72 (quote).

¹¹ Riley, "County Poor Farms in Minnesota," 73.

¹² Riley, "County Poor Farms in Minnesota," 81, 86 (quote).

¹³ Riley, "County Poor Farms in Minnesota," 50; Ethel McClure, *Facilities for the Care of the Infirm Aged in Nursing Homes, County Homes, and Homes for the Aged in Minnesota,* 31 (Minneapolis, 1950).

¹⁴ McClure, *Homes for Aged and Chronically Ill Persons, 1959,* 44.

¹⁵ McClure, *Homes for Aged and Chronically Ill Persons, 1959,* 23.

¹⁶ *Laws,* 1941, p. 1149–1153; McClure, *Homes for Aged and Chronically Ill Persons, 1959,* 27–29; Ray M. Amberg, "The Operations of Licensure Laws in Providing and Improving Hospital Service," in *Wisconsin Hospitals,* November, 1948, p. 1, a publication of the Wisconsin Hospital Association.

¹⁷ Bureau of Public Assistance, *Sheltered Care and Home Services,* 32; Austin, in *Survey Midmonthly,* 75:9; Viktor O. Wilson and Ethel McClure, "Complete Coverage Is Feature of New License Regulations in Minnesota," in *Hospitals,* May, 1944, p. 40–43, published by the American Hospital Association.

¹⁸ *Laws,* 1941, p. 1152; McClure, *Homes for Aged and Chronically Ill Persons, 1959,* 24; see also p. 43–45 for material on the preparation of standards in the next three paragraphs below.

¹⁹ *Laws,* 1951, p. 390–396. See p. 216, below.

²⁰ Department of Health, *Minnesota Directory of Licensed Hospitals and Related Institutions, 1942* (Minneapolis, 1942). These figures do not include the many facilities which were not clearly subject to the law or which were unable or unwilling to meet requirements.

²¹ *Laws,* 1943, p. 1030–1032; Department of Health, *Minnesota Directory of Licensed Hospitals and Related Institutions, 1944,* 30 (Minneapolis, 1944). The six county homes licensed as of July 1, 1944, were: Hennepin, Itasca, Ramsey, Redwood, St. Louis, and Steele. See list prepared by the author on July 1, 1944, in McClure Papers.

²² On fire inspection, see McClure, *Homes for Aged and Chronically Ill Persons, 1959,* 47. The first sprinkler system installed in a Minnesota home for the aged was that added to the Little Sisters of the Poor Home, St. Paul, in December, 1950.

²³ Department of Health, *Licensing Laws and Standards for Hospitals and Related Institutions,* 46 (quote) (Minneapolis, 1944). Although the law providing for the licensing of practical nurses *(Laws,* 1947, p. 626–629) became effective on August 1, 1948, the first examination was not conducted until February, 1949. See *Nursing Home News,* April, 1948, p. 3, a mimeographed quarterly issued by the Hospital Licensing Unit, Minnesota Department of Health. The MHS has a complete file.

²⁴ On the formation of the association, see McClure, *Homes for Aged and Chronically Ill Persons, 1959,* 69. On the training sessions here and in the next paragraph, see p. 61. See also *Nursing Home News,* December, 1950, p. 1 (quote).

²⁵ *Laws,* 1945, p. 532; McClure, *Homes for Aged and Chronically Ill Persons, 1959,* 82.

²⁶ For material cited here and below, see C. Stanley Clifton, "A Study of the Leisure Time Interests and Activities of Old Age Recipients in Commercial Rest Homes in Minnesota," 55, 80, 103, 104, 108, 220, 222, 225 (Ph.D. thesis, University of Minnesota, 1951).

²⁷ Division of Social Welfare, *Annual Reports*, 1949, p. 16; 1953, p. 19. The Hennepin County group worker was Jerome Kaplan. For an account of his activities, see Kaplan, *A Social Program for Older People* (Minneapolis, 1953).
²⁸ *Nursing Home News*, June, 1949, p. 2.
²⁹ *Nursing Home News*, June, 1950, p. 2; September, 1950, p. 2; December, 1950, p. 1, 4; March, 1951, p. 1.
³⁰ McClure, *Homes for Aged and Chronically Ill Persons, 1959*, 64, 65. For a report on the national study, see Commission on Hospital Care, *Hospital Care in the United States* (New York, 1947).
³¹ McClure, *Homes for Aged and Chronically Ill Persons, 1959*, 50 (quote); *Minnesota Welfare*, February, 1948, p. 26. For information on the boarding home fire, see *Minneapolis Star*, January 17, 1948, p. 1; January 20, 1948, p. 1.
³² *Minneapolis Tribune*, March 8, 1949, p. 1, 4. For many years proprietary homes in Minneapolis had been licensed by the city council under a procedure that required reports from local health, building-inspection, fire-prevention, and planning agencies. After the state hospital licensing law went into effect in 1942, it became evident that Minneapolis institutions would be required to have both state and city licenses, and the two health departments worked out a co-operative relationship on inspections. In the study made in 1948–49, workers from the state agency accompanied the city investigator on visits to homes.
³³ McClure, *Homes for Aged and Chronically Ill Persons, 1959*, 51; *Minneapolis Star*, February 19, 1949, p. 4; Minnesota House File 1574, mentioned in *House Journal*, 1949, p. 1245.
³⁴ *Minneapolis Star*, February 19, 1949, p. 4; *Laws*, 1949, p. 1579; United States, *Statutes at Large*, vol. 64, part 1, p. 549.
³⁵ McClure, *Facilities for the Care of the Infirm Aged in Nursing Homes, County Homes, and Homes for the Aged*, 31. The counties which were leasing their farms for private operation in December, 1949, were Beltrami, Brown, Chisago, Dakota, Dodge, Freeborn, Houston, Hubbard, Koochiching, Mower, Nicollet, Pine, and Wabasha. Counties still operating their homes were Blue Earth, Goodhue, Hennepin, Itasca, Lac qui Parle, Ramsey, Redwood, Rice, St. Louis, Steele, and Washington. The Rock County home was leased early in 1950. See county files, McClure Papers. On the closing of sanatoriums, here and below, see Division of Social Welfare, *Annual Reports*, 1945, p. 39; 1950, p. 30, 31. See also *Laws*, 1949, p. 123.
³⁶ Division of Social Welfare, *Annual Reports*, 1949, p. 15; *Nursing Home News*, June, 1949, p. 2 (quote).

CHAPTER 13 – REGULATIONS AND RATION BOOKS 1940–1950

¹ *Servants of Relief for Incurable Cancer*, 19, a pamphlet and other documents in Our Lady of Good Counsel Home file, McClure Papers; Leuchtenburg, et al., *New Deal and Global War*, 102.
² Lutheran Old People's Home, *Dedication Service, New Building, September 27, 1953*, copy in this home's file, McClure Papers; J. A. Aasgaard, circular letter to Madison district pastors, April 30, 1943 (quote), Madison Lutheran Old People's Home file, in the offices of the Division of Social Service, American Lutheran Church, Minneapolis.
³ Aasgaard, circular letter, April 30; H. M. Femrite to H. O. Shurson, July 23; Aasgaard to War Production Board, September 21; to R. R. Syrdal, October 1; to Femrite, October 5 — all dated 1943 and located in Madison Lutheran Old People's Home file, American Lutheran Church offices.

REFERENCE NOTES – CHAPTER 13   275

[4] Aasgaard to Syrdal, October 1, 1943 (quotes); M. O. Kraabel to Aasgaard, November 23, 1943; Syrdal to Aasgaard, April 7, 1944 — all in Madison Lutheran Old People's Home file, American Lutheran Church offices. The home was dedicated on June 18, 1944. See the home's file, McClure Papers, for a copy of the dedicatory program.

[5] Red Wing Seminary Memorial Home and Kenyon Sunset Home files, McClure Papers.

[6] Glenwood Home file, McClure Papers; Dahlen to "Dear Pastor," a circular letter dated December 30, 1946, in the Division of Social Service, American Lutheran Church offices; Nelson, *Lutheran Church Among Norwegian-Americans*, 2:312–314.

[7] *Farmers Independent* (Bagley), May 31, 1945; *Rock County Star Herald* (Luverne), October 29, 1959. On the society, see *Good Samaritan Handbook*, a pamphlet published by the central office in Sioux Falls, South Dakota, and A. J. Hoeger, Jr., to Mrs. June D. Holmquist, April 4, 1968 — both in McClure Papers. Although membership is limited to Lutherans, the society is unaffiliated with any specific church groups.

[8] *Farmers Independent*, May 31, June 7, August 23, October 11, 1945; Clearwater Sunset Home file, McClure Papers.

[9] Walker Methodist Home file, McClure Papers; E. W. Schwenius, "Norwegian-Danish Methodism in Minnesota," and Mrs. Campbell Keith, "The Walker Methodist Home," both in Pace, ed., *Our Fathers Built*, 129, 164, respectively.

[10] *New Prague Times*, June 5, 1947. Nine of the other ten homes opened in the 1940s were: Alliance Residence, Harriet House, Weddell Memorial Residence, Blaisdell Avenue Baptist Home, and Parkview Hospital (nonprofit owner), Minneapolis; Red River Valley Bible School and Home for the Aged, Thief River Falls; St. Joseph's Home, Fairmont; Bemidji Rest Home, Bemidji; and Samaritan Convalescent Hospital and Hotel, Rochester. The tenth — now the Franklin Nursing Home — was formerly the Hillcrest Surgical Hospital. It became a chronic disease hospital in 1935, but was later classified as a nursing home. Files on all these homes are in McClure Papers.

[11] Twin City Linnea Home, Minutes, January 13, 1942; January 12, 1943.

[12] Samuel I. Rosenman, comp., *The Public Papers and Addresses of Franklin D. Roosevelt, 1942*, 223 (New York, 1950); Imogene H. Putnam, *Volunteers in OPA*, 1 (Office of Price Administration, *Historical Reports on War Administration, General Publications*, no. 14 — Washington, D.C., 1947).

[13] William A. Nielander, *Wartime Food Rationing in the United States*, 106 (Baltimore, 1947); Judith Russell and Renee Fantin, *Studies in Food Rationing*, 9, 18, 72 (quote), 86, 87, 204 (Office of Price Administration, *Historical Reports on War Administration, General Publications*, no. 13 — Washington, D.C., 1947).

[14] Russell and Fantin, *Studies in Food Rationing*, 84, 92; Nielander, *Wartime Food Rationing*, 156; Women's Welfare League, Minutes, December 4, 1942 (quote).

[15] Russell and Fantin, *Studies in Food Rationing*, 93; McClure, *Homes for Aged and Chronically Ill Persons, 1959*, 69.

[16] Augustana Home, *Our Heritage*, 9, in McClure Papers.

[17] See, for example, Women's Welfare League, Minutes, May 14, 1943. On the inauguration of withholding, see Lillian Doris, ed., *The American Way in Taxation: Internal Revenue, 1862–1963*, 121 (Englewood Cliffs, N.J., 1963); United States, *Statutes at Large*, vol. 57, part 1, p. 126–150.

[18] Minneapolis Council of Social Agencies, *Agency Report: Care of the Aged*, 19, 20.

[19] Dates here and in next paragraph are drawn from appointment books in the possession of the author. See also McClure, *Homes for Aged and Chronically Ill Persons, 1959*, 61.

[20] Only a brief announcement was mailed by the Center for Continuation Study. The dates were May 17–19, 1943.

[21] McClure, *Homes for Aged and Chronically Ill Persons, 1959*, 62; University of Minnesota Center for Continuation Study, *Continuation Course in Care of the Aged* (Minneapolis, 1949). Robert G. Cerny's slide lecture on "Points to Consider in Building a New Home," discussed below, was not printed. The Minnesota Historical Society has copies of the Center for Continuation Study courses in *Care of the Aged in Institutional Homes* for 1949, 1950, 1952, 1954, and 1955.

[22] Frank H. Krusen, "Some Applications of Physical Medicine in Geriatrics," in Center for Continuation Study, *Care of the Aged in Institutional Homes*, 22–30; *Minneapolis Tribune*, September 6, 1947, p. 1; *Minneapolis Star*, September 5, 1947, p. 12.

[23] Ethel McClure, *The Care of Sick and Infirm Residents in Homes for the Aged in Minnesota*, 20 (Minneapolis, 1945).

[24] McClure, *Care of Sick and Infirm Residents*, 24.

[25] McClure, *Care of Sick and Infirm Residents*, 12–15.

[26] "What It Will Cost the Home in 1944," in *Ebenezer*, February, 1944, p. 10; McClure, *Facilities for the Care of the Infirm Aged in Nursing Homes, County Homes, and Homes for the Aged*, 11, 12; Walker Methodist Home file, McClure Papers.

[27] The four were: Church of God Home, St. Paul Park (closed in the early 1920s); Glenwood Old People's Home (1935); Elim Home, Minneapolis (1945); and New Prague Baptist Home, New Prague (1947).

CHAPTER 14 – PROGRESS IN THE FIFTIES 1950–1960

[1] John L. Thurston, "The Conference," in *Man and His Years: An Account of the First National Conference on Aging*, 6 (Raleigh, N.C., 1951).

[2] Oscar R. Ewing, "Our Aging Population," 1, 2, 4, and Thurston, 5–8, both in *Man and His Years*.

[3] *Man and His Years*, 171.

[4] Minnesota Commission on Aging, *Minnesota's Aging Citizens*, 1951, p. 4, 5, 67 (St. Paul, 1953); Minnesota Commission on Aging, *Minnesota's Aging Citizens*, 1953, p. 4 (St. Paul, 1955); Minnesota, *Laws*, 1951, p. 1084–1086; Minnesota Governor's Citizens Council on Aging, *Reports*, 1956, p. [1], 2; Bernard E. Nash and Ethel McClure, "Aging in Retrospect," in Rose, ed., *Aging in Minnesota*, 6–9. Created by executive order in 1956, the Governor's Citizens Council on Aging achieved statutory existence in 1961. See *Laws*, 1961, p. 737–739.

[5] Minnesota Commission on Aging, *Minnesota's Aging Citizens*, 1951, p. 12 (quotes), 34.

[6] United States, *Statutes at Large*, vol. 60, part 1, p. 1040–1049; Minnesota Department of Health, *Minnesota State Plan for Hospitals, Public Health Centers and Related Medical Facilities*, 1959–1960, p. [iii], 5, 72–75, 92–120 (Minneapolis, 1959). The amount of Hill-Burton money available for nursing homes was very limited, and in Minnesota priority was given to demonstration projects. By 1960 only four had received federal assistance: the Masonic Cancer Nursing Home on the University of Minnesota campus, the Bethesda Hospital Infirmary in St. Paul, the nursing home unit at the Wilder Residences in St. Paul, and a nursing home unit of the Granite Falls Municipal Hospital. Files on these four projects may be found in McClure Papers.

[7] Minnesota, *Laws*, 1951, p. 390–396; 1953, p. 593; McClure, *Homes for Aged and Chronically Ill Persons, 1959*, 40.

REFERENCE NOTES — CHAPTER 14   277

[8] See p. 199, above; Minnesota, *Laws,* 1951, p. 1019–1026, 1050; United States, *Statutes at Large,* vol. 64, part 1, p. 549.

[9] Minnesota Division of Social Welfare, *Annual Reports,* 1948, p. 31; Myers, *Invited and Conquered,* 414; *Lake Park Journal,* June 28, July 12, 1951. The other sanatoriums converted to nursing homes in the 1950s were Fair Oaks Lodge, Wadena, converted in 1952 to Shady Lane Rest Home, operated jointly by Wadena and Todd counties; Deerwood Sanatorium in Crow Wing County converted in 1952 to Cedar Brook Manor; Lake Julia Sanatorium at Puposky in Beltrami County converted in 1954 to Lake Julia Rest Home; Otter Tail County Sanatorium at Battle Lake converted in 1955 to Otter Tail County Nursing Home; Oakland Park Sanatorium at Thief River Falls converted in 1955 to Oakland Park Nursing Home under the joint sponsorship of Marshall, Pennington, and Roseau counties; Buena Vista Sanatorium at Wabasha converted in 1956 to Buena Vista Rest Home by Wabasha County; Trudeau Building of Nopeming Sanatorium in St. Louis County converted in 1957 to Trudeau Nursing Home Unit of Nopeming; and Glen Lake Sanatorium, Oak Terrace, which operated a Hennepin County nursing home in 1959–60. See files in McClure Papers.

[10] See Chisago County file, McClure Papers.

[11] See files on these county homes, McClure Papers.

[12] Ray Johnson, "County Home," in Minnesota Governor's Council on Aging, *Reports,* 1958, p. 62. One other county — Hubbard — purchased in 1955 a new nursing home building which had been erected for it by a private contractor. After leasing the structure for several years, the county took control in 1960. See Traverse and Hubbard County files, McClure Papers.

[13] Files on Pioneers' Infirmary and St. Louis County and Mesabi homes, McClure Papers; Minnesota Commission on Aging, *Minnesota's Aging Citizens,* 1953, p. 38.

[14] On the number of beds, see Department of Health, *Minnesota Directory of Licensed Hospitals and Related Institutions, 1953,* 13; *1957,* 18 (Minneapolis, 1953, 1957). See also St. Louis County homes file, McClure Papers.

[15] Work sheet listing homes opened in the 1950s and files on Tuff Memorial Home, Paul Watkins Memorial Methodist Home, Mary Rondorf Home, and Pioneer Memorial Home — all in McClure Papers; McDonald, *With Lamps Burning,* 263.

[16] Work sheet listing the nineteen new homes, McClure Papers; Commission on Aging, *Minnesota's Aging Citizens,* 1951, p. 47.

[17] For the suggestions and model floor plans prepared by the United States Public Health Service, see Neil F. McDonald and Marshall Shaffer, "Planning Suggestions and Demonstration Plans for Acute General Hospitals," in *Hospitals,* July, 1943, p. 33–68. A reprint of the article, with additional material subsequently developed including suggestions for nursing homes, was made available to architects and planning committees. The suggestions were originally prepared for use in the emergency health facilities construction program under the Lanham Act and were later adopted for use in the Hill-Burton construction program.

[18] Commission on Aging, *Minnesota's Aging Citizens,* 1953, p. 38, 39, 41; Minnesota Senate File 53, referred to in *Senate Journal,* 1957, p. 60, 1063, 1134; McClure, *Homes for Aged and Chronically Ill Persons, 1959,* 73; *Minnesota's Health,* January, 1957, p. 3, published monthly by the Minnesota Department of Health.

The first Minnesota home for the aged to be financed by a Federal Housing Administration loan was the Elders Home in New York Mills. The loan was approved in the fall of 1959, and the institution opened in October, 1960. By the summer of 1967, 15 Minnesota homes had been financed in this way. Elders

Home file, McClure Papers; *St. Paul Pioneer Press*, September 5, 1959, p. 6; interview of the author with R. W. Buskirk, deputy state director, Federal Housing Administration, August 7, 1967.

[19] This description of Tuff Memorial Home, which opened in 1959, is quoted from a brochure in the home's file, McClure Papers.

[20] McClure, *Homes for Aged and Chronically Ill Persons, 1959*, 74.

[21] McClure, *Homes for Aged and Chronically Ill Persons, 1959*, 72.

[22] McClure, *Homes for Aged and Chronically Ill Persons, 1959*, 69. The Department of Public Welfare adopted the standards for nursing homes that had been used by the State Department of Health. By the end of the decade virtually all of the seventeen county-owned homes had qualified and received licensure as nursing homes from the welfare department. The State Department of Health continued to license nonprofit and proprietary homes, in both the nursing and boarding care categories.

[23] McClure, *Homes for Aged and Chronically Ill Persons, 1959*, 70.

[24] Jerry Solon, et al., *Nursing Homes, Their Patients and Their Care*, 54, 56, 57 (United States Department of Health, Education, and Welfare, Public Health Service, *Monographs*, no. 46 — Washington, D.C., 1957).

[25] Commission on Aging, *Minnesota's Aging Citizens*, 1951, p. 34 (quote); Division of Social Welfare, *Annual Reports*, 1953, p. 19.

[26] Naime E. Wessin, "Successful Rehabilitation Program," in *Practical Nursing*, December, 1956, p. 10–13, published by the National Association for Practical Nurse Education; *Minnesota's Health*, May, 1953, p. 1.

[27] May Morrow, "Geriatrics-Nursing," in Minnesota Center for Continuation Study, *Care of the Aged in Institutional Homes*, 1950, p. 21.

[28] Quoted material here and in the next paragraph may be found in William Hoffman, "Preparing the Applicant for Group Living," in Center for Continuation Study, *Care of the Aged in Institutional Homes*, 1954, p. 21, 23.

[29] Abraham J. Heschel, "The Older Person and the Family in the Perspective of Jewish Tradition," in *Aging with a Future: Reports . . . from the White House Conference*, 42.

[30] Morton Leeds, "Let's Sponsor a Home for the Aged," in Morton Leeds and Herbert Shore, eds., *Geriatric Institutional Management*, 302 (New York, 1964).

[31] Material here and in the next paragraph is drawn from "History of St. Francis Home," [3–6, 9–11], McClure Papers; Sister Mary Laurice, "Program Development in Homes," in American Association for Homes for the Aging, *Conference Report No. 3*, 33–37, 39 (New York, [1964]). The quotation is on p. 33.

[32] Itasca County Nursing Home file, McClure Papers; *Grand Rapids Herald-Review*, November 18, 1958.

[33] *Grand Rapids Herald-Review*, November 24, 1959.

[34] "Institutional Programs and Social Services," in *Aging with a Future*, 99 (quote); Minneapolis Council of Social Agencies, *Agency Report: Care of the Aged*, 20.

[35] Arnold M. Rose, "Activities in Preparation for the White House Conference," in Rose, ed., *Aging in Minnesota*, 12–20. The quotation is on p. 16. See also *Minneapolis Tribune*, December 15, 1960, p. 13; Walker Methodist Home file, McClure Papers.

[36] Community Health and Welfare Council of Hennepin County, *Aging in Greater Minneapolis*, 16 (Minneapolis, 1963).

[37] Frank M. Rarig, "Development of the Wilder Residences," in Governor's Council on Aging, *Reports*, 1962, p. 59–61. The first unit at 512 Humboldt Avenue was ready for occupancy in 1961. For a description of it, see *St. Paul Dispatch*, October 14, 1960, Second Section, p. 1.

[38] *Bethesda News*, October, 1960, p. [1], February, 1962, p. [2] (quote), July,

1962, p. [1], published by the Bethesda Hospital Association; *General Rules for Woodland Apartments*, a leaflet, and other items in Bethesda Nursing Home file, McClure Papers.

[39] The Emmaus Home was opened by Augustana Lutheran Homes in 1953. See *Minneapolis Tribune*, September 3, 1953, Women's Section, p. 1; *Independent Review* (Litchfield), February 1, 1968; home's file, in McClure Papers.

[40] *Your Own Apartment at 2625 Park Avenue, Minneapolis*, (quote), a brochure in Teachers Home file, McClure Papers. See also *Minneapolis Tribune*, August 19, 1962, Women's Section, p. 20; Community Health and Welfare Council, *Residential Facilities for the Elderly in the Minneapolis Area*, 32 (Minneapolis, 1968).

[41] On the county committees, see Minnesota Governor's Citizens Council on Aging, *Community Action for the Aging in Minnesota*, 1–4 (St. Paul, 1961); *Laws*, 1957, p. 1024.

CHAPTER 15 – CHANGES AND CHALLENGES 1850–1960s

[1] For a provocative discussion of attitudes toward the aged, see Joel S. Torstenson, "Hazards of Aging in American Society," in Minnesota Governor's Conference on Aging, *Reports*, 1962, p. 53.

[2] Department of Health, *Minnesota Directory of Licensed Hospitals and Related Institutions, 1960*, III (Minneapolis, 1960).

[3] See Appendix, Table 1, below.

[4] Thurston, in *Man and His Years*, 6 (quote).

[5] Floyd B. Olson, quoted in McGrath and Delmont, *Olson*, 259.

[6] See Appendix, Table 1, below. See also McClure, *A Historical Directory of Minnesota Homes for the Aged*.

[7] Only seven Minnesota benevolent homes are known to have closed before 1960. Four were listed above in chapter 13, note 27. The other three were: Sacred Heart Home, Moorhead (1952); St. Ann's Home, Duluth, and Harriet House, Minneapolis (1956).

Between 1960 and 1967 at least thirteen homes were closed. Two were in the paths of proposed freeway construction. A half dozen were discontinued after their sponsors opened new and larger facilities. Most of the buildings which closed were very old or did not warrant the expenditures necessary to meet health and fire protection standards. The discontinued homes were: Ladies GAR Home, Anoka (1960); Red Wing Baptist Home, Red Wing, Weddell Memorial Baptist Home and Home for Convalescents, both in Minneapolis, North Memorial Nursing Home, Robbinsdale, St. James Nursing Home, St. James (1961); Alliance Residence No. 1, Minneapolis (1962); McCabe Guest Home, Duluth, Good Samaritan Home, Luverne (1963); Bethesda Lutheran Home for Invalids, St. Paul (1964); Crispus Attucks Home, St. Paul (1966); Mother Frances Rest Home, Mankato, Svithiod Home, Excelsior (1967). See McClure, *A Historical Directory of Minnesota Homes for the Aged*.

[8] *United States Census*, 1910, *Population*, 2:991.

[9] Jerry Solon and Anna Mae Baney, "Ownership and Size of Nursing Homes," in *Public Health Reports*, 9:437 (quote), (May, 1955).

[10] On applications from sick aged, see Morris, in *Aging with a Future*, 103. On housing opportunities for the elderly, including apartments connected with homes, see Lawrence Upton, "Housing: Its Place in Sheltered Care," in American Association for Homes for the Aging, *Conference Report No. 3*, 48–51.

[11] For discussions of these terms see, for example, Solomon Geld, "Toward a Definition of the Modern Home," and California Department of Social Welfare,

"Functions and Services of Homes," in Leeds and Shore, eds., *Geriatric Institutional Management,* 61–63, 118.

[12] 89 Congress, 1 session, *House Executive Documents,* no. 1, p. 5 (quote), (serial 12677–1). See also "Summary of Major Legislation for Older People Enacted by 89th Congress," in *Aging,* February, 1967, p. 10, a periodical issued by the United States Department of Health, Education, and Welfare.

[13] Bernard E. Nash, "A Prologue to Progress," a speech delivered at the Minnesota Governor's Conference on Aging in February, 1967. The author was present

[14] Department of Health, *Minnesota Directory of Licensed Hospitals and Related Institutions, 1960,* VII; *1965,* XV; *1968,* VII.

[15] *Minnesota's Health,* November, 1959, p. 3 (quote); United States, *Statutes at Large,* 79:286–423.

[16] Ollie A. Randall, "Congregate Living for Older People," in Geneva Mathiasen and Edward H. Noakes, eds., *Planning Homes for the Aged,* 4 (quote), (New York, 1959).

[17] Elmer L. Andersen, "A Welcome and a Challenge," in Governor's Council on Aging, *Reports,* 1962, p. 3.

[18] Ewing, in *Man and His Years,* 4.

[19] Morris, in *Aging with a Future,* 100.

[20] Leeds and Shore, eds., *Geriatric Institutional Management,* 413 (quote).

[21] Morris, in *Aging with a Future,* 110 (quote). See also Maurice E. Linden, "The New Philosophy of Care for the Aged," in Leeds and Shore, eds., *Geriatric Institutional Management,* 99.

Index

AASGAARD, REV. JOHAN A., 179, 202
Abbott, Grace, quoted, 161
Aftenro Home (Duluth), 142, 149
Aged, public aid, 1, 5, 6, 19, 41; county care, 1, 23, 24, 29, 30, 37, 38, 77, 78, 158, 234; family responsibility, 2, 29, 30, 31; state responsibility, 4–8, 20, 73–91, 95, 98–100, 101, 103, 129, 130, 132–139, 163, 168, 169, 170, 198, 239; outdoor relief, 6, 18, 29, 96, 168, 227; changing treatment, 6, 29, 80, 90, 93, 99, 102, 127, 131, 171, 189, 210; emotional aspects, 33, 63, 93, 131, 132, 141, 145, 146, 153, 240; chores in homes, 37, 93, 117, 148; number in population, 38, 52, 90, 91, 93, 126, 141, 157, 185, 186, 214, 233; unemployment problems, 126, 168, 185, 186, 233; pensions, 128, 129, 136, 137, 138, 139, 144, 158, 161, 180; recreation problem, 128, 145–150, 189, 195–197, 236, 238; infirmity question, 150, 152, 182; effect of social security, 164, 165, 171; community co-operation, 217, 230, 240; independent living, 229, 238. *See also* Hospitals, Medical and nursing care, Pensions, Poorhouses and poor farms, Rehabilitation, various types of homes
Aitkin County, 8, 97; poorhouse, 157, 166, 260n
Alcoholism, relation to pauperism, 1, 4, 23, 24, 36, 41, 105, 233
Alexandria, benevolent home, 203, 271n
Almshouses, word defined, 96, 159. *See also* Poorhouses and poor farms
Amberg, Ray M., 191

American Assn. for Old Age Security, 137
American Congress of Physical Medicine, 209
American Hospital Assn., 222
American Lutheran Church, 114, 262n
American Medical Assn., 222
American Public Health Assn., 222
American Public Welfare Assn., 223
American Social Science Assn., 74, 75
American Society for the Prevention of Cruelty to Animals, 52
Ancker Hospital (St. Paul), 188
Andersen, Gov. Elmer L., 241
Anoka, 52, 70, 147, 279n
Anoka County, 8, 77; poorhouse, 166, 259n
Appel, Rev. J. George, 110
Associated Charities of St. Paul, 88
Associated Conference for Officials Charged With Enforcement of Laws Relating to Children, 128
Asylums. *See* Poorhouses
Attucks, Crispus, 118; school and home, 48, 118, 119, 147, 279n
Atwater, Isaac, 55
Augustana Home (Minneapolis), 68, 69, 176, 181, 207
Augustana Synod, Minnesota Conference, benevolent homes, 110, 111, 120, 173
Austin, Nancy L., quoted, 169

BAGLEY, 203, 204
Baltimore and Ohio R.R., pension plan, 137
Bancroft, 29

281

Baptist church, benevolent homes, 143, 174, 205, 254n
Barr, Dr. Robert N., 196, 200
Baudette, 217
Bean, F. A., 143
Becker County, poorhouse, 89, 103, 166, 258n; nursing home, 217
Bell, David C., 76
Belle Plaine, 69
Beltrami County, poor farm, 166, 260n, 274n, 277n
Benedictine order. *See* Sisters of St. Benedict
Benevolent homes, private nonprofit, 40–50, 52–72, 108–124, 140–155, 172–184, 201–212, 253n, 275n; names, 42, 122, 149, 238; buildings, 44, 46, 48, 53, 55, 56, 57, 58, 59, 61, 63, 65, 66, 69, 70, 108, 109, 111, 114, 115, 116–119, 121, 122, 142, 143, 145, 150, 172, 173–175, 177, 179, 182, 201–210, 215, 221, 223, 235, 236; fees, 45, 47, 49, 57, 67, 115, 123, 127, 176, 181, 184, 211; fund raising, 45, 52, 53, 56, 61, 63, 66, 70, 114, 118, 121, 124, 148, 173, 204; admission policies, 47, 49, 57, 59, 65, 70, 108, 112, 117, 140, 154, 176, 182, 183; rules, 49, 117, 146; types of sponsors, 52, 54, 60, 67, 70, 108, 116, 141, 142; finances, 53, 71, 122, 124, 173, 175, 176, 178, 211, 220, 276n, 277n; origins, 54; bequests and gifts, 56, 58, 59, 63, 65, 68, 69, 142, 174, 175, 178, 229; attitudes toward, 57, 71, 117, 140, 144, 147, 153; legislative appropriations, 71, 86; state supervision, 85; for ethnic groups, 108–124; fraternal, 108, 119, 208, 279n; waiting lists, 127, 141, 172; number, 140, 141, 154, 172, 204, 212, 219, 234; place in community, 140, 225, 242; superintendents, 145, 207; residents, 145, 218, 235; recreation problem, 145–150, 181, 225–227, 238; matrons, 146; during *1930s*, 156, 172–184; effect of Social Security Act, 179, 180; overcrowding, 203; World War II problems, 205–207; conferences, 207–212; functions, 214; changing aspects, 215, 224, 232, 236, 241; closed, 276n, 279n. *See also* Medical and nursing care, various church organizations, and individual homes
Bennett, Abraham, 11, 12
Bennett, Mrs. Charles (Anna), 112
Benton, Mr. and Mrs. W. S., 60
Bergh, Henry, 52
Berry, Charles H., 75
Bethany Covenant Home (Minneapolis), 142, 149
Bethel Home (Mountain Lake), 110, 149
Bethesda Homes (Willmar), 116, 148, 177, 182
Bethesda Hospital (St. Paul), 111, 120, 264n
Bethesda Hospital Assn. (Crookston), 228
Bethesda Invalid Home (St. Paul), 120, 262n, 264n, 279n
Bethesda Old People's Home (Chisago City), 111
Big Stone County, 90, 259n
Bishop, Harriet E., 39, 40
Blaisdell Avenue Baptist Home (Minneapolis), 205
Blandin Foundation, 226
Bloomington, 143, 144, 147, 182
Blue Earth County, poor farm, 27, 80, 274n
Board of Control. *See* Minnesota Board of Control
Boas, Dr. Ernst P., 152
Boessling, Mrs. Sophia, 69
Boller, J. C., 94
Borger, Laurits H., 134
Boston (Mass.), first poorhouse, 4
Brace, Charles L., 83
Breckenridge, 225
Brisbo, Napoleon, 25, 26
Brist, F. Manley, 191
Brown, Rev. Frederick T., 43
Brown, John R., quoted, 127
Brown, Josephine C., quoted, 5
Brown County, relief problems, 29, 33, 34; poor farm, 34, 90, 101, 166, 260n, 274n
Buffalo (Minn.), 262n, 267n
Buhl, 218
Bullis, Mathew, quoted, 104
Burnquist, Gov. Joseph A. A., 134
Burton, Mary, 117
Busy Bee Club, 225

CADY, LOUVA M., 150
Campbell, William M., 75
Carleton, Will, author, 30, 31
Carver County, poor farm, 28, 35, 90

INDEX

Castle, Henry A., 86
Catholic church, 42, 47; aged care by nuns, 53, 54, 60–67; benevolent homes, 60, 109, 110, 120, 174. *See also* Orphanages, various orders
Chambers, Clarke A., quoted, 125, 144, 151
Charity Loan Society and Old Women's Home (St. Paul), 117
Chase, E. W., 75
Chesley, Dr. Albert J., 162
Chicago (Ill.), 137, 153
Child welfare, 158, 191; beginnings, 106, 128. *See also* Children, dependent; Orphanages
Children, dependent, public support, 1, 2, 4, 5, 73, 85, 233; apprentice system, 2, 6, 37; in poorhouses, 5, 23, 36, 37, 83, 85, 130, 132, 187; education, 5, 84; boarding care, 23, 83, 151, 175, 182; need for housing, 40, 43, 46; in benevolent homes, 44, 47, 49, 50, 52, 53, 54, 68, 116, 150, 204, 253n; humane societies, 52; state code, 106; federal aid, 125, 161. *See also* Child welfare, Orphanages
Children's Aid Society (N.Y.), 83, 84
Children's Home Society (Minneapolis), sponsors home, 54–58
Chippewa County, poor farm, 139, 258n
Chisago City, 111, 173
Chisago County, poor farm, 21, 166, 253n, 274n; Swedish settlement, 111; nursing home, 166, 217
Chisago Lutheran Home for Aged (Chisago City), 111
Christian Aid Society (Minneapolis), 40, 58. *See also* Woman's Christian Assn.
Christmas, 197
Church Home for Babies (Minneapolis), 67, 68
Church Home of Minnesota (St. Paul), 67, 68
Church of God Home (St. Paul Park), 154, 276n
Churches, sponsor benevolent homes, 42, 51–70, 108, 109, 114, 127, 143, 152, 154, 172–181, 182–184, 208, 219, 235, 236, 242, 243, 268n, 276n; ethnic aspect, 109, 141. *See also* various denominations and synods
Civil War, 21, 22, 24, 40, 70
Clark, Martin D., 17
Clark, Mary Vida, 106, 133
Clay County, nursing home, 217
Clearwater Sunset Home (Bagley), 204
Clifton, C. Stanley, 195, 196
Colter, Mrs. Alice J., 226
Commission on Chronic Illness, 222
Commission on Hospital Care, 197
Committee on Economic Security, 162
Community Chest, 124, 176, 178, 181, 237
Conference of Boards of Public Charities, 75
Congregational church, 76, 254n
Cook, A. P., 160
Cottage Hospital (Minneapolis), 67
Cottonwood County, poor farm, 259n, 260n
Coughlin, Sister Seraphine, 12
Counties and county boards, poor relief, 1, 4, 6, 7–14, 15, 18, 19, 20–23, 25, 33, 73, 74, 76, 81, 87, 88, 89, 92, 96, 106, 135, 158, 163, 186, 218; organized and reorganized, 8, 9, 15, 18; conferences, 92–96, 98, 128; welfare boards, 164, 165, 166, 167, 188, 191, 198, 220. *See also* Poorhouses and poor farms, individual counties
Cretin, Bishop Joseph, 11
Crookston, 228
Crow Wing County, poorhouse, 259n, 260n, 277n
Czechoslovak Baptist Charitable Assn. Home (New Prague), 143, 174

DAHL, DR. ELMER O., 182
Dahlen, Rev. Magnus A., 203
Dakota County, 8, 9; poorhouse, 24, 274n
Dana, Rev. Malcolm M., 75
Danebo Home (Minneapolis), 143, 182, 183
Danish element, 235; benevolent homes, 116, 143, 154, 175, 182, 183, 204
Davis, Cushman K., 48
Davis, James J., 129
Davis, Michael M., 152
Depressions and panics, *1857*, 14, 16, 19, 21, 178; *1870s*, 33, 36, 178; *1890s*, 52, 86, 87, 119, 178; *1920s*, 126, 127; *1930s*, 155, 156–184. *See also* Economic conditions
Deutsch Foundation, 151

284   MORE THAN A ROOF

Dix, Dorothea L., 4
Dodge County, poor farm, 26, 81, 166, 167, 274n; nursing home, 217
Dublin, Louis I., quoted, 126
Duluth, 160; humane society, 52; benevolent homes, 110, 142, 173, 175, 279n; hospitals, 188, 218. *See also* St. Louis County
Dwight, Theodore W., 74, 233

EAGLES, fraternal order, 138
Ebenezer Home (Buffalo), 262n, 267n
Ebenezer Home (Minneapolis), 121, 182, 183; founded, 115; funds, 116, 176, 180, 181, 211
Economic conditions, 101; in Civil War era, 21, 24, 27; during World War I, 123; effect on homes, 172–184; during World War II, 185, 186. *See also* Depressions
Eielsen Synod, 115
Ekstein, Andrew J., 101
Elim Home (Minneapolis), 204, 263n, 276n; name, 149
Elim Old People's Home (Princeton), 142; name, 149
Emmaus Lutheran Home (Litchfield), 229
England, poor laws, 1, 2, 6, 7, 19
Episcopal church, benevolent homes, 42, 67, 68, 254n
Erskine, 219
Ethnic groups, benevolent homes, 108–124, 141–152, 235, 236
Evangelical Lutheran Church, 203, 208
Evangelical Lutheran Good Samaritan Society, 203, 204, 279n
Evangelical Lutheran Synod, 69
Evans, Harry C., report, 129, 131, 132
Ewing, Oscar R., 213, 241
Excelsior, 142, 279n

FAIRMONT, 101
Faribault County, 90, 253n; poor farm, 29, 33
Faude, Rev. John Jacob, 68
Faulkner, Charles E., 94, 135
Federal Emergency Relief Administration (FERA), 158, 168
Fenlason, Anne F., 127, 136, 137, 147, 153
Ferderber, Dr. Murray B., 209
Fergstad, Mrs. Karl (Anna Qvale), 113, 148

Fergus Falls, 142
Fillmore County, poor farm, 28, 78, 80
Finke, Walter W., 190
Foley, Edna L., 151
Foley, Louis G., 99, 102, 130
Franciscan Sisters of the Blessed Virgin Mary of the Angels, 166, 174
Franciscan Sisters of the Immaculate Conception, 65, 66
Fraternal groups, benevolent homes, 108, 119, 127, 142, 143, 147, 153, 181, 182, 184, 208, 235, 236, 243, 279n; surveys, 129, 138; pension plans, 137
Frederik, crown prince of Denmark, 183
Freeborn County, poorhouse, 29, 35, 82, 259n, 274n
Freeman, Gov. Orville L., 226, 227
Frost, Robert, quoted, 159

GERIATRICS, 152, 209, 222, 242
German element, 28, 113, 117; benevolent homes, 109, 110, 141
German Mennonite Hospital (Mountain Lake), 110
Gervais, Benjamin, 9, 10
Gilbert, Bishop Mahlon N., 68
Glenwood Old People's Home, 114, 115, 179, 276n
Glidden, Mrs. Jane M., 55
Gloria Dei Home (Litchfield), 229
Good Samaritan Society, 203, 204, 279n
Goodhue, James M., 10
Goodhue County, poor farm, 22, 81, 88, 274n; benevolent homes, 203
Graham, Mrs. John A. (Amelia L.), 174
Grand Army of the Republic, 85. *See also* Ladies of the GAR Home
Grand Rapids (Minn.), 226
Grasshopper plagues, 34, 178
Green Acres Nursing Home (North Branch), 217, 253n

HAGGERNESS, REV. NILS S., 116
Hall, Elizabeth L., 229
Hall, Robert, 103
Hallock, 217
Hammill, Dr. Gerald P., 209
Hansen, Marie, 207
Harrison, Mrs. William M., 58, 59
Hart, Rev. Hastings H., state board secretary, 76–84, 85, 88, 89, 102, 120
Hauge's Synod, 115
Hazard, Thomas R., quoted, 5, 151

INDEX 285

Heen, Chris, 96
Hendry, Mrs. J. L., 93, 224
Hennepin County, 8, 154, 164, 228; poorhouse, 23, 48, 78–80, 105, 139, 147, 188, 199, 266n, 274n; hospital, 188; welfare board, 196, 198, 228; nursing home, 277n
Henry, Rev. O. A., 173, 174
Hill, James J., 64, 68, 114
Hill-Burton Law, 198, 215, 219, 276n, 277n
Hills (Minn.), home, 219
Hoeger, Rev. August J., 203
Hoffman, Isaac, quoted, 185
Hoffman, John A., quoted, 126
Home for Children and Aged Women (Minneapolis), 56–58, 123, 150, 182, 259n
Home for Convalescents (Minneapolis), 121, 207, 264n, 279n
Home for the Friendless (St. Paul), 47, 50, 54, 57, 58, 119; beginnings, 40–44; buildings, 45, 48; finances, 48, 49, 178
Homes for aged, criticized, 151; role, 152, 227; licensed, 216; special accommodations, 228; number, 240; changing aspect, 241. *See also* Benevolent homes, Nursing homes, Poorhouses and poor farms
Hopkins, Harry L., 158
Hopkins, poor farm, 24, 147, 188
Hospitals, county, 11, 16, 31, 33, 79, 188, 217, 218; general, 11, 37, 45, 67, 98, 111, 115, 120; mental, 12, 36; in Civil War, 40; increase, 42, 51, 214, 216; for aged, 58, 65, 66, 67, 69, 86, 103, 108, 109, 120, 122, 140, 141, 152, 174, 175, 182, 219, 228, 237; inspected, 98, 198, 240; chronic disease, 120, 188, 275n; convalescent, 121; relief work, 168; licensing, 171, 190–192; expenses, 176; auxiliaries, 197; architecture, 220; outpatients, 238; state, 253n. *See also* Medical and nursing care, individual hospitals
House of the Good Shepherd (St. Paul), 46, 61
Houston County, poorhouse, 36, 77, 102, 274n
Hubbard, Gov. Lucius, 75, 85
Hubbard County, 277n; poor farm, 166, 260n, 274n
Hultkrans, Rev. Carl A., 111, 120, 121
Hursh, Morris, 190

ILLINOIS, 88; poor laws, 6, 74
Immigrants and immigration, 109, 235; assistance and housing, 41, 43, 46; percentage of aged, 126; restricted, 125, 141. *See also* various ethnic groups
Indiana, 6, 165
Influenza epidemic, *1918–19*, 122, 123
Insane. *See* Mental illness
International Falls, 97
Invalidhem. *See* Bethesda Invalid Home
Iowa, 12, 130
Ireland, Archbishop John, 63
Isanti County, 8
Itasca County, 8, 9; poorhouse, 160, 188, 259n, 274n; poor and hospital commission, 164; nursing home, 217, 226
Ives, Gideon S., 119, 144

JACKSON, JAMES F., state board secretary, 88, 95, 189
Jarchow, George, 94
Jewish Home for the Aged (St. Paul), 116–118, 147
Johnson, Ray, quoted, 218
Johnston, Mrs. Daniel S. B., 46
Jones, Judge and Mrs. Edwin S., 58, 59
Jones-Harrison Home (Minneapolis), 53, 58–60, 122, 177
Jugan, Jeanne, 60, 62

KANDIYOHI COUNTY, poor farm, 260n
Kaplan, Jerome, 274n
Kelly, John, 105
Kelso, Robert W., quoted, 3
Kenyon Sunset Home (Kenyon), 203
Kindwall, Ida Nihlon, 112
King, Rev. and Mrs. James W., 118
Kittson County, poorhouse, 166, 260n; nursing home, 217
Knutson, Rev. M. S., 179
Koochiching County, 97; nursing home, 217; poor farm, 260n, 274n

LABOR, shortage, 193, 194; in World War II, 202, 205, 207. *See also* Unemployment
Lac qui Parle County, poor farm, 259n, 274n
Ladies Christian Union, 43, 44. *See also* Home for the Friendless
Ladies of the GAR Home (Anoka), 70, 147, 279n

Ladies Relief Assn., sponsors home, 44–46, 48. *See also* Home for the Friendless
La Du, Blanche L., 128, 130
Lake Auburn Home (Victoria), 143
Lake County, poor farm, 97, 166, 260n
Lake Louise, name, 14
Lake of the Woods County, nursing home, 217
Lake Park, 217
Lakeshore Lutheran Home for the Aged (Duluth), 173, 174
Lamberton, 116
Lampland, Oscar, 149
Lapp, John A., 126
Laurice, Sister Mary, 225
Le Bonne, Joseph, 11
Leeds, Morton, quoted, 225
Leonard, Dr. William H., 75
Le Sueur County, poorhouse, 27, 35, 90, 253n
Linnea Society, 112
Litchfield, 229
Little Falls, 65, 66
Little Sisters of the Poor, beginnings, 60; St. Paul home, 61–64, 149, 273n; Minneapolis home, 64, 176, 272n
Loretto Hospital (New Ulm), 110
Lundquist, G. A., quoted, 157
Lurie, H. L., quoted, 153
Lutheran church, welfare work, 53, 68; benevolent homes, 68, 69, 110, 111, 113, 114, 115, 116, 121, 123, 124, 142, 147, 148, 149, 173, 175, 176, 179, 180, 181, 182, 183, 202, 211, 254n, 264n; congregations, 68, 110, 111, 173, 175, 264n; hospitals, 111, 120, 264n; children's home, 175. *See also* individual synods
Lutheran Home Asylum (Lamberton), 116
Lutheran Home for the Aged (Belle Plaine), 69
Lutheran Old People's Home (Madison), 202
Lyngblomsten Home (St. Paul), 113, 114, 123, 124, 147, 148, 149, 182; name, 113
Lyngblomsten Society, 113, 114, 142
Lyon County, poorhouse, 77, 166, 258n

McCabe Guest Home (Duluth), 175, 279n
McLean, Nathaniel, 12, 13

Madison (Minn.), 202
Mankato, 52; benevolent home, 173, 279n
Marshall, William R., 47
Marshall County, 82, 90, 258n, 277n
Martin County, 82, 90; poorhouse, 166, 258n, 260n
Masons, benevolent home, 143, 144, 147, 182
Massachusetts, welfare work, 2, 3, 4, 7, 73, 120, 134
Medical and nursing care, of relief clients, 1, 6, 8, 11, 12, 17, 18, 19, 25, 37, 45, 80, 96, 233; of immigrants, 41; pesthouses, 97; of aged, 103, 104, 120, 121, 122, 131, 133, 150, 151, 152, 157, 165, 166, 169, 170, 178, 181, 182, 185, 186, 188, 190, 192, 193, 194, 199, 200, 204, 207, 208, 209, 210, 216, 228, 229, 236, 239, 240; in nursing homes, 168–170. *See also* Hospitals, Rehabilitation
Medicare, 238, 240
Medicine Lake, mission farm, 168
Men, as relief clients, 3, 5, 23, 25, 29, 30, 34; in benevolent organizations, 52, 54, 111, 115; in poorhouses, 53, 93, 105, 160, 168; in benevolent homes, 143, 203. *See also* Veterans
Mennonites, hospital, 110
Mental illness, public care, 1, 23, 24, 25, 74, 75, 96, 105, 133, 138, 219; in poorhouses, 4, 5, 6, 7, 14, 37, 81, 91, 130, 131, 132, 170, 233; in state hospitals, 12, 36, 38, 73, 253n; lack of facilities, 80, 81; in nursing homes, 170, 191, 192, 210
Merrill, Galen A., 85
Merritt, Thomas, 173
Mesabi Home (Buhl), 218
Methodist church, benevolent homes, 204, 208, 211, 227, 254n, 263n
Michigan, 30; poor laws, 6, 74; state school, 85
Mille Lacs County, 8; poor farm, 166, 260n
Miller Memorial Hospital (Duluth), 188
Minneapolis, 23, 51, 52, 62; benevolent homes, 37, 52, 53, 54, 56–60, 64, 67, 68, 69, 115, 116, 121, 122, 123, 142, 143, 147, 149, 150, 154, 176, 177, 178, 180, 181, 182, 183, 204, 205, 207, 208, 211, 227, 229, 272n, 275n, 276n, 279n; hos-

pitals, 67, 69, 86, 122, 128, 188, 191, 194, 197, 253n; soldiers' home, 70, 71, 86; board of education, 122; community fund, 124; nursing homes, 169, 188; health department, 198; conferences, 208; orphanages, 253n, 259n. *See also* Twin Cities

Minneapolis Council of Social Agencies, 181, 227

Minnehaha Park, soldiers' home, 70, 71, 86

Minnesota, statehood, 15; early poor relief, 15–19, 239; climate, 21, 31, 34, 41, 109, 158, 168, 178; population growth, 24, 90; correctional and welfare institutions, 36, 73–91, 134, 157, 158, 253n; number of aged, 38, 126, 157, 186; women in social work, 39–50, 51–72, 111–114, 116, 121, 142, 177, 197, 207, 219, 241, 242; humane societies, 52; health resort, 59; care of tuberculous, 103, 104, 134, 199; ethnic groups, 109–118, 235; percentage of poor, 130; pension law, 138, 159, 165; employment, 186; welfare planning, 227, 231. *See also* Minnesota legislature, Minnesota Territory, individual state institutions

Minnesota Assn. of Administrators of Homes for the Aged, 222

Minnesota Assn. of County Commissioners, 96, 103

Minnesota Assn. of Geriatric Homes, 222

Minnesota Assn. of Nursing Homes, 197, 222

Minnesota Board of Control of State Institutions, 95, 134; functions, 89, 135, 157, 163; inspections, 99, 101, 103, 127, 130, 169; children's bureau, 106; becomes SERA, 158

"Minnesota Children's Code," 106

Minnesota Commission on Aging, 134, 135, 214, 219, 223, 239

Minnesota Conference of Social Work, 126, 128, 130, 138

Minnesota Council of Church Women, 197

Minnesota Dept. of Health, 191, 192, 193, 196, 197, 198, 208, 210, 211, 216, 220, 223; child hygiene division, 191; training program, 194

Minnesota Dept. of Public Welfare, 222, 223

Minnesota Dept. of Social Security, 171. *See also* Minnesota Division of Social Welfare

Minnesota Division of Social Welfare, 171, 186, 190, 195, 200, 208, 222

Minnesota Governor's Citizens Council on Aging, 215, 229, 241

Minnesota Hospital Assn., 190

Minnesota legislature, 70, 71, 199, 220; township act, *1858*, 15, 18, 35, 252n; *1860*, 18; welfare measures, 20, 22, 24, 34, 35, 73, 82, 84, 85, 86, 89, 95, 104, 106, 127, 135, 158, 163, 164, 171, 214; poorhouse studies, 129, 131, 132, 137; pension laws, 138, 216, 234; reorganization act, *1939*, 171

Minnesota Masonic Home (Bloomington), 143, 144, 147, 182

Minnesota National Guard, 158

Minnesota Odd Fellows Home (Northfield), 119

Minnesota Soldiers' Home (Minneapolis), 70, 71, 85–87, 134, 147

Minnesota State Board of Corrections and Charities, established, 73, 75, 90; reports, 82, 87, 88, 168; replaced, 89, 95

Minnesota State Board of Medical Examiners, 170

Minnesota State Conference of Charities and Corrections, 96, 103; established, 89; functions, 92, 127

Minnesota State Medical Assn., 171, 190, 191

Minnesota Territory, poor relief system, 1–15; established, 7, 29, 213; counties, 8, 9, 21; legislature, 8, 15, 21; first poor farm, 10; growth, 10, 19; panic of *1857*, 14

Moorhead, 174, 279n

Moose, fraternal order, 129

Moravian church, home, 143

Morrill, Ashby C., 65

Morris, Dr. Robert, 242

Morrison County, poorhouse, 90, 259n

Mount, Mrs. E. B., 177

Mountain Lake, 110

Mower County, poor farm, 83, 253n, 265n, 274n

Murray, Archbishop John G., 201

Murray County, poor farm, 36, 82, 259n

NASH, BERNARD E., 239

National Conference of Charities, 37

National Conference of Social Work, 126
National Conference on Aging, *1950*, 213, 224, 234, 239, 241
Negroes, benevolent home, 108, 118, 279n
Nelson, Sen. Knute, 203
Nelson, Sister Cecelia, 68
Nelson-Glenwood Memorial Home (Alexandria), 203, 271n
New England, poor relief, 1, 2, 19
New Prague, 143, 174, 205, 276n
New Ulm, 110
New York, relief system, 4, 7, 14, 84, 120
Nicollet County, poor farm, 25, 80, 274n
Nicols, Kate, 48
Nininger, 25
Nonprofit homes. *See* Benevolent homes
Nordlin, George H., state senator, 129, 137, 162
Norman County, poor farm, 134, 139, 166
North Branch, 217, 253n
North Dakota, 130, 203
Northfield, 119, 144
Northwest Baptist Home Society, 143, 174, 205
Northwest Territory, 6, 7; relief system, 2, 5, 19
Norwegian-Danish Conference (Lutheran), 116, 204, 263n
Norwegian element, 24, 109, 235; benevolent homes, 113, 114, 115, 123, 124, 142, 147, 148, 149, 154, 182
Norwegian Synod (Norwegian Evangelical Lutheran Church of America), benevolent homes, 114, 115, 179, 202
Noyes, Daniel R., 47
Nurses, training, 122, 176, 194; establish rest homes, 169, 190
Nursing homes, county, 166–168, 199, 216–218, 226, 234, 237, 242, 253n, 274n, 277n; proprietary, 168–171, 187, 192, 223, 237, 274n; Minneapolis, 169, 188; regulated, 170, 171, 190, 192, 198, 216; number, 187, 199, 215–218, 232; idleness problem, 189, 195–197; buildings, 192, 219, 220, 221; scarcity, 200; staffs, 222, 223, 224; cooperation, 240

OAK GROVE HOUSE (Minneapolis), 59
Oak Ridge (Minneapolis), 223
O'Brien, William A., 208
Odd Fellows, benevolent home, 119, 144
Office of Price Administration (OPA), 206, 207
Ohio, welfare work, 6, 74, 120, 134
Ohio Synod, benevolent home, 110
Olav, crown prince of Norway, 183
Old age assistance. *See* Pensions
Olmsted County, poor farm, 27, 32, 82, 103
Olson, Gov. Floyd B., 157, 158
Orphanages, in East, 42; Protestant, 47, 54–58, 67, 68, 69, 116, 123, 150, 175, 182, 253n, 259n; Catholic, 47, 65, 66, 253n, 259n; state, 47, 253n, 258n; increase, 51; Negro, 118; criticized, 151; Twin Cities, 259n
Otter Tail County, 277n; poorhouse, 80, 166, 258n
Our Lady of Good Counsel Home (St. Paul), 201
Owatonna, 52, 85
Owens, John P., 15

PANICS. *See* Depressions
Parkview Hospital (Minneapolis), 188, 275n
Paupers and pauperism, classifications, 1, 4, 5, 6, 128, 133, 136, 233; attitudes, 15, 20, 30, 235; emotional aspects, 15, 30, 33, 131, 132; causes, 104, 128. *See also* Poorhouses and poor farms, Relief systems
Pennington County, 277n
Pennsylvania, poor laws, 6, 7, 74; commission on aging, 134; rehabilitation, 209
Pensions, mothers', 125, 132; old age, 128, 129, 134, 136, 137, 138, 144, 157, 158, 159, 161, 162, 163, 164, 168, 179, 181, 185, 186, 205, 210, 213, 216, 238, 239, 265n; clergymen's, 137; federal, 137; railroad, 137; trade union, 137; restrictions, 186, 191, 195, 199, 211; effects, 187, 216, 218, 234, 237. *See also* Social Security Act
Pesthouses, 97
Petri, Rev. Carl J., 68, 69
Pillsbury, Mrs. Charles S., 60
Pillsbury, John S., 58
Pillsbury, Mrs. John S., 55

INDEX 289

Pine County, 8; poorhouse, 101, 104, 139, 166, 260n, 274n
Pioneer Memorial Home (Erskine), 219
Pioneer Memorial Home (Fergus Falls), 142
Pioneer Nursing Home (Baudette), 217
Pioneers Infirmary (Virginia), 218
Pipestone County, poorhouse, 77, 259n
Plaut, W. Gunther, quoted, 117
Polk County, benevolent home, 219
Poor. *See* Paupers and pauperism, Poorhouses and poor farms, Relief systems
Poorhouses and poor farms, early Minnesota, 1–19; in East, 1, 2–5, 74; duties of residents, 2, 4, 8, 20, 22, 50, 83, 93, 94; superintendents and staffs, 2, 5, 10, 11, 12, 13, 15, 28, 77, 81, 82, 88, 89, 93–95, 100, 102, 105, 130, 138, 188; origin, 3; economic aspects, 3, 6, 8, 17, 22, 26, 27, 28, 32, 34, 35, 74, 81, 101, 102, 103, 106, 128, 130, 138; farming aspect, 3, 13, 17, 22, 26, 28, 31, 77, 78, 82, 93, 97, 100, 101, 102, 258n; living conditions, 4, 5, 6, 26, 27, 31, 45, 79, 80, 93, 94, 99, 131, 159, 160, 189; types of residents, 4, 6, 37, 53, 77, 80, 83, 90, 188; legislation for, 20, 22, 24, 35, 82; supervised, 73, 74, 76–78, 80–85, 87–90, 98, 188, 190; buildings and equipment, 77, 78–80, 87–89, 93, 97, 98, 99, 100–102, 106, 131, 132, 159, 217, 233, 265n; size, 82; proposed concentration, 82, 133; population, 87, 89, 90, 91, 129, 188, 266n; changes, 90, 92, 102, 125–139; proportion of aged, 91, 93, 127, 129, 157, 187; rules, 93, 94; community support, 95, 101; name, 96, 97; saloon problem, 105; in *1930s*, 156, 172; effect of social security, 164–168; leased, 166, 167, 199, 274n; importance, 186; decline, 187, 189, 193, 213, 214, 231, 232, 234, 237, 241, 260n; recreation problem, 189, 195–197; in *1860s*, 253n; in *1880s*, 258n, 259n; in *1890s*, 259n; *1900–19*, 260n; in *1940s*, 274n. *See also* Counties and county boards, Medical and nursing care, Relief systems, individual counties
Poor relief. *See* Relief systems
Population, growth: *1850s*, 21, 23; *1860s*, 22, 24; St. Louis County, *1864*, 21, 31; percentage of aged, 38, 52, 90, 126, 140, 157, 186; St. Paul, *1860s*, 41, *1870s*, 46; Minnesota, 52, 90, 110, 235; Little Falls, *1890*, 65; poverty surveys, 129, 130; percentage of infirm, 185
Poverty. *See* Paupers and pauperism, Relief systems
Presbyterian churches, St. Paul, 40, 43 254n
Princeton, 142
Proctor, John S., 13
Proprietary homes. *See* Nursing homes
Protestant Home of St. Paul, 40. *See also* Home for the Friendless
Public Works Administration, 160
Putnam, Frank E., 135

RAMSEY, GOV. ALEXANDER, 13, 47
Ramsey, Mrs. Isabel C., 59
Ramsey County, created, 8, 9; commissioners, 9–13, 157; relief system, 10, 15, 16, 17–19, 35; poor farms, 11, 13, 15, 17, 21, 36, 93, 104, 188, 266n, 274n; townships, 15; board of supervisors, 15, 16–18; hospital, 16, 33; pesthouse, 97; welfare board, 164
Randall, Ollie A., 240
Range Hospital Corp., 218
Rascher, Mr. and Mrs. William, 142
Rebekah Assembly of Minnesota, 120
Reconstruction Finance Corp., 157, 158
Red Wing, 22, 52; homes for aged, 74, 203, 279n
Redwood County, poorhouse, 82, 90, 217, 258n, 259n, 260n, 274n
Rehabilitation, of aged, 195, 209, 214, 215, 221, 223–227, 230
Relf, Sister Annette, 67
Relief systems, early Minnesota, 1–19, 233; financing, 1, 2, 6, 7, 8, 10; England, 1, 2, 6, 7, 19; local aspect, 1, 2, 7, 15, 16, 19; county, 1, 4, 6, 7–14, 19, 73, 74, 76, 87, 88, 92, 96, 128, 158; township, 1, 15, 18, 19, 35, 96; in East, 2, 3, 4, 5, 6, 7, 19, 42; housing, 2, 3, 4, 5, 6, 14; outdoor, 2, 3, 4, 5, 6, 14, 23, 25, 29, 32, 33, 34, 77, 86, 89, 96; apprenticing, 2, 7, 37; Midwest, 3, 4; costs, 3, 12, 25, 27, 28, 33, 81, 157; legislative measures, 20, 22, 24, 34, 35, 73, 82, 84, 85, 86, 89, 95, 104, 106, 127, 135, 158, 163, 164, 171, 214; private, 51–72; state supervision, 73–91, 133, 134; federal aid, 125; in *1920s*,

126; in *1930s*, 157; effect of World War II, 186. *See also* Counties and county boards, Medical and nursing care, Paupers and pauperism, Social Security Act
Renville County, poorhouse, 90, 259n
Rest homes. *See* Nursing homes
Reynolds, Reuben, 76
Rice, Edmund, 12
Rice, Henry M., 47
Rice County, poor farm, 253n, 274n
Riley, Sarah, 187
Robert, Louis, 9, 10, 11
Rochester, 52, 253n
Rock County, poorhouse, 77, 258n, 274n
Rondorf Home (Staples), 219
Roosevelt, Pres. Franklin D., 158, 162, 205
Rose, Arnold M., quoted, 227
Roseau County, 277n
Rubinow, Isaac M., quoted, 151, 153
Russell, Roswell P., 9
Rystrom, Mrs. E. M., 112

SACRED HEART HOME (Moorhead), 174, 279n
St. Alexander Home (New Ulm), 110
St. Ann's Home (Duluth), 110, 150, 175, 262n, 279n
St. Ansgar Hospital (Moorhead), 174
St. Barnabas Hospital (Minneapolis), 67
St. Benedict's Hospital (St. Cloud), 109
St. Cloud, 135; benevolent homes, 109, 141; hospitals, 109, 141
St. Elizabeth's Hospital (Wabasha), 141
St. Francis Home for the Aged (Breckenridge), 225
St. Francis Hospital and Home for the Aged (Shakopee), 166, 175
St. Gabriel Hospital (Little Falls), 66
St. James, benevolent home, 141, 279n; hospital, 141
St. John's Hospital (Springfield), 109, 262n
St. Joseph's Home (Minneapolis), 64
St. Joseph's Home for the Aged (St. Cloud), 109, 141
St. Joseph's Hospital (St. Paul), 11, 12, 17, 18, 45
St. Jude's Mission (Minneapolis), 67
St. Louis County, in Civil War, 21; county homes, 21, 31, 32, 77, 160, 188, 218, 224, 266n, 274n; growth, 21, 31; hospital, 31; pesthouse, 97; benevolent homes, 154; commissioners, 160; welfare board, 164, 188; nursing homes, 217, 218, 224, 277n
St. Luke's Hospital (Duluth), 218
St. Luke's Hospital (St. Paul), 47
St. Mary's Home (St. Paul), 175
St. Mary's Hospital (Duluth), 218
St. Otto's Home for the Aged (Little Falls), 65-67
St. Paul, 62; territorial capital, 8, 10, 19; hospitals, 11, 12, 45, 47, 111, 120, 188, 253n; indigents, 11, 16; jail, 12; port, 16, 24, 41; in panic of *1857*, 16; in *1859*, 18; population: *1860*, 19, *1867*, 41, *1870s*, 46; benevolent homes, 37, 40-50, 52, 54, 57, 58, 60-64, 67, 68, 108, 112, 113, 114, 116, 117, 118, 119, 120, 123, 124, 141, 147, 148, 149, 175, 178, 182, 201, 205, 228, 253n, 279n; city council, 41; social life, 46; orphanages, 47, 253n, 259n; business, 51; associated charities, 88; community chest, 124. *See also* Twin Cities
St. Paul Park, 154, 276n
St. Paul's Church Home (St. Paul), 141
St. Paul's Evangelical Church (St. Paul), 142
St. Raphael's Home for the Aged (St. Cloud), 141
St. Raphael's Hospital (St. Cloud), 109
Sanatoriums. *See* Tuberculosis
Sanborn, Frank B., 74, 75
Sanborn, John B., 135
Sanborn, Mrs. John B., 45
Sand Beach (Lake Park), sanatorium, 217, 261n
Savage, Marion W., 144
Scandinavian element, 46; benevolent homes, 110-116, 142, 147, 148, 154, 183. *See also* Danish element, Norwegian element, Swedish element
Scandinavian Union Relief Home (Minneapolis), 147, 181, 262n
Schwartzrock, Ferdinand, 110
Scott, Ebenezer D., 58, 59
Scott County, 77; poorhouse, 166, 175, 259n
Sears, Amelia, quoted, 137
Seng, Mrs. C. W. (Lillian), 142
Shakopee, 166, 175
Shearon, Marjorie, quoted, 181

INDEX   291

Sheltering Arms (Minneapolis), 67, 68, 259n
Sheppard-Towner Act, 125
Sibley, Henry H., 18, 47
Simpson, Sir George, 62
Sisters of Charity, 42, 166
Sisters of St. Benedict, hospital-homes, 109, 110, 141, 149, 175, 219
Sisters of St. Dominic Servants of Relief for Incurable Cancer, 201
Sisters of St. Francis of the Immaculate Conception, 174
Sisters of St. Joseph, 11, 12, 46
Sisters of the Sorrowful Mother, 141
Sisters of the Third Order of St. Francis of Our Lady of Lourdes, 141
Small Business Administration, 221
Social Security Act, *1935*, 162–169, 213, 234, 237, 239; effect on homes for aged, 179–181, 184; *1950* amendment, 216
Society of Brethren (Lutheran), 115, 263n
Sommars, Rev. Fred A., 204
South Dakota, 130
Springfield, 109
Staples, 219
Stasel, Alfred G., 191
State Conference of Charities. *See* Minnesota State Conference of Charities
State Emergency Relief Administration (SERA), 158
Stearns County, 35
Steele County, 217, 258n, 274n
Stevens, J. Walter, 88, 99
Stevens County, 82, 259n, 260n
Stevens Square (Minneapolis). *See* Children's Home Society
Stewart, Estelle M., author, 129, 159
Stillwater, 119, 253n; poor farm, 13, 21, 24, 25, 94, 139, 188; nursing home, 217
Sunnyside Rest Home (Lake Park), 217
Sunset home plan, 134–136
Svithiod Home (Excelsior), 142, 279n
Swedish element, 111, 235; benevolent homes, 109, 110, 112, 142, 154, 183
Swedish Evangelical Free Church, Covenant (Minneapolis), 142, 267n
Swedish Hospital (Minneapolis), 69
Swift County, 82, 90, 258n

TAXES AND TAXATION, 18, 158; income, 205, 207

Taylor, Dr. H. Longstreet, 104
Teachers Home, Inc. (Minneapolis), 229
Teachout, Rev. E. C., sunset home plan, 134–136
Thompson, Teman, 214
Todd County, 277n; poorhouse, 90, 96, 258n
Townsend, Dr. Francis, 161
Township Act, *1858*, 15, 18, 35, 252n
Townships, relief systems, 1, 19, 35, 94, 96, 252n
Transient Home for Girls (Minneapolis), 122
Traverse County, poor farm, 97, 260n; nursing home, 217
Truman, Pres. Harry S, 213
Tuberculosis, 59, 96, 103; sanatoriums, 104, 120, 134, 154, 199, 216, 217, 261n, 277n
Tuff Memorial Home (Hills), 219
Twain, Mark, quoted, 51
Twin Cities, social life, 56; nursing homes, 194; benevolent homes, 208. *See also* Minneapolis, St. Paul
Twin City Linnea Home for the Aged (St. Paul), 113, 147, 205; name, 112
Tyler, Jennie Pettyjohn, quoted, 25
Tyler Lutheran Home, 175, 182
Tyson, Helen G., quoted, 165

UNEMPLOYMENT, 176; *1920s*, 126; *1930s*, 156, 161, 168; remedies, 160; effect of World War II, 185, 186, 202, 205, 207; of aged, 233
Union City Mission (Minneapolis), 168
United Charities, St. Paul, 127; Chicago, 137
United Church of Christ, benevolent home, 267n
United Norwegian Lutheran Church, 115
U.S. Bureau of the Census, *1904, 1910* surveys, 145
U.S. Congress, 7; welfare measures, 86, 125, 157, 158, 160, 162, 199, 220, 221, 227, 238. *See also* Social Security Act
U.S. Dept. of Health, Education, and Welfare, 227
U.S. Dept. of Labor, statistics bureau, 129, 131, 139; studies of aged care, 145–147, 183, 195, 239
U.S. Public Health Service, 220
University of Chicago, 151

University of Minnesota, sociology department, 147; Center for Continuation Study, 208, 222; Mayo Foundation, 209; School of Architecture, 220
University of Minnesota Hospitals, 128, 191, 194, 197

VAN CLEVE, MRS. CHARLOTTE O., 51, 55
Vaněk, Joseph, 143
Vasaly, Charles E., 103, 135
Veterans, care, 70, 85–87, 239
Villincourt, Benois, career, 62
Virginia (Minn.), 218
Vocational High School (Minneapolis), 122
Vocational Nursing Home (Minneapolis), 122
Volunteer Visitors Program (Minneapolis), 197

WABASHA COUNTY, 141, 277n; poor farm, 28, 32, 78, 166, 274n
Waddell, C. B., 105
Wadena County, 277n
Wagner-Rainey bill, 157
Walker Methodist Residence and Nursing Home (Minneapolis), 204, 208, 211, 227
War Production Board, 202
Warner, Amos, quoted, 91
Washburn Memorial Orphan Asylum (Minneapolis), 56, 94, 135, 259n
Washington County, created, 8, 9; commissioners, 13; poor farm, 13, 21, 24, 25, 94, 139, 188, 274n; mentally ill, 14; nursing home, 217
Wasioja, 27
Watkins, C. S., 37
Watkins, Paul, 219
Wells, Henry R., 76
Wessin, Mr. and Mrs. H. Stanley, 223
West Hotel (Minneapolis), 56
Wheaton, 217
Wheeler, Mrs. Walter H., 177
Whipple, Bishop Henry B., 67, 68

White House Conference on Aging, *1961*, 227, 239, 242
Wilder Residences (St. Paul), 228, 276n
Wilkin County, 158; poor farm, 139, 260n
Willmar, 148, 177, 182
Wilson, Dr. Viktor O., 191
Winnebago Baptist Residence (Winnebago), 174
Winona, 47, 253n, 258n
Winona County, poorhouse, 78, 80, 94, 253n
Wisconsin, 7, 114; welfare work, 6, 7, 19, 74, 130, 134; pension program, 139
Woman suffrage, 106, 125
Woman's Christian Assn. (Minneapolis), 58, 59, 122, 177, 178; hospital, 122, 150. *See also* Jones-Harrison Home
Women, as relief clients, 1, 3, 4, 14, 23, 24, 37, 46, 47; in welfare work, 39–50, 51–72, 111–114, 116–118, 121, 142, 177, 197, 207, 219, 241, 242; in benevolent homes, 42, 44, 46, 49, 50, 53, 56, 57, 58, 68, 112, 116, 119, 123, 150
Women's Christian Home (St. Paul), 46, 47
Women's Welfare League (Minneapolis), 121, 169, 207
Woodland Apartments (Crookston), 228
Workmen's Compensation Act, 127
World War I, 122, 124; effect on benevolent homes, 123; rationing, 205–207
World War II, living conditions, 185–212; effect on unemployment, 185, 186, 193, 194, 202, 205; building restrictions, 201, 218; rationing, 205–207
Wright County, poorhouse, 105, 260n

YATES, JOHN V., 4, 5
Yellow Medicine County, 82; poorhouse, 77, 166, 259n

ZARDETTI, BISHOP OTTO, 65

About the Author

ETHEL MCCLURE is well qualified for the pioneering task of writing this first book-length study of the development of poor farms and benevolent homes for the aged in Minnesota. During the many years she served in the state's public health and welfare agencies, she visited many of the county poorhouses and most of the benevolent homes discussed in these pages, as well as hospitals and child-caring institutions. To this firsthand knowledge she has added approximately five years of research, gathering together much of the source material that now enriches the Minnesota Historical Society's collections on this topic.

The author, who lives in Minneapolis, holds a bachelor of science degree from Macalester College, St. Paul, a master's degree in public health from the University of Minnesota, and is a graduate of the Johns Hopkins Hospital School of Nursing, Baltimore. Beginning her career as a visiting nurse in Chicago, she then worked as a nurse and teacher for the Grenfell Mission in Newfoundland and Labrador.

She began her employment with the state of Minnesota as a field worker for the children's bureau of the Board of Control of State Institutions. In 1939 she became supervisor of maternity hospitals for the Minnesota division of social welfare; from 1942 until her retirement in 1960 she was hospital licensing supervisor for the department of health. For nearly three years she served as research associate for the Governor's Citizens Council on Aging, and she was a member of Minnesota's delegation to the 1961 White House Conference on Aging.

Among Miss McClure's previous publications are booklets entitled *Homes for Aged and Chronically Ill Persons in Minnesota: Their Development and Licensure* (1959) and *The Care of Sick*

MORE THAN A ROOF

and Infirm Residents in Homes for the Aged in Minnesota (1945), both published by the Minnesota department of health, and articles in hospital and nursing journals and in *Minnesota History*.

Miss McClure was a cowinner of the Solon J. Buck award for the best article published in *Minnesota History* in 1963 for her account of "An Unlamented Era: County Poor Farms in Minnesota," which appeared in December of that year. She is also the compiler of a booklet entitled *A Historical Directory of Minnesota Homes for the Aged*, which gives the dates of founding, names of sponsors, and other detailed information about all public and nonprofit homes known to have opened in Minnesota from 1854 to July 1, 1968. This is her first book.

A HISTORICAL DIRECTORY
of Minnesota Homes for the Aged

Compiled by

Ethel McClure

Minnesota Historical Society · St. Paul · 1968

COPYRIGHT, 1968 © by the MINNESOTA HISTORICAL SOCIETY

Library of Congress Catalog Number: 68-65927

Introduction

This directory lists all nonprofit and public homes for older persons which are known to have opened in Minnesota between 1854 and July 1, 1968. Even though every effort has been made to locate these homes, it seems probable that some have inadvertently been missed, since information about such institutions is scattered and often unobtainable. The compilation includes county poor farms, homes for the aged, long-term nursing homes, and hospital units which are licensed by the Minnesota Department of Health under either the nursing home or the boarding care home classification. Some hospital units either failed to respond to questionnaires or indicated that the facility was only incidentally involved in care of old people. These were not included. Nonprofit apartments for the elderly are listed if they provide meal service and are similar in other phases of operation to the traditional home for the aged. Institutions are arranged alphabetically within counties under their most recent name and address.

The purpose of the directory is to preserve for ready reference the main historical facts about these facilities. Included are the original name and location of each institution with later changes, dates of opening and closing (if closed), the sponsoring organization, and the previous use of the original building if it was not a new structure. Because the annual directories issued by the Minnesota Health Department give bed capacity, administrator's name, and the type of care for which the institution is licensed, these items have been omitted.

The information given herein has been compiled from questionnaires, descriptive brochures, annual reports, and other material supplied by the homes. It has been supplemented by research in newspapers, government reports, county and church histories, and many miscellaneous documents. The material received, together with references to the other sources consulted, will be found in the individual institution and county files among the Ethel McClure Papers in the manuscripts collection of the Minnesota Historical Society.

In identifying sponsoring organizations, problems are created by changing names, mergers, and shifting responsibilities among various boards, societies, and agencies within religious groups. In the entries the name of the founding body has been given as it existed at the time, as well as the name of the organization presently responsible for the institution or responsible at the date of closing. Inaccuracies may occur, since the information received was frequently vague, and it was impossible to check in detail the management of each institution. Often, too, responsibility is divided or not clearly defined.

The following paragraphs attempt to identify and describe the groups which sponsor more than five homes in Minnesota. Abbreviations here indicated are used throughout the directory.

AMERICAN LUTHERAN CHURCH (ALC)

The first home for the aged opened in the state by a Norwegian Lutheran church body was the Glenwood Old People's Home, started in 1914 by the Norwegian Synod. In 1917 this synod merged with two other groups to form the Norwegian Lutheran Church of America, renamed in 1946 the Evangelical Lutheran Church. Its institutions were supervised by a board of charities. In

1960 the Evangelical Lutheran Church became part of the American Lutheran Church, and its homes were placed under the supervision of a department of services for the aging within the ALC Division of Social Service. Individual homes are sponsored by the congregations of the area, and each home has its own local board, but all are listed in this directory as being associated with the church.

ASSEMBLY HOMES, INC.

Assembly Homes, a nonprofit corporation, was organized in the early 1960s by members of the Assembly of God Church. Its headquarters are in Glenwood, Minnesota, where its first institution — the Assembly of God Home — was opened.

EVANGELICAL LUTHERAN GOOD SAMARITAN SOCIETY (GSS)

This organization, founded through the efforts of the Reverend August J. Hoeger, has its headquarters in Sioux Falls, South Dakota. Its first Minnesota facility was the Clearwater Sunset Home, opened at Bagley in 1945. While Good Samaritan homes are owned and administered by the society, they are maintained with local support and are established only at the invitation of the community. Membership in the society is limited to Lutherans, but it is not owned or subsidized by any church body.

LUTHERAN CHURCH IN AMERICA (LCA) — MINNESOTA SYNOD

At the time its first Minnesota homes for old people were established, this group was known as the Minnesota Conference, Augustana Lutheran Church — often referred to as the Lutheran Minnesota Conference. Until 1923 its charitable agencies were operated by various societies and boards, but in that year their administration was centralized under the Board of Christian Service. With the merger of several church bodies in 1962 to form the Lutheran Church in America, these institutions were placed under the Board of Social Ministry of the Minnesota Synod of the LCA. Also under the LCA, but not directly governed by the board, are a number of homes sponsored by associated congregations.

LUTHERAN CHURCH IN AMERICA (LCA) — RED RIVER VALLEY SYNOD

The Red River Valley Conference, comprising some ninety-one congregations formerly a part of the Minnesota Conference, Augustana Lutheran Church, was organized separately in 1912. This conference, too, had a social service board — the Board of Charities. In 1963 it became the Board of Social Ministry of the Red River Valley Synod of the LCA.

LUTHERAN CHURCH — MISSOURI SYNOD (LCMS)

State congregations of this church body are in two districts: Minnesota South District, with headquarters in Minneapolis, and Minnesota North District, with headquarters in Brainerd. Most of the homes associated with it are sponsored by groups of congregations in the area served.

NORTHWEST BAPTIST HOME SOCIETY

This organization was formed at Winnebago, Minnesota, in June, 1930, by Baptist leaders from Iowa, Minnesota, Nebraska, and the Dakotas for the purpose of establishing homes for the aged in these states. Headquarters of the group is in Minneapolis.

ROMAN CATHOLIC ORDERS

Most of the Catholic homes in Minnesota are either staffed or sponsored by an order of nuns. Some sixteen separate groups are active in this work in the state. Entries generally specify the headquarters, since this is usually the administrative center from which work in the homes is conducted. One of the first religious orders to serve the state's aged was the Little Sisters of the Poor, which opened its St. Paul home in 1883 and St. Joseph's Home in Minneapolis five years later. A large number of homes is now served by Sisters of the Order of St. Benedict, including groups headquartered at St. Paul, St. Joseph, Duluth, and Crookston, and by the Franciscan Sisters of the Immaculate Conception, with headquarters at Little Falls. Franciscan groups located in St. Paul and Rochester, Minnesota, and in Warwick, New York, are also active in the state, as are several other orders which operate one or two homes each.

Directory of Homes for the Aged

AITKIN

Aitkin Community Hospital and Convalescent and Nursing Care Unit. 301 Minnesota Ave. S., Aitkin. July 1, 1963—Opened as Aitkin Community Nursing Home by a nonprofit community association. Operated by the hospital.

Aitkin County Poor Farm. Aitkin. 1904–36.

ANOKA

Anoka County Poor Farm. Anoka. 1898–1936. Opened on a rented farm; land purchased, 1899.

Crestview Lutheran Home. 4444 Reservoir Blvd., Columbia Heights. April, 1952—Opened in an existing dwelling by Minneapolis Lutheran Mission Auxiliary. Now operated by 21 congregations of the LCMS, Minnesota South District. A new addition was built in 1968.

Ladies of the G.A.R. Home. 427 W. Main St., Anoka. 1899–February, 1960. Was operated by the Minnesota Department, Ladies of the Grand Army of the Republic.

BECKER

Becker County Poor Farm. Detroit Lakes. 1883–1940. First opened in a log cabin on farm; moved to town, 1889. Building destroyed by fire and new poorhouse erected, 1900. Leased as Torgerson Boarding Home, 1936–40.

Emmanuel Nursing Home. Detroit Lakes. October 1, 1964—Opened in a new building by Board of Social Ministry, Red River Valley Synod, LCA.

Sunnyside Rest Home. Lake Park. July, 1951—Operated by Becker and Clay counties in building formerly used by Sand Beach Tuberculosis Sanatorium.

BELTRAMI

Beltrami County Poor Farm. Bemidji. 1901–51. Land purchased, 1901; poorhouse leased to City of Bemidji, 1909; returned to county and new building erected, 1919. Leased as Spears Boarding Home, 1936–51.

Bemidji Hospital Convalescent and Nursing Care Unit. 803 Dewey Ave., Bemidji. 1964—Occupies new addition to Bemidji Hospital.

Bemidji Rest Home. 1437 Irvine Ave., Bemidji. 1946–64. A former proprietary rest home taken over by a nonprofit association in 1946 and transferred to Lutheran (now Bemidji) Hospital in 1958.

Good Samaritan Center. Kelliher. April 20, 1964—Opened by GSS in a new building.

Lake Julia Rest Home. Puposky. 1954—Operated by Beltrami County in building formerly used by Lake Julia Tuberculosis Sanatorium.

BENTON

Good Shepherd Lutheran Home. 1115 4th Ave. N., Sauk Rapids. December, 1963 — Opened in a new building by 12 congregations of the LCMS, Minnesota North District.

BIG STONE

Clinton Good Samaritan Center. Clinton. April 20, 1964 — Opened in a new building by the GSS.

Holy Trinity Home. Graceville. March 12, 1966 — Operated by Missionary Benedictine Sisters, Graceville, in connection with Holy Trinity Hospital. Occupies building formerly used by hospital.

BLUE EARTH

Blue Earth County Poor Farm. Mankato. 1867 — New building erected, 1890. Leased as Albert Wurster Boarding Home, 1957. In operation as boarding and lodging house, Pearl Dodge, licensee, 1968.

Mankato Lutheran Home for Aged. 718 Mound Ave., Mankato. November, 1937—Opened by Minnesota Conference, Augustana Lutheran Church (now Minnesota Synod, LCA) in a new building.

Mapleton Community Home. Mapleton. February, 1965—Opened in a new building by a nonprofit community organization.

Mother Frances Rest Home. 401 N. 5th St., Mankato. 1953–April, 1967. Was operated by Sisters of the Sorrowful Mother, Milwaukee, Wisconsin, in a building formerly used by St. Joseph's Hospital.

BROWN

Brown County Poor Farm. New Ulm. 1903–65. New building erected, 1908. Leased as a boarding home, 1938–65. Operated by a succession of lessees.

Divine Providence Community Home. St. Mary and Lake Sts., Sleepy Eye. October, 1960—Operated by Daughters of St. Mary of Providence, Chicago, Illinois, in a building erected by the local community.

Highland Manor. 405 N. Highland Ave., New Ulm. September, 1959 — Opened in a new building by New Ulm Memorial Foundation.

St. Alexander Home. 1324 5th St. N., New Ulm. 1913 — Opened by Sisters of the Poor Handmaids of Jesus Christ (now Ancilla Domini Sisters) in a building formerly used by St. Alexander's Hospital. Although the hospital had earlier cared for aged persons, the home did not achieve separate identity until 1913. Now operated in connection with Loretto Hospital.

St. John Lutheran Home. Springfield. 1901—Opened by a local group as part of a new hospital. In 1917 ownership was transferred to Lutheran Synod of Ohio and other states. In 1958 hospital was closed and entire building was taken over for nursing home. Now an institution of the ALC.

Union Hospital Convalescent and Nursing Care Unit. 7th St. and Broadway, New Ulm. April, 1957 — Occupies a section of Union Hospital.

CARLTON

Community Memorial Hospital and Convalescent Nursing Care Section. Skyline Blvd., Cloquet. March 1, 1965—Opened by the hospital association in a new building.

Mercy Hospital Nursing Home. Moose Lake. May 11, 1964 — Opened by Moose Lake Community Hospital District in a new building and operated in connection with Mercy Hospital.

CARVER

Carver County Poor Farm. Dahlgren. 1870–77.

Elim Home. Watertown. July 1, 1968—Former proprietary nursing home taken over by North Central District Association, Evangelical Free Church of America.

Lake Auburn Home for Aged. Rte. 1, Excelsior. November 11, 1928—Opened in a new building by Western District, Moravian Church in America.

Nightingale Nursing Home. 232 S. Elm St., Waconia. June, 1955—Opened by Waconia Hospital in a building formerly used as a nurses' home. Took over old hospital building in 1963.

CASS

Ah-gwah-ching Nursing Home. Ah-gwah-ching. 1962—Operated by the State of Minnesota for the care of senile patients transferred from state mental hospitals. A section of the former state sanatorium for tuberculosis patients was used from 1956 for care of the elderly, and the entire building was converted in 1962.

Good Samaritan Home. Pine River. February, 1957—Opened by the GSS in a new building.

CHIPPEWA

Chippewa County Poor Farm. Montevideo. 1883–1927.

Clara City Community Nursing Home. 1012 Division St. N., Clara City. March 7, 1966—Opened in a new building by the Village of Clara City.

Luther Haven Nursing Home. E. Highway 7, Montevideo. June, 1964—Opened in a new building by congregations of the ALC.

CHISAGO

Chisago County Poor Farm. See Green Acres Nursing Home.

Chisago Lutheran Home for Aged. Chisago City. November, 1904—Opened in a new building as Bethesda Old People's Home by Minnesota Conference, Augustana Lutheran Church (now Minnesota Synod, LCA).

Green Acres Nursing Home. Rte. 1, North Branch. 1868—Former Chisago County Poor Farm, now operated as a county nursing home. Poor farm was first opened on a farm near Sunrise and moved to North Branch, 1904. Leased as Fairview Rest Home, 1938–48, and as Green Acres Rest Home, 1948–54, when it was returned to county operation under the present name.

CLAY

Barnesville Nursing Home. Barnesville. May, 1965—Opened by Assembly Homes in a new building.

Eventide Lutheran Home. 1405 S. 7th St., Moorhead. June 1, 1951—Opened in a new building by congregations of the Moorhead Circuit, Evangelical Lutheran Church (now ALC).

Sacred Heart Home. Moorhead. 1930–52. Opened in an addition to St. Ansgar Hospital by Franciscan Sisters of the Immaculate Conception, Little Falls.

Viking Manor Nursing Home. Ulen. January 17, 1966—Opened in a new building by Village of Ulen.

CLEARWATER

Clearwater Sunset Home. Bagley. September, 1945—Opened by a local organization under direction of the GSS in a former residence.

Good Samaritan Center. Clearbrook. January, 1952—Opened as Good Samaritan Home in a new building. Operated by GSS.

COOK

North Shore Nursing Home. Grand Marais. April, 1965—Operated by Cook County in connection with North Shore Hospital. Occupies a new building.

COTTONWOOD

Bethel Hospital facilities. Mountain Lake.
    Bethel Hospital Nursing Care Unit. 1960—
    Bethel Hospital Old People's Home. 1904–50.
    Eventide Home. 1950—
Hospital was opened, 1904, in a former school building by a local organization. Old People's Home was part of hospital until 1921, when a new hospital was built and the home occupied the old building. It was replaced by Eventide Home, opened in 1950 in a new building. The Nursing Care Unit, opened when a new hospital building was completed in 1960, occupies the hospital built in 1921. Originally associated with the Mennonite church, the institutions are now operated by the Bethel Hospital Association.

Cottonwood County Poor Farm. Great Bend Township. 1887–1903.

Good Samaritan Center. 306 N. 10th St., Mountain Lake. February 28, 1966—Opened by GSS in an existing building.

Senior Citizens Home. Westbrook. August 5, 1962—Opened in a new building by the GSS.

Sogge Memorial Good Samaritan Center. W. 6th St., Windom. January 15, 1958—Opened in a new building by the GSS.

CROW WING

Cedarbrook Manor. Rte. 6, Deerwood. November, 1952—Operated in the former Deerwood Tuberculosis Sanatorium by Crow Wing County, which bought out Aitkin County's share in the building.

Crow Wing County Poor Farm. Brainerd. 1888–1913.

Good Samaritan Center. 803 Kingwood St., Brainerd. March, 1963—Opened by the GSS in building formerly used by Northwestern Hospital, to which a new wing had been added.

DAKOTA

Dakota County Poor Farm. Farmington. 1866–1952. First opened at Nininger; moved to Vermillion, 1880; moved to farm purchased north of Farmington, 1895; building destroyed by fire and new poorhouse erected, 1897. Leased as Henry Ulvi Boarding Home, 1947–52.

Haven Homes. 930 W. 16th St., Hastings. November 16, 1967—Operated in a new building by a nonprofit corporation.

Inver Grove Nursing Home. 4700 S. Robert Trail, South St. Paul. May 17, 1964—Opened in a new building by Assembly Homes.

Regina Nursing Home and Residence. Nininger Road, Hastings. November 16, 1965—Operated in connection with Regina Memorial Hospital by Sisters of Charity of Our Lady, Mother of Mercy, Hastings.

Sanford Memorial Nursing Home. 913 Main St., Farmington. February 27, 1967—Opened by Sanford Hospital in a new building. Operated in connection with the hospital.

DODGE

Dodge County Poor Farm. See **Fairview Nursing Home.**

Fairview Nursing Home. Dodge Center. 1869—Former Dodge County Poor Farm, now operated as county nursing home. Poor farm first opened at Wasioja and later moved to Dodge Center; new building erected about 1927. Leased as Fairview Rest Home, 1938–52, when it was returned to county operation under present name.

DOUGLAS

Bethany Home. 1020 Lark St., Alexandria. January, 1917—Opened in a new building by Red River Valley Conference, Augustana Lutheran Church (now Red River Valley Synod of LCA).

Community Memorial Home. Osakis. 1963—Opened by a nonprofit community organization in a new building.

Knute Nelson Memorial Home. 420 12th Ave. E., Alexandria. April, 1948—Opened as Knute Nelson–Glenwood Memorial Home by Evangelical Lutheran Church (now ALC) in a homestead willed by Nelson to the church. Separate building erected in 1958.

Our Lady of Mercy Home. 700 Cedar St., Alexandria. August, 1962—Operated by Franciscan Sisters of the Immaculate Conception, Little Falls, in building formerly used by Tanquist Hospital.

FARIBAULT

St. Luke's Lutheran Home. 1219 S. Ramsey St., Blue Earth. April 16, 1963—Operated in a new building by congregations of the ALC.

Winnebago Baptist Residence. 217 W. North, Winnebago. 1931—Opened by Northwest Baptist Home Society in a former college dormitory.

FILLMORE

Fillmore County Poor Farm. Canton. 1868–1943. Opened in a new building, which burned, 1893; second new building erected, 1896.

Good Shepherd Lutheran Home. Rushford. September 13, 1965—Opened in a new building by congregations of the ALC.

Green Lea Manor. Mabel. December 27, 1961—Operated by Village of Mabel in a new building.

FREEBORN

Freeborn County Poor Farm. Albert Lea. 1870–75, 1889–1953. New building erected, 1916. Leased as Hill Top Rest Home, 1947?–53. See **Good Samaritan Center.**

Good Samaritan Center. Rte. 2, Albert Lea. 1953—Opened by the GSS in former poor farm leased from county. Building was later purchased by the society and a new nursing home added.

St. John's Lutheran Home. Luther Place, Albert Lea. January 2, 1962— Opened in new building by congregations of the ALC.

GOODHUE

Community Home. 433 Mill St., Zumbrota. November 11, 1964—Opened by Village of Zumbrota in a new building and operated in connection with the Zumbrota Community Hospital.

Community Hospital Nursing Home. 1116 W. Mill St., Cannon Falls. November 3, 1958—Opened by City of Cannon Falls in a wing attached to the hospital.

Goodhue County Poor Farm. Red Wing. 1864–1963. Opened in an existing farmhouse; new building erected, 1867; destroyed by fire, 1889; second new building erected, 1891.

Kenyon Sunset Home. 127 2nd St., Kenyon. December 1, 1949—Opened by Evangelical Lutheran Church (now ALC) in an existing residence. Operated in connection with **Red Wing Seminary Memorial Home.**

Pine Haven Nursing Home. Washington St., Pine Island. August 3, 1964— Opened by Village of Pine Island in a new building.

Red Wing Baptist Home. College Bluff, Red Wing. 1914–61. Originally a city-operated institution, the home was transferred in 1939 to the Northwest Baptist Home Society.

Red Wing Seminary Memorial Home. 906 College Ave., Red Wing. May, 1943—Opened by Evangelical Lutheran Church (now ALC) in a building that was formerly used as a residence for the president of Red Wing Seminary and College.

GRANT

Community Memorial Hospital Convalescent and Nursing Care Unit. Elbow Lake. January 5, 1962—Administered by nonprofit corporation operating the community hospital.

Hoffman Nursing Home. Hoffman. August, 1964—Operated in a new building by Assembly Homes.

HENNEPIN

Alliance Residence No. 1. 3101 Aldrich Ave. S., Minneapolis. 1946–April 15, 1962. Opened in a residential building by Christian and Missionary Alliance Church, **Minneapolis.**

Alliance Residence. 3101 Lyndale Ave. S., Minneapolis. 1951—Opened as Alliance Residence No. 2, in an existing apartment building, by Christian and Missionary Alliance Church, Minneapolis.

Augustana Home of Minneapolis. 1007 E. 14th St., Minneapolis. November, 1896—Opened as a home for aged, young women, and children in a dwelling at 1307 8th St. S. by Ladies Aid Society, First Augustana Lutheran Church (changed in 1908 to Women's Mission Association). Moved within Minneapolis several times. In 1918 home renamed Augustana Mission Colony. Services to children and young women discontinued, 1952, 1960. In 1960 membership in organization made available to other Augustana Lutheran churches in area and present name adopted.

Baptist Residence. 512 N. 49th Ave., Minneapolis. March, 1961 — Opened by Northwest Baptist Home Society in a former hospital building.

Bethany Covenant Home. 2309 Hayes St. N.E., Minneapolis. 1929—Opened in a former residence by Northwest Mission Society (now Northwest Conference of Evangelical Covenant Church of America).

Blaisdell Avenue Baptist Home. 2118 Blaisdell Ave., Minneapolis. June, 1947—Opened in a former residence by Northwest Baptist Home Society.

Calhoun Beach Manor. 2730 W. Lake St., Minneapolis. January 5, 1963— Opened by United Church Homes in a converted hotel building. Apartment-type facility providing meals and other services.

Colonial Acres. 5825 St. Croix Ave., Golden Valley. February 7, 1962— Opened in a new building by a nonprofit organization.

Danebo Home. 3030 W. River Road, Minneapolis. May, 1925—Opened in a new building by a Danish-American organization.

Ebenezer Home Society facilities. Minneapolis.
    Ebenezer Home. 2545 Portland Ave. May 7, 1917—
    John Field Hall. 2647 Oakland Ave. 1950—
    Luther Hall and Annex. 2631-2636 Park Ave. 1960—
Ebenezer Home was first opened at 3017 Portland Ave. by a men's organization representing six Norwegian Lutheran church bodies. Moved in 1919 to a new building on the present site. All of the society's facilities are now under the ALC.

Elim Old People's Home. 934 14th Ave. S., Minneapolis. 1914–45. Was operated by Norwegian-Danish Conference of the Methodist Church.

Fairview Hospital Extended Care Unit. 2312 S. 6th St., Minneapolis. 1963— Opened by the board of trustees as an addition to the hospital.

First Christian Church Residence. 2300 Stevens Ave. S., Minneapolis. 1965— Opened in a new building by the First Christian Church of Minneapolis.

Franklin Nursing Home. 501 Franklin Ave. W., Minneapolis. 1935 — Former Hillcrest Hospital, converted into Franklin Public Hospital, a chronic disease facility, and later Franklin Nursing Home.

Harriet House. 2200 Harriet Ave., Minneapolis. 1947–June, 1956. Was operated by Women's Welfare League of Minneapolis in building formerly used as a girls' club.

Hennepin County Poor Farm. Hopkins. 1864–1953. Large addition erected, 1884; new building completed, October, 1926.

Home for Convalescents. 100 Clifton Ave., Minneapolis. October 1, 1913– October, 1961. Operated by Women's Welfare League. Occupied several residential buildings before acquiring final quarters in former Charles M. Loring mansion.

Jones-Harrison Home. 3700 Cedar Lake Ave., Minneapolis. May 29, 1888— Opened by Woman's Christian Association in a former hotel-sanatorium, later replaced by several new buildings.

Maranatha Conservative Baptist Home. 5401 69th Ave. N., Brooklyn Center. May 1, 1963—Operated by Twin City Association of Conservative Baptist Churches in a new building.

Martin Luther Manor. 1401 E. 100th St., Bloomington. September 27, 1961— Opened by congregations of the Northwest Synod, United Lutheran Church in America, in a new building. Accepted in 1963 as an institution of the Minnesota Synod, LCA.

Minnesota Masonic Home. 11400 Normandale Road, Bloomington. August, 1920—Opened in a former residence; moved to new building, September, 1927. Operated by a nonprofit corporation.

Minnesota Veterans Home. 51st St. and Minnehaha Ave., Minneapolis. 1887—Opened as Minnesota Soldiers Home; renamed in 1967. Operated by State of Minnesota.

Mission Farms Nursing Home. 3401 E. Medicine Lake Blvd., Minneapolis. 1927—Opened by Union City Mission of Minneapolis as a self-help project for needy men. Infirmary service was gradually developed, and in 1964 the most substantial building was converted to a nursing home.

Mount Olivet Lutheran Church facilities. Minneapolis.
    Mount Olivet Home. February, 1958–June, 1965.
    Mount Olivet Senior Citizens Home. 5517 Lyndale Ave. S. September, 1960—
    Careview Home. 5515 Lyndale Ave. S. October, 1965—
Mount Olivet Home was formerly Vocational Nursing Home. The Senior Citizens Home is a new residential-type building, and Careview Home, also new, is designed for intensive nursing care. It is operated under a separate corporation.

North Memorial Hospital Unit. 3220 Lowry Ave. N., Robbinsdale. 1955–61. Nursing home unit was operated by hospital in building formerly used as nurses' dormitory.

Oak Terrace Nursing Home. Oak Terrace. 1959—Opened by Hennepin County as Glen Lake Sanatorium County Nursing Home in a section of the Glen Lake Tuberculosis Sanatorium. Entire property turned over to State of Minnesota in 1961 and nursing care unit given new name.

Parkview Nursing Home. 512 N. 49th Ave., Minneapolis. 1923-59. Opened as Parkview Sanitarium by City of Minneapolis in former Hopewell Hospital building. Leased in 1946 to Parkview Hospital Association. In 1956 sold to Parkview Nursing Home, Inc., a proprietary corporation, and closed in 1959.

Queen Nursing Home. 300 Queen Ave. N., Minneapolis. August, 1956— Opened by Children's Hospital of Minneapolis in building formerly used by Maternity Hospital. Transferred to a proprietary corporation in 1963.

St. Joseph's Home for Aged. 215 Broadway, N.E., Minneapolis. 1889— Opened by Little Sisters of the Poor in an existing dwelling at 313 3rd St. N.E. Moved to new building at present location, 1896.

St. Olaf Residence. 2912 Fremont Ave. N., Minneapolis. September 1, 1964— Operated in a new building by a nonprofit church-related organization. Is an institution of the ALC.

St. Therese Nursing Home. New Hope. January 9, 1968—Opened by Sisters of St. Benedict, St. Paul's Priory, St. Paul, in a new building erected by the community.

Stevens Square. 101 E. 32nd St., Minneapolis. 1881—Opened as a children's home by Children's Home Society of Minneapolis. Reorganized as Home for Children and Aged Women, 1886, in a new building. Separate women's building erected, 1922; children's service discontinued, 1935; renamed and new building added, 1959.

Svithiod Home. Excelsior. 1928–October, 1967. Was opened in a new building by Independent Order of Svithiod, Chicago, for aged members of the organization.

Teachers Homes. 2625 Park Ave., Minneapolis. July, 1962—Opened by an organization of active and retired teachers. The apartment-type building provides limited dining room service and infirmary care to members.

Union Home for the Aged. 1507 Lowry Ave., N.E., Minneapolis. 1915—Opened in a residential building as Scandinavian Union Relief Home by a women's organization. Renamed in 1961.

Vocational Nursing Home. 5511 Lyndale Ave. S., Minneapolis. 1927–58. Formerly Woman's Christian Association Hospital, which was taken over by graduates of its practical nursing school and moved to an existing sanatorium building on Lyndale Avenue. In 1958 ownership was transferred to Mount Olivet Lutheran Church. See **Mount Olivet Nursing Home.**

Walker Methodist Residence and Nursing Home. 3701 Bryant Ave. S., Minneapolis. November, 1945—Opened by Methodist Conference of Minnesota in former Harriet Walker Hospital building.

Weddell Memorial Baptist Home. 2201 Pillsbury Ave., Minneapolis. December, 1944–March 15, 1961. Was opened as Minneapolis Baptist Home by the Northwest Baptist Home Society and renamed in honor of a donor.

Woman's Christian Association Hospital. 1700 3rd Ave. S., Minneapolis. 1919–27. Opened by the Woman's Christian Association to provide training in practical nursing in co-operation with the Minneapolis Board of Education. Was taken over by an association of nursing graduates in 1927. See **Vocational Nursing Home.**

HOUSTON

Caledonia Community Hospital Convalescent and Nursing Care Unit. Blue Spruce Summit. December 17, 1962—Operated in connection with the hospital.

Houston County Poor Farm. Caledonia. 1878—First opened in a tavern building in Union Township. Present site purchased and building erected, 1902; replaced by new building, 1906. Leased as Evergreen Rest Home, 1944–? In 1968 is being operated as a boarding and lodging house.

Tweeten Memorial Hospital Convalescent Home. Spring Grove. August, 1963—Opened in a new building by a nonprofit organization. Operated in connection with the hospital.

Valley View Nursing Home of Houston. Houston. October 30, 1967—Operated in a new building by Village of Houston.

HUBBARD

Hubbard County Poor Farm. Park Rapids. 1906–55. Opened in a new building. Leased, 1937–55, by a succession of lessees, usually going under name of Hubbard County Poor Farm (or Home).

Sunset Home. W. 5th St., Park Rapids. 1955 — Purchased by Hubbard County from a private builder; operated 1955–60 on a lease-type arrangement; county assumed direct operation about 1960.

ISANTI

Grand View Christian Home. 800 2nd Ave. N.W., Cambridge. October 22, 1963 — Opened in a new building by an organization of congregations in the East Central District, Minnesota Baptist Conference, St. Paul.

ITASCA

Itasca County Poor Farm. See **Itasca Nursing Home.**

Itasca Nursing Home. 924 County Home Road, Grand Rapids. 1896 — Former Itasca County Poor Farm, now operated as county nursing home. New poorhouse building erected 1935; converted to nursing home, 1957.

JACKSON

Good Samaritan Sunset Home. 600 West St., Jackson. 1956 — Opened in a new building by the GSS.

Jackson Municipal Hospital Convalescent and Nursing Care Unit. North Highway, Jackson. April 10, 1967 — Opened by City of Jackson in a new building. Operated in connection with the municipal hospital.

KANDIYOHI

Bethesda Homes facilities. Willmar.
> **Bethesda Country Home.** Rte. 1. 1910 —
> **Bethesda Nursing Home.** 1012 E. 3rd St. June, 1953 —

The Country Home was operated in connection with a children's home, discontinued in 1939. Became responsibility of Lutheran Free Church, 1928. Nursing Home was opened in a new building. Both became institutions of the ALC, 1961.

Christian Rest Home. 1801 Willmar Ave., Willmar. October 26, 1965 — Opened in a new building by Christian Rest Home Association.

Kandiyohi County Poor Farm. Willmar. 1907–13.

KITTSON

Kittson County Nursing Home. Hallock. April, 1959 — Operated by Kittson County in a former hospital building.

Kittson County Poor Farm. Hallock. 1910–37.

KOOCHICHING

Falls Nursing Home. International Falls. 1956 — Opened by county in former county poor farm. New building in different location opened May 1, 1963.

Koochiching County Poor Farm. International Falls. 1908–63. Leased, 1942–56, and operated by county as a nursing home, 1956–63. See **Falls Nursing Home.**

Littlefork Municipal Hospital Nursing Home. Littlefork. June, 1964—Opened by Village of Littlefork in a building formerly occupied by the municipal hospital.

LAC QUI PARLE

Lac qui Parle County Poor Farm. Madison. 1889—Opened in new building. Leased in 1950s as Frank Cox Boarding Home.

Madison Lutheran Home. 900 3rd Ave., Madison. March, 1944—Opened by Norwegian Lutheran Church of America (now ALC) in a former dormitory building, to which a new addition was later made.

LAKE

Community Health Center Nursing Home. 426 1st Ave., Two Harbors. July, 1957—Opened by Community Health Center in building formerly used by Two Harbors Hospital.

Lake County Poorhouse. Two Harbors. 1913–39.

LAKE OF THE WOODS

Pioneer Nursing Home. Baudette. June, 1954—Formerly a co-operative home operated by old-age assistance recipients. Operated by county as Pioneer Rest Home 1954–63, when new building was completed and present name was adopted.

LE SUEUR

Garden View Home. 621 S. 4th St., Le Sueur. August 1, 1967—Operated by Minnesota Valley Memorial Hospital in a new building connected with the hospital.

Kasota Valley Lutheran Home. Kasota. September, 1951—Opened in an existing building by Evangelical Lutheran Synod, Mankato.

Le Sueur County Poor Farm. Kilkenny Township. 1868–80.

LINCOLN

Divine Providence Home. Ivanhoe. April 3, 1967—Operated by Schoenstatt Sisters of Mary, Madison, Wisconsin, in a new building connected with Divine Providence Hospital.

Hendricks Retirement Home. E. Lincoln St., Hendricks. November 3, 1958—Opened by Hendricks Community Hospital Association in building formerly used by hospital.

Tyler Lutheran Home. Tyler. 1936—Opened as Tyler Old People's Home by Danish Evangelical Lutheran congregations in the area in a building formerly used as a children's home. Now operated by Tyler Lutheran Home Corporation.

Tyler Nursing Home. Tyler. February 15, 1960—Opened by Village of Tyler in building formerly used by Tyler Hospital.

LYON

Christian Manor Nursing Home. 502 5th St. E., Tracy. September 9, 1966—Opened in a new building by General Benevolent Association of Churches of Christ and Christian Churches of Minnesota (headquarters, Willmar).

Louis Weiner Memorial Hospital Nursing Home Unit. Marshall. 1964—Opened by City of Marshall in a new building connected with the hospital.

Lyon County Poor Farm. Marshall. 1883-1936. Occupied a farmhouse built in 1884 for use as a poorhouse.

Marshall Chronic and Convalescent Home. 208 S. 4th St., Marshall. July, 1951-1964. Was owned by City of Marshall and operated by Louis Weiner Memorial Hospital.

Tracy Nursing Home. 2nd and Emory, Tracy. May 16, 1966—Opened by community organization in building formerly used by Tracy Hospital.

McLEOD

Burns Manor Municipal Nursing Home. North High Drive, Hutchinson. April 23, 1965—Opened by City of Hutchinson in a new building.

Glenhaven. Silver Lake Road, Glencoe. October, 1967—Former proprietary nursing home, purchased by City of Glencoe.

St. Mary's Hospital and Home. 551 4th Ave. N., Winsted. January, 1960—Opened by Sisters of St. Benedict, St. Paul's Priory, St. Paul, in a new building erected by the community. Operated in connection with the hospital.

MARSHALL

Emmaus Lutheran Home. 554 E. Wentzel Ave., Warren. March, 1961—Opened by Red River Valley Conference of the Augustana Lutheran Church (now Red River Valley Synod, LCA) in building formerly used by Warren Hospital.

Good Samaritan Center. 410 S. McKinley, Warren. October, 1952—Opened as the Good Samaritan Home in a building formerly used by North Star College. Operated by the GSS.

MARTIN

Lakeview Methodist Home. 610 Summit Dr., Fairmont. June, 1964—Opened in a new building by the Southwest District of Minnesota Annual Conference of the United Methodist Church.

Martin County Poor Farm. Fairmont. 1915-37. See **St. Joseph's Home.**

St. Joseph's Home. Rte. 1, Fairmont. September, 1949—Opened in building formerly used by Martin County Poor Farm. Operated by Sisters of Charity of Our Lady Mother of Mercy, Holland.

Trimont Nursing Home. Trimont. March 1, 1964—Opened in a new building by the Village of Trimont.

MEEKER

Augustana Lutheran Homes facilities. Litchfield.
    Emmaus Home. 204 N. Holcombe. 1953—

Gloria Dei Manor. 218 N. Holcombe. 1964—
Bethany Nursing Home. 203 N. Armstrong. 1966—
This complex of homes, sponsored by congregations of the Minnesota Synod, LCA, provides boarding care, nursing, and rental units. Emmaus Home occupies the building formerly used by Litchfield Hospital. The other two were opened in new structures.
Dassel Lakeside Community Home. Dassel. August 19, 1963—Opened in new building by Village of Dassel.

MILLE LACS

Community Mercy Hospital Convalescent and Nursing Care Unit. Onamia. September, 1962—Opened as Bethany Home by Franciscan Sisters of the Immaculate Conception, Little Falls. Occupies a new building adjoining the hospital.
Elim Home. 101 S. 7th Ave., Princeton. 1927 — Opened in a residence by Minnesota District Society of the Swedish Evangelical Free Church (now North Central District Association, Evangelical Free Church of America).
Elim Home. 730 2nd St. S.E., Milaca. July 15, 1964—Opened in a new building by the North Central District Association, Evangelical Free Church of America.
Mille Lacs County Poor Farm. Milaca. 1910-49. Leased as George Wills Rest Home 1936-42, and as Arne Swenson Rest Home 1942-49. Building destroyed by fire, 1949.

MORRISON

Lutheran Senior Citizens Home. 1200 1st Ave. N.E., Little Falls. May, 1964—Opened by nonprofit corporation in a new building.
Morrison County Poor Farm. Little Falls? 1887-89.
St. Mary's Villa Nursing Home. 1st Ave. S.E., Pierz. April, 1961—Opened by St. Joseph's Church of Pierz (Roman Catholic parish) in a new building. Staffed by Franciscan Sisters of the Poor, Warwick, New York.
St. Otto's Home for Aged. 8th Ave. and 2nd St., Little Falls. 1891—Opened by Franciscan Sisters of the Immaculate Conception, Little Falls, in combined convent, hospital, and orphanage building. New orphanage built, 1895, and new hospital, 1916. Home for aged moved into orphanage building, 1925, after latter operation was transferred to St. Cloud.

MOWER

Comforcare Nursing Home. 205 14th St. N.W., Austin. December, 1963—A former proprietary home, purchased by Assembly Homes.
Meadow Manor Nursing Home. Grand Meadow. February 10, 1964—Opened by Village of Grand Meadow in a new building.
Mower County Poor Farm. Austin. 1868-1963. First opened in LeRoy Township; later moved to Lansing Township. New building erected in 1917. Leased as Cedar Valley Rest Home, 1946-63. Closed 1963, and property used as home for wayward boys.

Sacred Heart Hospice. 1200 12th St. S.W., Austin. June 30, 1964—Opened in a new building owned by the Diocese of Winona. Staffed and operated by the Sisters of St. Francis, Congregation of Our Lady of Lourdes, Rochester.

St. Mark's Lutheran Home. 400 15th Ave. S.W., Austin. January, 1963—Opened in a new building by congregations of the ALC.

MURRAY

Maple Lawn Nursing Home. 400 Maple Lawn Drive, Fulda. June 8, 1964—Opened in a new building by a community nonprofit organization.

Murray County Poor Farm. 1896–May 1, 1944.

NICOLLET

Community Hospital Nursing Care Unit. 618 Broadway, St. Peter. January, 1960—Operated by City of St. Peter in building formerly used by hospital.

Grandview Nursing Home. 830 N. Sunrise Dr., St. Peter. January 25, 1967—Opened in a new building by Assembly Homes.

Lafayette Good Samaritan Home. Lafayette. July, 1959—Opened in a new building by GSS.

Nicollet County Poor Farm. Nicollet. 1867–1958. Opened first in Granby Township; moved to farm near Nicollet and new building erected, 1899. Leased as Chester Webster Boarding Home, 1946–49, and as James Stevenson Boarding Home, 1949–58.

NORMAN

John Wimmer Memorial Home. 200 4th St. E., Ada. June 2, 1965—Opened by City of Ada and operated in connection with the Ada Municipal Hospital.

Lutheran Memorial Home. Twin Valley. April, 1950—Opened in a new building by the Evangelical Lutheran Church (now ALC).

Norman County Poor Farm. Lake Ida Township. 1926–43. Leased as Ole Orvik's Boarding Home, 1937–43. Destroyed by fire, June 18, 1943.

Town Hall Estates Nursing Home. Twin Valley. January, 1966—Opened as Twin Valley Manor by American Religious Town Hall Meeting, St. Paul, in a new building.

OLMSTED

Madonna Towers. 4001 19th Ave. N.W., Rochester. February, 1967—Opened in a new apartment-type building with meal service and nursing care center. Operated by Oblates of Mary Immaculate, Central United States Province, St. Paul.

Olmsted County Poor Farm. Rochester. 1868–1944. First opened in Marion Township; moved to Rochester Township, 1874; new building erected, 1896.

Samaritan Nursing Home. 25 7th St. N.W., Rochester. 1921—Operated by the Brotherhood of the Evangelical Church of Peace of Rochester in a new building.

Town Hall Estates. 607 E. Center St., Rochester. October, 1966—Opened in a new building as Rochester Senior Citizens Manor by the American Religious Town Hall Meeting, St. Paul.

OTTER TAIL

Broen Memorial Home. 420 Alcott Ave. E., Fergus Falls. 1957—Opened by Church of the Lutheran Brethren in building formerly used as a school.

Elders Home. New York Mills. October, 1960—Opened in a new building by a nonprofit community organization.

Good Samaritan Home. 119 Broadway, Pelican Rapids. 1953—Opened by GSS in building formerly used as Dr. Peter Boysen's Hospital, to which a new addition was later made.

Otter Tail County Nursing Home. Battle Lake. 1955—Operated by Otter Tail County in building formerly used by Otter Tail County Tuberculosis Sanatorium.

Otter Tail County Poor Farm. Fergus Falls. 1881-1938.

Pelican Valley Health Center Nursing Home. 211 E. Mill St., Pelican Rapids. September, 1963—Operated by Pelican Valley Health Center as a unit of its hospital.

Pioneer Memorial Home. 1006 S. Sheridan, Fergus Falls. December, 1928— Opened in a new building by an organization of members of Lutheran congregations in area. Now an institution of the ALC.

St. James Home. 665 3rd St. S.W., Perham. March, 1960—Opened by Franciscan Sisters of the Immaculate Conception, Little Falls, in a building formerly used by St. James Hospital. The home is operated in connection with the new hospital.

St. William's Rest Home. Parkers Prairie. September, 1960—Operated by Church of St. William (Roman Catholic parish) Parkers Prairie, in former St. Raphael's Hospital building.

PENNINGTON

Oakland Park Nursing Home. Thief River Falls. 1955 — Operated by Pennington, Marshall, Red Lake, and Roseau counties in building formerly used by Oakland Park Tuberculosis Sanatorium.

Valley Home. Highway 32 and S. Arnold, Thief River Falls. 1944—Opened as Red River Valley Bible School and Home for Aged at 404 N. Horace, by an organization of Baptist churches. In 1955 was transferred to Valley Christian Home Society (nondenominational); organization was renamed Valley Home Society in 1961. On August 30, 1963, home was moved to a new building at the present site.

PINE

Pine County Nursing Home. Washington St., Sandstone. August, 1962— Operated by Pine County in a new building in connection with the Pine County Memorial Hospital.

Pine County Poor Farm. Hinckley. 1907—Leased as Bowe's Boarding Home, 1937-57, and as Holznagel Boarding Care Home, 1957—

PIPESTONE

Good Samaritan Home. N. Hiawatha Ave., Pipestone. November, 1958— Operated by the GSS in a former Indian school hospital building.

Pipestone County Hospital Nursing Home Unit. 911 5th Ave. S.W., Pipestone. July, 1965—Operated by Pipestone County in a former hospital building.

Pipestone County Poor Farm. Pipestone. 1884–1944. Opened in temporary poorhouse building erected in Pipestone. Moved to farm, 1890–92.

POLK

Bethesda Nursing Home and Woodland Apartments. 423 Woodland Ave., Crookston. June, 1953—Nursing home opened by Bethesda Hospital Association in former hospital building. Apartments opened February, 1962.

Fair Meadow Nursing Home. Fertile. March, 1967—Operated in a new building by Village of Fertile.

Fosston Municipal Nursing Home. Fosston. November, 1961 — Operated by Village of Fosston in building formerly used by Fosston Hospital.

Good Samaritan Nursing Center. 210 20th Ave. N., East Grand Forks. September, 1965—Opened in a new building by the GSS.

Perpetual Help Boarding Care Home. 725 6th St. N.E., Fosston. April, 1966—Opened in a dwelling by Our Lady of Perpetual Help Church (Roman Catholic parish), Fosston.

Pioneer Memorial Home. Highways 2 and 59, Erskine. March 1, 1950—Operated by a nonprofit association in a building formerly used as a roadhouse, to which new structure was later added.

St. Francis Hospital Convalescent and Nursing Care Unit. 516 Walsh St., Crookston. January, 1962—Operated in wing of hospital by Sisters of St. Benedict, Crookston.

St. Vincent's Rest Home. 223 E. 7th St., Crookston. June, 1950—Operated by Sisters of St. Benedict, Crookston, in building formerly used by St. Vincent's Hospital.

POPE

Assembly of God Nursing Home. 223 E. Minnesota Ave., Glenwood. 1958–64? Proprietary nursing home purchased by Minnesota Assembly of God District Council; affiliated with Assembly Homes.

Glenwood Old People's Home. Glenwood. December, 1914–1935. Was opened by Norwegian Synod (later Norwegian Lutheran Church of America) in building formerly used by Glenwood Academy.

Glenwood Retirement Home. 719 S.E. 2nd St., Glenwood. October 15, 1963—Opened by ALC in a new building.

Lakeview Nursing Home. Franklin at Birch. Glenwood. 1963—Opened by Assembly Homes in a new building.

Minnewaska Lutheran Home. Starbuck. August 11, 1961—Operated in a new building by a community organization separate from, but co-operating with, Minnewaska Hospital.

RAMSEY

Bethesda Lutheran Home for Invalids. 249 E. 9th St., St. Paul 1914–July, 1964. Was opened as Bethesda Invalid Home (or Invalidhem) by Minnesota

Conference, Augustana Lutheran Church (now Minnesota Synod, LCA) in resort building at Lake Gervais. Moved to former Bethesda Hospital building in 1932. Name changed, 1957.

Bethesda Lutheran Hospital Convalescent and Nursing Care Unit. 559 Capitol Blvd., St. Paul. January, 1960—Opened as Bethesda Lutheran Infirmary by Minnesota Conference, Augustana Lutheran Church (now Minnesota Synod, LCA) in new building connected with Bethesda Lutheran Hospital.

Central Towers. 20 E. Exchange St., St. Paul. January 25, 1966 — Apartment-type facility with dining room, operated in new building by Central Presbyterian Church.

Church Home of Minnesota. 1879 Feronia Ave., St. Paul. 1894—Established by Sister Annette Relf in an existing dwelling; sponsorship assumed by Episcopal diocese, 1897. After several moves, located at present site in 1920.

Church of God Old People's Home. St. Paul Park. 1908–1920s. Opened by members of Church of God, St. Paul Park, in new building; destroyed by fire, November, 1917; moved to former college dormitory; turned over to Church of God of Andersonville, Indiana, in 1920 and closed shortly afterwards.

Crispus Attucks Home. 469 Collins St., St. Paul. 1908–66. Opened as part of an industrial school for boys. Occupied several St. Paul residences before moving to building vacated by Home for the Friendless (now Protestant Home) in 1916. Children's care discontinued, 1919.

Jewish Home for the Aged of the Northwest. 1554 Midway Pkwy., St. Paul. June 14, 1908—Opened in a former residence by organization of Jewish societies, superseding the Charity Loan Society and Old Women's Home. Enlarged to include Minneapolis Jewish community, and home moved, 1923, to new building on present site.

Little Sisters of the Poor Home. 90 Wilkin St., St. Paul. October, 1883— Opened by Little Sisters of the Poor in building formerly used by House of the Good Shepherd, and later replaced.

Lutheran Home. 121 Virginia St., St. Paul. May, 1953—Opened by the St. Paul Lutheran Chaplaincy Auxiliary (composed of women from 18 congregations of the LCMS, Minnesota South District).

Lyngblomsten Retirement Center. 1298 N. Pascal St., St. Paul. November 5, 1912—Opened in a new building as Lyngblomsten Home by an organization of Norwegian-American women. Merged with ALC in the early 1960s.

Our Lady of Good Counsel Home. 2076 St. Anthony Ave., St. Paul. December, 1941—Operated by Sisters of St. Dominic Servants of Relief for Incurable Cancer, Hawthorne, New York. Occupies building formerly used for offices.

Presbyterian Homes. 3220 Lake Johanna Blvd., St. Paul. June, 1955—Operated in a new building by Synod of Minnesota Presbyterian Church.

Protestant Home of St. Paul. 753 E. 7th St., St. Paul. 1868—Opened by Ladies Christian Union of the City of St. Paul, later changed to Ladies Relief Association. Organization and home renamed Home for the Friendless, 1877. First opened in existing residence at 47 Walnut St. New building erected, 1883, at 469 Collins St., and 1916, at present site. Took present name in 1935.

Ramsey County Home. 2000 White Bear Ave., St. Paul. 1854—Former Ramsey County Poor Farm, now operated by Ramsey County and City of

St. Paul as a nursing home. Poor farm first opened at Mounds View; moved to Pig's Eye, 1857, and to Rose Township, 1865; site became part of state fair grounds, 1883. Institution was moved to present location and a new building was erected, 1885.

Ramsey County Poor Farm. See **Ramsey County Home.**

St. Mary's Home. 1925 Norfolk Ave., St. Paul. October, 1936—Opened in a new building by Franciscan Sisters of the Blessed Virgin Mary of the Angels, St. Paul.

St. Paul's Church Home. 484 Ashland Ave., St. Paul. 1925—Opened as Evangelical St. Paul's Home by members of the church. Occupied former hotel on present site in 1927, after several moves. New main building erected, 1962. Affiliated with United Church of Christ.

Sholom Residence. 1620 Randolph Ave., St. Paul. June, 1950—Dwelling at 45 S. St. Albans was acquired by Daughters of Abraham and transferred to Sholom Residence, Inc., a nonprofit community organization. The Daughters of Abraham became the Women's Auxiliary with representation on the governing board. In February, 1958, the operation was moved to a new building on the present site.

Twin City Linnea Home for Aged. 2040 Como Ave., St. Paul. February, 1918—Opened by Twin City Linnea Society, an organization of Swedish-American women, in new building.

Wilder Residences facilities. 512 Humboldt Ave., St. Paul.
  The Infirmary. February, 1961—
  The Apartments. May, 1965 —
  The Residence. November, 1966—
Operated by Amherst H. Wilder Foundation in new buildings.

RED LAKE

Hillcrest Nursing Home. Red Lake Falls. March, 1960—Opened by Red Lake County in a new building.

REDWOOD

Gil-Mor Manor. Morgan. October, 1961—Opened in a new building by Morgan Memorial Foundation, a community nonprofit organization.

Parkview Home. 401 County State Aid Highway 9, Belview. November 1, 1965—Opened in new building by Village of Belview.

Redwood County Nursing Home. Redwood Falls. 1909—Former Redwood County Poor Farm, now operated as a county nursing home. First poor farm, opened in 1889, was operated intermittently, and closed in 1899. Second poorhouse was opened in new building on present site, 1909. Converted to a nursing home in the 1950s.

Redwood County Poor Farm. See **Redwood County Nursing Home.**

Sunwood Nursing Home. 200 S. De Kalb, Redwood Falls. August 1, 1962— Opened in a new building by Assembly Homes.

Wabasso Nursing Home. Wabasso. September, 1965—Opened in a new building by the Village of Wabasso.

RENVILLE

Ren-Villa Nursing Home. Renville. 1963—Opened by the City of Renville in a new building.

Renville County Poor Farm. Olivia. 1891-99. Occupied existing farmhouse.

RICE

Faribault Manor Nursing Home. 1738 Hulett Ave., Faribault. May, 1965—Opened in a new building by Mennonite Care Centers, Inc., International Falls, Minnesota.

Minnesota Odd Fellows Home. 815 Forest Ave., Northfield. 1900—Opened in a new building by Independent Order of Odd Fellows. Originally combined with an orphanage, which is now closed.

Northfield City Hospital and H. O. Dilley Convalescent and Nursing Care Unit. 800 W. 2nd St., Northfield. August, 1963—Opened in new building attached to hospital. Operated by City of Northfield.

Rice County Poor Farm. Faribault. 1866-1953. New building erected, 1903.

St. Lucas Geriatric and Convalescent Care Center. 503 E. Division St., Faribault. April, 1960—Opened by St. Lucas Health and Welfare Association in building formerly used by St. Lucas Deaconess Hospital, to which a large addition had been made. Connected with but not operated by Rice County District 1 Hospital.

ROCK

Good Samaritan Home. See **Rock County Poor Farm.**

Mary Jane Brown Nursing Home. 110 S. Walnut Ave., Luverne. October, 1959—Opened in new building by the GSS.

Rock County Poor Farm. Luverne. 1881-1963. Leased for farm operation some time prior to 1936. Building leased to GSS, 1950-63, for operation as Good Samaritan Home.

Tuff Memorial Home. Hills. 1959—Opened in new building by Evangelical Lutheran Church (now ALC).

ROSEAU

Greenbush Community Hospital Convalescent and Nursing Care Unit. Greenbush. June 5, 1962—Opened by Greenbush Community Hospital Association in new wing of the hospital.

Roseau Area Hospital District facilities. Roseau.
    Sheltering Oaks Home. August 19, 1960—
    Eventide Home. 1963?—
Sheltering Oaks Home occupies a building started by the Lutheran Benevolent Association but transferred to the hospital before completion. It is connected with a new hospital erected in 1962. Eventide Home occupies the building formerly used by Roseau Community Hospital.

Warroad Nursing Home. Lake St., Warroad. June, 1962—Opened by Village of Warroad in building formerly used by Warroad Municipal Hospital. Operated in connection with present hospital, to which it is attached.

ST. LOUIS

Aftenro Home. 1425 N. 19th Ave. E., Duluth. May, 1921—Opened in a new building by Aftenro Society, an organization of Norwegian-American women, originally a branch of Lyngblomsten Society.

Cook Community Hospital Convalescent and Nursing Care Unit. 3rd and Cedar St., Cook. December 24, 1964—Opened by Village of Cook in new building and operated in connection with the hospital.

Ely-Bloomenson Community Hospital Convalescent and Nursing Care Unit. 328 W. Conan St., Ely. July 17, 1967—Opened in a new building by same nonprofit corporation which operates the hospital.

Eveleth Fitzgerald Community Hospital Unit. McKinley Ave., Eveleth. May, 1967—Opened by community hospital corporation as extended care facility.

Hibbing General Hospital Convalescent and Nursing Care Unit. 2015 4th Ave. E., Hibbing. 1957—Opened as Hibbing General Hospital Nursing Home by Benedictine Sisters Benevolent Association, Duluth. Converted to an extended care facility in 1966.

Lakeshore Lutheran Home for the Aged. 4002 London Road, Duluth. June, 1930—Opened in a former residence by Minnesota Conference, Augustana Lutheran Church (now Minnesota Synod, LCA).

McCabe Residence. 2125 Abbotsford Ave., Duluth. June, 1939–October, 1963. Was operated in a former dwelling by Benedictine Sisters Benevolent Association, Duluth.

Mesabi Home. Jones St., Buhl. December, 1953—Opened in building formerly used as county hospital. Operated by Range Hospital Corporation, headquarters in Virginia.

Nopeming Sanatorium, Trudeau and Chateau Nursing Home Units. Nopeming. 1957—Operated by St. Louis County in sections of the sanatorium no longer needed for tuberculosis patients. Second unit was opened in 1961.

Pioneers' Infirmary. See **Virginia Municipal Hospital Unit.**

St. Ann's Home. 2002 W. 3rd St., Duluth. 1910–November, 1956. Was opened by Benedictine Sisters Benevolent Association in building formerly used by St. James Orphanage and before that by St. Mary's Hospital. After its closing, the remaining residents were transferred to a section of St. Mary's Hospital, which was operated temporarily as a nursing unit.

St. Ann's Home. 330 E. 3rd St., Duluth. October, 1963—A new apartment-type building with meal service, built by Diocese of Duluth and administered by Benedictine Sisters Benevolent Association.

St. Louis County Poor Farm. See St. Louis County Welfare Medical Care Facilities.

St. Louis County Welfare Medical Care facilities. Duluth.
    Cook Nursing Unit. 2501 Rice Lake Road. 1902—
    Morrow Nursing Unit. 1621 Arlington Ave. 1934—
    Chris Jensen Nursing Unit. 1967—
Former St. Louis County Poor Farm plus additional facilities, now operated as county nursing home. Poor farm was first opened in 1873; new building erected, 1902. In 1934 the poorhouse was renamed Cook Home. In the same year a former industrial school was remodeled as a rest home and opened under the name Arlington Home. After the new Chris Jensen Nursing Unit was added in 1967 the present names were adopted.

St. Luke's Hospital Infirmary. 915 E. 1st St., Duluth. 1951—Opened by hospital in an addition erected by St. Louis County for welfare clients.

St. Mary's Hospital Infirmary. 407 E. 3rd St., Duluth. 1958?—Opened by hospital in an addition erected by St. Louis County for care of welfare clients.

Virginia Municipal Hospital Unit. Virginia. September, 1950—Opened as Pioneers' Infirmary by Range Hospital Corporation in a building erected by St. Louis County and connected with Virginia Municipal Hospital. Since June, 1967, it has been operated by the hospital under the present name.

White Community Hospital Unit. Aurora. January 16, 1961—Operated by hospital in a wing of new hospital building.

SCOTT

Lutheran Home for the Aged. Belle Plaine. November, 1898—Opened by Evangelical Lutheran Synod of Wisconsin, Minnesota, and Michigan (now Wisconsin Evangelical Lutheran Synod) in a new building. Originally cared for both children and aged; children's service gradually discontinued.

New Prague Baptist Home. New Prague. 1925-47. First opened as Czechoslovak Baptist Home by Czechoslovak Baptist Charitable Association of America. Transferred to Northwest Baptist Home Society and renamed, May, 1938. Occupied a former residence.

Queen of Peace Nursing Home. 301 2nd St. N.E., New Prague. September, 1963—Opened by Sisters of St. Benedict, St. Joseph, Minnesota, in a new building. Operated in connection with Queen of Peace Hospital.

St. Francis Home. 304 W. 4th St., Shakopee. November, 1938—Opened by Franciscan Sisters of the Blessed Virgin Mary of the Angels, St. Paul, in building formerly used by Scott County Poorhouse.

St. Francis Hospital Unit. Shakopee. 1964?-October, 1965. Operated by Franciscan Sisters of the Blessed Virgin Mary of the Angels in a section of St. Francis Hospital.

St. Paul's Lutheran Home for Senior Citizens. Prior Lake. June 10, 1963— Operated by a nonprofit church-related organization.

Scott County Poorhouse. Shakopee. 1889-1938. Opened in building formerly used by an academy. Sold to Sisters of St. Francis. See **St. Francis Home.**

Shakopee Friendship Manor. 1340 W. 3rd Ave., Shakopee. June, 1965— Opened in new building by Friendship Homes, Inc., Jamestown, North Dakota.

Valleyview Sanitarium. Jordan. December 27, 1950—Operated by Minnesota Valleyview Hospital Association in building formerly used by a private sanatorium.

SHERBURNE

Elk River Nursing Home. 400 Evans Ave., Elk River. November 1, 1965— Opened in new building by Guardian Angels Foundation, an organization founded by Trinity Episcopal Church, Elk River. Same group operates Riverview Apartments for the aged, with priority for nursing home care.

St. Joseph Home for the Aged. 1824 Minnesota Blvd. S.E., St. Cloud. May, 1900—Opened by the Sisters of St. Benedict, St. Joseph, Minnesota, in former hospital building.

SIBLEY

Good Samaritan Home. Gaylord. 1953—Opened by GSS in a former hospital.

Winthrop Community Home. Winthrop. June 17, 1965—Opened by Assembly Homes in a new building.

STEARNS

Assumption Nursing Home. Cold Spring. September 21, 1963—Opened by St. Boniface Church (Roman Catholic parish) in new building. Staffed by Sisters of St. Benedict, St. Joseph, Minnesota.

Belgrade Nursing Home. Belgrade. May 1, 1965—Opened in a new building by a nonprofit corporation.

Good Samaritan Home. 311 Washburn, Paynesville. 1955 — Opened by GSS in a former hospital building.

Koronis Manor Convalescent Home. Paynesville. November 3, 1964 — Operated by Paynesville Community Hospital in a new building attached to the hospital and erected by the Village of Paynesville.

Mother of Mercy Nursing Home. Albany. August, 1959 — Opened by Church of the Seven Dolors (Roman Catholic parish) in a new building. Staffed by Sisters of St. Benedict, St. Joseph, Minnesota.

Pine Villa. 11 N. 5th Ave. W., Melrose. December 1, 1961 — Opened by City of Melrose in new building attached to Melrose Hospital.

St. Michael's Extended Care Facility. N. Elm St., Sauk Centre. May, 1967 — Opened by Franciscan Sisters of the Immaculate Conception, Little Falls, in a converted section of St. Michael's Hospital.

St. Raphael's Home. 511 9th Ave. N., St. Cloud. 1928 — Opened by Sisters of St. Benedict, St. Joseph, Minnesota, in a former hospital building.

Sarepta Home for Aged. Sauk Centre. 1910 — Opened by Church of the Lutheran Brethren in an existing residence.

STEELE

Cedarview Rest Home. 1409 S. Cedar, Owatonna. 1880 — Former Steele County Poor Farm, now operated as county nursing home. Poor farm first opened in Havana Township; moved to present site in 1917 and new poorhouse erected. Converted to nursing home about 1958.

Steele County Poor Farm. See **Cedarview Rest Home.**

STEVENS

Stevens County Poor Farm. Morris. 1896–1911.

Villa of St. Francis Nursing Home. W. 10th St., Morris. August 1, 1963 — Opened by Assumption Church (Roman Catholic parish) in new building. Staffed by Franciscan Sisters of the Poor of the St. Anthony Province, Warwick, New York.

SWIFT

Appleton Municipal Hospital and Nursing Home. Schlieman and Behl Sts., Appleton. April, 1965 — Opened by Village of Appleton in a new addition to the hospital.

TODD

Bertha Boarding Care Home. Bertha. January, 1965 — Opened by Village of Bertha in a former hospital building.

Long Prairie Memorial Nursing Home. 20 9th St. S.E., Long Prairie. April 7, 1966 — Operated by Village of Long Prairie in connection with Memorial Hospital.

Mary Rondorf Home. 222 5th St. N., Staples. June, 1953 — Opened by Sacred Heart Church of Staples (Roman Catholic parish) in existing apartment buildings. Staffed by Sisters of St. Benedict, St. Joseph, Minnesota.

Memorial Community Hospital Convalescent and Nursing Care Unit. 1965 — Opened by Village of Bertha in section of new hospital building.

St. Mary's Home. 310 2nd Ave., Long Prairie. 1958–68. Was operated by Sisters of St. Benedict, St. Joseph, in former hospital building.

Todd County Poor Farm. Long Prairie. 1882–85. Building destroyed by fire, 1884, and inmates cared for in overseer's home until institution closed.

TRAVERSE

Traverse County Nursing Home. Wheaton. January, 1959 — Opened in a new building by Traverse County.

WABASHA

Buena Vista Rest Home. Wabasha. 1956 — Operated as a nursing home by Wabasha County in building formerly used by Buena Vista Sanatorium for tuberculosis patients.

St. Elizabeth Hospital Nursing and Boarding Care Home. 1200 5th Grant Blvd., Wabasha. 1920 — Opened by Sisters of the Sorrowful Mother, Milwaukee, Wisconsin, in section of St. Elizabeth Hospital. The former hospital was converted in 1962 to a nursing home.

Wabasha County Poor Farm. Wabasha. 1867–1956. First opened in Hyde Park Township; moved to Wabasha, 1873. Leased as John Ziendt Rest Home, 1936–38; Elizabeth Baker Rest Home, 1938–49; Harold Matteson Rest Home, 1949–56.

WADENA

Green Pine Acres Nursing Home. Menagha. May 1, 1965 — Opened in new building by Village of Menagha.

Shady Lane Rest Home. Wadena. 1952 — Operated by Wadena and Todd counties in building formerly used by Fair Oaks Lodge Tuberculosis Sanatorium.

WASECA

Janesville Nursing Home. 102 E. North St., Janesville. October 1, 1965 — Opened in new building by Village of Janesville.

WASHINGTON

Croixdale Residence. 334 N. 7th Ave., Bayport. June, 1961 — Operated in a new building by Washington County Association for Senior Citizens.

Pine Point Nursing Home. Stillwater. 1858 — Former Washington County Poor Farm, now operated as a county nursing home. Poorhouse building erected in 1925 was converted to nursing care and renamed in 1954.

Washington County Poor Farm. See **Pine Point Nursing Home.**

WATONWAN

Luther Memorial Home. 221 6th St., Madelia. May, 1959 — Opened in a new building by congregations affiiliated with the ALC.

Pleasantview Good Samaritan Home. 1000 S. 2nd St., St. James. July 1, 1963 — Opened by GSS in a new building.

St. James Home. 405 N. Armstrong Blvd., St. James. October, 1922–1961. Was operated by Sisters of St. Francis, Congregation of Our Lady of Lourdes, Rochester, as part of St. James Hospital. Occupied former hospital-sanatorium building.

WILKIN

St. Francis Home for the Aged. 415 Oregon Ave., Breckenridge. September 23, 1952 — Opened by Franciscan Sisters of the Immaculate Conception, Little Falls, in building formerly used by St. Francis Hospital.

Wilkin County Poor Farm. Breckenridge. 1909–29.

WINONA

Community Memorial Hospital Convalescent and Rehabilitation Unit. 855 Mankato Ave., Winona. February 7, 1966 — Opened by Winona General Hospital Association in new building attached to hospital.

Paul Watkins Memorial Methodist Home. 175 E. Wabasha, Winona. January, 1959 — Opened by the Methodist Church, Minnesota Conference, in an existing residence.

Saint Anne Hospice. 1347 W. Broadway, Winona. February, 1962 — Opened by Sisters of St. Francis, Congregation of Our Lady of Lourdes, Rochester, in new building.

Sauer Memorial Home. 1635 Service Drive, Winona. April 18, 1966 — Opened by an organization of Lutheran men in a new building.

Winona County Poor Farm. Winona. 1868–1941. First opened in Burns Valley; moved to farm near Winona and new poorhouse erected, 1904.

WRIGHT

Ebenezer Home for the Aged. 310 Lake Blvd., Buffalo. June, 1918 — Opened by Northwest Mission Society (later Northwest Conference of the Evangelical Covenant Church of America) in a former residence.

Retirement Center of Wright County. 3rd Ave. S., Buffalo. November, 1962 — Opened by a nonprofit organization.

Wright County Poor Farm. Buffalo. 1909–42.

YELLOW MEDICINE

Clarkfield Nursing Home. Clarkfield. January, 1960 — Opened in new building by Assembly Homes.

Granite Falls Manor. 10th Ave., Granite Falls. September 1, 1960 — Opened by City of Granite Falls in new building connected with the Granite Falls Municipal Hospital.

Senior Haven. Canby. October, 1963—Opened by Canby Community Hospital District No. 1 in a former hospital building.

Yellow Medicine County Poor Farm. 1888?–1936.

www.ingramcontent.com/pod-product-compliance
Lightning Source LLC
Chambersburg PA
CBHW020941230426
43666CB00005B/116